Guy Claxton is an internationally renowned writer, consultant, lecturer and academic, specialising in creativity, education and the mind. He has a double first in Natural Science from Cambridge, a doctorate in Psychology from Oxford and has held the post of Visiting Professor in Learning Science at the University of Bristol since 1993.

The Wayward Mind

*An Intimate History
of the Unconscious*

GUY CLAXTON

ABACUS

First published in Great Britain in January 2005 by Little, Brown
This paperback edition published in February 2006 by Abacus

A CIP catalogue record for this book
is available from the British Library.

ISBN 0 349 11654 7

Every effort has been made to trace copyright holders in all the
copyright material in this book. The publisher regrets any oversight and
will be pleased to rectify any omission in future editions. Quotation
from 'The Silent Pool' by Harold Monro by permission of
Gerald Duckworth & Co. Ltd.

Typeset in Garamond by M Rules
Printed and bound in Great Britain
by Clays Ltd, St Ives plc

Abacus
An imprint of
Time Warner Book Group UK
Brettenham House
Lancaster Place
London WC2E 7EN

www.twbg.co.uk

Contents

For Rod

Preface

I don't know about you, but my mind has a mind of its own. It wanders off while I'm trying to concentrate. It refuses to stop churning over the day while I'm trying to get to sleep. At night it creates movies that range from the exceedingly tedious to the embarrassingly bizarre. It comes up with tunes and phrases that I didn't intend, and often didn't want. It tells me that someone has come into the room when I've got the headphones on and my eyes shut and I'm miles away – and often it's right. It forgets well-known names at crucial moments. It feels hurt or angry out of all proportion. It is a royal pain in the ass sometimes. But, apparently, it is the only mind I've got.

Maybe yours conforms more neatly and obediently to the standard definition of what a mind is supposed to be: conscious, predictable, biddable, orderly. Maybe you have no wild flights of fancy, know nobody who's been unaccountably depressed, have no interest in hypnosis or mysticism. If waywardness of mind is not something you know, something that concerns you, then better save your money. You will be one of a small minority, perhaps a lucky one, whose minds are transparent to them, and do what they say.

From the dawn of history, most people have been more like me than you. The waywardness of mind has puzzled and troubled people, and all human societies – and chimps, for all I know – have told themselves stories to give comfort, and the illusion, at least, of control, in the face of their own aberration. Three types of culprit recur in these stories. First there are gods, and the multitude of supernatural sprites and forces that go with them. My hallucinations are punishments or blessings, orchestrated by Tinkerbell or the Good Lord. Then there is 'the unconscious', or rather the unconsciouses, for there are many different versions that have been dreamed up to account for different kinds of weirdness. And finally, and most recently, there is the brain. Maybe there are no real demons, no id, and it's all down to a serotonin imbalance in the frontal lobes.

In this book I have tried to chart the historical ups and downs of these three ways of approaching the wayward mind, from ancient images of the 'underworld' to contemporary neuroscience. All three are at least two thousand years old. Freud, whether he knew it (or admitted it) or not, was not the architect of the unconscious but its archaeologist. Rudimentary neuroscience was being used to explain dreams by Aristotle. And of course the supernatural world, a strong presence in ancient Egypt, is still very much alive today. Tracking the shifting balance of power between god, id and brain over more than two millennia, and over the face of the Earth, makes an intriguing journey.

The full horror of the mind's waywardness reveals itself when you try to meditate. Sit down quietly, and try to follow the sensations in your chest as you breathe slowly in and out. What could be simpler? But when I try it, as I do, within seconds I am over the hills and far away. Most days it's like an explosion in a fireworks factory in here. My carefully constructed image of control and rationality is regularly blown to smithereens. To any human being this is troubling, but to a cognitive scientist it is deeply unnerving, for I see that most of my actual experience has been tacitly airbrushed out of the subject I profess and the psychology curriculum we set before our students.

In 1997 I wrote a book that pulled together many of the previously disparate bits and pieces that cognitive science has unearthed about what we now call the 'intelligent unconscious'. It was called *Hare Brain, Tortoise Mind: Why Intelligence Increases When You Think Less.* Its theme was that science shows, beyond a shadow of a doubt, that we know much more than we know we know, and we make use of it, all the time, without realising it. But writing *Hare Brain* made it clear to me that I was only scratching the surface of the unconscious, both culturally and historically. If words for 'the unconscious' were only invented in the nineteenth century, how had people gone about explaining their oddities before? How did people in non-European societies do it? Had the boundary between 'normal' and 'odd' shifted over time, and therefore had the *function* of the unconscious – or whatever alternative people had been using – changed? What was the relationship between supernatural, psychological and biological explanations? And which of these, at the beginning of the third millennium after Christ, did we still need? What kind of ragbag of notions were we heir to, and could they be tidied up and thinned out? If we start from a fuller, more accurate picture of our psychological lives, wayward warts and all, how does our image of the mind itself have to change in order to accommodate this inconvenient richness? And, in the end, does it matter? Does it make any difference to how twenty-first century life is actually lived, or is it just another scholarly displacement activity?

Questions like these started to tug me out of my familiar psychological habitat and into the stranger worlds of intellectual history, cultural anthropology, literature and even spirituality – for 'religious experiences' kept recurring as perennial forms of unusual, inexplicable experience. The journey was full of surprises. Egyptian mythology of four thousand years ago seemed to have formulated answers to some of these questions that, once you scratched them, turned out to be startlingly modern. There were fascinating parallels between the psychologies of Homer's Greece and contemporary Polynesia. I met sides of Pythagoras and St Augustine I never knew existed, and, of course, found that

Shakespeare had strewn his plays with prescient images of the unconscious. Descartes, normally the arch-villain of the epistemological piece, turned out to be intensely aware of the non-rational aspects of his own experience. He was arguably the first person to write on the subject of 'transference', for example. And many recent suggestions about the overall modus operandi of the brain were being widely discussed more than a hundred years ago – in slightly more poetic language, it is true, but sounding astonishingly contemporary for all that.

When I started, I thought I was going to be able to conclude that we were ready to do away with both the supernatural and the psychological, and put it all down to the brain. But now I am not so sure, and my conclusions will disappoint my more evangelical neuroscientific colleagues. Yes, we can now make a good stab at showing how the brain could make us hear voices, feel depressed, lose the thread and come up with insights. We can even begin to hazard an idea about how romantic and religious experiences of awe and unity might reflect unusual machinations in the cerebral cortex. But the neural language of the 'wet-ware' is not well suited to talking about the quality of experience – especially that which puzzles us. Nor will it help with thorny issues like 'legal responsibility'. Yes, there is more to me than meets the rational 'I', and this recognition threatens to undermine a sharp distinction between 'diminished responsibility' and 'being in one's right mind'. But societies need to run on Wise Fictions as well as Scientific Truths, and we may not be done with our ids, or even with our gods, just yet.

It has been an exhilarating journey, and a challenging one as well, and I have needed a lot of help, which I am happy to acknowledge here. So thank you, in different ways, to Peter Abbs, Sebastian Bailey, Christopher Ball, Stephen Batchelor, Susan Blackmore, Alan Bleakley, Pascal Boyer, Felicity Bryan, Malcolm Carr, Margaret Carr, Rita Carter, John Cleese, Marcus Cook, Steve Cox, Roy D'Andrade, Jean Decety, Janine Edge, Keri Facer, Peter

Fenwick, Jeffrey Gray, Susan Greenfield, Steve Guise, Sean Hardie, Charlotte Hardman, Anne Hollingworth, Martin Hughes, Nicholas Humphrey, Dick Joyce, Annette Karmiloff-Smith, Barry Kemp, Jenny King, Thanassis Kostikas, Ruth Leitch, David Lorimer, Bill Lucas, Tasha Mundy, Judith Nesbitt, Bernie Neville, Imogen Newman, Natasha Owen, Anne Phillips, Andrew Powell, Jonathan Schooler, Linda Silverman, Victoria Trow, Tim Whiting and Timothy Wilson. And to Rod Jenkinson, extraordinarily generous, creative and wayward man, who laboured mightily outside while I was writing inside, and to whom this book is dedicated.

Of course, any errors that remain are due to them, and all the good bits are down to me. Oh sorry – that should be the other way round. You see. There it goes again . . .

1

On Making Up Your Mind: What the Unconscious Is For

Faith, if it bears any relation to the natural world, implies faith in the unconscious. If there is a God, he must speak there; if there is a healing power, it must operate there; if there is a principle of ordering in the organic realm, its most powerful manifestation must be found there . . . The conscious mind will enjoy no peace until it can rejoice in a fuller understanding of its own unconscious sources.

– Lancelot Law Whyte, *The Unconscious Before Freud*[1]

Last night I dreamed I was in a lift descending through a fissure in the rock by the side of the Clifton Suspension Bridge in Bristol, fearful of being crushed. I wonder what it means. On my way home from the university that afternoon, my car had travelled twenty miles on the motorway without my being aware of a single other vehicle. I'd like to know who was driving while 'I' was elsewhere. Sometimes my spirits are bleak for no apparent reason, and I feel perplexed and powerless. Occasionally I say or write something that strikes me as witty or interesting – yet it came to me out of the blue, and I feel slightly fraudulent taking the credit.

There are many aspects of human experience that seem at odds with 'common sense'. Dreams, mood swings, creativity, the

'automatic pilot' are just a few. They all reveal us to be less knowledgeable about our own minds, and less in control of them, than
we would like – than we think we ought to be. Vaguely unsettled,
we either brush them off, or feel the need to propose some kind of
explanation. There is an urge to make them comprehensible – to
domesticate, through words, events that have an uncomfortable
whiff of wildness about them. Societies differ in what they count
as 'common sense', and therefore in the particular oddities of
experience that stand in need of comprehension. And they differ
too in the kinds of account that they offer. For some, madness, like
drought, reflects the machinations of an angry god. For others, it
stems from the self-destructive churnings of the unconscious
mind. Creative insight may be a gift from a generous Muse; or it
may reflect the fortuitous closing of a neural circuit in the brain.

This book is about the range of such explanations that human
societies have concocted, and how they have changed and developed over time. Broadly, we have moved from 'outward' to
'inward' stories: from gods, fairies and supernatural forces, to subconscious archetypes and neurotransmitters. But the historical
progression is by no means smooth, and though the balance shifts,
many kinds of story have always coexisted, and continue to do so.
Something remarkably like 'the unconscious' existed four thousand years ago in ancient Egypt, while belief in 'spirits' is still very
much alive, and some members of the Royal College of
Psychiatrists practise exorcism in London to this day.

It would be easy to get into an argument about which of these
kinds of agents is 'real' and which 'made up', but such a debate
would generate more heat than light. Instead, I treat them all as
hypothetical – as ingenious human inventions that do a more or
less good job of assuaging the anxiety or satisfying the perplexity
that our own mental states sometimes induce. We are inveterate
story-tellers, and telling stories is the survival strategy that, perhaps
more than any other, distinguishes our species. When we feel our
grasp on events beginning to slip, when we start to feel confused,

we gather together and ask: 'How come?' And the explanations we concoct give us the illusion – and sometimes even the reality – of re-establishing control. As Daniel Dennett has nicely put it, 'our fundamental tactic of self-protection, self-control and self-definition is not spinning webs or building dams, but telling stories'. And while some of these stories concern the causes of metal fatigue, or the failure of the harvest, others, some of the most important, concern our own psychology and physiology – why and how we think and feel and act and see the way we do.

In trying to account for the uncanny aspects of our experience, we spin tales about our minds. To do so, we reach, just as the metallurgist and the agriculturalist do, for images and metaphors to extend our grasp. Is metal like a 'sheet'? Were the locusts, in some sense, like a 'plague'? Is memory like a wax tablet, as it was for Plato, or a scroll, as it was for the early Middle Ages, or a library, as it was in the 1960s, or a microchip, as for many people it is now?

And what do such images tell us, implicitly or explicitly, about the nature of 'the unconscious', and its relationship to consciousness? If the mind is a tablet of wax, could it contain faint impressions of old memories that have been overwritten, like a palimpsest? Freud himself once compared the mind to a 'mystic writing pad' – one of those toys where you can 'magically' erase what you have written on the plastic window, though its impression remains on a hidden pad beneath. Is the mind like an abattoir, with a clean, bright reception area, and thick soundproofing to prevent the ruckus of suffering from penetrating into the foyer? Is it like a television set, that does nothing but pick up and display broadcasts from 'beyond'? Is it a computer, in which the dumb screen of consciousness does nothing itself, but merely displays occasional messages from the intelligent innards that are themselves entirely dark and inaccessible? Or is the mind simply the brain, with no ghost in the machine at all, as many cognitive scientists today would have us believe?

These shifting images of the mind, and its unconscious regions, are not innocent accessories to our mental life, for they actually determine how we experience the world, and react to it. They steer and skew the use we make of the resources we were born with, leading us to exercise and value some aspects of our natural endowment, and to neglect others. A good Cartesian, for whom the very idea of 'unconscious intelligence' is an oxymoron, can have no interest at all in developing her 'sixth sense', because the possibility simply does not compute. A Romantic like William Blake, on the other hand, sees only coldness and calculation in Reason, and wants nothing to do with it. If you believe that 'intelligence' is innately fixed, there is no point in trying to get smarter, but if you believe that your mental muscles can strengthen with exercise, then sweating over a problem can be as beneficial a workout for your mind as twenty minutes on the treadmill is for your heart.

There is another way in which our psychological tales impact on the way we live. Telling ourselves explanatory stories has two functions. They give us ideas to try out, that might improve our ability to predict and control the world. Whether they do so is a test of how accurate the stories are. If the harvest failed, as the shaman said, because the gods were angry, and the sacrifice of a couple of virgins is a good way of appeasing them, then do the crops grow better next year or not? If profits are down, as the expensive consultants said, because we have too many layers of management, then that contemporary form of ritual sacrifice called 're-engineering' ought to do the trick. Does it?

The problem is that stories do not just generate hypotheses for action; they also console and reassure in themselves. And the need to hold on to a comforting myth may turn out to be more important than testing its accuracy. Our cultural narratives make sense of confusion, they give meaning and dignity to adversity, they offer pattern and design where all we could see was chance and misfortune. So the beliefs we hold about 'spirit possession' or telepathy or the meaning of dreams can very easily become self-fulfilling and self-protecting. And the resources of the mind then have to be dedicated to ensuring that whatever happens, we don't turn out to have been wrong. The cool rationalist writes off her spooky premonition as a meaningless coincidence, while the parapsychologist seizes on the very same coincidence as further proof of his psychic powers.

Mental myths have repercussions for societies as well as for individuals. If Plato's *Republic* had ever come into being, those most given to deliberation would have done well, and those of a more poetic bent rather badly. (We do, in fact, live in a flawed version of Plato's world.) Institutions grow up that enshrine and develop a view of mind. British justice assumes that truth will emerge from a form of argumentation that has to have the appearance – though often only that – of dispassionate logic and impartial weighing of evidence. Intuition has no value unless it is supplanted by proof. Wisdom, or what in a Maori meeting would be called *mana*, has no place in a court of law. It cannot be assayed. It does not count. In a Buddhist art class, skill and perception emerge slowly from experience, and so patient copying is prescribed. In a progressive primary school, such repetition would be seen as 'boring' and 'deadening', and creative daubing would be encouraged from the word go. Whether a culture's 'folk psychology', as it is called, incorporates an image of the unconscious, and what kind of image it is, makes a real difference to how life is lived. Whether, at the beginning of the twenty-first century, we possess an accurate and coherent image of the mind's invisible foundations, or a comforting but valueless collection of archaic fragments, turns out to matter a great deal.

Every society has its characteristic stock of stories, whether they concern the age by which daughters should be married, the right way to cook rice, or the import of dreams. And a great deal of work goes in to encouraging children, as they grow up, to spin these stories for themselves. For the web of meaning that you weave for yourself comes out not as opinion or conjecture, but as reality. We spin our tales, but in doing so, our tales also spin us. They magic into existence the worlds of meaning we inhabit.[2]

There are two types of story that people learn to spin: implicit ones, which we call 'common sense', and explicit ones, which we call 'explanations'.[3] The implicit – dare I say, unconscious – ones determine everyday habits and values. They are often not spelled out, but they underlie a society's intuitive judgements about what is 'normal', 'obvious', 'intelligent', 'proper', 'good' or 'true', and conversely, what is to be treated as 'stupid', 'naughty', 'ugly' or 'wicked'. *Of course* one does not expose the soles of one's feet to a superior person. It is *unthinkable* for a man to share a bed with a child who is not his own. How *ridiculous* to wear (or not to wear) one's cap like that. Common sense gives people the unthinking code of thought and conduct by which they recognise each other, and through which the cohesion of their culture (or their subculture) is maintained. As monkeys service their relationships by mutual grooming, and dogs leave chemical messages on trees, so we maintain the bonds, and beat the bounds, of our worlds by trading judgements. To be one of us, you must laugh at our sexist jokes, or admire the same fashion designers.

It is the painstaking work of the anthropologist to gently unearth the story, the tissue of belief, that lies below unquestioned common sense – the carcass of commitment that frames what people *act as if* they believed, without knowing that they do. Indeed, they are often horrified if confronted with this skeleton directly. Dorothy Holland and Naomi Quinn took three years to reconstruct the 'presuppositional framework', to use fancy language, that underpinned the judgements that female American college students made about relationships and men.[4] Behind the banter and the gossip, it turned out, lay a mercilessly commercial view of what was being traded for what, and what kinds of bargain it was proper to strike. Crudely, the more *attractive* the woman, the more she merited an *enviable* man who was appropriately *attentive* and *appreciative* of her good looks. Any deviance was ruthlessly identified, judged and labelled, distinguishing misfits into those who were desirable but insufficiently attentive, for example – 'jocks' and 'hunks' – from those who were over-attentive but lacked the requisite status – 'nerds' or 'dweebs'. A woman who did not abide by the rules and chose badly was in real danger of being cruelly censured herself (a 'slag', a 'princess'). Confronted with this model, many of the young women were deeply offended that they could be thought so cynical, yet that was indisputably what they acted as if they believed. Where does the presuppositional framework of a female sophomore live? It certainly lives in the sharp gossip of her milieu. But it must surely also live inside her head – in an 'unconscious' part of her mind that may be very different from the Freudian subconscious.

Our Western common-sense view of our psychology is equally hard to explicate, but the cognitive anthropologist Roy D'Andrade of the University of California has tackled it. For European cultures since the eighteenth century, people have been seen as possessing something called a 'mind', which is their organ of intelligence. This organ is closely associated with the brain, but it is not the same. (The nineteenth-century satirist Ambrose Bierce defined the mind as 'a curious form of matter secreted by the brain'.) It is also a kind of mental place where states of mind happen – the well-lit office of consciousness – and who we are, each of us, is essentially the 'chief executive' whose office this is. This is where all the interesting, intelligent, bits of us go on – where we 'ponder', 'plan', 'decide', 'intend' and issue speaking or marching orders to the muscles of our throats and feet to put our plans into action.[5]

On this model, conscious states, especially rational thoughts, are the causes of actions – except occasionally, when we are 'absent-minded', or mad, or when we suddenly 'change our minds' (though exactly who changed what remains rather a mystery). 'I didn't mean to' works (sometimes) as an excuse for kids, but not for grown-ups. Perception shows us the world as it is, except occasionally, and memories are accurate records of our real history, except occasionally. The perceptual world is 'outside', while memories, like thoughts and feelings, are 'inside'. Emotions are not made by the mind in the way thoughts are, but they can colour or cloud its operations. 'Bad' feelings are a nuisance, and it is one of the jobs of the mind to control them – a job at which it is not always very good. Introspection means looking in on the workings of the mind, and we can do this pretty well on the whole. 'The unconscious', on the orthodox view, doesn't exist, or if it does, it is better not to think about it (like the bishop of Worcester's wife who, when told of Darwin's theory of evolution, said she hoped it was not true, but that if it was, it didn't get about).

But cultures vary a lot in their implicit psychology. The closest the Illongot, a Filipino tribe, get to a concept of the mind is *rinawa*, but *rinawa* leaves the body and roams about during sleep, and gets thinner as you get older. The Japanese *kokoro* is like mind, but it is located in the heart and is not distinguished from the body.[6] In 2001 a Pakistani mother successfully claimed asylum in the USA for herself and her ten-year-old autistic son. Back home, his condition had been interpreted as 'a curse from Allah', and the boy had been 'forced to undergo various degrading and dangerous mystical treatments'. In Chicago she expected quite a different set of interpretations and reactions.[7]

And cultures change over time. Now, we see our set of judgements as obvious or even 'enlightened', as compared with 'back then', when people saw the world in ways that were much more 'primitive' and 'crude'. It was not till 1975 that, as a result of a notorious postal ballot of members of the American Psychiatric Association, homosexuality was removed from the prestigious Diagnostic and Statistical Manual of Mental Disorders. For the Kpelle people of Africa, the core of 'intelligence' is the ability to remember and reproduce myths and folk tales correctly. For applicants to an American MBA programme it is the ability to solve abstract logical puzzles that bear no relation to their real concerns, fast, under pressure. For Swiss psychologist Jean Piaget it was 'knowing what to do when you don't know what to do'. Take your pick.

Though definitions of 'normality', and the lineaments of common sense, vary over space and time, they always leave an uncomfortable penumbra of human experiences unaccounted for – oddities that seem to challenge the tacit consensus. We cannot tell a story about what is 'normal' without also bringing into existence the abnormal, the deviant, the perverse, the uncanny, the odd. And it is here that the second kind of stories – the explicit 'explanations' – are required to protect and buttress common sense. When life gets dangerous and unpredictable, it pays to have such a story, one that will tell you how to proceed, as well as offering the comfort of comprehension. If the danger passes, so too does the need to explain. Before their fishing boats had motors, it was hazardous for a community of Portuguese fishermen to negotiate the bar at the entrance to their harbour. There were many witches and spirits living there, whose powers caused boats to capsize. But when motors came, it was much easier to cross the bar – and almost overnight the witches, and all the rituals they demanded, disappeared.[8]

If it is dangerous not to have a theory about the wrecking of boats or the failure of the crops, how much more so to be at sea about oneself? 'If I'm so sensible, how come I did such a stupid thing?', we are obliged to ask. And we answer: I must have been stressed. I was beside myself. I was obsessed, or perhaps possessed. A vindictive god whispered into my ear. A mischievous gremlin led me astray. The ley lines were strong, the feng shui wrong, or the planets misaligned ... Some supportive account is trotted out that explains, or explains away, the apparent rent in my rationality. It is here, in the shadows, just outside the walls of common sense, that notions of the unconscious make their camp. They are part of an armoury of ideas, ancillary tales, that buttress the unarticulated, consensual view of human nature.

As common sense varies over time and place, so do its appendices, or its apocrypha. For the Balinese, the experience of being 'possessed' by the spirit of another person is commonplace and unexceptionable. For a Christian mystic it could have been a mysterious blessing. For a nineteenth-century medium it was a communication channel to the 'other side'. For a contemporary stage hypnotist it is a trick. In the British colonies, or the American South, a century or two ago, the minds of the natives or slaves were unquestionably feebler than those of their lords and masters. Only a fool would have doubted it. Today, it is the psychological racist who looks stupid and perverse. The orthodoxy has been inverted. As Alexander Pope wrote in *The Dunciad*,

> What's now apocrypha, my wit,
> In time to come may pass for holy writ.

But however the explanatory landscape has changed, there is a collection of psychological oddities – varieties of the uncanny – that crop up again and again, requiring a coat of explanatory whitewash. There is random bad luck that seems egregiously unreasonable or unfair. There are surges of physical energy, strength or emotion that seem to well up from nowhere: uncharacteristic acts of bravery, or the overwhelming passions of love, for example. There are experiences that seem to confuse reality and imagination: visual hallucinations, or voices inside your head that tell you what to do. There are, so we are told, experiences of grace, when personality drops away and an oceanic peace relieves people of all anxiety and dissatisfaction. There are moments of inspiration or creativity, in which genuinely novel and valuable ideas just erupt into consciousness without any train of thought leading up to them. There are moments of decision, perhaps life-changing ones, that likewise come out of the blue. And there are subtler intimations of knowing, such as inklings, hunches and aesthetic feelings that again have no rational antecedents, but which can turn your stomach or make your hair stand on end with excitement.

There are the self-defeating or self-destructive impulses that characterise obsessive and compulsive behaviour. There are periods of melancholy or mania that have no apparent cause. There is cruelty that seems so monstrous that 'human nature' alone is inadequate to explain it. There are Freudian slips, in which our less creditable natures seem for a moment to grab control of our tongues and spill the beans. There are dreams and visions that come pregnant with symbolic and elusive significance. There are altered states of consciousness, in which normal self-control seems to be handed over to another, as in hypnosis or possession or trance. There is the paranormal: the world of telepathy and precognition. There are the age-old questions of what makes the difference between a live person and a dead body, and whether there is a 'somewhere' that the 'whatever-it-is' decamps to after death. There is the 'automatic pilot' that seems to be able to do very smart things while consciousness is elsewhere. There is subliminal perception, and the 'sixth sense' that tells you, without any apparent information, that there is someone else in the room. There are puzzling neurological phenomena, such as 'blindsight', in which people can inexplicably see or hear, but have no *experience* of vision or sound. If you add them up, there is a mountain of such details that do not square with our common sense and stand in need of an alternative story.

Some of these concocted stories look outward, to the hypothetical forces of evil or feng shui, or to the interventions of quasi-human beings such as ancestor-spirits or the gods. But others look inward, and posit dark corners of the human psyche, soul or mind that influence us without our knowing. We call these 'the unconscious', but really we are not talking about a single invisible entity, a psychological *éminence grise* that is behind all the puzzling phenomena. No, what we are pointing to is a motley collection of such agencies that are called into existence, one by one, when we need them to do a particular explanatory job. The 'unconscious' of subliminal perception is not the same as the unconscious of creativity, or of Freudian neurosis, or of a momentary mystical meeting with the Godhead. The truth is that, after millennia of story-telling, we have inherited a glory-hole of notions that is in urgent need of a clear-out.

My holiday reading contained *The Dead Lagoon*, an Aurelio Zen detective story by Michael Dibdin, *Atonement* by Ian McEwan, a collection of old Jeeves and Wooster yarns to cheer me up, and a copy of the *Independent* newspaper. I did not have to search very hard for traces of these various unconsciouses in popular culture. Jeeves, as usual, turned out to be rather more *au courant* than his master. In one of the stories, Bertie Wooster had woken to find the solution to a knotty social problem clear in his mind. Jeeves opined sagely that 'it must have been your unconscious, sir'. Bertie, impressed as ever, mused to himself: 'I never actually knew I had an unconscious mind . . . but I suppose I must have done all along, without realizing it.' Even by the 1930s, the creative unconscious was familiar enough to make jokes about.

In Dibdin's thriller, there are several versions of the unconscious on display to choose from. Zen's mind throws up elusive ideas that 'scurry about on the fringes of consciousness'. Uncannily finding his way around Venice, a city he has not visited for decades, he is guided by 'an intimate, subconscious knowledge . . . built up over years of boyhood exploration'. Why he has returned there he is not sure, but suspects that 'painful, murky matters which he kept filed away in an inaccessible portion of his mind' are behind his pilgrimage. Here we have the unconscious as the shadowlands of intuition, as the sedimentary rock of physical memory, and as the locked ward of repression. They share a name, but perhaps they have no more to do with each other than do Tony Blair, Lionel Blair and the Blair Witch Project.

Ian McEwan gives us a different kind of unconscious again – one that functions as a kind of non-verbal organ of learning. In the

"MY DEAR - HE SIMPLY TWISTED MY SUBCONSCIOUS ROUND HIS LITTLE FINGER."

This cartoon from Punch *magazine (1938) is typical of the ambivalence aroused by the un- or sub-conscious. As with hypnotism, the fear is that those who understand this dark terrain will have power over those who do not.*

opening pages of *Atonement*, we meet a small boy who has wet the bed. He is being made to wash his sodden sheets, but why? McEwan explains that 'this was not represented to the boy as a punishment, the idea being to instruct his unconscious that future lapses would entail inconvenience and hard work.'

In the *Independent*, a retired lawyer is interviewed about his remarkable success in a TV quiz show.[9] Does he have any tips for the reader? Yes he does, and they rely on learning to trust the 'feeling of knowing' an answer that leaps into the mind faster than the answer itself. 'The subconscious knows things your conscious mind doesn't. You may hear a question, and think you ought to know the answer, so you buzz. After you've buzzed, you're thinking, What the hell is the answer? You open your mouth to say something – anything – and your subconscious takes over and the answer comes out.' Here is a different unconscious again, an intelligent one which can, like an on-line librarian, make a lightning check of the catalogue to see if the requisite knowledge is in stock, deliver an answer into consciousness, and then take a few extra seconds to scurry out into the library itself to fetch the book from the shelf. (Of course, if the book turns out to have been misplaced or stolen, you are left gasping for air, as contestants on quiz shows sometimes are.)

And despite our ambivalence about the unconscious, there is no question but that our language is full of allusions to it. 'He's just compensating for being short.' 'That boy's obsessed with his teddy-bear.' 'She tries so hard, she must have a complex about failure.' 'He's too introverted to be a good salesman.' 'Her cheerfulness is just a persona.' 'That's just a projection.' 'You're a bit paranoid.' We psychologise ourselves, probing down into the mud-banks of our own partial self-awareness, and second-guess each other, happily attributing to our friends motives and mental states that we think they are unconscious of. This bowdlerised Freudian lexicon we use all the time.

So over the centuries, each different group of oddities has

spawned its own set of stories and its own family of images. For Plato, as for Freud, dreams revealed a kind of hidden sub-personality, libidinous, greedy and uncivilised, that managed to slip past the censors under cover of sleep and romp and growl in the mind of the dreamer. For Aristotle the unconscious was the animating spirit, the inner 'form' of the human being, while for the early Christian Church it was the soul, the buried scrap of pure divinity, the immaculate memento of His glory, which God had hidden in every human heart. For the European Middle Ages, the unconscious was the 'book of the heart', with the cryptic Word of God on one page, the recto if you like, waiting to be deciphered, and the dubious record of one's own life, the raw material for reflection and repentance, on the verso facing it.

Shakespeare's unconscious had 'an unknown bottom, like the Bay of Portugal', and was the turbid depths of the mind, into which one had to peer in order to discern one's true desires and motives. For the Romantics, the unconscious was the dark tunnel that connected everyone's personal soul to the energy and wonder of Nature. While for the mystics, of whatever religious stripe, the unconscious was The Cloud of Unknowing, the Godhead, the impenetrable wellspring out of which all experience continuously and spontaneously gushed. And for the more sober, cognitively inclined, like Leibniz and Herbart, the unconscious was the sub-merged bulk of the iceberg of the mind, without which the conscious tip had neither meaning nor stability. Or it was the wings of the theatre of consciousness, the 'behind the scenes' where the scripts were written and rehearsed.

Heir to so many different 'tales of the unexpected', no wonder our current folk psychology is confused and incoherent. If we are to broaden Freud's narrow, pathologised vision of the unconscious to include the many other forms of the uncanny, and to move towards a picture of the human mind that embraces and gives coherence to all its different modes, from the sharpest, most rational, to the mystical and the murky, we have several tasks before us. First we have to tease out the tangled skein of images that we have already, lay them out, and see clearly what jobs they have been doing. And then we have to see if they can be woven together into a stronger fabric. That is what I shall go on to do in the remainder of this book.

I shall suggest that current thinking in neuroscience can help us with this task. There are ways of thinking about the brain, and its wider connections with the body as a whole, that enable us to begin to construct a common explanation for creativity *and* repression, subliminal perception *and* mystical experience. We might even, at a stretch, be able to include the fairies at the bottom of the garden, and the voices of the gods echoing across from Mount Olympus, within the brain itself. But in the end I shall conclude that the brain alone is not enough. We do need both inner and outer kinds of explanation: both the amygdala and the Devil. For gods and demons are public figures, and they serve a social function, as well as a psychological one. The brain can do a lot, as an explanatory idea; but it does not, and I argue will not, help us regulate our world as well as the spirits do. The pendulum has swung just about as far towards the 'inward', the psychological and neurological, as it can, and we shall gain, I think, by allowing it to swing back just a little towards the social and the mythic.

Whether I am right about that or not, it is certainly time to take a cool overarching look at the unconscious, not least because it has been the subject of so much misunderstanding, antipathy and derision. It is all too easy for an uncomfortable Reason to poke fun at the simplifications and excesses of our vernacular version of Freud, for example. Michael Bywater, nominating the unconscious as one of his 'Things we could have done without in the last 1000 years', tells the story of a 'highly regarded Freudian analyst' who, while driving, had to brake sharply, and was struck hard by the car behind. Later, she announced to her family her surmise that this incident must have 'meant' that she had a deep-seated unconscious desire to experience sodomy. For Bywater, even entertaining the idea of the unconscious leads, as inexorably as pot leads to crack, to crack-pot ideas, spiralling self-absorption and the desire to excuse Slobodan Milosevic his crimes on the grounds of inadequate potty training. Any idea – evolution, nuclear fission, as well as the unconscious – can be made to look silly or dangerous in the wrong hands, but that does not mean, of course, that it is not a useful tool for thought if treated intelligently.[10]

At least in its popular versions, the unconscious has always been greeted with ambivalence. Its exotic and mysterious nature makes it intriguing, while at the same time it seems to strike at the heart of our common sense. The possibility that I, *qua* conscious reasoner, am not in charge is highly disconcerting. And although we need stories to tie up the loose ends of experience, we are bound to view those accounts with mixed feelings, precisely because their subject matter is the uncanny: that which cannot be 'kenned' within normal beliefs. To the extent that I am identified with an image of myself as self-aware, self-willed and rational, I am going to be hostile to the suggestion that I do not know myself as clearly as I think, and that I am run, more than I think, by motives that are obscure and often shameful. The unconscious, whatever else it is, is undomesticated and unpredictable. It threatens to subvert my carefully crafted and strongly maintained public image, to remind me of things I'd rather forget, or suggest the existence of things I hadn't even thought I had. Better to pooh-pooh the whole idea. Better to attribute such things, if I have to deal with them at all, to the gods and pixies. At least they are beyond my control, and I can maintain the idea, fictional though it may be, of being master in my own house.

Academic psychology has been particularly antagonistic to the unconscious, for obvious reasons. It can be, as William James called it, 'the sovereign means for believing whatever one likes in psychology, and of turning what might become a science into a tumbling ground for whimsies', though James was himself fascinated by the less conscious and non-conscious regions of the mind. In his monumental *Principles of Psychology*, a few pages after he lays out his 'Ten Objections to the Unconscious', we find him happily admitting that 'the recesses of feeling, the darker, blinder strata of character, are the only places in the world where we catch real fact in the making.'[11] But he put his finger on the key anxiety, which continues to this day: that any talk of the unconscious opens a fatal chink in psychology's claim to be a science. Once we admit, not that Freud was right, but even that he had a point, that hard-won scientific status is put in jeopardy. Even the names of university departments matter. To this day, the sign outside the Cambridge University Department of Psychology warns you that you are entering 'The Psychological Laboratory'. And Oxford still has only a Department of *Experimental* Psychology, for no other kind can be admitted. Edward Titchener, one of the founding fathers of scientific psychology, warned in 1917 that if we make the mistake of 'inventing an unconscious mind . . . we voluntarily leave the sphere of fact for the sphere of fiction'.[12]

The fact that creating and testing the utility of such explanatory fictions is the very essence of science was not widely appreciated in the early twentieth century. It is not *having* wacky ideas that is unscientific: on the contrary, they are vital. It is either *rejecting* or *clinging* to them in the absence of evidence that undermines the scientific enterprise. Who would have thought that space could contain 'black holes', or that the idea could be made mathematically precise and empirically powerful? Surely 'antimatter' belongs to the outer reaches of the literary genre called 'science fiction', not to learned Fellows of the Royal Society? The fact that no one has ever seen 'gravity' is neither here nor there. It works so well as an explanatory fiction that it has an honourable place in the pantheon of Common Sense, as well as in the physics lab. 'Germs' and 'atoms', like gods and fairies, ultimately stand or fall on whether it helps to attribute puzzling phenomena to their behind-the-scenes existence, and if it does, and enough people agree, we can call them 'real'. They were useful ideas long before they were made precise. Inventing 'atoms' helps us get a handle on the fact that two lumps of ordinary-looking metal, if brought together in just the right way, will produce a surprisingly big bang. Disease theory makes sense of the unlikely relationship between small, innocuous-looking water snails and the decimation of whole populations through bilharzia. And so it is with the unconscious. The fact that you will not find an Unconscious in a glass case in the British Museum, nor even if you take the top off someone's head and look inside, is neither here nor there.

Academics from William James in the 1890s to Douglas Holander in the 1990s have fired a variety of arguments at the very idea of the unconscious. They agreed that if it dared to strike at the heart of human being's most prized possession – free will – it obviously, self-evidently, had to be wrong. They said it undermined the vital notion of personal responsibility, and therefore law and order. It might be all right in the hands of the intelligentsia, but they argued that it would blow up in the faces of the *hoi polloi*. They said it was a logical impossibility: it was absurd to claim that you could both 'know' something, and not know it, at the same time. They said it was totally anecdotal and based on flawed research – and, indeed, pointed out some instances where it was. All of these arguments have some force, and all apply to certain claims about the unconscious that are inflated or lax. None of them, as we shall see, is conclusive. And when all the different kinds of evidence are put together, the case for the utility, and even the validity, of the unconscious becomes irrefutable.

It is too much to suggest a conscious conspiracy, but, as Freud would say, there may be some unconscious motivation behind the fact that the different strands of the unconscious have never before been tied together. 'Divide and rule' is an age-old strategy, and the rule of Reason has been buttressed and prolonged by the fragmentation, as much as the denial, of the sources of evidence for the unconscious. The dominant Freudian model makes the unconscious scary, alien and abstruse: something whose existence we grudgingly acknowledge – preferably in other people – when there is madness in the air. Meanwhile, when they are not being ignored, other branches of the unconscious are treated as isolated curiosities, consigned to the fairground sideshow of *The X-Files* or forming the basis of dodgy music-hall acts, sandwiched between the magician and the juggler.

To be fair, there have been attempts to tie some of the threads of the unconscious together. Freud's original version was designed to account for subliminal perception just as much as psychopathology. His 'Project for a Scientific Psychology', written in 1895, sketched out a synoptic view of the unconscious, but he soon abandoned this wider project and narrowed his focus, perhaps wisely, to neurosis and the meaning of dreams. Jung's unconscious aimed to incorporate other forms of symbolism, as well as varieties of mysticism, but he had no interest in the more mundane functions that have excited so much recent interest amongst cognitive scientists, who, in their turn, disdain the mystical and poetic. In general, conceptions of the unconscious have been more like a collection of separate but adjacent mine workings, rather than an interconnected network of catacombs. Taken as a whole, our current folk psychology is a jumble of different, incompatible notions that we draw on in an ad hoc way. It is a Heath Robinson machine assembled from the remains of a dozen different traditions by a bunch of clowns.

It is time to see if it might be possible to tell a more elegant tale, one in which the different subplots of the unconscious are given greater prominence, and welded into a tighter, more convincing narrative. If we dare to put them all together and stare them in the face, I shall argue that they no longer form an exotic string of marginalia round common sense, but mount an irresistible challenge to it. To resolve it, we have to turn the image of our minds on its head. And I shall try to persuade you that we shall be better off as a result: able to function more intelligently in the face of the peculiar, complicated mental demands that twenty-first century living makes on us every day.

History does not, of course, repeat itself. But once before, an unbalanced, over-rational model of the mind threatened to hold sway, and the people rejected it, with dire consequences. At the end of the third century BC, Greek rationalism appeared on the verge of final triumph.[13] Clear, methodical thinking was held up as the royal road to overcoming personal difficulties and living a moral life. And what happened? The citizens of Athens fled in their droves from the burden of thinking for themselves into the arms of a host of New Age gurus and shysters. E. R. Dodds published his masterly study of *The Greeks and the Irrational* in the aftermath of the Second World War, and he, like Freud, was deeply afraid that the suppression of the unconscious was partly to blame for the mayhem that he had witnessed. As I write, the tension between Islam and the West seems to increase daily, while the British prime minister's barrister wife is ridiculed for her relationship with a New Age adviser. It would be absurd to draw facile parallels, but I wonder if, again, we are seeing a link between social events and an unbalanced and incoherent picture of the mind.

My enterprise may be timely for another reason. There is, at the moment, a frenzy of interest in 'consciousness'. Both academic and popular books are pouring from the pens of cognitive scientists, each more eager than the last to convince us that they have figured out how consciousness evolved, how brains make it, and what it is for. They form an impressive selection of carts, but we are still, unfortunately, waiting for the horse. For it is not 'the unconscious' that is a late embellishment to the human mind, it is consciousness itself. We were unconscious beings long before the glimmerings of consciousness appeared, and most of our intelligent lives are still lived without reflection or premeditation. After all this time, the intricate process that culminates in the rapid depression of my keyboard keys remains entirely mysterious to me – and I am delighted that my conscious awareness does not have to bother itself with all that detail. It is as plain as the nose on my face (which, of course, I cannot see) that I am not privy to most of what I am, nor should I be. The bulk of me is inaccessible, So how can we hope to talk sense about the tip of the iceberg if there is a conspiracy of silence about the vastly greater bulk below the water-line, or if we demonise or scoff at it? Time to pay attention to the horse, so that we can tell what we are hitching our carts to.

To be sure, words for unconscious events entered European languages only in the eighteenth century, but that is because they had been neither necessary nor possible before. Not possible, because the explicit conceptualising of unconscious mental states needed a well-developed notion of the mind as 'the organ of intel-ligence' to hook onto, and that notion itself only developed during the seventeenth and eighteenth centuries. In 1712 Sir Richard Blackmore had used the word 'unconscious' to mean generally 'unheeding' or 'unaware' of an aspect of the world ('Through every dark recess they pursue their flight, unconscious of the road'). But it was the Scottish judge Lord Kames, in 1751, who first talked of being conscious or unconscious *of our own mental processes*. And it was not till the middle of the following century that the noun, *the* unconscious, made its appearance, first in German ('das Unbewusste') and then in English.

And not necessary, because, before the seventeenth century, the fact that people were not entirely transparent to themselves was so commonplace that it had not needed stressing. Only in the after-math of Descartes' rejection of the very idea of 'unconscious intelligence' was a special word required, to point insistently at all the phenomena that had been quietly airbrushed out of the mental picture. An old idea that had been *implicit* in a host of images and myths and ways of talking was suddenly explicitly denied, and so had to be explicitly reasserted. One new word, bobbing like a buoy on the surface of eighteenth- and nineteenth-century cul-ture – but so many different theories and understandings, both old and new, dangling off it, waiting to be hauled up into the light. The unconscious was all the rage in the fashionable salons of mid-nineteenth-century London and Paris. Repression and the archetypes were topics of widespread discussion long before Freud and Jung's successful rebranding of them. But speculations were wild and confused. It was not till the back end of the twentieth century that solid evidence began to be collected, and the painstaking work of integrating all the different senses of the unconscious could begin.

From the beginning, explicit versions of the unconscious were confused and contested, and people invented new words to try to distinguish their version from their rivals'. The word 'unconscious' rapidly began to acquire connotations that different users of the term did not intend and did not like. For some, like Samuel Butler, it had become, in the hands of German Romantics such as Schopenhauer, unbearably grandiose and mystical; while for others, it threatened to supplant the 'soul' itself. As early as 1832, the equivalent term 'subconscious' made its appearance in the historical works of Thomas De Quincey. While commending the Emperor Hadrian for his 'elevated' view of human nature, De Quincey noted that his thought was 'not without some subconscious influence, received directly or indirectly from Christianity'. And it was not long before those whose primary interest was in subliminal perception tried to avoid all unnecessary theoretical baggage by talking of the 'preconscious'. Freud, of course, was to co-opt all of these terms and muddy their meanings still further. Empirical psychologists these days have distanced themselves from Freud by talking of the 'cognitive unconscious', or simply referring to 'non-conscious' processes. In the same spirit I, in my earlier book *Hare Brain, Tortoise Mind*, floated the idea of the 'undermind', but I now think there are quite enough words already, and I shall take my chances of rousing unwanted associations in the reader's mind, by using the generic 'unconscious' to refer to the whole tangled family of ideas.

One last set of caveats, before we embark on our tour round the history of the unconscious, in order that expectations are not set too high. The topic is huge, and I have been highly selective. A truly comprehensive history waits to be written, and when it is, it will be several volumes thick. I offer only 'edited highlights', landmarks that seem to capture something essential about the times, or which represent a jump or a new direction in the way the unconscious is seen. Some obvious traditions, characters and ideas are given rather shorter shrift than you might expect, and this is sometimes because their stories are widely known, or have been given fuller treatment by others, and sometimes because there simply wasn't room. The Judaic mystical tradition, to pick just one, contains much that is relevant, though I'm afraid you won't find it here. Plotinus and Aquinas deserved much greater space than they have got, as did Schopenhauer. And much of nineteenth-century psychiatry and twentieth-century psychotherapy is skated over, the former because Henri Ellenberger has given it an exhaustive treatment in his magisterial *The Discovery of the Unconscious*, and the latter because the 'mind, body and spirit' shelves in your local bookstore are already groaning with it. Eric Berne and Fritz Perls should be here, and a good many of the post-Freudians and post-Jungians. But there we are.

A more serious warning concerns the kind of evidence I have drawn upon, and what weight it will bear. When we go back before the seventeenth century, and certainly back to classical times and beyond, it is very hard to know exactly how the mass of people perceived their lives, and what they actually believed. In the Middle Ages, for example, it is entirely possible that people talked and thought in private in a different way than they did 'in public', just as people used to do in the Soviet Union, for fear of reprisals from the oppressive powers of State or Church. On the other hand, many of the theological or philosophical writings which have been preserved may not have touched the lives of ordinary folk at all, nor represent their experience. Such writings were often

avant-garde and arcane. What the average Athenian knew about
Plato, and what they thought of him if they did, I can't say with
any great conviction. Emerson tells a nice story about lending a
copy of Plato's *Republic* to a farmer friend, who expressed his surprise, on returning the book, that it had had so many of his own
ideas in it. But I don't know what his fifth-century BC counterpart
would have said. Nevertheless, I have drawn on these writings, as
well as on the literature, poetry, drama and art of different periods.
It is possible to distil out of a song or a play indications of their
implicit models of the mind – how life-and-death decision-
making is depicted in the plays of Euripides, for example – and it
may well be that these capture the prevailing folk psychologies
better than the more didactic writing of the time. Nevertheless, I
am not a trained historian, nor an anthropologist, so I advise you
to test the strength of some of my arguments, as best you can,
before you put your full weight on them.[14]

In this opening chapter my aim has been to give a sense of the
scope and the purpose of the book. In a nutshell, the unconscious
has a relatively short history as a word – though still a good deal
longer than Freud would have had us believe – but an extremely
long and complex one as an idea. People have always had the need
to tell stories about the oddities of their experience, and though
the precise nature of these oddities, and of the stories concocted to
account for them, has varied across cultures and over time, variations on the theme of the unconscious occur time and again.
Sometimes these variations are metaphorical and elliptical. When
people have invoked the gods, or constructed an underworld, we
cannot always know for certain whether they have seen them as
real external entities, or as externalised images of inner processes,
or both. Often the latter, I am sure. Over the last six millennia,
there has been a trend towards internalisation, but many societies
and individuals have bucked that trend. In other instances – that
of St Augustine, for example – it is absolutely clear that the source
of the mystery is being firmly located within, and astonishingly

modern forms of introspection, and psychological conceptualisation, have been developed.

The earliest attempts to tell stories about the uncanny placed its source outside the person, in mythologised landscapes, and person-like gods and spirits. Over the course of history, those sources have been moved inside, into the inner recesses of heart and brain. Mount Olympus has become a metaphorical microchip. But it is with the outside that we must begin. Enough with the overview. Now it is time to get down to work. And to do that we have to roll up our sleeves, unwrap our amateur archaeologist's trowel, and dig back some four thousand years into the sophisticated mythological world of ancient Egypt.

2

The Supernatural: Magical Landscapes and Invisible Puppeteers

> There *are* such things as ghosts. People everywhere have always known that. And we believe in them every bit as much as Homer did. Only now we call them by different names. Memory. The Unconscious.
>
> – Donna Tartt, *The Secret History*

Westward, where the sun sinks every evening, lies the underground realm of the unconscious – and the dead. Every night, while we sleep in darkness, the burning sun, below the horizon, traverses the subterranean ocean of Nun, brightening the secret world of the mummified, and revitalising the tired bodies and minds of the merely asleep. The Sun God Ra, himself weary and grey from the rigours of the day, sails across this vast expanse of water in his golden ship, and enters the anus of Apophis, the evil but life-giving serpent. Passing through Apophis from tail to head, Ra both overcomes the wicked snake and is himself rejuvenated, eventually re-emerging from the serpent's mouth refreshed and ready to rise again in the East to light another day. The dark intestine of Apophis is both nurturing and dangerous. Nun is both the 'Lake of Life', reinspiring the virtuous, and the 'Lake of Fire', the prototype of Hell, in which the wicked are forever punished. And the most wicked of all are imprisoned in the uttermost depths of the lake, where no light ever reaches, and from where no cry of horror can ever escape. Into this world, every night, slips my *Ka*, the invisible source of my own life energy, to follow Ra on his voyage, and to reap the benefits of rejuvenation for myself. And as my *Ka* progresses, so its bizarre adventures, and its encounters with the ancestors and the gods, are beamed back to my sleeping body by the Nile, and kindle its *Ba*, its dormant consciousness, into dreams and visions.[1]

Two thousand years before Christ, with the Pyramid of Cheops and the Great Sphinx already nearing their thousandth birthdays, the ancient Egyptians of the Middle Kingdom in the Nile valley had some aspects of the unconscious pretty well worked out. Using imagery familiar to a nation of boatmen, they created a mythic world that was at once a cautionary moral cosmology and a psychology that provided a rather sophisticated account of both dying and dreaming. Both Inner and Outer were accommodated. In the world of Nun you would find gods and monsters, symbolic animals and archetypes, and also rudimentary facets of what would come to be called the psyche, both conscious and unconscious, happily (or not so happily) living side by side. Aspects of life, good, bad and indifferent, are temporarily raised into the light of consciousness by the passage of Ra before sinking back into darkness again. There are intimations of forces so dark and powerful that they must never be brought into the daylight of consciousness at all. There are harbingers of the incipient conflicts of Freud, and also the archetypal, godly wisdom of Jung.

It is from these promising and picturesque beginnings that the four-thousand-year history of the unconscious must set out. Its own journey has not been uneventful, and, like the Sun God, it has been through cycles of enervation and refreshment, neglect and prominence. In the last two hundred years the scientific method has at last begun to put the unconscious on a firm empirical footing. Much progress has recently been made, though not

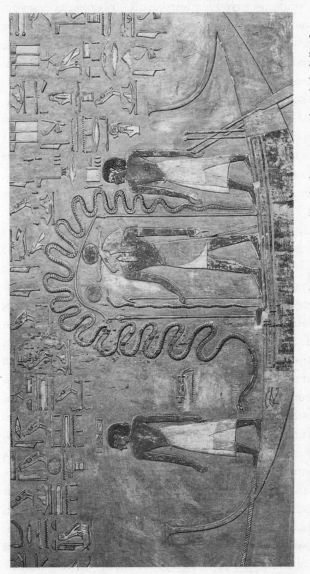

The Egyptian sun god Ra undergoes his nightly journey of regeneration, as his solar barque passes through the belly of the serpent Apophis. This limestone wall painting was discovered in the tomb of King Seti the First, and dates from the New Kingdom, circa 1200 BC.

necessarily in the directions that the Freudians would have us believe. But things have been lost as well – richness, poetry and, perhaps most importantly of all, coherence. At the onset of the twenty-first century, we have some well-worked-out titbits of the unconscious; but hardly such a Big Picture as the ancient Egyptians seem to have devised.

All we can have of the unconscious are metaphors and theories, of course. We cannot stand it up against the wall and take its photograph. And these symbolic images have to derive from the world as it is known. The modern world is full of existing concepts and artefacts from which we can draw metaphorical inspiration – water pumps and digital computers help us get a handle on the workings of our hearts and minds. But in the absence of such tangible forms of technology, you have to draw on what you know: landscape, the weather, the rhythms of nature and, of course, other people. And in the absence of much understanding of the 'interiority' of people – of their physiology and anatomy, as much as their psychology – you tend to turn outward, and seek explanations for the oddities of human nature not in the individual 'mind', for that idea was not yet thinkable, but in visible shapes and behaviours. You look at the land, you listen to the thunder, you observe your friends and your rulers, and you bend them, in your collective imagination as a society, as much as you need, into a set of forces and players that can underwrite metaphorical stories about how it is that dreams and death, madness and misfortune, come to be. Hence the Lake of Fire. And hence the gods.

We can roughly divide these sources of analogy into two: the natural world of landscape, weather and animals, and the human world of power, wisdom, trust and influence. As we shall see, both of these have carried through until the present day. The unconscious is still conceived of partly as a 'place', partly as a set of impersonal forces, and partly as a collection of sub-personalities. What was originally outward-looking has become psychologised, though the metaphorical roots of the unconscious remain visible.

But let us first sample some of the more vivid of these metaphors, and explore how and why the outer began to be internalised. To do so, we shall have to make some leaps through space and time. But to start with, let's go back to the metaphors derived from the nature and the land.

Certain geographical features and locations lend themselves to modelling the unconscious. Fast-forward some 1,500 years from the ancient Egyptians, and listen to Plato in the *Phaedo* basing his detailed description of the Underworld explicitly on his first-hand knowledge of the volcanoes and underground waterways of the island of Sicily.

> Underneath the earth there are ever-flowing rivers of an
> immense size, some with hot waters, others with cold. And there
> is much fire, and great rivers of fire, and many rivers of liquid
> mud – some purer, others more turbid – just like in Sicily with
> its rivers of mud flowing ahead of the lava, and then the stream
> of lava itself. These fill each of the regions in the Underworld . . .
> and they all move up and down according to a kind of see-saw
> motion inside the earth . . . The regions in the hollows of the
> earth are all joined to each other by channels . . . with
> interconnecting passages through which much water flows from
> one place to another as if into mixing bowls or craters.[2]

As it was for the Egyptians, the Greek kingdom of Hades was simultaneously mythic and geographic; social and psychological. There is no point in trying to decide whether such images are meant to be taken literally or symbolically – as *logos* or *mythos* – because such distinctions were not made anything like as firmly as the global Euro-mind likes to make them today. Layers of meaning comfortably coexisted and intermingled: real terrain was imbued with symbolic meaning (as it still is for many indigenous peoples), while mythic figures and events were more than mere fictions. So it is hard not to read Plato's description of the natural catacombs of Sicily, at some level, as painting a remarkably prescient picture of what today would be called the 'modular mind'. (The archaeologist Steven Mithen, author of *The Prehistory of the Mind*, remarks: 'If you wish to know about the mind, do not ask only psychologists and philosophers; make sure you also ask an archaeologist.')[3] Nevertheless, we must suppose that people took these images, as they did their parables and legends, at very different levels, many, perhaps, being content with a rather literal reading, while others were more aware of their psychological resonances. The Greeks were certainly as puzzled as we are by the sudden, dramatic way in which emotions can 'boil over', and people 'blow their tops', and what better metaphor to reach for than a volcano, whose fearsome eruptions of fire and steam betoken turbulent interactions between fire and water running through the earth, the world's unconscious, below?

Plato himself demonstrates how intricately these layers of meaning are woven together. In his mythological landscape there is a subterranean river called the Cocytus whose colour is described as *kyanos*, midnight blue. Etymologically the Cocytus is the river of grief, and in Greek religion and literature, *kyanos* was itself the colour of mourning. Just as the unpredictability of Mount Etna mirrors an abrupt outburst of anger, so the outpouring of the Cocytus provides an image of the uncontrollable welling up of tears. True, these are not images that give you a great deal of purchase on the problem of what to do about these wayward passions, but at least they offer the slight comfort of being able to construe your emotional outbursts as natural phenomena (rather than as personal failings). And the gods and goddesses are woven into Plato's story too. Persephone was, according to legend, given the island of Sicily by Zeus as some compensation for having been raped by Hades; and the spring at Syracuse, where Hades was said to have snatched Persephone, was known as *Kyane*, the Midnight Spring, after the tears shed by Demeter at the loss of Persephone, her daughter.

The underground provides a natural metaphor for creativity, as well as for emotion. Volcanoes are creative – new configurations of the landscape result from their molten flows of lava. The forces of nature are productive as well as destructive. The ground is the source of precious minerals, and the wellspring of blossoms, as well as of earthquakes and floods. So we should not be surprised to find 'going down into the earth' being used, down the ages, as a symbol for harnessing the creative power of the unconscious.

A modern example is provided by the nineteenth-century fairy tale 'The Three Feathers'. In order to decide which of his three sons should inherit his realm, an old king set them the task of finding the finest carpet. Three feathers launched from the castle tower indicated which way they should head: one west, one north, and the third, belonging to the youngest brother, the 'dummy', fell to earth close to the castle wall. He sits down, dejected, by the feather, but then notices a trapdoor, leading down into the earth. He descends and comes to a room in which sits a big toad, who gives him the most beautiful carpet, which, of course, much surpasses the feeble offerings of the other two brothers, who had thought their younger brother so stupid that they need not bother to look very hard. The older brothers protest and persuade their father that further tests are needed . . . and so the story progresses, until finally Dummy is given the crown, and rules 'for a long time, and with great wisdom'. The supposed 'dummy', not too proud to dig into his own mental back yard, his unconscious, creates works of great beauty, while the discursive intellect roams far and wide, and comes home with nothing original. Bruno Bettelheim comments: 'Going down into the darkness of the earth is a descent into the netherworld . . . this is a tale of Dummy embarking on exploring his unconscious mind . . . The story suggest the limitations of an intellect that is not founded on, and supported by, the powers of the unconscious.'[4]

We should not forget, however, that the more sinister, deathly side of the unconscious is also, to this day, symbolised by the underworld. Comics and cartoons make constant use of the device. It's in Dungeons that you find Dragons. H. G. Wells's classic story *The Time Machine*, you recall, creates an eerie relationship between the childlike Eloi who live above ground, apparently blessed and playful, and the mole-like Morlocks, scuttling in the dark, fearful of the light, to be pitied for their lot – or so the Time Traveller thinks to begin with. Only slowly and with horror does it dawn on him where the power actually lies, and who is really in control. (*The Time Machine* was first published in 1895, the same year that Freud was writing his 'Project for a Scientific Psychology', and both Freud and Wells were touched by the pessimism about human nature that marked the *fin-de-siècle* years. There is little doubt that Wells's fantasy deserved to be shelved under 'psycho-mythology' rather than 'science fiction'.)

There are many other aspects of nature that can be pressed into metaphorical service. The tangible forces of wind and thunder and magnetism constitute prototypes from which more ethereal counterparts such as 'the wrath of the Lord', or even perhaps the invisible power of feng shui, can be derived, and held responsible for creativity and madness, strange attraction or undeserved misfortune. While from Aesop's fables and the witch's black cat to Uncle Remus and the Brothers Grimm, with their wise toads and wild trolls, authors down the ages have imbued animals with humanlike traits and good or bad intent, and used them to gain a spurious handle on the otherwise inexplicable, or to do their moral work. Like Dr Dolittle, Siberian shamans talk to the animals, or even turn themselves into birds or dogs, and through such means gain apparent access to the esoteric knowledge of the supranormal world.[5]

In many of these nature-based analogues, 'down' – down into the earth, down the phylogenetic scale – is one of the dominant metaphors for the oddities of human experience. 'Dark' is another. Wherever you look, both externalised and internalised versions of the unconscious draw on either or both of these symbolic dimensions. The underworld is not only a subterranean place of punishment and interment; it is the place – the nightly journey of Ra notwithstanding – where, to echo a coarse expression, 'the sun don't shine'. Darkness is scary: it is where the creatures of the night have the advantage, where gollums hiss and wolves howl. And it is the state that invites the projections of our own unconscious fears. All cats are grey in the dark, but they are likely to be savage, too. Aristotle observed that 'in some young people, even if their eyes are wide open and it is dark, many moving shapes appear, so that they often cover their heads in fright'.[6] In the dark is where ghosts appear, and night-time is when the dim flickering of a candle flings monsters into the far corners of rooms.

For our forebears, until just a century ago, the crepuscular world was much more real and familiar than it is for us, and therefore a readier source both of scary apparitions and of metaphorical inspiration. Darkness was a daily part of life for adults and children alike, and in using the dark as an image they were, perhaps, weaving the idea of the unconscious – of the central, continuous presence of mystery, the inability to 'see', in the midst of life – into the explanatory fabric of their stories. It is only with the coming of electric light that darkness itself has become a virtual stranger, or at least an option. People who know they can reach out for the light switch are never as truly in the dark as those who have to pick their way carefully across the room to bed. We flood the night with light, and close our eyes almost before we have flicked off the bedside lamp to sleep, and in doing so, reduce our acquaintance with the ambiguous, projective quality of the gloaming, in which we can rub shoulders with ghosts, as well as feel the elusive beauty of the Old Masters. Walter de la Mare, in the introductory essay to *Behold, This Dreamer!*, his anthology of poetry celebrating the unconscious, reminds us that 'to resort to candles even for a few hours is to realise what an aid their gentle light can be to quiet of mind and quiet talk – let alone the beauty thus conferred on quiet face and musing eye.'[7] In the twilight, our imaginations are more

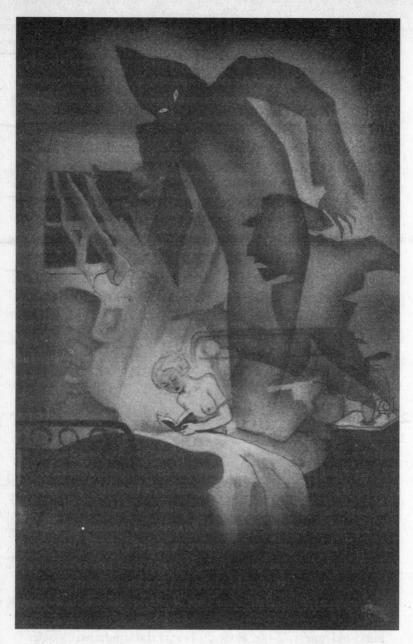

Even after electric lights had become widely available, the imaginative potential of the gloaming retained its hold. In this image by the artist Le Chantre, published in Fantasio *magazine in 1934, the localised illumination of the lamp leaves plenty of dark corners into which the thriller reader can project her imaginings.*

restless and alert, more on the *qui vive*, and our conscious minds brush more adventurously and intimately against their own unconscious lining.

Impersonal nature provides a source of vivid imagery for the wilder reaches of human nature, but, as I say, it does not offer much in the way of practical suggestions for coping with them better. Unless you have first imbued nature with humanlike feelings and responses, there is little point in pleading with a volcano or trying to outwit a lake. But you can with people. If your disconcerting mood swings are caused not by natural forces but by whimsical, humanlike beings, albeit invisible ones, you can attempt to persuade them to cut it out, or get someone to intercede with them on your behalf. Gods may not be real, but they do at least suggest things that you could try. They stop you feeling so damn helpless, whether the problem be a plague of locusts or a sudden, disastrous, loss of nerve. So enters into the historical record the supernatural world of beings that are like us – but not exactly; human in form, but possessed of exaggerated powers: immortality, precognition, superhuman strength, flight. Zeus or Aphrodite, God or the Devil, goblins or incubi, Batman or the Bunyip: a million malign or benign quasi-people can be conjured up to account for your bad luck, your hallucinations, your burst of genius – or simply to keep you in line.

Even in the haunting bright-dark world of Nun, it is the heroic, humanlike figure of Ra that draws our attention – and to whom we can offer praise and sacrifice, on the off chance he'll see us right. The gods were not invented, initially, to explain our psychological oddities, but to assist with the management of the natural, and increasingly the social, worlds. You cannot control the wind, or the tidal rip around the sandbar at the mouth of the harbour – but if there is a god of the weather or the sea, *they* can, and they might, perhaps, be talked into running their affairs in a more accommodating fashion.

An animistic world is one in which insecurity is ameliorated by the appearance of influence or control. And this appearance, though an illusion, is not without an abundance of supporting evidence. If rain comes after the rain-dance, that proves the rain god is there, and listening. If it doesn't, that proves that he finds us unworthy, or is angry, or has more important things on his mind, and we have to make a bigger sacrifice, or repent our sins more sincerely. Eventually our luck will change, and when it does, it will provide us with yet more dramatic proof of the long-term virtues of faith and prayer. Such selective perception – driven by what psychologists call our 'confirmatory bias' – is ubiquitous, and arguably the most powerful influence on the shaping of our systems of belief.[8] It is precisely because believing is seeing (our perception is 'theory-laden') that seeing is believing (our experience seems, so often, to validate our beliefs).[9] Keep betting on good old Number 17 and sure enough, if you are not bankrupt or dead long since, your faith will be rewarded . . .

To see why the gods and spirits emerged as they did, we have to dig a little deeper into the prehistory of the human mind. Perhaps 100,000 years ago, way back in the Pleistocene era, human intelligence began a dramatic process of escalation. And the main reason, according to the British psychologist Nicholas Humphrey, was the need to figure out what your friends and acquaintances were thinking.[10] If you could distil your experience of individuals into internal models of their habits and dispositions, you could put yourself in their shoes, infer what they were up to, anticipate what they might do next, and beat them to the draw. We got to be so smart, says Humphrey, because we all became amateur psychologists and social poker-players, reading meaning, and potential advantage, into the twitch of an eyebrow or the tapping of a foot. (Chimpanzees too display some of this 'Machiavellian intelligence', but they lack the genes to capitalise upon it as massively as we human beings have done. One of the characteristics of autistic people, it is said, is precisely their inability to make and use these mental models of other people.)[11]

To fulfil your evolutionary destiny, for example, it is important to be able to tell the difference between predators – those who wish you harm; prey – those who can serve your own purposes; and protectors – those you can trust in your hour of need. Many mammals are born oriented to these crucial distinctions, and programmed to refine and develop both their perceptiveness and the sophistication of their responses, through play with their friends and relations. Feline cubs and kittens take turns to play these roles with their brothers and sisters.[12] But life gets very much more interesting when those around you can switch unpredictably between these roles and start to play the game for real. Then you need to develop both specific knowledge of individuals' idiosyncrasies, and the general skills of the mind-reader. (It is also useful if you can learn how to conceal your own plans and issue misleading signals that throw your rivals off the scent, but the evolution of deception is another story.)

The most important people to be able to suss out are, of course, the most powerful: the kings and queens of your social world. It pays you to observe them, and listen to them, carefully, so you can intuitively distil out their desires and dispositions more accurately, and thus placate or manipulate them more effectively – knowing (as children and employees do today) when to ask for a raise, or to kowtow in order to avoid being picked as the sacrificial victim. You learn when and how to adopt their habits, and when and how to mirror their assertiveness with your own display of submission. You learn how they think, and how to think like them. Though you have no idea that this is what you are doing, in the psychological language of today we might say (as I suggested a moment ago) that your brain builds a little working model of significant others, and runs this model, in critical situations, in order to hear and see how they are likely to behave.

To help you stay one jump ahead, you may literally hear their voice, issuing their commands or prohibitions, in your head. And when they die, their voices can continue to be produced by the microchip in your own mind. And the Princeton psychologist Julian Jaynes has suggested that it is precisely through those mental models, and their hallucinated pronouncements, that dead kings provided the initial bases for the voices of immortal gods. There is certainly evidence, dating as far back as 9000 BC, that tribal rulers continued after their death to be active presences, their corpses being preserved and displayed for all to see – and perhaps to 'hear' as well. And such rule from beyond the grave could easily have formed the basis on which memories of real figures turned into reverence for supernatural ones. Jaynes suggests, for example, that the great Egyptian god Osiris was, in essence, 'the hallucinated voice of a dead king whose admonitions could still carry weight'.[13]

People who lived three thousand years ago or so, suggests Jaynes, had brains that were wired a little differently from yours and mine. They had not yet acquired the trick of attenuating these internally generated voices to distinguish them from 'real' ones, so they heard them just as if they were the voices of real people talking to them. They possessed, to use Jaynes's phrase, a 'bicameral mind', with two 'chambers', one which generated the voices, and one which heard them, and the latter could not tell, simply from the quality of the heard voice, when it was having a genuine conversation and when it was picking up self-generated activity. Except that, when you are listening to the internalised voice, there is nobody around – you can't see anybody else's lips moving. So they must be there, but you just can't see them. With such a mentality, it makes perfect sense to plug the explanatory vacuum with a real, but invisible, god or a spirit. And if you have not one but a variety of voices in your head – or if people around you are hearing different ones – your pantheon expands, and your sense of living in a populated supernatural world strengthens and stabilises.[14]

Of course, in Jaynes's 'Just So story' it is not long before the already powerful in society notice that it suits them just fine for people to be tuning in to the voice of the 'gods'. If the dictates and judgements of these invisible beings just happen to coincide with their own interests, they will have 'God on their side'. Better still, keep the pronouncements of the gods vague and gnomic, and they can set themselves up as intermediaries and interpreters, thus consolidating their public mandate, and ensuring that they don't get caught out. If the gods sound like kings, people will respond like 'subjects'; if they sound like stern but loving parents, people will tend to trust them and do what they say. What's more, if these invisible beings are omniscient, and can see inside you, you have not just to be careful about what you do, for fear of 'divine retribution', you even have to try to control what you think and feel. Put the judge inside people's own minds, and you will have less dissent to deal with.[15]

Some of these beings are more fully, richly humanlike than others. In many societies in Africa, for example, the voices are explicitly heard as those of revered ancestors, and though they may have acquired some superhuman characteristics, they remain recognisably 'like us'. Whether the Greek pantheon was originally based on historical figures or not, the residents of Mount Olympus too, for all their immortality, are essentially souped-up human beings. But not all societies followed the Greeks in casting their gods in such obviously human form. Herodotus, for example, points out that the Persians 'have no images of the gods, no temples, no altars, and consider the use of them as a sign of folly. This comes, I think, from their not believing the gods to have the same nature with men as the Greeks imagine.'[16] But – to anticipate the argument – the more distinctly human these ancillary beings are, the easier it will turn out to be, perhaps, to shrink them and place them inside one's own heart or mind, as mysterious little 'sub-personalities' of one's own.

Today we tend to think of hearing voices as a sign of mental disorder, but throughout history it has been a common, and often beneficial, experience. Though they had little else in common, Pythagoras, St Augustine, Galileo and Joan of Arc all experienced compelling auditory hallucinations, and for the last two thousand years it has been taken as a sign of being favoured as often as it has been associated with madness. Even today, around 2 million people in Britain claim to hear voices regularly, and as many as one in five of the population hear them occasionally. In fact, a good many of us hear voices, quite routinely: we hear our own, as 'thought', when we 'talk to ourselves' in our heads, and we have mental conversations with a variety of others as we rerun unsatisfactory conversations, or 'wonder what Granny would have said'. The only difference is that we usually distinguish these 'imaginary' voices from 'real' ones, and we do so largely on the basis of their being less intense or distinct. Sometimes though, particularly at times of stress, this distinction breaks down, and we hear the voices with unaccustomed clarity and power. And then we may experience them as godlike – or at least as commandingly parental. 'I don't know if it is my mother,' said one woman, 'I just know it sounds like her . . . putting down what I've done, or criticising me, or saying that what I'm doing is for the wrong reasons.' The same mental mechanism that allowed our forebears to hear from the gods is clearly still part of our modern make-up.[17]

In a society such as classical Greece, hearing voices, and believing them to come from powerful, but invisible, others, is not just an individual matter. Public legends and myths cloak these supernatural beings, if not with solid flesh, at least with histories. Stories were told, embellished and passed on, and in these narratives the gods and goddesses became the cast of the world's first, and arguably longest-running, soap opera. They did not just have individual resonance and existence; over the centuries, they took part in dozens of sagas and story-lines that – just like the contemporary gods and antigods of *Friends* or *Neighbours* – made them seem even more 'like us'. As Daniel Dennett reminded us in the previous chapter, it is deeply in our nature to represent our myths in narratives rather than in neat conceptual categories.[18] Zeus revealed his character – both his power and his vulnerability – in his ongoing domestic disputes with Hera, and through his interventions in the adventures of the Argonauts, rather than in a simple pen-portrait. The idea of an abstracted 'personality', like that of an organ of intelligence called the 'mind', was not yet part of the Greek psychology. People existed in context, and in action, and in Homer the gods therefore manifested in stories. Their influence on human affairs appeared in the context of human dramas – battles, tragedies, moments of crucial decision and indecision. In dreams they tended to restrict their remarks to current dilemmas – though whether they were genuinely trying to be helpful, or were mischievously leading their victims astray, was for the individual to attempt to sort out.

By the time of the great epics of classical Greece, the *Iliad* and the *Odyssey* – still half a millennium before any conception of the individual *psyche* – the supernatural world of the gods was firmly in place. This semi-fictional domain had, originally, two jobs to do. The first was to provide a set of agreed interpretations for the vicissitudes of meteorological fortune – harvests, floods, earthquakes and the like – and agreed methods for trying to improve things. Zeus was responsible for the weather, Poseidon for the sea, Demeter for the harvest, and the junior ranks of nymphs, dryads, naiads and so forth for individual trees, springs and meadows. And the gods' second function was to provide a moral framework for social conduct that reinforced and stabilised a certain *status quo*. The latter function, we might imagine, was in part carried out through the internalised voices of authority – the beginnings of what would develop, over the ensuing two and a half millennia, into the 'super-ego' or the voice of conscience.

But now the pantheon was ready to undertake a third major function in Greek society, one that echoed and developed the multi-layered mythology of ancient Egypt. It could be drawn upon to provide an explanation for the recurrent oddities of human experience, and in doing so, it sowed the seeds of the unconscious, and of psychology itself. For as well as being in charge of different aspects of the environment – wind, flocks, the sea – the gods had begun to develop distinct temperaments, and to concern themselves with particular realms of experience where common sense seemed to break down. When Agamemnon tries to explain why, in a moment of 'madness', he stole the beautiful slave Briseis who had been given to Achilles as a prize, he firmly declares: 'I am not the cause. No; Zeus and Moira and the Fury that walks in darkness are the cause, who cast fierce blindness into [me].'[19]

Though the cumulative sagas of Olympus and its outposts had left the characters of individual gods and goddesses obscured under layers of conflicting story-lines and legends, it is still possible to discern their psychological functions, and even to find their traces in our everyday language. Though Pan was the protector of flocks, his mischief was also responsible for their occasional, apparently unmotivated outbursts of *pan-ic* – and by extension, he could induce unaccountable terror in human beings too.[20] It was Aphrodite's whisper in your ear that filled you with the *aphrodisiac* madness that made sensible people behave in the wild, ridiculous or destructive manner of the love-struck, and also marked the way to the ecstasies of sexual passion. Hermes was the overstepper of boundaries, god of magic, capable of inducing alchemical – that is, *hermetic* – changes in people's personalities; and also, as Mercury, god of the *mercurial*, responsible for the mysteries of whimsy, cunning and deceit. When people behaved out of character, Hermes had been at work. Creativity, whether *muse-ical*, or worthy of a place in a *muse-eum*, or not, depended on gaining privileged information from one of the Muses. The kinds of altered states of consciousness associated with being 'out of your head' on drugs, drink or the powerful *bacchanalian* energies of drumming and dance were the province of Dionysus.

Not all gods have left these linguistic traces, but their special responsibility for an aspect of human oddity remains clear. If your anticipation of the future turned out to be uncannily accurate, that could only be because Apollo, the god of prophecy, had told you in a dream. Athena was often, in the *Iliad*, depicted as the conveyor of unexpected courage or power, *menos*. During one battle, she injected a triple dose of *menos* into the chest of her protégé Diomedes, giving him a much-needed surge of confidence and spunk. When anyone performed a normally difficult feat with ease, it would have been due to such a divinely heightened surge of *menos*. Behind each of the oddities of human experience the Homeric Greeks could clearly discern the shadowy influence of one of the gods. Where we today would point to the repressed memory of childhood trauma, or to the novel linking of two circuits in the brain, the Greeks would have seen the hand of Hermes or Calliope.

Here is not the place to attempt a detailed history of the supernatural.[21] It must suffice to state the obvious: that the invention of supernatural realms, and their use in accounting for the oddities of human experience, neither started nor stopped with the Greeks. Most human cultures throughout history, and across the world, have created and elaborated such systems of belief, and continue to do so. The attempt to distinguish clearly between the inner and outer, and the real and imaginary, characteristic of the post-Enlightenment Euro-mind is culturally and historically unusual. Just as we happily accept the reality of invisible entities and forces such as 'quarks', 'gravity', or indeed 'the unconscious', so the everyday world of pre-Renaissance Europe was peopled with angels and demons, and the forces of Good and Evil were every bit as real and influential as those of 'the market' or of 'globalisation' are today.

In European history the extended family of the Greek gods and goddesses, heroes and heroines, began to lose its status from around the sixth century BC onwards, under the influence of three opposing trends. The first was the rise of the more elaborate psychology, and the development of the concept of the 'soul', which we shall explore in the next chapter. The second was the increase in trade and travel, and with it the appreciation that the Greek deities were not universal. The fact that other peoples had quite different ways of carving up the supernatural territory, and of accounting for madness, magic or creativity, inevitably led to a weakening of certainty and belief, as pluralism always does. And the third was the progressive implosion of an antiquated and over-elaborated mythology into a single divine being. The pantheon collapsed under its own weight of legend and detail, and was gradually replaced by a single, more ethereal, less robustly human deity – the early prototype of the King of Kings and Lord of Lords, the theological *capo di tutti capi* who would in time elide with the Jehovah of the Jewish Old Testament, and turn into the central 'immortal, invisible God only Wise' of the Christian Church. Xenophanes was one of the first to proclaim: 'One god there is, midst gods and men the greatest, in form not like to mortals; he without toil rules all things; ever unmoved in one place he abideth.'

Whereas the Greek pantheon – what the Australian psychologist Bernie Neville refers to as 'Olympus Inc.' – constituted a rather flat, distributed management structure, the Christian, and later Islamic, organisations became rather more layered and hierarchical. At the top, Chairman of the Board, sat God or Allah, but in order to reach and regulate human affairs, a variety of senior, middle and junior managers had to be appointed. Some of these, like the angels, were definitely supernatural, and it was their job to carry messages from God to the world (the word 'angel' derives from the Greek equivalent of the Hebrew word for messenger). Some spirits were recruited or poached from rival religions. ('Remember,' said Pope Gregory the Great, 'you must not interfere with any traditional belief or religious observance that can be harmonised with Christianity.') Like the ancient kings-turned-deities, many of these were originally saints: real, legendary sages and prophets who had been turned into divine or semi-divine beings with the passing of time. And then came popes, bishops and the whole hierarchy of the living clergy, custodians and communicators of God's messages and intent. And on the opposing team there were also the hordes of demons and devils, also arranged in hierarchies, from Satan, chief antagonist of Christ in Christianity, downwards, which personified and externalised the seamy sides of human nature: greed, cruelty, selfishness, lust, treachery and the rest.

It was all very well placing the sources of puzzling experiences outside in the supernatural realm, but there remained the problem of exactly how the denizens of that world exerted their influence. If it is the gods that make us mad, just how do they do it? Tales of their existence had to be supplemented with some understanding of how they communicated with 'mere mortals'. There are various possibilities. The first, which we have already explored, is that they speak directly to me, and tell me what to do, or talk me into doing things that might turn out to be disastrous. They could do this either directly, in a state of trance or in my dreams, or indirectly, through a medium or intermediary of some sort. In principle, as we have seen, such talk posed no more problem to understand than did a face-to-face conversation between two 'real' people. However sometimes – increasingly, argues Julian Jaynes, from the eighth century BC onwards – people felt or dreamed or behaved oddly *without* having heard any such voices. Therefore there had to be other ways in which people could conceivably be swayed by gods and spirits. The second possibility is that they might just mess about with my mind or my emotions directly but remotely, like someone jamming a radio broadcast, without having the courtesy to let me know what they are up to, so that I just find myself besotted, inspired or melancholic without any sense of 'why' or 'how come'. The action of the god is inferred, but without any direct evidence. This feels unsatisfyingly hypothetical and abstract, though, and the search for better answers began to open up questions about what was *inside* people that *made* them susceptible to those influences.

The simplest possibility, one which didn't require much in the way of 'psychology', was that a god or a spirit had physically slipped inside you and had taken over the controls. This itself raises some awkward questions. Is Zeus so small that he can slip into me without my feeling anything? That doesn't square with my sense of him as huge and powerful. And – like a child beginning to wonder how one Father Christmas can be simultaneously sliding down millions of chimneys all over the world – it can seem implausible that God is concerning himself so wholeheartedly with little me. So the idea arose, certainly as far back as classical Greece, that a person could be infiltrated not by God or Satan himself, but by some junior devil or proxy agent – a dirty rag, perhaps, or a mouse – which had been charged up with the deity's benign, or more usually malevolent, intent. A full-size devil would literally be hard to swallow, but a little imp could more plausibly be introduced into you without your knowing, and once installed, like a computer virus, could boost or pervert the workings of your own mind and body, dissolving your courage at a crucial moment, or seizing control of your vocal cords and causing you to blaspheme 'against your will'.

As well as requiring little in the way of psychological understanding, this notion of 'possession' had the added social advantage that the ensuing oddities of speech or action were not directly your fault (any more than the spots are your 'fault' when you have caught chickenpox). People might reckon that it was your own shortcomings that had made the demon choose to invade you in the first place, but there might be the chance that you could blame your bad or mad behaviour on a purely capricious invader, and escape even this residual responsibility. It may well be for this reason that the phenomenon of possession has proved so robust throughout history. It has been particularly popular, for example, amongst young women in sexually repressive societies, such as seventeenth-century Britain, France or Puritan New England, or the *fin-de-siècle* Viennese bourgeois world from which the vast majority of Freud's 'hysterical' female patients were drawn. Being possessed, you might be able to get away with behaving badly or selfishly, cursing your enemies, yelling and crying, and even, if you were lucky, questioning the authority of the Holy Father or the Good Lord himself.

Demonic possession invites exorcism, of course, and this too can be traced back to classical Greece and the 'incubation temples' that were found throughout the Western Mediterranean and Asia Minor from around 1000 BC. Wherever possession occurred, some form of exorcism or 'spirit release' rituals were also to be found, and these took many forms and served a variety of social as well as personal functions. For example, if the infecting agent is conceptualised in physical rather than ethereal terms – if it is a real, dirty thing that has got inside you – then exorcism can involve retrieving and displaying it. John Monro, one of the dynasty that ran the 'Bedlam' hospital in East London in the eighteenth century, described in his notebook a Mr Walker, who, having undergone an exorcism ritual, 'told me that the Devil left him this morning about four o'clock, that he had been with him seven years, was brown, and of a size between a mouse and a rat'.[22] Even today, on the small island of Mayotte, which lies between Mozambique and Madagascar in the Indian Ocean, the most common form of exorcism involves the healer locating and extracting a small parcel of rotting or revolting items – dirt, nail clippings, broken glass or faecal matter – from the body of the patient, or, if that is too difficult to carry off, from his or her house or property. The package is triumphantly displayed, slit open and tossed to the ground, whereupon the invasive force is supposed to – and frequently does – give up its hold on its victim.[23]

The effectiveness of the exorcism seems to depend – just as it does in therapy – on the personal and professional authority of the practitioner. Priests and shamans are on their mettle to prove that they, and any religious or therapeutic institution which they represent, are more powerful than the demon itself. The exorcist has to be a person of considerable personal authority (or possessing a high degree of 'animal magnetism', as Anton Mesmer would have put it), but personal charisma is often judged insufficient. The term 'exorcise' itself derives from the Greek for an oath, and exorcism involves not merely 'casting out' the devil, but putting him 'on oath' by invoking the irresistible power of the highest religious authority available. In a Christian exorcism, for instance, the exorcist begins his (exorcists are invariably male) ritual with a formula such as: 'I adjure thee, most evil spirit, by almighty God . . .'

Typically there follows a bit of toing and froing between the exorcist and the devil, maybe involving some bargaining about time scales for eviction, or compensation of various sorts. In the case of fifteen-year-old Nicole Obry, possessed by Beelzebub (no less) in 1566, the devil insisted that a dark prince of his rank could only be exorcised by a bishop, and that he would not leave her except in the cathedral of Laon, or 'that great brothel' as he caustically referred to it. There were so many exorcisms of Nicole, sometimes both a matinee and an evening show on the same day, and they were so well publicised, that some 150,000 people were claimed to have watched her.

During these exorcisms, Beelzebub proved extremely adept at publicly revealing the secret sins of the onlookers – so much so that priests were stationed at every pillar in the cathedral to receive the private confession of the thousands who feared that they would otherwise be exposed in front of the crowd. Beelzebub also issued a stream of witty and wounding jibes against the Huguenots, the rival Church. But eventually, in this case as in others, God's superior power is grudgingly acknowledged, and the devil says 'Oh, alright then' and slinks off, much to the evident relief – though possibly the private disappointment – of the victim. (Nicole Obry had developed such an appetite for fame that some ten years later she became temporarily 'blind' – and could be cured by nothing less than the head of John the Baptist!)

A successful exorcism boosts the credibility of the exorcist who,

Possession by spirits and devils was widespread in sixteenth- and seventeenth-century Europe, and exorcists were almost as much in demand as psychotherapists are today. In this Italian fresco, dating from 1610, Saint Bartholomew is extracting the offending spirit from a possessed boy.

through winning the ethical battle of wills, affirms yet again the power and rectitude of the organisation for which he works. Certainly in France in the sixteenth century, exorcisms were carried out by Catholics with the purpose of confuting the Huguenots, and were written up and distributed widely with that expressed aim. And there are clear indications of deception and more or less conscious collusion between the possessed person and the exorcist. Perhaps the victim starts out with some genuine illness – often epilepsy, or some visual or auditory hallucinations. She is treated kindly and allowed some latitude that she would not otherwise enjoy. Someone suggests that she is 'possessed', and she becomes even more the centre of attention. Consciously or unconsciously she begins to shape her aberrant behaviour to the expectations of her religious community, and may even learn how to simulate fits when the occasion demands. The local priest brings in an eminent exorcist, who is delighted at the prospect of another propaganda coup against his religious rivals. With the help of informants, he may feed the victim with knowledge of the peccadilloes of her community, for public revelation in the voice of Beelzebub. And so the collusion builds.[24]

Had Nicole's fits and outbursts been attributed to a straightforward medical condition such as epilepsy or Tourette's Syndrome, or to unconscious neurosis stemming from childhood trauma, neither she nor her priest would have reaped the benefit that the diagnosis of possession made possible. It may be that the medical or psychopathological diagnoses would be, in some sense, truer, but that advantage has to be set against the substantial social investments that may be at stake. The historical movement between an 'outer' view, that of possession, and an 'inner', that of physiology, or of the unconscious, has to be seen in the light of these complex webs of pros and cons.

Here is an example of one of the points I stressed in the previous chapter: how the acceptability of different explanations for oddity is affected by historical drifts in what counts as unexceptionable common sense. The early Christian Church actually condemned some supernatural interpretations of odd behaviour. The Council of Ancyra in AD 314 ordered that 'priests everywhere should teach that they know this 'night-flying' to be false, and that such phantasms are sent by the evil spirits who delude them in dreams'. The synod of Paderborn in AD 785 decreed that 'whoever being fooled by the devil maintains in accordance with pagan beliefs that witches exist, and causes them to be burned at the stake, shall be punished with death'. (Note, however, that 'the devil' and 'evil spirits' are accepted as real, at the same time as 'phantasms' and 'witches' are said not to be.) Some writers insisted that 'spirits' often had a perfectly straightforward physical basis – if you could pin it down. The French sceptic Pierre Massé noted in 1573 that 'you shall read in the legend how in the night time Incubus came to a ladies bed side and made hot love unto her; whereat she being offended cried out so loud that companie came and found him under the bed in the likeness of the holie bishop Sylvanus.'[25]

Now we are more inclined to join Massé in smiling benignly at people's lack of scientific sophistication. In doing so, however, we may underestimate, from our highly individualistic perspective, the positive social and cultural value of the supernatural stance. There are many instances in which the treatment of cases of possession or madness by shamans and healers, when observed closely, turns out to recognise and work with the social dimensions of illness, both mental and physical, in sophisticated ways. In a classic case, a member of the Ndembu tribe in what was then Rhodesia became agoraphobic and paranoid. The 'healer' saw that the naturally timid man was caught in a social web that demanded a degree of assertiveness that he could not muster – but diagnosed the cause as an embedded incisor from having been bitten by an *ihamba*, a ancestor spirit. The cure, however, involved a complex social ritual in which the man's wife and mother-in-law, as well as the village as a whole, were required to acknowledge their demanding and unsympathetic relationships with the man. After the 'removal' of the incisor, the patient seemed cured, and village harmony and tolerance increased. Victor Turner, the anthropologist who recorded this incident, commented that 'the Ndembu "doctor" sees his task less as curing an individual patient than as remedying the ills of a corporate group. The sickness of a patient is mainly a sign that "something is rotten" in the corporate body.' It is likely that people will 'buy into' such social and personal self-examination more willingly if they believe that, by doing so, they are helping to effect a supernatural cure. There is probably less shame, and therefore less resistance, that way.[26]

In orthodox Christianity, the vast majority of cases of possession were seen as negative, and deliberately so. A claim that someone was 'enthused' – possessed by God – could be much more unwelcome to the priesthood than the idea of being invaded by a force of evil. If God could enter directly into a layperson's being, the power of the clergy to act as interpreters and mediators was in jeopardy. But across the world, not all cases of possession have been seen as demonic, by any means. To take a contemporary example, possession in Bali is generally seen as a pleasurable and valuable experience. It is more likely to be construed as a temporary 'altered state of consciousness', rather than a long-term infestation in need of urgent expert treatment.[27] Instead of being used exclusively to account for 'bad' behaviour such as convulsions, tantrums or blasphemy, the notion of possession in Bali is used to explain more positive oddities, such as the 'magical' power of a traditional healer, or an unexpected burst of wisdom or insight in an otherwise ordinary member of society. It can also be used to legitimise a kind of zombie-like behaviour – unreactive, impassive and lethargic – reminiscent of what Western psychiatry would call profound depression, called *ngramang sawang*. Often this is seen as being brought on by an identifiable emotional trauma, or even by simple fatigue, but if it does not clear up within the expected time-course, then it can be attributed to possession.

In general, the experiences associated with possession vary from culture to culture, but where there is a strong belief in the power of spirits and demons, their intervention is widely used as a way of making sense of periods of deviant behaviour, and even to legitimate some 'time out' from normal conventions and expectations for the affected person. Possession and its aftermath may require such periods of indulgence and recuperation in the same way that a diagnosis of 'neurasthenia' allowed retreating to a sanatorium in the nineteenth century, or 'alienation' today may legitimate a thrice-weekly visit to a kind person who will be unswervingly interested in you for an hour.

Throughout human history, the supernatural world has been invoked to account for many of the oddities of human nature that, in the twentieth century, would come to be laid instead at the door of the unconscious. Mania and melancholy, creativity and religious experience, blasphemy and greed, dreams and visions, can all be readily put down to the work of the gods and spirits. Causes and explanations are sought outwards, in the whims and wise judgements of humanlike agents and naturelike forces. But, as we have seen, the question begins insistently to arise of how it is that these agents make contact with and gain control of the individual. They can speak to me, but if they are not physically present, and I can hear no voice, what is it in me that receives the messages and resonates to them? Or they can invade me, physically wresting control from 'me'. But what exactly is going on? How does that power struggle play itself out? In what kind of inner world do I and the invader meet to do battle? Sooner or later, even if they are equipped with a sophisticated supernatural world, questions of interiority, of psychology, arise. The development of ideas about the psyche, the soul, and eventually the mind, is inevitable. And along with them, like their shadow, emerges the unconscious itself.

All societies, from the ancient Egyptians to the present day, have found some aspects of their experience and behaviour intensely puzzling, and have created systems of belief that offer a real or imaginary handle on them. For the classical Greeks, it was the Olympian gods. For many of the peoples of Africa and Polynesia it was the spirits of nature and of their ancestors. For seventeenth century Europeans it was God and Satan and their angels and demons who were at work. They all had a partly reassuring and partly uneasy relationship with a variety of beings who could be understood as rather like them. Today's Euro-mind experiences many of the same kinds of puzzlement about itself, but has largely opted, instead, for an equally ambivalent relationship with a bunch of theoretically postulated internal systems (whose behaviour is essentially rather like theirs) – the Ego, Super-Ego and Id; Archetypes and the Collective Unconscious. It is to the historical prototypes of these mysterious inner agents that we must now turn.

3

The Invention of the Soul: Glimmerings of the Unconscious

The god to whom a man proves devout, that is his own soul turned inside out.

– Goethe[1]

Death is one of the most fundamentally and universally puzzling aspects of human life. The newly dead body of a friend or relation is like them in a way, and yet utterly unlike them in its stillness. Where has all that energy, all that personality, gone? What was it that they had while alive, and so obviously have no more? Surely there must be some force, some principle of life, that has disappeared? Surely this must be associated with the breath, the first and last vestige of life: the *pneuma*, the spirit? Surely this spirit cannot simply have been extinguished; surely it must have moved on, rather than been snuffed out. But where has it gone? If I cannot see the departed any more, but can still hear their voice talking to me, surely their spirit lives on in some immaterial world? Otto Rank said: 'The primitive belief in souls is originally nothing else than a kind of belief in immortality, which energetically denies the power of death . . . the thought of death is rendered supportable by assuring oneself of a second life, after this one . . .'[2]

Sleep is also odd. A sleeping person is unresponsive, yet not

quite in the way that a corpse is. Grandmother's body will not
reanimate, however loudly I shout or cry, but my husband's will.
When my children sleep they are still, but not that still: their
breathing remains, and in the morning they are back, miraculously refreshed and full of tales of the night's journeys. Where has
that replenishment come from? What inner battery has been
recharged? And where did they go, and who were those strangers
who came to them in their sleep? What makes them conscious?
What feeds their fantasies? What makes them dream? Slipping
off the blinkers of familiarity, we too can feel the urgency of such
questions, and the perplexity that humankind must have felt in
the face of such everyday miracles ever since we began to wonder
about anything at all, and to start to spin our stories in response.
In these speculative narratives are to be found the beginnings both
of mythology and of psychology.

I started the previous chapter with an image from Egyptian
mythology of four thousand years ago. In that mythic underworld
are loud symbolic echoes of the unconscious. But those echoes are
there, much more literally, in the primitive psychology which
accompanied it. There was no division in ancient Egypt, such as
we are used to, between 'soul' and 'body'. The Egyptians of the
Middle Kingdom had no equivalent of the Greek word *psyche*. But
they did divide their inwardness, as we saw, into *Ba* and *Ka*. *Ba* is
the principle of consciousness. When unconscious, through fainting or in sleep, it is *Ba* that has temporarily gone AWOL. And *Ka*
is the fundamental source of life energy. It is the 'mains' into
which we are still plugged while asleep. It is life-giving, and full of
life – but not conscious. *Ka* is that unconscious life-support system
which makes consciousness possible. *Ka* connects 'downwards' to
the rejuvenating power of *Nun* and the underworld. *Ba* connects
upwards to the world of fancy and dream. This is a psychological
theory, albeit a simple one, in which each of those basic puzzles of
existence is 'answered' by the invention of an entity that reifies it.
What is the principle of vitality? *Ka*. What is the principle of

consciousness? *Ba*. These mental constructs are different in kind and in sophistication, but not in essence, from their great-great-ever-so-great-descendants the ego and the id.[3]

Such proto-psychologies are neither recent nor particularly Western. They are to be found throughout human societies, from ancient to modern, and across all continents. The anthropologist Robin Horton has shown that these kinds of binary mental divisions are characteristic of the indigenous psychologies of West Africa, for example, though where the mind is 'cut' depends very much on what key oddities are being explained, within any particular culture. West African Kalabari society is much exercised by the paradox of personal dissonance: often one finds oneself doing or saying something quite different from what one expected or intended. How is it, as Eliot wondered too, that 'Between the conception/And the creation/Between the emotion/And the response/Falls the Shadow'?

In order to construct an explanation for this, the Kalabari divide the psyche into the *biomgbo*, which corresponds roughly to the conscious mind, and the *teme*, which represents a kind of unconscious, though one that is very different from the ancient Egyptian *Ka*. The *teme* is one's implicit destiny, a set of unconscious commitments which have been established prior to birth, and which may support, or may undermine, more conscious intentions throughout life. In a previous existence, for example, a person may have achieved an exalted position in society, only to experience a disastrous fall from grace, as a result of which the *teme* may have decided never to aspire to high status again. Now, the person who has inherited this *teme*, though striving consciously to 'make something of himself', finds, time and again, that he sabotages his own advancement. He continually, inadvertently, puts his foot in it, and his *biomgbo* hasn't a clue what is going on. Eventually, in desperation, he may seek the help of the local diviner, who uncovers the *teme*'s buried self-destructive commitments, and endeavours to banish them through an elaborate ritual.[4]

The Kalabari unconscious emerges as quite distinct from the ancient Egyptian one, because it is not centrally designed to account for the universal facts of life, death, sleep and dreaming, so much as the equally perplexing slippage between conscious intentions and actual achievement. And though the Kalabari place the unconscious decision point in a previous life, rather than in the early experience of the individual, their answer is astonishingly Freudian in feel.

What is attributed to the unconscious, within any society, tends to reflect the 'mixed messages' that are structurally present in the way that society functions. In Kalabari society there are strong explicit injunctions to gain competitive advantage over one's fellows in quite an assertive fashion. However, it is actually dangerous to live up to these 'ideals' because of the fear that rivals will retaliate by using lethal sorcery. The tendency to pull your social punches is therefore quite strong, as is one's fear of being thought in breach of social norms if one does so. Their model of the mind offers a way out of this dilemma: you can behave as timidly as you would like to, and avoid any personalised social stigma, if it turns out that your lack of assertion is not due to simple cowardice, but is part of the 'spoken destiny' associated with your *teme*. In Freud's Vienna, by contrast, it was not self-assertion, but sexuality, that was rendered problematic by the mixed cultural messages of the time, so it is no surprise that his conscious/unconscious division is drawn in libidinous, rather than competitive, terms. Though – for reasons we shall explore in the next two chapters – Freud's psychology startled its European audience considerably, the essence of his view would have been, as Robin Horton puts it, *vieux jeu* in West Africa.

In these rudimentary accounts of the various oddities of human nature lurk the seeds of the soul and the spirit, many aspects of which underlie the *explicit* images of the unconscious that would begin to emerge and blossom in European culture from the late seventeenth century onwards. Over the course of the preceding

European history from Plato to Descartes, such seeds proliferated and gathered increasingly complex, and sometimes conflicting, layers of meaning, so that, in the eventual reaction to Descartes' summary ablation of all things unconscious, not one but a whole range of different images of the inaccessible depths of the mind would begin to bloom. To trace, in outline, the development of the European view of the unconscious, and its place in the mind, we must go back to classical Greece, to the ninth-century BC world of Homer and his account of the Trojan Wars in the *Iliad*. From there, we can follow the gradual formulation, over the last millennium before Christ, of the first explicit idea of the unconscious as an intangible 'thing' that human beings possess. It was called the *psyche*, or the soul.

Homer's use of the word *psyche* had nothing of the mind about it: it was simply the original Greek term for the invisible life-force that animates a body when it is alive, and leaves it when it dies. All the more interesting oddities of human conduct are down to the gods. But 'Homer' (if there ever was such an individual: scholars now suggest that the *Iliad* and the *Odyssey* were the work of different hands) must be counted one of the remote grandfathers of psychology, because he did address the question of what it was, inside people, that resonated to the wishes of Zeus or Athena. If their voices could not always be heard, he reasoned that there must be some other internal mechanisms for receiving – unconsciously – distant broadcasts of divine wisdom or intent. When Aphrodite presses her remote control and makes me fall head over heels in love with an ass, there has to be a sensor in me that picks up the signal. And this sensor was not, for Homer, associated with the *psyche*, the life-force, but with the *phrenes* (translated in the *Iliad* as the lungs, though later also as the midriff or the diaphragm) and also with the *ker* or *kradie*, the physical heart. The receiving apparatuses were bodily, and the way the gods affected you was primarily physical and emotional: through a quickening of the pulse, a rush of blood, an intake of breath, a tensing of the stomach, a pounding of the heart. Although *psyche* was the underlying life-force, the centre of tangible, and variable, vitality, *thymos* – and also of consciousness – was the *phrenes*. The *kradie* was more usually seen as the seat of passion.[5]

These 'organs of feeling and perception' do not, in the *Iliad*, fit together into any kind of coherent bodily system (let alone a psychological one). The person, in both their psychological and physical natures, is seen as a loose, unintegrated collection of parts – they are, in the contemporary parlance, 'modularised'. There is as little sense of the 'body as a whole' as there is of an overall entity called the 'mind'. The art of the time typically depicts the body, to quote Julian Jaynes, as 'an assembly of strangely articulated limbs, the joints underdrawn, and the torso almost separated from the hips'.[6] The human being is not yet a smoothly conducted symphony orchestra; he is a small group of stringed instruments, each of which is plucked by individual gods, and the thrumming of which impels him to act in a characteristic way. There is no internal centre of volition and decision. (Though today we have a very well-developed sense of such a conscious instigator inside, we should note that we still make good use of the kinds of phraseology that would have been typical of Homeric man: 'It struck me that . . .', 'I was driven to . . .', 'What possessed me . . .', and so on.) We might say that these organs, internal but not under any centralised, personal control, function as an ensemble of 'unconsciousnesses' whose job it was, as it is now, to account for otherwise inexplicable impulses and experiences. As one would expect, the gods and their remote resonators are invoked predominantly under conditions of stress and confusion – exactly when we tend to behave and feel in ways that are out of character, and therefore potentially threatening to our 'common sense'.[7]

The *Odyssey* continues to use the rather crude, piecemeal anatomical knowledge of the time as the basic metaphor for the organs of feeling and perception – but now these organs begin to

Not until the eighth century BC did Greek artists add the human form to their repertoire of ceramic decorations. In this Dipylon amphora, for example, human beings were depicted in a way that was highly stylized and disjointed. Limbs and torso exist almost as separate elements of the person, juxtaposed but not combined.

be seen as potential *sources*, rather than just the receptors, of extreme or uncanny forms of experience. With this, history takes another important step towards the invention of the semi-autonomous interior agents that will people the unconscious of Freud and many others. It is now some rather mysterious quality of your own *phrenes* that determines whether you will act wisely or badly. In the *Odyssey*, Clytemnestra is able to resist Aegisthus because her *phrenes* are *agathai*, godly, or good. Penelope's faithfulness and loyalty to the absent Odysseus are also down to her *agathai phrenes*. In descriptions such as these, the internal organ becomes not just the local source of feeling, but a moral agent, capable of behaving in either a 'higher' or a 'lower' manner. Though not yet cloven into 'good soul' and 'bad soul', a hairline fracture has been introduced that, by the time of Plato, will have expanded into humankind's major, enduring psychological fissure.[8]

If the *phrenes* are not always well behaved, they are not always straightforward either. In fact, in the *Odyssey* they become the seat of deceit, the place where private knowledge and personal secrets are held. In the *Iliad*, people do not have secrets, but the *Odyssey* – like many of the later plays of Euripides and Aristophanes – is centrally about dissembling and deception. And instead of a goddess feeding secret knowledge to her favoured hero, it is now the hero's own *phrenes* that are the depository of such knowledge. There is still a way to go before people are capable of *self*-deception, of concealing knowledge, desires and so on even from themselves, but the idea of the inner vault of secrets moves us another significant step in the direction of the personal unconscious.

If you want to, you can see glimmerings of the psychological unconscious in the way the word *psyche* is used in Homer to explain minor, less dramatic mysteries and oddities. Inexplicable bursts of courage or bouts of confusion are down to the gods, but a sneeze comes straight from the *psyche*. The *psyche* is sometimes, in Homer, located in the head, and this is obviously where those mini-mysteries called sneezes arise. A violent explosion occurs in

the head, for no apparent reason, over which one has no conscious or voluntary control – a small oddity in need of an
explanation! A sneeze was often interpreted as prophetic. When
Telemachus sneezes as his mother Penelope is voicing her wish that
Odysseus should hurry home and wreak vengeance on her enemies, she takes it as a clear sign that her wish will come true.
Richard Onians, author of *The Origins of European Thought*, one
of the seminal works on the Greek mind, notes that a sneeze was
'a sign from a power with other knowledge', and comments:
'*Psyche* seems to have served for the early Greeks many of the purposes which the concept of the Unconscious serves for us.'[9] In one
of its meanings at least, *psyche* starts out as just one of the ensemble of 'organs' that are used to explain strange occurrences.

Let me take another jump out of my chronological story to note
that similar kinds of 'ensemble psychology' are still very much
alive today. In New Zealand, Maori psychology has a similar
'exploded' view of the person, with different kinds of impulse or
emotion being attributed to a variety of real or hypothetical internal organs. As with many other folk psychologies, one of the
prime concerns is to give a reassuring account of the fickleness or
unpredictability of things, including human behaviour. In order to
preserve the sense of an idealised 'core self' that is untroubled by
such whimsicality, the oddities are attributed to a range of body
parts. In Maori, you *can* say 'one speaks' or 'one takes', but it is as
common to say 'the mouth speaks' or 'the hand takes'. Each organ
has 'a mind of its own': the eyes direct the muscles in order to protect the body; the tongue decides what is good to eat, and so
protects the stomach. *Ngakau*, roughly the intestines, is associated
with a variety of feelings, and also clarity of awareness. *Ngakau* is
not under personal control: instead of saying 'I changed my mind',
Maori would tend to say 'another *ngakau* unfolds'. *Manawa*, like
the Greek *thymos*, is a kind of variable vitality that is associated
with breathing and the lungs, and this is seen as the seat of a

range of puzzling conditions. Supreme courage reflects 'great *manawa*' through deep, steady breathing, while 'closed *manawa*', shallow or disrupted breathing, can be the cause of depression, or of paralysing anxiety.[10]

Two of these organs, less closely tied to specific areas of the body, are of particular interest in terms of the unconscious. *Wairua* is the 'vital spirit' that survives death and makes for the underworld, but it is also, during life, capable of going walkabout and recovering memories, gathering dreams or generating intuitions. It has an independent life, and is linked to the fickleness of mental awareness, and to things insubstantial or unseen – and thus to subliminal perception and the 'sixth sense'. After having forgotten the end of a song, the next day a Maori man said: 'I can now finish the song. My *wairua* found it last night.' Another man heard someone singing in the night and interpreted this as his *wairua* having detected some impending misfortune. He explained that 'the singer knows nothing of the coming trouble, he cannot perceive it, but his *wairua* knows all about it, and thus prompts him to sing'. The second 'organ', *tipua*, is a kind of indwelling spirit used to account for a variety of strange characteristics or behaviours. Sickness that defies normal remedies may be due to *tipua*, as could a feeling of intense anxiety (which would otherwise be experienced, in Maori culture, as shameful). The first Europeans to arrive in New Zealand were called *tipua* because they looked so odd.

In some cases, these Maori concepts, like the Homeric ones, toggle between being inward and outward. They are components of the person that can both generate unusual feelings and also act as receivers from outside – or even be the outside influence itself. A *tipua* can be a kind of goblin that has decided to mess you about, as well as the organ through which it affects you. However, the internal limbs and organs of the body can also be centres of intelligence and influence in their own right, as they were in the *Odyssey*. They do not need to be activated by external agents. And this, as we have seen, is what happened to the Greek organs, to the *phrenes* and the *kradie*.

But back to the story line. By the seventh century BC, the Greek gods were beginning to lose their influence, and the bodily organs were taking over more and more of their authority and their explanatory functions. Creativity, for example, was coming to be seen as a quality that originated within the person, rather than from the gods. Terpander, the inventor of the drinking song according to Pindar, called for inspiration not on the Muses, but on his own *phrenes*. 'Of the Far-flinging Lord come sing to me, O *Phrenes*', he pleaded to his own organs. In the *Odyssey* it was still more common for the gods to beam songs down, to be picked up by the *phrenes*; now, Terpander is speaking to his own *phrenes* as if it were they, not the Muses, that were the mysterious fount of his creativity. Note that he does not yet identify with his organs – they remain somewhat autonomous, and have to be coaxed into delivering the goods, just as the gods did.[11]

So by 600 BC the nucleus of the soul has already been formed. Several originally different hypothetical entities, dreamed up to make sense of different kinds of puzzle, have begun to fuse together. First, there is the idea of an animating spirit – the whatever-it-is that makes live things live. This spirit can also be taken not just as the source of life but of movement and of action. Then comes the idea that this spirit does not go out, like a candle flame, at death, but continues to exist in a supernatural realm, an underworld or a heaven, and can, perhaps, retake human form. And it is plausible, and economical, to identify this ethereal 'something' with the other ethereal something that makes us conscious, and which temporarily decamps when we faint or sleep. If there is a supernatural realm where dead souls go, then it seems rather a waste if sleeping ones cannot go there too, and bring back reports of strange lands and bizarre experiences in the form of dreams. Thus, while none of these ideas logically requires each other, they certainly fit together very smoothly. In particular, the idea that such a soul exists, separately from the body, strongly invites the idea that there are occult realms to which it has access. There are powers of movement and clairvoyance which defy the conventional laws of space and time and which enable it to gain superhuman knowledge. And there can be a Hades – or if you are lucky an Elysium – where departed souls can foregather and recoup before occupying another body.[12]

This figment of the human imagination – the immortal, animating, conscious soul – neatly mops up quite a few of the core mysteries of human existence, and provides a measure of reassurance, in the midst of all kinds of seemingly chaotic and senseless events. Not least, the fear of death is mitigated by the belief that it is not, after all, The End.[13] Immortality also helps with the blatant conundrum of inequity. The vicissitudes of life make a mockery of any simplistic belief in fairness. Bad deeds go unpunished; tyrants frequently prosper; the virtuous get cancer and their children go off the rails for no apparent reason. 'It's not fair!' is one of the most primitive human cries, and not just of children. Life after death helps to even up the score: to preserve faith in ultimate fairness – in two ways. It holds out the promise that virtue will be rewarded, and evil punished, in the 'afterlife'. And reincarnation expands the time-scale, so that, even if life wasn't fair this time around, things will even up in the long run. You may have lost the first couple of games, one of them on a terrible line-call, but over a five-set match justice will be done. And even if it isn't, the Great All-Seeing Video Referee in the Sky will spot the shenanigans of your cheating opponent and send him to the Sin Bin.

There was another stimulus for the emergence of the idea of the individual soul. In a stable, clannish society, the idea of justice over the long term can be provided by the inheritance of guilt; the sins of the fathers and mothers can fall onto the children and grand-children. Good and bad fortune are totalled over the generations of a family. But in the Archaic Age of classical Greece, around

600–450 BC, especially in Athens, family ties were being broken, and therefore the moral accounting unit had to become the individual rather than the clan. So the only way for the moral accounts to even out was to allow the individual, or their proxy, the soul, to accumulate credits and demerits as it passed from life to life. Put all of these elements together, and you are well on the way to believing in a multi-functional, but essentially coherent, ghost in the machine. But why would I come to think of that ghost as quintessentially Me?[14]

For the classical Greeks, as for the Kalabari of West Africa, one of the core mysteries of humankind is the prevalence of inner conflict. I think I want to succeed but I keep screwing up. I want to settle down but my relationships are a continual disaster. I want to be liked, but I want to have my own way. The experience of being in two minds, or of being apparently in one mind, but somehow not following through, is far from being an exclusively modern or a Western one. In the face of his *kradie*'s impulsive desire to kill the maids who are larking about with his enemies, Odysseus sternly admonishes the seat of his own rage: 'Endure, my heart; you once bore an even baser thing, when the Cyclops devoured your comrades. But still you endured, till your guile found a way.'[15] Even in Homer, people sometimes found a cooler internal voice, with which, seemingly, they could identify more closely than they did with their various, more clearly located, organs. Though still small, it was this voice that would develop, over the ensuing centuries, into Socrates' rational core of the soul.

That calmer, more dispassionate internal voice would become the hub from which all the other elements of the soul would radiate. We know it well today. 'Come on, André; you can serve better than this', we say to ourselves, urging on our more impulsive or more wayward parts a better course. The difference between Odysseus and André is that André is more firmly convinced that the rational voice is him.

Socrates and Plato would set the seal on the pre-eminence of reason. But they could hardly have done so without the lyric poets and playwrights paving the way. Aristophanes' and Euripides' dramatisation of intense moments of inner conflict, accompanied by the dispassionate human voice of the chorus, reflected back to their audiences possible ways of construing their own indecision. The chorus offers wise commentary, and even dares to argue with the gods, as when, in *Medea*, it says: 'may I know the blessing of a heart that is not passion's slave . . . may the dread Cyprian [Aphrodite] never inflict upon me quarrelsome moods and insatiable strife.'

Euripides loves the set pieces, the grand moments of conflict – prototypically, Medea's agonising over whether to kill her children by Jason as revenge for his infidelity. But he also was the first soap-opera writer, revelling in the foibles and indiscretions of his characters. Even the gods got cut down to size – and by taking the mickey, Euripides helped considerably to undermine their already waning authority still further. Medea, though she is a mortal, takes on much of the authority that would traditionally have been the gods' (appearing, at one point in the play, above the stage in a magical chariot drawn by dragons). But she possesses a developed version of Odysseus' reflective voice. 'What a perverse creature I am', she says to Jason – though she is being disingenuous in saying so. And she reminds herself that she is alone and friendless in a foreign country: 'When I reflected on this, I realized the full extent of my folly and the futility of my anger . . . I admit to a lack of sense earlier; I have now come to a better understanding of my situation'. Medea is a mistress of deception, but she is here also coming alive to the possibility of *self*-deception. She sees herself as capable of misconstruing situations, forgetting important considerations, getting it wrong.

But in Medea's implicit psychodynamics, 'the unconscious' remains her 'heart', which is under the sway of external forces. The three agencies which she invokes or makes use of are Aphrodite, 'the Cyprian', who inflicts on her her jealous rage and murderous

This 1759 portrait of the renowned actress Mademoiselle Clairon, defiant but well coiffed, as Medea was painted by Charles-Angre Loo. Euripedes places Medea somwehere between the gods and 'mere mortals'. She agonises like a human being, but also has some of the 'larger-than-life' attributes of the Olympians.

intent; her *kradie*, her heart, where these passions are received and felt, and her own reflective voice, supported by that of the chorus, that consciously weighs up the pros and cons. Unlike Socrates' rational eye, however, Medea's sees, but cannot act. It is perceptive, but, in the face of the irresistible alliance of Aphrodite and her own heart, she is powerless. 'I have no choice, old man, none at all,' she says to her tutor. 'This is what the gods and I devised, I and my foolish heart' ('I' here seems to be a cipher or an address – it signals more the location of the drama than an active 'player' in its own right). And a little later: 'I am well aware how terrible a crime I am about to commit, but my passion is master of my reason.' This moral sensibility is expressed in a voice that is Medea's own. She is not beholden to the gods for this awareness. And this signals a new development in Greek psychology – the birth of the personal conscience, soon to be incorporated into the agglomeration of the soul, and eventually to grow into the compartment of the unconscious called by Freud the super-ego. It has a voice, it can bleat perceptively, but like a newborn lamb, it is, in Medea, weak and unsteady on its feet. Its bones have not had time to set, and it does not have any of the strength that it was beginning to develop in the work of Socrates. Medea has *scruples*, but they do not yet count for much.[16]

Medea has no equivalent of the Kalabari's *teme*; a personal heritage bends her, unconsciously, one way rather than another. Her inbuilt tendency towards mayhem or self-destruction remains generic and unexplained. Unlike Gordon Burns in *Happy Like Murderers*, his exploration of the pathogenic backgrounds of Fred and Rosemary West, Euripides shows no interest in any aspects of Medea's personal history that might have predisposed her to evil, or even made her more available as the Cyprian's instrument.[17] If Medea has been brutalised, it is through the irresistible power of Aphrodite's passion, not as a result of her abusive childhood. Though her psychology is more elaborated than that even of Odysseus, and she possesses a moral voice that he never had, the source of her trouble is still, when push comes to shove, placed outside.

By the time of Medea, the lyric poets had already begun to describe and celebrate the marvels and idiosyncrasies of individual experience. Though she embodies a new self-awareness, Medea, like her fictionalised predecessors, became interesting, worthy of observation and comment, only in moments of crisis and conflict. She remains archetypal. But when Sappho declares 'Some say an army of horsemen is the fairest thing on the black earth, others an army of foot-soldiers, and others a navy of ships – but I say, the fairest thing is the one I love',[18] she is asserting her right to personal taste. She revels in her love, and in its difference from others'. And her experience becomes interesting, not as an accessory to action, but in its own right. 'When I look at you but once, my speech ceases to obey me; my tongue is broken, a subtle fire creeps under my skin, my eyes see nothing, and my ears begin to ring.'[19] In such descriptions, another ingredient of 'the mind' or the 'soul' begins to emerge – the ability, and perhaps also the inclination, to decouple experience from the immediate pressures of decision and action, and savour it for what it is.

Experience becomes an object of richer description and rumination, because attention is not driven so powerfully, or so continually, by the need to act. The soul thus begins to develop another facet: its identity as an observer, as well as a doer. It is no coincidence that these poets focus so often on personal, romantic love. For the Greeks, as it would be for the Romantics, and still is for us, the power and passion, sometimes even the madness, of love is as compelling a mystery as death or dreaming. Aphrodite and Eros are still available as handy sources of explanation. 'Once more Eros, looser of limbs, drives me about, a bitter-sweet creature who puts me at a loss . . .',[20] says Sappho. Like Medea, she loses her composure and her wits in the face of the almost meteorological forces which are battering her. Their power perplexes both of them – but for Sappho, unlike Medea, the forces are amorous, not murderous. Though

Sappho's poem predates Euripides' play by some fifty years, the range of what is to be considered odd, in need of explanation, is extended in her poetry, and her examination of the phenomena is, if anything, even more meticulous, more personal, than Medea's.

The state of confusion, of not being able to see clearly either the course of events or the dynamics of one's own heart, has always been of interest to the Greeks. In Homer, as you would expect, confusion, *ate*, is deliberately sent by the gods to make things difficult for you. But in Sappho, confusion, especially in the sense of not being able to see to the bottom of one's own feelings and desires, becomes a more personal trait, captured in metaphors that are vivid but not supernatural. A storm stirs the heart, she says. The soul is shaken, as the winds swoop down on the oaks upon the mountain. Wine hits the mind like lightning. These images attempt not so much to offer a real cause for the emotion as to capture its quality and intensity.

It was also during the sixth century BC that the idea of the 'mind' as the seat of consciousness and thinking first makes its appearance. In the works of Solon of Athens, the *noos* (or *nous* as it later came to be spelled) takes on something much closer to the modern usage of the word 'mind'. In Homer, *noos* referred to something like the 'field of view', but in the hands of Solon this outward, literal view of perception is turned metaphorically inwards. The field of view is now one that contains thoughts and feelings, as well as sights and sounds, and *nous* becomes both the mental 'space' in which such experiences occur, and the organ of thinking, reflection and discernment. It may well have been Solon who coined the injunction to 'know thyself', an idea that would have made no sense to a Homeric hero. And how can one know oneself? Julian Jaynes explains: 'By initiating *by oneself* memories of one's actions and feelings and looking at them together, with an analog "I", conceptualising them, sorting them out into characteristics, and narratizing so as to know what one is likely to do. One must "see" "oneself" as in an imaginary "space" . . .'21

Belief in the immortality of souls, and in their ability to relocate from one body to another, was central to the views of Pythagoras and his followers in Croton, in Southern Italy, around 530 BC. Although none of Pythagoras' own writings survive, Porphyry's *Life of Pythagoras*, written in the second century AD, records that 'it became very well known to everyone that he said, first, that the soul is immortal, then, that it changes into other kinds of animals.'[22] And it was Pythagoras who first saw the soul not purely as an individual entity, but as a part of a wider cosmic or godly soul that permeated the universe. In a human being, one speck of this cosmic soul had broken off, one handful of the divine spirit had coagulated and become 'entombed' in a human body, which could not but cloud and corrupt it. This cut-off speck of soul yearned to be reconnected to the Whole, and it was people's job to work to cleanse and purify themselves, so as to assist this reconnection. In a very significant development, the soul is now seen as the 'real person', temporarily incarcerated in the birdcage of the body, longing to be set free and to fly home. But only when it had been purified completely, through a succession of lives, could this desired reunion take place. Till then, like a dull pupil, the soul was condemned to be 'held back', transmigrating from life to life, until it was mature enough to pass the 'final examination', and be awarded its heavenly degree. More than anyone, then, Pythagoras was responsible for the final splitting of soul from body, and for making the ethereal soul both more 'real', more 'worthy' and more 'spiritual' than the poor, coarse, corruptible, unreliable body.

Well before Plato's famous metaphor of the shadows on the cave wall, it was Pythagoras who turned the world, and especially the person, upside down and inside out. That which was visible and tangible was to be disdained, and that which was merely an idea was to be taken as the only true and worthwhile reality. Behind mucky, complicated, changeable appearance lurked, if one could only understand it well enough, the divine, pristine, eternal forms that were the only things on which one could truly rely, and which embodied the everlasting principles of order, justice and harmony. Not surprisingly, this order and harmony were revealed most clearly in the idealised figures and formulae of mathematics, and the clean uncluttered lines of music. The soul became that scrap of abstract beauty and wisdom with which every human being was endowed, but which became buried under the mounting pile of ordinary memory and experience. Here is a draft version of the soul that is the prototype of the Cartesian mind: inner, mysterious, abstract and ideal.[23]

This internal *éminence grise*, the power – and the glory – behind the mundane throne of everyday life, was rendered even more mysterious by Heraclitus. Like Pythagoras, whose theories he roundly condemned, Heraclitus left little in the way of authenticated writings, just a few rather gnomic 'fragments' and aphorisms. One of his fragments reads: 'Soul is the vaporization out of which everything else is composed; moreover, it is the least corporeal of things and is in ceaseless flux.' For Heraclitus, soul is the 'thin stuff' out of which everything material is made, his guiding image is of a complex, evanescent plasma, not a set of lasting, lapidary forms. (Rather as Einstein reconciled matter and energy by making the latter the 'thin stuff' which could congeal, from time to time, into the former.)

With Heraclitus, we find the depth and unknowability of the soul being emphasised. In other fragments, he writes: 'you will not discover the limits of the soul, even if you travel along every path there is, so deep is its nature', and 'the soul of man is a far country, which can be neither approached nor explored.' Put Pythagoras and Heraclitus together and you have a soul, an inner 'reality', that is hard to know – because it is both 'higher' and 'deeper' than the ordinary stuff of everyday – but which it is our job to know. Hence the injunction to 'know thyself', and hence the difficult and perplexing nature of the task. By the fifth century BC, the idea that the soul is 'deep' and hard to plumb had taken a firm hold on the Greek mind. In 490 BC Pelasgus, the protagonist of Aeschylus' play *Suppliants*, is faced with a tough problem. 'Now we must think deeply about salvation,' he says, 'as a diver descends to the depth.'[24] No god comes to his aid. The soul is the place where answers are to be found, and the soul is also the tool for digging. Individual cognition takes the place of divine intercession. And the mind begins to have its dual character, as both the instrument of knowing, and that which is itself hard to know. The unconscious takes another big step forward, and is separated more distinctly from its calmer, wiser twin, reason.

As the soul, at least in its 'higher' manifestation, became more clearly abstract and unitary, so, commensurately, did the Divine essence, off whose old block the soul was a personalised chip. If you have dozens of gods, as the Homeric heroes had, and each of them potentially leaves a token of themselves inside people, the 'soul', *in toto*, becomes hopelessly multiple and confused. It becomes hard for it to do the explanatory jobs for which it was originally invented, let alone any more sophisticated ones. So collapsing all the gods into one supreme Force would clearly support the soul in its narrative work. Happily, that was exactly what various influential thinkers of the fifth century BC proposed. Heraclitus called it the *logos* – the prototype of St John's 'In the beginning was the Word' – while Parmenides spoke of the One, and Anaxagoras of the universal *Nous*. And, as part of this rationalisation of the deities, the single supreme being also began to grow more idealised and remote. An increasingly abstract chip must derive from an ever more abstract block, presumably. So, whereas the old Olympians, were really 'quite like us' in form, stature and character, the God of the fifth century began to dissolve. Xenophanes, whom I quoted in Chapter 2, wrote: 'One God there is, midst gods and men the greatest; in form not like to mortals; he without toil rules all things; ever unmoved in one place he abideth.'[25] And as this new Lord of Lords took hold of the popular imagination, so the Olympian colony of old gods rapidly found themselves pensioned off, demoted to running their own small temples and oracles.

Around 500 BC, the soul also takes a cognitive turn. *Psyche* begins to coalesce with *nous*, which has acquired the sense both of the hypothetical mental space of reflection, and the active agent who reflects therein. To the moral, divine and mysterious connotations of the soul are added intellectual ones. The way that the soul knows good, and God, is through cogitation and reflection, and the 'mind' is that aspect of the soul which provides the tools for this inquiry. Though empirical science is still only on the horizon, within philosophical circles, experience loses ground, as a way of knowing, to thinking. Experience is associated with the body, and the body is tainted and untrustworthy. It can only tell you of Appearances, not of Reality. It is not by gazing out of your windows that truth will come to you, but by earnestly mulling over what you already know, in the seclusion of your inner sanctum.

The habit of reflection also grows out of the ethical understanding that bad actions are often impulsive, and that a moral life therefore involves learning to check those impulses, and give yourself time to think. Such an idea is already present in the *Iliad*. At one point, Athena assists Achilles not by directly controlling his temper, but by reminding him of the rewards of restraint: 'For I say to you – and it will surely be fulfilled: three times as many beautiful gifts will in the end accrue to you in recompense for this insult, if only you hold yourself in check.' Later the appeal to material advantage will be replaced by more uplifting moral sentiments – you are more likely to behave 'rightly' if you pause. And all the more so if you use that pause to think through the possible results of your action. The sage Chilon coined the maxim *hora telos*, 'See the end, consider the consequences.' Through planning, mistakes are avoided and general well-being enhanced. By the time of Socrates, a moral life was indelibly associated with *sophrosyne*, a life of moderation and restraint. Here is another reason why the beneficial core of the soul becomes detached from impulse, emotion and the body, the latter becoming more disowned and id-like, while the former begins to turn into something recognisably like the ego.

With Socrates and Plato, the tool of reason becomes sharper and more effective, its use more disciplined, and its goal more theoretical and less immediately practical. Partly, perhaps, as a result of the greater affluence and security that the Greek city states provided, the goal of knowledge shifted from the desire to control the wayward forces of nature (and of your fellow citizens) to the discovery of the means of virtuous living – that is, the promotion of the well-being of your eternal soul.[26] Bertrand Russell saw Plato as combining previous trends in the evolution of the soul, and blending them finally, inextricably with Reason.[27] If Truth is to be found in deep understanding, in intellectual penetration of the veil of appearances, then the pre-eminent tool with which to conduct the search has to be rationality itself.

And, as Plato says in the *Phaedrus*, 'The region of which I speak is the abode of the reality with which true knowledge is concerned, a reality without colour or shape, intangible but utterly real, apprehensible only by intellect which is the pilot of the soul.'[28] You cannot apply the most rigorous thinking to the complex, dynamic mess of the actual world, just as you cannot apply mathematics to the behaviour of atoms in any but the simplest, most idealised cases. Algebra does not work except in the magical world of x and y. So the purest thinking demands the invention of a world of pure forms that hypothetically lies behind, and is an idealisation of, the actual world of diapers and missed appointments. For Plato, as it was for Pythagoras and will be for Descartes, mathematics offered the most beautiful example of order and deduction. Pity that everyday life is not like that at all. At home, we argue about whether this or that decision was a 'good' one. In Plato's world, the definite article has to be invented so that we can talk late into the night about 'The Good', *tout court*.

In the Socratic world, Reason recruits Will, and the more clearly one's Reason has helped one to see The Good, through the smoke and between the mirrors of Appearances, the more powerful one's Will will be. To understand, one has to proceed slowly and methodically, defining words precisely and unearthing and inter-rogating potential confusions and misunderstandings. In Socrates' hands, logical analysis becomes the tool that trips you up time and again, revealing that you do not really know what you are talking about. And if you cannot explain yourself to Socrates' satisfaction, you clearly don't know Right from Wrong. Exuberant spontaneity is always flawed and suspect, and any flight of fancy can be shot down with an arrow called 'What do you mean by . . .' Finally, the Greek confidence in the power of the intellect sweeps the board. It is the same in many classrooms still.

The stage is set for Plato's historic tripartite model of the *psyche*. Soul had been, and continued to be, split into two, in a variety of ways, but it had never been divided into three before, and in so doing, Plato established a model that was to hold sway in Europe right up to the present day.

> Let us compare the soul to a winged charioteer and his team acting together . . . The ruling power in us men drives a pair of horses, one of [which] is fine and good and of noble stock, and the other the opposite in every way . . . The horse that is harnessed on the senior side is upright and clean-limbed; he holds his neck high and has a somewhat hooked nose; his colour is white with black eyes; his thirst for honour is tempered by restraint and modesty; he is a friend to genuine renown and needs no whip . . . The other horse is crooked, lumbering, ill-made; his coat is black and eyes a bloodshot grey; wantonness and boastfulness are his companions, and he is hairy-eared and deaf, hardly controllable even with the whip . . . So in our case, the task of the charioteer is necessarily a difficult and unpleasant business.[29]

The relationship between the three players in this moral tableau seems to be based on a straightforward trial of strength. When I catch sight of my current lust-object (says Plato), the white horse is 'constrained by a sense of shame' and holds back, while the black 'rushes forward prancing' and 'makes mention (to the lad in question) of the sweetness of physical love'. The charioteer is doing his best to tug on the reins by focusing on the memory of 'absolute beauty' (rather than on the practical delights of consummation) but the black horse no sooner recovers from the pain of the bit 'than he bursts into angry abuse, reproaching the driver and his fellow horse for their cowardice'. (In choosing a 'dark horse' for his id, Plato was drawing on imagery that was already common currency, and which we mentioned in chapter 1. From Homer on, the bodily, emotional and unbridled side on human beings had often been symbolised by animals, while Greek literature is full of allusions to joy as 'light', 'bright' or 'lofty', and to pain and unhappiness as 'heavy' and 'dark'.)

Plato's chariot offers a picture of a soul in conflict, but interestingly, though one of his protagonists is dark, the picture itself has no dark corners. The two horses and their master are transparent to each other. There is conflict, but no unconscious. Though this metaphor of Plato's captures something of the general dynamics of the mind, it does not incorporate the notion – already familiar in Athens from the writings of Heraclitus and others – that the soul has unknown depths; human beings remain largely a mystery to themselves, and self-knowledge is hard won. It is also worth remarking that Plato's chariot seems only to be wheeled out to account for the conspicuous perversity of human nature; when things are going according to plan, it stays safely in the garage.

In his later writings, however, Plato does seem to recognise that the black horse has a side to him that is sneaky and cryptic, as well as wild and lustful. He is willing to do things in dreams, for instance, that he would not dare to do under the watchful eye of the charioteer. In *The Republic*, Socrates is talking to Adeimantus

about the difference between wholesome desires and those which
have to be controlled. The latter, he explains, are

> those which are awake when the rest of the soul, the rational,
> gentle and dominant part, is asleep; then the wild beast within
> us, gorged with meat or drink, starts frisking about, shakes off
> sleep and goes forth to satisfy his desires [in dreams]; and there is
> no conceivable folly or crime – having sex with all and sundry,
> even his mother, rampaging and murdering – which at such a
> time, when he has parted company with all shame and sense,
> this part of a man may not be ready to commit.

Just as now we have our beliefs about the dream-unleashing properties of certain habits and foodstuffs – some say toasted cheese,
for example – so Plato thought that over-indulgence at dinnertime
would fatally weaken the vigilance of the rational guards posted at
the mouth of the unconscious, allowing the beast to slip past and
run amok.[30]

In the *Timaeus*, Plato sums up the model of the soul that was to
define human nature throughout the Middle Ages, and on, even
to the present day, though it no longer carries the unquestioning
cultural assent that it had for so long. Those agencies that created
man, whatever they were, said Plato,

> received the immortal principle of the soul; and around this they
> proceeded to fashion a mortal body, and made it to be the
> vehicle of the soul, and constructed within the body a soul of a
> different nature, which was mortal, subject to terrible and
> irresistible affections – first of all, pleasure, the greatest
> incitement of evil; and then, pain, which deters from good; also
> rashness and fear, two foolish counsellors; anger, hard to be
> appeased; and hope, easily led astray. These they mingled with
> irrational sense and with all-daring love according to necessary
> laws, and so framed man.[31]

'The unexamined life is not worth living', said Socrates, but, for many people, the over-examined life becomes unbearably self-conscious and stilted. In the hands of others, the ideas of Socrates and Plato became woefully one-sided and collapsed into a tabloid version. The idea that the best plan is always to figure things out in advance, decide what to do, and then do it – that deliberation is father to the moral or the effective act – became the principal, explicit article of faith. Comprehension had to precede competence, and if one acted without due consideration, one was likely to act badly or ineptly. Though Plato is largely to blame for this caricature, he himself tempered his respect for reason with some understanding of the valid vigour of the 'black horse'. Aristotle, too, knew that 'no one could sustain the life of pure reason for more than very brief periods'. He and his students made space for the irrational in their studies. But many of the Stoics and the Epicureans did not. Their ideal was *ataraxia*, the ability to live entirely free from 'disturbing passions', and their asceticism became, in the hands of many adherents, if not in those of the founders Zeno and Epicurus, extreme and life-denying. Their goal was to cleanse the mind so that it became 'passionless, pitiless, and perfect'.[32] The soul, being of God, could contain no imperfections, and so the young shoot of the unconscious was weeded out.

This exaggerated faith in reason – the belief that the best kind of person is someone who lives like a philosopher – together with its corollary denial of the unconscious, would resurface with Descartes in the seventeenth century, and it provoked then the same kind of reaction that it did in Greece in the last three centuries before Christ. It is hard work to live the ponderous life, and it is not to everyone's taste, so, however much they might agree with it in principle, people in practice reverted, in large numbers, to the delights of spontaneity and the simplistic reassurances of the supernatural. Much of the populace had never really paid more than lip-service to the supremacy of reason anyway, and in the third century BC, far from reason sweeping the board, there was an upsurge of interest in astrology, charms, and all kinds of weird and wonderful cults. Gilbert Murray said that such New Age beliefs and practices 'fell upon the Hellenistic mind as a new disease falls upon some remote island people'.[33]

The old gods were gone, and the rigid determinism of astrological fate proved more appealing than the new rationalism, with its burden of individual reflection and responsibility. The trade in magical charms, healing crystals, plausible gurus and medical quackery boomed. Amulets promised protection against 'every malice of a frightening dream or of beings in the air', or 'enemies, accusers, robbers and terrors'. Just as in the twentieth century AD, or the Romantic rebellion against Descartes and Locke in the eighteenth, people voted on the threatened hegemony of reason with their mystical feet.[34] When figuring out the ethical implications of genetically modified crops, or the genome project, gets too hard, it may be time for a little aromatherapy and a quick check on the horoscope.

When the domain of the unconscious is too much excluded – when no framework is allowed, except a condemnatory one, within which to acknowledge and explore the scary but exciting world of dreaming and abandon – then it seems that forms of social resistance break out that may be more worrisome than the outlawed oddities themselves. As one of Donna Tartt's characters explains in *The Secret History*:

The Greeks, you know, really weren't very different from us. They were very formal people, extraordinarily civilised, rather repressed. And yet they were frequently swept away *en masse* by the wildest enthusiasms – dancing, frenzies, slaughter, visions . . . The revellers were apparently hurled back into a non-rational, pre-intellectual state, where the personality was replaced by something completely different – and by 'different' I mean something to all appearances not human . . . I thought of the

Bacchae, a play whose violence and savagery made me uneasy, as did the sadism of its bloodthirsty god . . . it was a triumph of barbarism over reason: dark, chaotic, inexplicable.[35]

Plato's black horse with the hairy ears, in other words, back with a vengeance.

If one reaction to the de-liberated, devitalised soul-mind of the Stoics was a retreat into the supernatural, another, which also pre-figured eighteenth-century Romantic views of the unconscious, was provided by Aristotle. His notion of soul did not transcend the body, and was not set in opposition to it; it was immanent and inherent in biology. Bodies could be described in terms of their visible parts and organs, but they were also characterised by what these days we might call their 'design specifications': their typical functions, the way they grow, their inbuilt portfolio of needs and threats, and the resources with which they are endowed by nature for dealing with those innate interests and priorities. Soul, for Aristotle, was not the godly flame that kindled animation in the coarse, damp matter of the body, but this hierarchy of processes, with the basic metabolic functions of eating and breathing at the bottom, the faculties of motion and sensation in the middle, and the power of reasoning – the level that only human beings, of all the animals, possessed – at the top. Just as burglars are commonly supposed to 'give themselves away' through their inability to break out of a characteristic modus operandi, their 'm.o.', so each species can be identified by its trademark habits and faculties, and that is its 'soul'.

Aristotle, too, was more the careful observer of the quirks of human psychology than the finger-wagging moralist. He was per-haps the first to ponder the mystery of remembrance and forgetting. In *De memoria et reminiscentia*, he observes that there are occasions when we see something, and do not instantly know whether it is familiar or not. The feeling of recognition is elusive, until, at some unpredictable moment, 'we get a sudden idea and recollect that we have, in fact, heard or seen something formerly'. Sometimes, he notes, we can retrieve something by systematically searching our memories; at other times, it just mysteriously pops into our heads, presumably from the interior place where it has been lurking.[36] Thus in Aristotle, we have the seeds of the intellectual, rather than the emotional, approach to the unconscious – one that is rooted in biology rather than theology, and which takes a broad, dispassionate, but not unaffectionate approach to the soul-mind, rather than a strongly dualistic, moral and judgemental one.

Two hundred years before the birth of Christ, almost all of the basic elements of, and approaches to, the unconscious were in place, mostly constellated around the various views of the soul that were competing for popular recognition. All of these building blocks of psychology had been motivated, in one way or another, by the desire to make sense of the characteristic oddities of human nature. From the unnerving, dispiriting stillness of death, and the fundamental desire for people to receive their 'just deserts', came ideas of soul as the eternal flame, the divine spirit, breathing life into the body and accumulating bonus or penalty points from life to life. From dreams came the possibility that this sentient essence could detach itself from the sleeping body and take off for nightly adventures in other worlds. From the lyric poets' discovery of the ability to wonder at, and articulate, their own unfolding experience developed the idea of the soul as the inner eye, the observer sitting, watching, in the corner of a mental space where perceptions and feelings and inner voices paraded themselves. From the intriguing differences between people came the idea of soul as the carrier of personality, while from equally fascinating observations of sameness arose Aristotle's subtle notion of the soul as the 'm.o.' of the species.

From the concentration of the supernatural forces into a single abstract divinity grew the idea of the soul as 'God's viceroy' within each human heart. From the experience of being torn and conflicted came the idea of the soul as the battleground between a higher and a lower nature; and from the etherialisation of God, and of Reality, came the idea that the soul itself was immaterial, and that one's 'better side' issued from this abstract, godly source, while one's 'worse side' was coarse and bestial and physical. And finally, the Good Bit, or the God Bit, became associated with the exercise of calm methodical reason, 'passionless, pitiless and perfect', applying itself to moral questions in the same way that a mathematician applies herself to the solution of an algebraic equation. Put these elements together into a mental kaleidoscope, and give them a twist, and the mind, the soul, the psyche as a whole, takes on one constellation; give it a shake, and a different pattern emerges. In some of these patterns, the soul incorporates the animal and the emotional – as, in some Christian theologies, Satan is seen as an essential agent of God's work, part of the divine plan. In others, the soul crystal fractures, with one part forming itself around only the Good Bits, and others – sometimes making two, sometimes three, in all – forming different kinds of entity that impact upon each other in different ways.

Though the idea of a mental place called 'the unconscious', the wings, the 'behind the scenes' of the mental theatre of consciousness, was not yet well worked out, hardly even explicit, it is there in the language and imagery of classical Greece in all essentials. The image of the conscious mind as the well-lit office behind the windows of the eyes, where sits a small intelligent being, 'me', who observes and thinks and decides and issues orders to the dumb menial called the 'body' – that strange idea will not be fully formulated in Europe until the seventeenth century. Modern notions of the unconscious, especially Freud's, are parasitic on this view, designed to complement it, so it is inevitable that we see them, too, only in outline and by allusion in ancient Greek culture. But the id and the super-ego are there in embryo, ready to explain why the poor old ego, the thoughtful realist, the charioteer, has such a hard time of it.

In the Western world, these kaleidoscopic views continued to be shaken and debated for a millennium and a half, though little essentially new was to be added until the fifteenth and sixteenth centuries. Technical debates recurred in Christianity about the precise relation of soul to body, but while these had great theological significance, the psychology remained relatively undeveloped. If you look for the unconscious in traditional Christian doctrine, you can find it. One can read the power of the unconscious into the appearance of shame and self-consciousness in the Garden of Eden, when the physical and the feminine become allied with the reptilian. One can read the fruit of the tree of knowledge as the awful post-Homeric realisation that what you thought was the voice of God telling you what to do was actually your own ventriloquism. I thought I was just doing the Lord's Work, but actually, it's down to me. One can see the unconscious in Jesus' temptation by the Devil in the metaphorical wildness, the 'badlands', of the Wilderness.

But for the most part, the oddities of human experience continue to be externalised, and some of the promising beginnings of psychology in Greece remain sidelined and neglected until the Renaissance. The supernatural world continues to have great power and 'reality' for ordinary folk throughout the Middle Ages. God and His angels, Satan and his demons, Heaven and Hell, the magical power of relics and the spiritual authority of the exorcist – all these serve to keep the common people in fear of retribution, keen to observe the rules, and to distract them from delving into the rich idiosyncrasies of their own experience. All that was to change quite rapidly over the three centuries from 1400 to 1700.

4

The Dumb Menial: The Unconscious Refined, Banished and Bouncing Back

One should say '*it* thinks', just as one says 'it rains'. To say *cogito* is
already too much, as soon as one translates it by '*I* think'.
– G. C. Lichtenberg[1]

The Middle Ages, so it seems, were times of certainty, stoicism and
hard work, both physical and moral. The major questions of existence were definitively answered by the Church. God had created
the world in six days. It was big, round, flat, surrounded by water,
and for man's (*sic*) benefit. It was composed of four elements,
earth, air, fire and water, and people were composed of corresponding 'humours': blood, phlegm, black bile and yellow bile.
The balance of these determined your temperament, and if they
got out of balance, you became ill, physically or mentally.
Everything had its place in the Great Chain of Being, with human
beings above all the animals and below the angels, which mediated
between them and God. People had a body, a mind and a spirit or
soul, though precisely what the relationship was between these
ingredients was unclear, and you didn't ask. Very clever holy
people argued about this, and they told you what the answers
were.

It was people's job to get on stoically with their hard lives, to believe what their priests told them, to repent of their sins, and, for the more sophisticated, to use Reason to try to distil Truth and Knowledge from the corrupted, treacherous raw material of the Senses, Memory and Imagination. It was all going to stop at the Last Judgement when the ledger of your life would be audited and your heavenly or hellish fate determined. Nothing was what it seemed: natural impulses were 'evil', primitive, self-serving clergy cared deeply for your soul, everything – a lone magpie, a late frost, an abscess on your neck – was imbued with symbolic significance which had to be divined, and only the invisible was really real.

There were, however, two psychological images, widely known throughout the medieval period, that are well worth noting, for they are the only ones, before the Renaissance, that deduce the existence of unconscious mental activities and structures from direct observation, and attempt to picture explicitly what might be going on behind the mental scenes. The first is the mirror of Plotinus, the third-century AD Neoplatonist philosopher. Plotinus was of a psychological bent, and his observations left him in no doubt that unconscious processes occurred all the time. 'Feelings can be present without our being aware of them', he said; and 'the absence of conscious perception is no proof of the absence of mental activity'. To explain what to him was the obvious fact that we become aware of the processes of thought only when we pay attention to them, he imagined that there was the equivalent of a mirror in the soul the angle of which determined whether the soul's activity was reflected into consciousness or not.

When [this mirror] is present in the soul, wherein the images of reflection and of the mind are mirrored, these latter are seen, and the higher recognition is present that the mind and soul are active. But when [the mirror] is broken [or displaced], on account of the disturbed harmony of the organism, then the

mind and the soul think without the mirror image, and then
thought is present without an inner image of itself.[2]

Interestingly, Plotinus placed the mirror inside the person, but
saw consciousness itself as external. The mirror was, as it were,
reflecting the light of an outer 'sun' onto the private activities of
the soul, and thereby illuminating them.

The second guiding image was of memory as a repository of
knowledge that was sometimes hard to search: the dark catacombs
of the mind, perhaps, or the 'book of the heart', whose writing was
not always easy to decipher. The catacomb image is due to
Augustine, who, like Plotinus, thought of human beings psychologically, as well as physically. He knew that his 'spiritual work'
involved being scrupulously honest with himself – but he also
knew that this was far from easy, and that his own mind was likely
to play hide-and-seek with itself, and conceal painful memories
and insights from him.

> Thou, O Lord, didst turn me towards myself, taking me from
> behind my back, where I had placed myself while unwilling to
> exercise self-scrutiny; and Thou did set me face to face with
> myself . . . and I beheld and loathed myself; and whither to fly
> from myself I discovered not.

For Augustine, one of the roles that God played in his life was
clearly that of a psychotherapist, forcing him to attend to aspects
of himself from which he would much rather avert his gaze. In
acknowledging 'that which is deliberately unattended', Augustine
lays one of the first paving stones on the road that will lead, in the
nineteenth century, to the crucial concept of repression. The idea
that the mind is motivated deliberately to conceal things from
itself – that it creates its own unconscious regions – begins with
Augustine.

In order to explain how he could hide from himself, Augustine created his catacomb model of memory, which contains all our thoughts and experiences, and also 'anything else that has been entrusted to it for safe keeping'. When he tries to recall something, the response of the internal archivist is variable. 'Some things it produces immediately; some are forthcoming only after a delay, *as though they were being brought forth from some inner hiding place* . . . And if, for a short space of time, I cease to give them my attention, they sink back and recede again into the more remote cells of my memory . . .' Here is the beginning of yet another clear version of the unconscious in all but name: as mental contents that are inaccessible, but not *deliberately* hidden away. And the immensity and partial inscrutability of memory, in Augustine's image, help to account for the mystery that lies at the core of every soul:

> Memory is a vast, immeasurable sanctuary. Who can plumb its depths? And yet it is a faculty of my soul. Although it is part of my nature, I cannot totally grasp all that I am. This means, then, that the mind is too narrow to contain itself entirely. But where is that part of it which it does not itself contain? . . . I am lost in wonder when I consider this problem. It bewilders me. Men go out and gaze in astonishment at high mountains, the huge waves of the sea, the broad reaches of rivers, the ocean that encircles the world, or the stars in their courses. But they pay no attention to themselves.[3]

(Note that Augustine's puzzlement is compounded by the unrecognised ambiguity of the word 'mind' [or 'soul', as the word was used then]. 'The mind is too narrow to contain itself' does indeed sound paradoxical – but only if you fail to distinguish 'mind' *qua* 'consciousness' from 'mind' *qua* 'memory store'. This confusion bedevils our vocabulary to this day.)

For Augustine, memory contains two kinds of things: personal records, and 'anything else which has been entrusted to it for safe keeping' – by which Augustine meant, of course, the Word of

God, with which every soul came into the world pre-configured, as it were, like Windows on a new computer, or like a divine instruction manual. Indeed, Augustine complemented his image of the catacombs with the equally compelling image of a book, 'the book of the heart', in which the left-hand pages came pre-printed with the Word of God – though in rather weak and watery ink that could fade or smudge and become hard to read – and the right-hand pages were filled in with the daily diary of your own thoughts and deeds, good and bad, as you went along. Your job was to keep deciphering the divine instructions, as best you could, and to keep rereading your diary, so that you could repent fully of your sins. You tried to live as good a life as possible, so the disparity between the verso and the recto was kept as small as possible.

Such images were widespread, even in the fourth century. Augustine's contemporary, St Ambrose of Milan, enjoined his congregation not to let their sins overwrite the pre-existing holy script in their heart-soul. 'If you have lived righteously, God's writing shall remain . . . see that you do not erase it and write with the ink of your evil deeds.'[4] A century earlier, when 'books' were still predominantly scrolls, the Egyptian philosopher Origen wrote: 'these books are now rolled up and hidden in the heart, containing written records of our deeds, and marked, so to speak, with the reproofs of conscience, and still known to no one but God.'[5] For Origen, God, it seems, has more direct access to these records than we do ourselves. He can speed-read in the dark; we have to unfold the scrolls laboriously and peer uncertainly at their faint inscriptions in the flickering candlelight of our own consciousness. Only at the Last Trump will all be revealed about ourselves, to ourselves. 'That full meaning shall remain hidden until revelation of an ending which is not of our own device', said Augustine. The unconscious soul is still largely divine territory, but for Augustine it is more subtle and detailed than the mere fleck of holiness at the centre of every human life which it had been before. Now it has a structure and a dynamics of its own.[6]

The 'book of the heart', represented as a literally heart-shaped book in this Flemish portrait by the Master of Sainte Gedule, c. 1485. Images of this kind were common during the fifteenth century, and earlier.

Later in the Middle Ages it became clearer still what exactly the point of self-scrutiny was. The psychological function of repentance became sharper. Isaac of Stella, abbot of the Cistercian monastery at Étoile, explained that the goal is to understand more fully whence, and how, our sins arise. We ruminate on what we have done in order to infer why we did it: to know ourselves more accurately, and thus, because we will not like what we see, to be drawn to God more strongly. We read the book of the heart, said Isaac, in order to find 'the source of all that rises within us, the origins of thoughts and feelings, the roots of desires and urges, as well as of suggestions and pleasures'. Isaac was preaching seven hundred years before Sigmund Freud was conceived.[7]

So people who lived in the Middle Ages did have some quite powerful images of their interiority, and these images emphasised, in certain ways, the fact that we are mysterious to ourselves, and that self-knowledge was only to be won through effort, and with the grace of God. But all of this was firmly contained within a moral and emotional framework of fear and hope: fear that your sins will be found out, and that they will prove too weighty to allow you access to Paradise; hope that sufficient diligence and piety might get you there after all. Introspection was not of interest for its own sake, and people's sense of their own personality was correspondingly much less differentiated than ours. Even in the world of entertainment, there were songs and stories of human conduct aplenty, but (like the Greek epics, or today's cartoons) they generally told of one-dimensional characters – 'greedy', 'shrewd', 'brave' – behaving cunningly or treacherously or nobly in the face of various trials and tribulations.

The thin end of the wedge that began to prise this world of conformity and uniformity apart was, perhaps, the discovery (or maybe the invention) of a new, more personal, quality of tenderness in human relationships. Around the time of Chaucer, a host of words that originally had theological meanings became used in a more intimate, affectionate, homely way: *amorous, dalliance, debonair, delight, pleasure, beauty, compassion, passion, patience.* A whole range of feelings that had been evoked by, and directed towards, the divine, now became available for talking about human relationships. Owen Barfield, in his elegant and authoritative study of *History in English Words*, suggests that the accretion of such small shifts began to open up 'a new consciousness of the individual human soul. On the one hand the sense of its independent *being* and activity, of bottomless depths and soaring heights within it, to be explored with fear or trembling, or with hope and joy – with *delight* and *mirth*, or with *agony, anguish, despair, repentance* – and on the other hand that feeling of its being an *inner* world.' (I have followed Barfield in italicising key words with newly emergent possibilities of meaning.)[8]

People were slowly waking up to the idea that they could think for themselves, but of course the rise of independent thought did not occur without opposition. For the Church, ordinary people's growing doubts about its previously unquestioned authority was a profound threat that needed to be held in check, and the Inquisition emerged as the first Orwellian 'thought police', ruthlessly intent on prying into people's minds and trampling their budding doubts and questions to death. But what today is called 'the decline of deference' proved too strong to stem. Over the next two centuries, throughout Europe, even the public world of the troubadours and story-tellers came to model greater subtlety, autonomy, and even self-acceptance in human hearts and affairs. Tales such as Boccaccio's *Decameron* appeared that were much more scurrilous, disrespectful and even raunchy. People dared to celebrate registers of sensuality and playfulness that the Church had been at pains – literally – to condemn. The clergy and nobility came in for much more perceptive and critical ragging. A richer, more psychological vocabulary became available in which to discuss people's underlying – and often unworthy – motives, and to dissect their characters and their foibles. The characters, though, remained if not one- then two-dimensional, functioning, as Ian Watt in *The Rise of the Novel* put it, only as 'necessary devices for the presentation of an amusing situation.'[9]

Not that the Church gave up without a fight. It remained highly dangerous publicly to question almost any aspect of Christian doctrine, let alone the very existence of God. It would not be till far into the eighteenth century that even the boldest of sceptical philosophers would dare to 'come out' on the subject of the immortality of the soul, for example. Some of their predecessors did go so far as to hint at the possibility of heresy, and talked, in guarded, general terms of the need to conceal one's true questions and opinions. John Toland published an essay in 1696 that discussed the many philosophers, including Pythagoras and Plato, who 'took care not to reveal their true judgment save secretly to very few, for fear of the rage and violence of the superstitious'. Even Jesus, he pointed out, cloaked his messages in parables. The sixteenth-century Italian physician Gerolamo Cardano, discussing the vexed question of the immortality of the soul, declared that 'all wise men, even if they do not believe it themselves, agree publicly with the vulgar'. Sir Walter Raleigh, a closet fan of Machiavelli, counselled that 'wise men should be like Coffers with double bottoms: which when others look into, being opened, they see not all that they hold'.[10]

In general, though, few were reckless enough in their own lives even to allude to such potent mixtures of heresy and dissimulation. But the very presence of private doubt, coupled with the growing awareness of the *essential* privacy of experience, further enriched the soil in which the idea of *self*-deception – and with it, the concept of a part of the mind *deliberately* hidden from its owner – would germinate and blossom into an even more variegated conception than Augustine had been able to produce. Though he had been very well aware of the devious ways of self-deception, the linguistic and conceptual resources available to him were strictly limited.

One of the movements in the fifteenth century, which was to improve the situation considerably, was the increasingly open

interest in the possibilities of inter- as well as intra-personal deception. Freed from the obsessive need to be keeping both eyes on
what you *ought* to be doing, obsessively tracking the accumulating
credits and debits on your soul's spiritual bank account, people
took a keener interest in what they, and their neighbours, actually
were doing. If what I do can be used as a clue to what, underneath,
I am feeling and wanting and fearing, so I can use the minutiae of
other people's actions – *the* tapping foot, the sideways glance – to
infer what may be on their minds. And if it turns out that we both
want the same thing, this gives me the edge. People have always
had this Machiavellian side to them. Even animals such as chimpanzees have been shown to have it.[11] But never had it been raised
to such a high, and conscious, art as it was in the time of the arch-
manipulator, Machiavelli himself.

On 17 May 1521, Niccolò Machiavelli confessed privately to
his friend Francesco Guicciardini: 'for a long time I have not said
what I believed, nor do I ever believe what I say, and if indeed
sometimes I do happen to tell the truth, I hide it among so many
lies that it is hard to find.' In *The Prince*, published eight years earlier, he explains that the effective ruler has to be ruthlessly realistic
about the motives and fears of his subjects. 'For this it may be said
of men generally: they are ungrateful, fickle, feigners and dissemblers, avoiders of danger, eager for gain.' And he must use this
knowledge as a basis for manipulation, whilst always appearing to
be honest and transparent. He must have the skill and the gall to
beat these amateur dissemblers at their own game. 'Those best able
to imitate the fox have succeeded best. For foxiness should be well
concealed; one must be a great feigner and dissembler.'[12] This, it
must be said, was not a particularly esoteric point of view. A
widely circulated sixteenth-century maxim declared *nescit vivere
qui nescit dissimulare*. 'He who doesn't know how to lie doesn't
know how to live.' But Machiavelli was exemplary in his cold-eyed
dissection of his fellow human beings' lack of self-awareness, and
therefore their openness to manipulation.[13]

A natural corollary of this increasingly sophisticated interest in manipulation was a greater degree of self-control and skill in impression management. And as the art of dissembling grew more common and more subtle, so, inevitably, people became more aware of the disparity between their inner experience – of avarice or anger, say – and their outward appearance of generosity or forgiveness. The protagonist of Molière's *Tartuffe* raised laughs by ineptly trying to cover his greed and ambition with a veneer of pious belief. By then, ordinary folk had become much more sensitive to the disparity between experience and appearance, and adept at exploiting it.

And then, at the end of the sixteenth century, came Shakespeare. He knew all about deception. He fed Lady Macbeth the advice she passed on to her husband:

> To beguile the time,
> Look like the time; bear welcome in your eye,
> Your hand, your tongue. Look like th'innocent flower,
> But be the serpent under't.
>
> (*Macbeth*, I.5)

But his understanding of self-deception enabled him also to draw together many of the emerging strands of the unconscious, and describe them clearly through his characters' mouths. Often they are found trying to see through the shadowy depths of their own minds in order to find the cause of their feelings, fears or desires. Achilles says: 'My mind is troubled, like a fountain stirr'd; And I myself see not the bottom of it' (*Troilus and Cressida*, III.3). *The Merchant of Venice* starts with Antonio ruminating aloud about his current depression:

> In sooth I know not why I am so sad:
> It wearies me; you say it wearies you;
> But how I caught it, found it, or came by it,

What stuff 'tis made of, whereof it is born,
I am to learn;
And such a want-wit sadness makes of me,
That I have much ado to know myself.

(*Merchant of Venice*, I.1)

He is confused, but he can no longer confidently blame it on external agencies. We have come a long way from Homer's Achilles, or even Medea. Homer's heroes explained their perplexity by claiming that Aphrodite or Athena has filled their *kradie* with *ate*. For Antonio, it is *his* confusion, and his wits that he has to rely on if the confusion is to be dispelled. It may be – to put a Freudian spin on it – that his depression is masking what he does not want to admit to himself: his attraction to Bassanio. Shakespeare's heroes soliloquise about their plight, as Medea did, but by comparison her analysis, though agonised, is crude and angular, lacking the curves and nuances that Shakespeare so delicately explores.

Certainly, love, for Shakespeare, is often associated with a feeling of unplumbable depth. Rosalind longs to convince Celia 'how many fathoms deep' she is in love with Orlando. 'But it cannot be sounded; my affection hath an unknown bottom, like the Bay of Portugal.' To which Celia, the friend with the tart tongue, replies: 'Or rather, bottomless; that as fast as you can pour affection in, it runs out' (*As You Like It*, IV.1). Rosalind may experience her love as infinite, but, her friend reminds her, she still has the insecurity of the lover, the insatiable need for reassuring signs that the love is reciprocated. In a couple of lines, the mind has become both a well of untold depth, and a leaky bucket! How sophisticated a piece of psychology is that?

Three hundred years before Freud, audiences at The Globe were being taught that it is ideas and thoughts that can get inside you and 'possess' you, not quasi-physical agents such as hobgoblins or rats. Iago is so consumed with jealousy of Othello that 'the thought thereof doth, like a poisonous mineral, gnaw my innards'

(*Othello*, II.1). Lady Macbeth's guilt becomes so unbearable that her husband pleads with the doctor:

> 'Canst thou not minister to a mind diseased;
> Pluck from the memory a rooted sorrow;
> Raze out the written troubles of the brain;
> And with some sweet oblivious antidote
> Cleanse the stuff'd bosom of that perilous stuff which weighs
>   upon the heart?'

To which the doctor, like any good therapist, replies: 'Therein the patient must minister to himself' (*Macbeth*, V.3).

Actually, Shakespeare does have a favourite form of therapy: sleep. As in the incubation temples of ancient Greece, it is 'sleep that knits up the ravell'd sleave of care'. Sleep is the 'balm of hurt minds, great nature's second course, chief nourisher of life's feast' (*Macbeth*, II.2). Visitors to Bohemia, we are told at the beginning of *The Winter's Tale*, are routinely given 'sleepy drinks', so that their critical minds will be quietened, and their stay made all the more pleasant. Loss of sleep is one of the consequences of wickedness – 'Since Cassius first did whet me against Caesar I have not slept,' complains Brutus in *Julius Caesar* (II.3). The Shakespearean scholar John Vyvyan comments that: 'In many passages Shakespeare associated healing with sleep; and, therefore, with a reconstruction in what we now call the unconscious.'[14] More generally, he says: 'It would not surprise me if Shakespeare knew more about psychoanalysis, under a different name, than our psychiatrists, or their patients, have yet dreamed of.'[15]

Shakespeare knows how often perception is tilted by subliminal thoughts, desires and feelings. There are 'dark-working sorcerers that change the mind' (*Comedy of Errors*, I.2) inside as well as out. When the Prince says 'I never thought to hear you speak again', his father suggests, unkindly but perceptively, that 'Thy wish was father, Harry, to that thought' (*King Henry IV*, Part 2,

IV.5). When Gloster turns up at the room in the Tower of London where King Henry VI is held, Henry is, quite rightly, rather wary. Gloster, aiming to unsettle him further, says: 'Suspicion always haunts the guilty mind; The thief doth fear each bush an officer' *(King Henry VI,* Part 3, V.6). Clearly Shakespeare himself has experience of such perceptual 'mistakes', for he returns to the theme in *A Midsummer Night's Dream* (V.1): 'Or in the night, imagining some fear, How easy is a bush supposed a bear.'[16]

Not just perception, but impulses and actions too, are fuelled by unconscious desires, and Shakespeare may have been the first to articulate the complex psychological notions of projection, 'reaction formation' and other defence mechanisms. King Lear, mad, and making little sense, is yet able, as mad people are supposed to do, to squeeze out gems of insight. A propos nothing that is going on, Lear blurts out:

> Thou rascal beadle, hold thy bloody hand:
> Why dost thou lash that whore? Strip thine own back;
> Thou hotly lust'st to use her in that kind
> For which thou whipp'st her.
>
> *(King Lear,* IV.6)[17]

It is the beadle's own projected lust that he is unconsciously lashing so viciously, and Shakespeare also means us, perhaps, to hear the mad Lear's lament on the lack of self-knowledge that had led to the cruelty and mayhem which surround him.

Plato identified four kinds of 'madness': lunatic, poetic, romantic and divine. Shakespeare fears to tackle the divine, but he agrees, in *A Midsummer Night's Dream,* that the other three are very much of a kind, all stemming from hyperactive imaginations.

> The lunatic, the lover and the poet
> Are of imagination all compact:
> One sees more devils than vast hell can hold,

This watercolour by Eugene Delacroix, from the mid-nineteenth century, captures the reflective quality of Hamlet's conversation with Horatio as they muse on the skull of Yorick in the graveyard, in Act V, scene 1 of Shakespeare's Hamlet.

That is the madman: the lover, all as frantic,

See Helen's beauty in a brow of Egypt:

The poet's eye, in a fine frenzy rolling,

Doth glance from heaven to earth, from earth to heaven;

And as imagination bodies forth

The forms of things unknown, the poet's pen

Turns them to shapes, and gives to airy nothing

A local habitation and a name.

(A Midsummer Night's Dream, V.1)

He might well have included dreams in this catalogue of inflamed fantasies, for in the celebrated 'Queen Mab' speech in *Romeo and Juliet* he has Mercutio perform a pretty severe hatchet job on Romeo's feeble attempt to justify his unaccountable reluctance to go to dinner with the Capulets on the basis of a 'prophetic dream'. Mercutio pretends to have had a significant dream too, but he claims 'that dreamers often lie' and goes on, mockingly, to say 'I see Queen Mab hath been with you' , she who 'gallops o'er a courtier's nose, And then dreams he of smelling out a suit' and other such nonsense. Romeo protests: 'thou talkst of nothing', to which Mercutio replies: 'True, I talk of dreams, Which are the children of an idle brain, Begot of nothing but vain fantasy' *(Romeo and Juliet*, I.4). As in many other things, Shakespeare has a peculiarly modern attitude to things of the mind, and an attitude that is at the very least ambivalent about the supernatural.

If the unconscious is the turbid bottom of the lake of the mind, you have to be peering down into the lake to notice it. The habit of introspection, of *trying* to see through to the non-obvious origins of feelings and desires, is almost a prerequisite for the discovery, in experience, of the inner mystery. Augustine noticed his own opacity, but it was Shakespeare, again, who raised the articulation of inner processes to a higher level. Richard II, languishing in the dungeon of Pomfret Castle, has plenty of time to reflect on his own mental processes. He develops an analogy between the busy social world of the court, and his solitary state, peopled only by his own thoughts:

> My brain I'll prove the female to my soul;
> My soul, the father; and these two beget
> A generation of still-breeding thoughts.
> And these same thoughts people this little world;
> In humours like the people of this world,
> For no thought is contented . . .
>
> Thus play I, in one person, many people,
> And none contented. Sometimes I am king:
> Then treason makes me wish myself a beggar,
> And so I am: Then crushing penury
> Persuades me I was better when a king;
> Then am I king'd again: and by and by,
> Think that I am unking'd by Bolingbroke,
> And straight am nothing.
>
> (*King Richard II*, V.5)

And so on and so on, sounding, for all the world, like a contemporary meditator, recounting the ceaseless pattering of tiny thoughts during a session on her cushion. Richard's thought-children represent complementary, and often conflicting, sides of his soul, the voices of the quasi-human sub-personalities which are the inhabitants of his unconscious. Indeed, the idea of a 'king' surrounded by a complex, rebellious court, full of intrigue, is a fruitful image of the internal tussles between the ego, who must, in the end, act as wisely as it can, and the myriad constraints and cabals that are plotting to achieve their own ends, and whispering misdirections, behind the scenes.

Richard, and Shakespeare himself, is here 'feeling his way through a twilight of self-knowledge',[18] limbering up, perhaps, for the virtuoso introspection that we will find some seventeen years later in the mouth of Prospero, and in his relationship with his own id personified in Caliban. Indeed, we might see many of Shakespeare's characters as archetypes, symbolising and externalising the basic voices within a single soul: the beautiful young women, the Princess Dianas, who stand for Love – Ophelia, Desdemona; the aged counsellors standing for Wisdom – Polonius, Gonzalo; and the personified 'faults' in a person's soul that bring them down – of which Iago and even Caliban himself could be examples. Jung will call these archetypes the Anima, the Wise Old Man and the Shadow, respectively, but Shakespeare got there first.[19]

As the mature Shakespeare was working on perhaps his most intricate psychological study, *The Tempest*, across the English Channel a young scholar from La Haye in Touraine was beginning to lay the foundations of an approach to psychology from which almost all of Shakespeare's subtlety would be removed. Like Shakespeare, René Descartes was heir to five of the great movements of the early seventeenth century: individualism, introspection, improvement, doubt and separation. People were becoming intensely interested not just in how good or bad they were, or their mutual potential as threats or resources, but in the details of each other's experience. The memoirs of soldiers, diplomats and missionaries were selling like hot cakes. The questions of how people as unique individuals were different, and, despite that, how they were the same underneath, were much debated. These travellers' tales were of interest not just because they fed this interest in difference, but because they also contained the writer's thoughts and reflections: they struggled to explore their own experiences, as well as simply relate it. They contained the seeds of introspection.

There was developing, also, a corollary interest in the possibilities and processes of self-improvement, not just in the Christian, moralised sense, but in the sense that 'travel broadened the mind', and people's views and expectations were capable of change. Until 1620, *improve* had been a legal term that meant enclosing and cultivating waste ground; now people could 'improve' themselves. News of other societies stimulated an interest in historical change: the startling idea that whole peoples evolved over historical time. It had not always been 'like this'. Francis Bacon's 'method of induction' encouraged people to look around them, and put their beliefs to the test of systematically observed fact. Luther's defiant 'Here I stand; I can do no other' had echoed down the sixteenth century as a call to independent thinking. And all this was fuelled by the increasing legitimacy of doubt. Where words like *curious* and *inquisitive* had previously carried an air of pious disapproval, they now signalled a welcome enthusiasm for discovery and learning.

Such developments impacted on people's sense of themselves in the world. Throughout the Middle Ages, as it had been in ancient Greece, the distinction between Inner and Outer had not been anything like as sharply drawn, or felt, as it is today. The link between the four ingredients of the world, and the four humours out of which people were constituted, was strong. The stars and planets were seen as living bodies, capable of influencing – i.e. 'flowing into' – human beings. But by focusing more on the psychological, the people of the seventeenth century started to feel a clearer sense of the physical world as something alien and foreign. Subjectivity and objectivity were shearing apart. A process began in which the sense of being 'in and of the world', of being, if you like, an ecologically embedded element of the wider system, started to implode, sucking the sense of self inside, away from the land and the sky, away even from one's own flesh and blood, down into the shadowy, private world of thoughts and feelings. The connective tissue of the soul that tied people to the world was being severed, and being replaced by a cold, mechanical universe on the one side, and millions of separate 'selves' and 'minds' on the other.[20]

Into this climate stepped Descartes, doubting everything, taking nothing on trust, bent on discovering, by the power of his own observation and intellect alone, what was true and reliable, and what was corrupt and changeable, both in the world and in human nature. Externally, his project was Platonic and Pythagorean: he wanted to turn the universe into abstract, elegant, beautiful combinations of numbers and equations. He wanted to cut through the dull detail of actual motions and collisions to the clean, clear skeleton of natural laws on which that messy flesh was hung. And so, too, with human beings. What, if anything, did human beings possess that was indubitably 'of the soul', and therefore of the divine? How much of what they needed, and did, and felt and thought, could be plausibly delegated to some insentient biological machinery? And what would be left, incapable of issuing from merely physical processes and causes, and therefore indicative of a different sphere entirely? What could he not conceive of himself as being *without*? What could not be pared away by the scalpel of doubt?

Descartes was hamstrung in this honourable quest in a number of ways. First, little was known directly about the body, and what it was capable of doing 'by itself', so he was always liable to underestimate its capacities. Second, there was only a small range of rather crude technological devices available for him to use as metaphorical tools to help him conceptualise the body: clockwork and hydraulic machines, in the main. He had no way, for example, of thinking about how consciousness could *conceivably* be produced by a physical system. He saw the body as a kind of clever hydraulic automaton, in which movements were due to muscles being 'pumped up' by a mysterious fluid that flowed from the brain along the narrow 'tubes' that were the nerves. Lacking any understanding of the intricacy and power of the brain, there was obviously no way in which such a mechanism could account for the ability to talk, think or be conscious.

Third, he lived in a conceptual world in which the most important and obvious things were *things*: things that did things to each other, but retained their identities through such interactions, like balls on a billiard table, for instance. Entities were primary, and instigatory; processes and changes were secondary and consequential. So he was predisposed to look for some kind of thinglike agency as the root of humanness. (He was always looking to put the 'entity' into 'identity' – and to take the 'id' out, at the same time.) And finally, his belief in the soul – his commitment to the venerable idea of the divine microchip implanted inside us by God – turned out to be unshakeable. Convinced that there *must* be something that could not be reduced to the physical, he naturally (as we all do; Descartes was far from exceptional in this) found what he set out to find.

To cut a long story short, he discovered, looking at himself through this set of lenses, that he could doubt pretty much everything that might be a candidate for 'quintessential humanness'. The one thing he could not doubt was that he was having the conscious experience of doubting and thinking. He inferred three things from this observation, all, in fact, false. First, he concluded that there had to be a 'Him' – an inner entity behind the scenes who was *doing* the doubting and thinking. Second, he deduced that the essential characteristic of this 'Him' was that it engaged in such conscious scrutiny and reasoning. And third, he assumed that the physical stuff of which he was composed was incapable in principle of underwriting this conscious, thinking 'self'. If you look at the body, on the one hand, consisting entirely, as far as one can tell, of meat and goo of various kinds, and at the 'mind', on the other, with its rarefied reflections and cogitations, it does indeed seem preposterous, even today, that the former should be able to generate the latter. *Of course* they are different kinds of stuff – what Descartes called *res extensa*, material stuff, and *res cogitans*, thinking stuff.

Like many before him, Descartes had a slight problem with perception, being clearly of the world of consciousness, yet tied rather too closely for comfort to the bodily world of senses and appetites. But a quick adjustment of the meaning of the word 'thought' seemed to fix that. 'Thought is a word that covers everything that exists in us in such a way that we are immediately conscious of it. Thus all the operations of will, intellect, imagination *and of the senses* are thoughts,' he declared in the *Meditations*. Thinking is redefined as 'consciousness'. With this, he was home and dry. 'What then am I?' he asks rhetorically. 'A thing which thinks. What is a thing that thinks? It is a thing which doubts, understands, conceives, affirms, denies, wills, refuses, which also imagines and feels.' And, in case there is any doubt, he wrote to his friend and mentor Mersenne: 'As to the proposition . . . that nothing can be in me, that is, in my mind, of which I am not conscious, I have proved it in the *Meditations*, and it follows from the fact that the soul is distinct from the body, and that its essence is to think.'

At a stroke, more or less, 'soul' is rendered no longer numinous and mysterious; it has been dejuiced, desiccated and transformed into the 'cognitivised' notion of 'mind'. This 'mind' has, to Descartes' satisfaction, been confirmed as completely separate from the body, as well as from the entire physical world, and has become the hypothetical 'organ of intelligence' based exclusively in consciousness, and, ideally, in the methodical exercise of conscious reason. The body is left, therefore, as a mere unconscious, unintelligent machine. It is where desires and emotions have their being, and thus they too are lacking in anything that one could conceivably call intelligence, let alone 'spirit'. And the sanitised mind becomes the natural home of my 'identity'; the well-lit mental space, somewhere behind the eyes, where 'I' sit, like the Chief Executive, in a big leather chair, watching what comes before me, making decisions, and issuing orders for the dumb menial of the body to carry out. Introspection is direct, unproblematic and, in principle at least, complete and accurate ('I know clearly that there is nothing more easy for me to know than my own mind'). The conscious observer, thinker and instigator *is*

Who I Am. So there is no such thing as 'the unconscious' (apart from the physiological robotics of the body). The very idea of an unconscious mental state or process is inconceivable; and if there *were* to be any such thing (which there wasn't) it would most certainly not be intelligent, and it could not possibly be anything to do with 'me'. QED.[21]

Such is the conventional image of Descartes' legacy: the terrible crystallisation of misunderstandings which he packaged and passed down to European, and increasingly global, culture. The picture is largely fair. But not entirely, for Descartes himself was less attached to his shrunken image of human nature than one might think, and also more open to other aspects of human experience. The American philosopher Amelie Rorty has suggested that Descartes' dualism may have reflected political as much as intellectual concerns. He clearly understood the opposition of the French Church to scientific developments and had moved to Holland to avoid possible persecution. Perhaps he also reasoned that overt questioning of the reality of the soul would have provoked a crackdown on scientific work as a whole. Patricia Churchland suggests that some of Descartes' arguments are so riddled with obvious flaws that they may have been deliberately 'planted as clues for the discerning reader'.[22] The attempt to solve the core problem of dualism – how do the body and soul 'talk' to each other? – by having them communicate via the pineal gland, on the grounds that there is only one pineal gland and two of everything else, is patently absurd, for example. (Descartes himself says, late on in the *Meditations*, that 'I am joined to my body . . . so compoundly and intermingled with [it] that I form, as it were, a single whole with it.' So what price his precious dualism?)[23]

In several places, Descartes acknowledges the reality, the importance even, of forms of experience which are airbrushed out of his Official Doctrine (as Gilbert Ryle calls it). He well knew of the value of intuition, and the surprising wisdom it was capable of delivering, but chose to attribute this form of knowing to God rather than to the mind. And in the Second Meditation he acknowledges an even bigger problem: that, despite being careful and honest, it is still possible for him to be mistaken about things. How does Descartes deal with this? He claims that 'there is some deceiver both very powerful and very cunning, who constantly uses all his wiles to deceive me'. Who is it? Well, it can't be God, because, a little later, he asserts that 'it is impossible that he should ever deceive me', and he refuses to take the obvious alternative – that it is 'the Devil'. But if it is a part of Descartes himself, it cannot be 'the body', for the body is dumb, and this agency is highly intelligent: 'malicious and cunning, who employs all his efforts and industry to deceive me'. So it has to be a part of his own mind – a part that begins to look suspiciously like a version of the unconscious – a part subsequently expurgated from the Official Doctrine.

Elsewhere he talks of 'thoughts which sprang up hitherto spontaneously in my mind', and of the fact that something could be 'presented to my mind without my consent being required . . . and that it was in no way in my power not to perceive it'. He sees clearly that many judgements and conclusions *arrive* in consciousness, but are not *worked out* there. 'I observed that the judgements I was in the habit of making about these objects were formed in me before I had the leisure to weigh and consider the reasons which might oblige me to make them.' And again he acknowledges that there might be more to his own mind than has been allowed to meet his eye: 'Although the ideas . . . do not depend on my will, I do not think that one should conclude on that account that they came from things different from myself, since *perhaps some faculty might be found in me, although it is hitherto unknown to me, which caused and produced them.*'[24] No sooner is the unconscious kicked out of the front door than it sidles in again though the back – even in Descartes' own writing!

We could even argue that it was Descartes who first described the phenomenon of transference, or something close to it – which the contemporary psychoanalyst Janet Malcolm calls Freud's 'most original and radical discovery'.[25] Three years before his death in 1650, Descartes described this charming insight in a letter to his friend Canut:

When I was a child, I loved a girl of my own age, who was somewhat cross-eyed; as a result of which, the impression which sight made on my brain when I looked at her divergent eyes was so joined to that which also stirred in me the passion of love, that long afterwards, whenever I looked at cross-eyed persons, I felt more inclined to love them than to love others. Simply because they had this defect: and nevertheless I did not know that this was the reason . . . Thus, when we are led to love someone without knowing the reason, we may suppose that this is because they have some point of resemblance with someone whom we loved previously, even though we do not know what it is . . .[26]

Better-known is Descartes' respect for his own dreams. He recounts how the whole course of his life's work was set as a result of a series of dreams on the night of 10 November 1619. The third of these was a 'lucid dream', a dream in which the dreamer is aware that he is dreaming. In it, Descartes found himself trying to interpret the earlier dreams. In this third dream he was reading from two significant books, a dictionary and a book of poetry, in particular a poem entitled 'Est et Non' ('It is and it isn't'). The dictionary, he decided, in the dream, stood for scientific and philosophical knowledge, while the poetic anthology stood for non-intellectual wisdom. Later Descartes recorded, referring to himself in the third person: 'the Poets . . . were full of sentences more serious, more felt, and better expressed than those which are found in the Philosophers. He attributed this marvel to the divine nature of Enthusiasm ["being filled with God"] and to the power of the Imagination, which brings out the seeds of wisdom . . . as

Reason cannot'. The poem 'Est et Non', he went on, stood for truth and falsehood in human knowledge, and especially, paradoxically, in science. Indeed, 'it was the Spirit of Truth which had wanted to open to him the treasures of all the sciences by this dream'. It was, to Descartes, as if 'Olympus had spoken through his unconscious', and the High Priest of Rationality took the message very seriously.[27] Overall, we have to conclude that the Official Doctrine was more Procrustean bed than complete picture, and that much of what did not fit – and of which Descartes himself was vividly aware – had to be ignored, twisted or explained away. What we cannot be sure of is how much of this distortion was knowing and tactical, and how much was an unintentional reflection of his rationalistic missionary zeal.

Almost immediately after its publication, the Official Doctrine attracted both defenders and opponents. John Locke, in his *Essay Concerning Human Understanding*, strongly reaffirmed Descartes' welding together of 'mind', 'consciousness', 'intelligence' and personal identity. The essence of a person, he wrote,

> is a thinking intelligent being, that has reason and reflection, and can consider itself the same thinking thing in different times and places; which it does only by that consciousness that is inseparable from thinking and, it seems to me, essential to it: it being impossible for anyone to perceive without perceiving that he does perceive. When we see, hear, smell, taste, feel, meditate, or will anything, we know that we do so . . . Consciousness always accompanies thinking, and it is that that makes everyone to be what he calls 'self'.[28]

A little later, in the early eighteenth century, David Hume would assert tersely that 'the perceptions of the mind are perfectly known', and 'consciousness never deceives'.[29]

It was Hume, also, who articulated most clearly the image of the mind as a mental 'space': 'a kind of theatre, where several perceptions successively make their appearance, pass, re-pass, glide away, and mingle in an infinite variety of postures and situations'.[30] But even Hume realised that the metaphor of a theatre *stage* immediately demands that there be unseen *wings* to the stage, and technicians, and rehearsal rooms. 'The comparison of the theatre must not mislead us . . . we [don't have] the most distant notion of the place where these scenes are represented, or of the materials of which it is composed.'[31]

The idea that everyone has a brightly lit mind which comprises both the workshop and the workforce of intelligence, and that the Head Thinker in this set-up is the most crucial role that 'I' have to play, rapidly consolidated itself as the core of European Common Sense. People soon came to experience themselves through this working model so naturally and continuously that the model itself dissolved in everyday life and became invisible. And it was a central belief of this model that it was complete, and left nothing over to explain, so phenomena that were inconvenient to it were continually ignored or explained away, as Descartes himself had had to do. Yet they were everywhere. Lapses of consciousness, for example, such as occurred with head injury, fainting, sleep or even just a moment of blankness, were commonplace, yet, on the Official Doctrine, they had to mean that 'I' did not exist during those periods. The fact that ideas, as Descartes himself had noted, often 'popped into your mind' or 'occurred to you' meant that consciousness was frequently the display cabinet of the mind, not its engine room. Slips of the tongue, mundane intuitions, dreams themselves: dozens of times a day people's experience refused to lie down quietly on Descartes' Procrustean bed and allow its feet to be chopped off to make it fit. Yet, amazingly, many people did not notice – and still don't. The Official Doctrine turned, as 'common sense' does, into what American psychologist Charles Tart calls 'the consensual trance'.

But some people *did* notice that their sense of self was being shrunk to fit the oversimplified Cartesian view of mind, self and soul, and their voices were soon raised in protest. Hardly was the ink dry on Locke's *Essay* than the English Platonist John Norris was defiantly echoing Plotinus' observation that 'we may have ideas of which we are not conscious', and 'there are infinitely more ideas impressed on our minds than we can possibly attend to'.[32]

In France Blaise Pascal, an acquaintance of Descartes, himself a highly skilled and rigorous thinker, refused to accept that that was all that he was. In his *Pensées* he observed that the inner depth of human nature and the seat of true knowledge was rarely convinced by reason, and often swayed by rhetoric. 'The instrument by which persuasion is brought about is not demonstration [i.e. proof] alone. How few things are demonstrated! [It is] custom [that] makes our strongest proofs and . . . draws the unthinking mind after it.' And, in his most famous reminder of the fact that we often have much ado to know ourselves: 'The heart has its reasons of which reason itself knows nothing.'

Like Pascal, Benedict de Spinoza and Thomas Hobbes insisted on basing their views of the mind on how it *actually* appeared to work, rather than on an a priori set of dubious assumptions about how it was *supposed* to work. In his *Political Treatise* of 1678, for example, Spinoza poked fun at Descartes and his predecessors for their judgemental attitude towards human emotions, and for thinking that, by bewailing the real and exalting the impossibly idealistic, 'they are doing something wonderful'. Instead, he said,

I have laboured carefully, not to mock, lament or execrate, but to understand human action; and to this end I have looked upon passions such as love, hatred, anger, envy, ambition, pity, and the other perturbations of the mind not in the light of vices of human nature, but as properties, just as pertinent to it, as are heat, cold, storm, thunder and the like to the nature of the atmosphere, which phenomena, though inconvenient, are yet necessary.[33]

Without the example of Spinoza and Machiavelli, the rapid rise of interest, by novelists as much as philosophers, in what *is*, in human nature, rather than what *ought* to be, would not have occurred as rapidly as it did.

Spinoza and Hobbes both noted that the emergent idea of 'free will', as being the ability of the mind-agent to concoct and instigate courses of action that were not completely constrained by events, took no account of Pascal's unconscious 'heart'. Spinoza said it straight out: 'Men regard themselves as free, since they are aware of their will and their desires, and do not even in dream think of the causes which determine their desiring and willing, as they do not know them.' On the Official Doctrine, if you do not know them, they can't exist, and therefore any explanatory gap, in accounting for why you did what you did, had to be plugged with the 'soul', or with God. Hobbes put it rather more poetically:

A wooden top that is lashed by the boys, and runs about sometimes to one wall, sometimes to another, sometimes spinning, sometimes hitting men on the shins, if it were sensible of its own motion, would think it proceeded from its own will, unless it felt what lashed it. And is a man any wiser, when he runs to one place for a benefice, to another for a bargain, and troubles the world with writing errors and requiring answers, because he thinks he doth it without any cause other than his own will, and seeth not what are the lashings that cause his will?[34]

Confusingly, David Hume himself, he of 'consciousness never deceives', in a later work goes even further than Pascal, Spinoza and Hobbes in recognising that we are not just ignorant of some of our influences and motives, but that we may actively conceal some and promote others in order to present a more favourable image of ourselves to our own eyes. In doing so, he echoes Augustine, and again anticipates Freud. 'Our predominant motive or intention is, indeed, frequently concealed from ourselves when it is mingled and confounded with other motives which the mind, from vanity or self-conceit, is desirous of supposing more prevalent.' This is a significant passage, not just for its modern take on self-deception, but also because it may be the first time that 'the mind' itself is credited with humanlike motives and psychological stratagems. It is not just the inner theatre now; it has become a Machiavellian humanoid being that lies behind and motivates the overt machinations of impression- and consciousness-management – exactly the kind of internalised 'god' or 'demon' that Freud was to make such use of in his theorising. Hume even recommends dream analysis as 'an excellent method of becoming acquainted with our own hearts . . . The generosity or baseness of our temper, our meekness or cruelty, our courage or pusillanimity, influence the fictions of the imagination with the most unbounded liberty, and discover [i.e. reveal] themselves in the most glaring colours.'[35]

Hume recognises the impact that unconscious traits and motives have on dreams, but he imagines that their expression is unhindered. He underestimates the inner opposition that there may be, and the psychic struggle – as experienced, for instance, by Plato's charioteer – to prevent those forces from making themselves known. However, that struggle, too – yet another ingredient of the Freudian mix – was being written about at the time. In 1644, three years after the publication of Descartes' *Meditations*, and also in Paris, Sir Kenelm Digby, son of one of the conspirators in the Gunpowder Plot, produced a treatise in which he strongly reaffirmed the censoring function of reason. He warns of occasions when 'the multitude and violence of those spirits which Passion sendeth boyling up to the fantasie is so great [that Reason is] not able for the present to balance them and stay their impetuosity'.[36]

So the first wave of anti-Cartesian protest insisted on reminding the world of what it knew only too well, and what Shakespeare had taken as read: that the mind is not transparent to itself.

Descartes' attempt to present the mind as being like a clock in a glass case, with all its workings perfectly and unproblematically available for inspection, doesn't wash. It is not how we experience ourselves. It is not progress to try to replace messy but accurate observations with a tidy, idealised but phoney theory.

There were several more movements that came into being as reactions to the Official Doctrine, and we must, perhaps, be grateful that Descartes' flawed attempt to conceptualise the mind forced other people, over the ensuing three centuries, to think more carefully about the variety of ways in which the rich oddities of their experience demanded a reinstatement, and a development, of conceptions of the unconscious, in order to accommodate them. The three main trends were, roughly, the Romantic, the psychopathological and the cognitive, and it is the growth of each of these, from the eighteenth century on, that the next three chapters aim to chart.

5

The 'Inner Africa': Romanticism, Mysticism and Dreams

> The unconscious is really the largest realm in our minds, and just on account of this unconsciousness is the inner Africa, whose unknown boundaries may extend far away.
>
> – Jean Paul, 1804[1]

Let me tell you a little more about that dream: the one where I was in a lift descending through a shaft in the rocky gorge by the side of Isambard Kingdom Brunel's magnificent Clifton Suspension Bridge in Bristol. I was feeling afraid, but also rather excited and 'suspense-ful'. When I awoke, I was left with the feeling that the dream was 'significant' in some way. But how was I to go about making sense of it? I remembered that I had been in such a lift, not long before, that ran down through the cliff from a rather smart hotel in La Gomera, one of the Canary Islands, to the beach below – near to the small apartment, right on the seafront, where I was staying. I had walked up the road to have a look at the hotel, and had found it very snooty and unfriendly – not my kind of place at all. I then found the lift, which would be my short-cut home, but only hotel residents had a key to it, so I lurked about and squashed in, nervously, with the next family going down. My musings also revived strong feeling about the bridge in Bristol, which I actually drive over quite frequently. It has been a favoured spot for suicide jumps, and – though far from suicidal – I sometimes feel a potent mixture of fearful vertigo and mysterious attraction in high places that one could jump off.

Lying in bed, chewing over the dream, I realised that I had already generated enough emotional memories and associations to fuel a dozen 'interpretations'. It might be about feeling 'suspended' in my job at Bristol University. It might be about having to face something fearful before I could 'go home'. It might be about dying. It might be about realising that I do not feel that I belong in 'high places', and feel much more sure – or 'shore'? – down by the sea, where I can see things closer at hand, rather than (from the top of the cliff) way off on the horizon. Any of these could give me food for thought. But were any of them actually latent in the dream? Was my unconscious trying to send me coded messages about my priorities in life, last night? Or am I – no less valuably, perhaps – simply creating these interpretations with the help of my waking mind, and pasting them back over the top of the innocent, maybe even meaningless, dream? Am I deciphering the dream, or simply using it like a Rorschach ink-blot, or a chicken's entrails, as a blurry, messy invitation to generate and inspect my own projections? Is it true that the unconscious is an invisible gnomic guru, a disembodied voice spouting wise riddles for us to crack, if only we are smart enough?

Such questions are the stuff of this chapter, which explores whether we can get closer to the unconscious, to where it lives, what it knows, and why we have it, by looking at some of the various unusual and exotic voices – dreams, symbols, experiences of awe or selflessness – that have been attributed to it. I shall focus for the moment largely on such positive voices: the ones that, in the eighteenth and nineteenth centuries, were of great interest to the European Romantics and which, throughout other cultures and over longer spans of history, have been the subject of many forms of aesthetic, mystical and religious experience. The 'inner Africa' symbolised, for Europe at the beginning of the nineteenth century, the realm of the exotic, the mysterious and the uncharted, rather than that which was wild or frightening. We shall get back to the dark side of the unconscious in chapter 6.

Right from the start, one of the most strongly recurring themes in the history of the unconscious has been its apparent power to offer insight and wise advice through dreams and visions, and to do so in a way that is allusive. Where the conscious mind speaks prose – and, if Descartes had anything to do with it, flat, unambiguous, logical prose at that – the voice of the unconscious is poetic and symbolic. It hints at the future, or at the buried recesses of our own nature, or even at the universal, archetypal themes of human existence. But because it does it so indirectly, it is up to 'us', to a secondary, more conscious process, to infer and clarify its intent. Right back in the fourth century AD, Gregory of Nyssa captured this elliptical quality of dreams in a metaphor that anticipated our current concern with 'smoke and mirrors':

> As naturally happens with fire when it is heaped over with chaff, and no breath fans the flames – it neither consumes what lies beside it, nor is entirely quenched, but instead of flame it rises through the air in the form of smoke . . . In the same way, the mind, when hidden by the inaction of the senses in sleep, is neither able to shine through them, nor yet is quite extinguished, but has, so to say, a smouldering activity . . . it cannot make its meaning clear by direct methods, so that the information of the matter in hand should be plain and evident, but its declaration of the future is ambiguous and doubtful – what those who interpret such things call an 'enigma'.[2]

Opinion has always been divided as to whether all dreams are inherently significant, or none, or only some. If they are 'significant', are they reliable, or even divine, in nature, or mischievous and misleading, implanted by the Devil for the sole purpose of leading us astray and causing us confusion and distress, or making us do bad things 'against our true nature'? And – crucially, because we are prone to error, and the Devil is cunning – how do we tell the significant from the meaningless, and the trustworthy from the treacherous? For some, it has been self-evident that dreams are always of interest. Rabbi Chisda in the Talmud says 'the dream that is not interpreted is like a letter which is not read.'

Plato, too, tended to see dreams as inherently meaningful, though some reflected the rampaging of the 'lawless wild beast nature that peers out in sleep', while others offered wise counsel. For example, he had Socrates, while in prison awaiting his execution, explain to Cebes that he had had a recurrent dream throughout his life that he should 'make and cultivate music'. Previously Socrates had taken this to refer to his particular 'music' of philosophy – but now, as philosophy was a bit of a sore subject, he had decided to follow its suggestion more literally, and was in the process of composing a variety of hymns and poems. Which kind of dream you have, says Plato, depends on whether you have dined with restraint, and 'awakened your rational powers' before nodding off, or not.[3]

For Aristotle, more the cool observer than the righteous moralist or amateur dietitian, dreams reflected residual reverberations of the day's sense impressions, sometimes clear, when the mind is very calm and these faint traces are able to be seen, and sometimes distorted by other aspects of temperament or emotion – melancholy, fever, intoxication – so that 'the visions appear confused and monstrous', like images broken on the surface of ruffled water. If dreams appear prophetic, Aristotle counsels suspicion of any supernatural interpretation. His rational mind sees two alternative possibilities. The first, quite ingenious, is that during sleep one may have explored an anticipated scenario and tried out various possible responses in one's mind's eye – so that, if the rehearsed response subsequently occurs (which may have been rendered more likely by the dry run), there may attach to it a feeling of *déjà vu*, which, in the absence of a conscious memory of the rehearsal, can be interpreted as an uncanny prediction ('I just knew this was going to happen . . .'). The second possibility is that apparent prophecies are 'to be classed as mere coincidences, especially all such as are extravagant . . . As regards these, it is natural that the fact should stand [out] as it does, whenever a person, on mentioning something, finds the very thing mentioned come to pass. Why, indeed, should this not happen in sleep? The probability is, rather, that many such things should happen.'

Aristotle's second possibility is the first resort of sceptics today, as then: killjoys who point out that our powers of selective memory, selective attention and selective interpretation are quite equal to the task of highlighting cases of apparent prophecy, and ignoring all the times when what we dreamed did not occur.[4] Cicero, like many others, went even further in denying that dreams held any interest whatsoever:

> If it is impossible by experiments and observations to arrive at a
> sure interpretation of them, the consequence is that dreams are
> not entitled to any credit or respect whatever. Let us reject,
> therefore, this divination of dreams, as well as all other kinds.
> For, to speak truly, that superstition has extended itself through
> all nations, and has oppressed the intellectual energies of all men,
> and has betrayed them into endless imbecilities.[5]

Lucretius, in around 55 BC, took a step towards the Freudian view of dreams when he argued that it was not *any* recent experiences that found their way into dreams, but only ones linked to current concerns or needs. Dreams represented the fulfilment of wishes, though he did not (as Plato had, and Freud would) divide these wishes into 'acceptable' and 'unacceptable'. 'Whatever be the pursuit to which one clings with devotion . . . it is generally the same things that we seem to encounter in dreams.' A prime example would be the 'wet dreams' of adolescents, he said. 'Those into the boiling currents of whose age seed is for the first time passing, when the ripe fullness of days has produced it in their limbs' are most likely to encounter in their dreams 'a glorious face and a beautiful bloom which stirs and excites the frame'.[6]

Over the years, systems for categorising and interpreting dreams became more complex, if not always more soundly based. Artemidorus in the second century AD restricted the term 'dream' to night-time experiences in which the dreamer 'discovers the truth under a hidden figure, as when Jacob interpreted Pharaoh's dream of the seven lean cattle that should devour the seven fat ones'. Dreams were to be distinguished from Visions or precognitions; Oracles, in which an Angel speaks directly to you; Phantasies, which happen 'when the affections are so vehement that they ascend up to the brain during sleep and meet with the more watchful spirits'; and mere Apparitions that present themselves 'to weak infants and ancient men who fancy they see chimeras approaching to intimidate or offend them'. Were you to conjoin Phantasies and Dreams proper, you would have many of the elements of the psychoanalytic view of dreams as disguised wish-fulfilment.[7]

Many systems for interpreting dream (and other mythic or artistic) symbols have come and gone, and many have prefigured the fanciful, prurient and overconfident tone of some of the more enthusiastic present-day psychological code-breakers. The Talmud tells us, for example, that someone who dreams of watering an olive tree with olive oil is expressing, in a disguised form, his incestuous desire. Dreaming of having sex with your mother, however, means that the dreamer is destined to become wise! Then, as now, it was quite possible for everything to be stood on its head and back again, so that the possibilities of interpretation are limited only by the creativity, perversity and stamina of the interpreter. For Freud, the penis is symbolised by neck-ties, umbrellas, snakes, airplanes and flames, amongst many other things. Landscapes are 'invariably the genitals of the dreamer's mother',[8] an idea which will doubtless enrich your next visit to the Tate Britain art gallery to look at all those wonderful Constables and Turners.

It is interesting that we seem to have made little progress in deciding whether the meanings of dreams are discovered or imputed. It is still largely a matter of assertion and personal belief. For example, in his 1999 book on *The Unconscious* Antony Easthope recounts Freud's analysis of the nonsense word '*Maistollmutz*' which featured in one of his female patient's dreams. It can be deconstructed, says Freud, into *mais*, maize, *toll*, mad, *mannstoll*, nymphomania, *Meissen*, a porcelain bird, the English Miss, the Yiddish *mies*, disgusting, and so on. It doesn't take a trained psychoanalyst to see where Freud is heading. But what is of interest here is the word Easthope uses to indicate his evaluation of this creative activity – Freud does not 'speculate' or 'suggest' or even 'argue': he '*shows*', says Easthope, that these connotations are 'what counts' about the word. Likewise, Freud's assertions that fire stands for the penis and a fireplace for the vagina is somehow '*confirmed*' by pointing to the crude, misogynist expression (used by English males of a certain type to remind each other that it is OK to have sex with women whom they do not find attractive) that 'You don't look at the mantelpiece when you're stoking the fire.' We might raise our eyebrows a little at what is accepted as 'evidence' by some of symbolism's enthusiasts.[9]

The question of whether the dream interpreter is a subtle diviner of meaning, or a creative projector of it, can never be finally settled. Even if we could show that 'Freud made it all up', that would not prove that the meaning was not *also* inherent in the dream. The difficulty of deciding this issue is illustrated by the different interpretations possible of an experiment on dream interpretation, cited by Erich Fromm (a 'believer') in his book *The Forgotten Language*. Apparently, people under hypnosis are more likely to find dreams that are presented to them meaningful, and are more willing to offer symbolic interpretations of them, than people who are not hypnotised. From this, Fromm concludes that 'we all possess *the gift to understand symbolic language*, but that this knowledge becomes operative only in the state of dissociation brought on by hypnosis' (emphasis added). There is an alternative explanation, however: that hypnosis simply induces a state of mind in which one is more ready, willing and able to 'think poetically', that is, to make broader associations and to see links between ideas that do not follow the normal, conventional tramlines of thought. It does not have to be that we all possess a pre-installed Symbolic Dictionary to which hypnosis gives us access. We may simply enter a more dreamy state of mind in which – surprise, surprise – some of the same associative possibilities tend to occur to different people.

The latter possibility is strengthened by a study of long-term meditators, which showed (yes, 'showed', because this was a properly controlled piece of scientific research) that different types of meditation alter the meditators' propensity for giving fanciful responses to Rorschach blots in different ways. One form of Buddhist meditation called 'one-pointedness' cultivates the ability to inhibit the spontaneous ramblings of the mind, and maintain a concentrated focus on a single object or idea for extended periods of time. When presented with the ink-blots, people emerging from a three-month 'one-pointedness' retreat described the blobs with literal accuracy, and could not be induced to make any projected elaborations. One subject said: 'The meditation has wiped out all the interpretive stuff on top of the raw perception.'

A second group, however, had spent three months practising 'mindfulness', in which one learns to maintain a stance of disinterested observation while allowing the mind to run around as much as it likes. When confronted with the meaningless blot, these people spontaneously spewed out dozens of highly fanciful and often obscene 'interpretations', while protesting that they were perfectly aware that none of these was in any sense 'real'. ('This I see as a circumcised penis . . . thrusting up between these two red spaces . . . as though they were two twin creatures with

An 'inkblot' image, designed as a 'projective test' to diagnose patients' state of mind, by Hermann Rorschach in the early 20th century. Rorschach, nicknamed 'Kleck' – 'Inkblot' – at school, made this technique famous, though he actually borrowed it from Szyman Hens. Like Freud, Rorschach was both a staunch psychoanalyst and given to fanciful over-interpretation of his subjects' fantasies.

little paws . . . wanting to pounce on it . . .') Their disposition to create meaning had been not suppressed but disinhibited, while the one-pointedness practitioners had placed their meaning-seeking tendencies firmly under control.[10] There is no reason to suppose that the two groups differed in the bundled symbolic software with which they were born.

On the basis of such studies, it is hard to discount the possibility that Freud's main gift was not so much the accuracy of his insights into his patients' conditions, as his undoubted creativity in being able to generate and rationalise an impressive range of sophisticated 'double entendres' which conformed to (rather than 'confirmed') his theoretical suspicions. Indeed, with such a fecund imagination, and such an interest in the effects of the sexually inhibited society in which he lived, it would be very surprising if some of his diagnoses had *not* rung bells with some of his patients.

One could go on illustrating differing opinions about the origins and meanings of dreams throughout history, and across cultures, *ad infinitum*. For two thousand years people have argued about the significance of dreams – how many types there were, whether they came from a full stomach or a benign god, whether symbols had universal meanings, or had to be taken in the light of the individual's life and concerns – and have made little progress. St Thomas Aquinas said there were four types and some came from God. Hobbes believed all dreams were caused by bodily stimuli. Voltaire said that they were all nonsense. Kant, quaintly, thought that the best dreams were absolutely clear and transparent, but that, unfortunately, because such dreams occurred only in the deepest levels of sleep, we could never remember these big fish, and ended up only ever catching the shallower and more obscure minnows! Emerson voiced a rather Freudian view when he said that 'we call the Phantoms that arise [in dreams] the creation of our fancy, but they act like mutineers, and fire on their commander . . . Wise and sometimes terrible hints shall in them be thrown to the man out of a quite unknown intelligence.' And:

'Sleep takes off the costume of circumstance, arms us with a terrible freedom, so that every will rushes to a deed.'[11]

Today's approaches tend to be hybrid. A mixture of ongoing concerns and the impressions of the preceding day remain active at night, and fragments may rise to the surface of the mind, some of which are quite inconsequential, while others are charged with emotional significance. As the normal constraints of reasonableness, decorum and the maintenance of a favourable self-image are relaxed in sleep, so these fragments initiate a spontaneous, imaginative process that tries to weave them into the semblance of a coherent story. On waking, only some parts of this story remain available – again, plausibly, those parts which carry the motivational charge – and these reduced and selected passages may then form the raw material of a more conscious attempt to reconstruct and articulate 'the dream'. So by the time we have a 'dream' ready to recount to our therapist, or to a researcher, we already have a highly wrought product that has been through several phases of construction and interpretation, some of it quite automatic and some much more conscious and deliberate.[12]

We shall return to consider the fabrication of dreams in more detail when we come to look at the unconscious in the light of current brain-science. For now, we might simply note that these more sophisticated theories of dreaming and the unconscious have their precedents too. To pick just one out of dozens . . . Marin Cureau de la Chambre, physician to Cardinal Richelieu and Louis XIV, writing at the same time as Descartes, saw the soul as a thinly disguised kind of central nervous system 'which is present everywhere in the body, readily notices everything which happens there, and communicates it to the imagination'. However, 'since this [internal] knowledge is obscure and confused, it does not instruct the imagination clearly, but only gives it a general view'. And, says La Chambre, these 'outlines' are not only incomplete representations of the bodily and sensory states of affairs, they are also biased and distorted by the character and preoccupations of the dreamer. So when, for example, 'the bile has been stirred up, even though the soul does not know what it is, it does know that it is a warm and ardent humour, and from the report which it then gives to the imagination, the latter imagines the brilliant colours, the flames and conflagrations . . . the plans for assault and combat, the imaginary enemies . . . which conform to this vague notion which it has received'.[13]

The Romantic backlash to the Cartesian ablation of the unconscious took up this age-old interest in the dense actuality of dreams with great enthusiasm. The Romantics obstinately asserted that human experience, in all its gloriously messy detail, was of interest in its own right, and not merely as an overlay that obscured the ideals of Pure Truth and Eternal Knowledge. This led to a natural fascination with dreams, and the development of methods by which one could get to know them better – 'befriend them', as the archetypal psychologist James Hillman says – rather than attempt to plunder them for their knowledge. To try to smelt the imaginative ore of a dream down into a rectangular brick of understanding is to miss the point, as much as it would be to insist that Turner's magnificently abstract *Norham Castle* be replaced with a brief, framed description of the artist's intention. (Or, as Duke Ellington famously said to a dumb interviewer, 'If I could say it, I wouldn't have to play it.')

An early advocate of this befriending process was William Smellie, the Scottish printer and first compiler of the *Encyclopaedia Britannica*, in his *Philosophy of Natural History*, published in 1979; four years after his death. Though David Hume had already noted that reflecting on dreams was 'an excellent method of becoming acquainted with our own hearts', Smellie added a more detailed rationale, and clearer instructions about how to do it. Human beings, he said 'are so artful in disguising the real motives of their actions' that trying to 'know oneself' in waking mode is almost a waste of time. 'An inquiry into the natural tendency of imagination while awake would engage us in a struggle with all the obstacles to self-knowledge formerly suggested.' In dreams, though, the pressures towards self-deception are lessened, and the mind is therefore 'less inclined to palliate its real motives . . . and in general more open and candid'. As dreams are hard to catch in the morning light, however, we should practise doing so by writing them down, not in a *diary* but a *nocturnal*. 'The mere habit of writing, so ductile is the human mind, will soon make him both more attentive to his dreams, and increase his faculty in remembering them' – a form of learning to which many contemporary dream-watchers will attest.[14]

Fifty years later, still six years before the birth of Sigmund Freud, the poet and dramatist Christian Friedrich Hebbel advised a very modern approach to dream interpretation: to use dreams as a baited hook with which to fish in one's own unconscious for all the allusions, big and small, that might be drawn up to the surface of the mind by its lure. 'If a man would collect his dreams and would examine them, and would add to the dreams which he is now having all the thoughts he has in association with them, all the reminiscences, all the pictures he can grasp from them, and if he would combine these with the dreams he has had in the past, he would be able to understand himself much better by this than by means of any other kind of psychology.' Though Hebbel was living at the time in Vienna, and though there is evidence that Freud did read some of Hebbel's plays, we do not know if this pre-scient passage ever came Freud's way. It may well have done.[15]

However, the induction and interpretation of significant dreams, both as therapeutic responses to various kinds of illness and as a method for seeking spiritual depth in one's experience, had long held an honourable and popular place in classical Greece, as well as, earlier still, in ancient Egypt. The practice probably began in the ancient Egyptian civilisation of Kemet, spread down the Nile, and thence into the Mediterranean worlds of Greece, Rome and the Near East. In the hundreds of 'sleep temples' that existed around the sixth century BC, often in caves or other dramatic natural settings, seekers after truth, clarity or simply emotional relief would go through elaborate preparatory rituals of cleansing and fasting, and then be hypnotically induced into a kind of trance on the borderlands of wakefulness and sleep. In the sleeping-waking dreams that often ensued, it was said that people would directly experience the Amenta underworld, as it was known in Egypt, or what Carl Jung would come to refer to as the 'collective unconscious'. When they were reawakened, so it was claimed, people would have achieved a lasting reunification of their conscious and unconscious domains in a way that would enhance well-being and deliver valuable insight.[16]

In Greece, at the beginning of the fifth century BC, Parmenides wrote a poem that summarises his experiences of 'incubation' is such an Asclepian shrine. A group of young women come to lead him down into the Mansions of Night, the very depths of the depths of the kingdom of Hades, Tartarus, where even the gods fear to go, following in the footsteps of Orpheus. Darkness, he explains, symbolises ignorance and confusion: to experience the highest wisdom one must be prepared to pass through the black night of one's own incomprehension (or, perhaps, as the anonymous fourteenth-century English mystic would call it, the dark *Cloud of Unknowing*, or, in the Gospel of St John, the darkness that 'comprehendeth not' the light). After his preparations, Parmenides lies down in the *pholeos*, the 'lair' of the unconscious, and enters into the dream-trance state, knowing nothing, thinking nothing, emptying himself, so that the deep wisdom of the 'collective unconscious' may be drawn into the vacuum of his consciousness. And there, in Tartarus, Parmenides is instructed by the being he has been taken to meet: Persephone, wife of Hades. 'And the goddess welcomed me kindly, and took my right hand in hers', and she told him that he was there to 'learn all things: both the unshaken heart of persuasive Truth and the opinions of mortals, in which there's nothing that can be truthfully trusted at all'. Interestingly, the principal deity of these shrines was Apollo,

This fifth-century BC marble relief shows Asclepius, together with his female assistants, inducing the healing incubatory trance in a drowsy patient.

known today as the divine embodiment of rationality, but then also the god of knowledge gained through quiet insight or 'suspended animation'.[17]

The origins of the Romantic spirit, in the broadest sense, thus go back at least to classical Greece. Indeed, the French philosopher Pierre Hadot has recently argued, in a scholarly and convincing fashion, that the development of Socratic reasoning itself has been misunderstood by the philosophers and commentators of our own rationalistic age. More often than not, as in the case of Pythagoras, which we have already briefly looked at, reason was not seen as a tool with which to supersede more personal, emotional or even spiritual forms of knowing, but as an adjunct to them. Right down to the Stoics and Epicureans, including Socrates and Plato, says Hadot, the aim of philosophy was pragmatic: to find increasingly satisfactory ways of living. Reason was one such path, which, with Socrates, became the dominant, but still not the exclusive, one. But the deliberate induction of certain kinds of prized experience was – for Parmenides and Zeno, as much as for Keats, Shelley and Blake – of equal, if not greater, significance. In fact the Romantics, in their reaction to the rampant rationalism of their time, tended to be more polarised than the Greeks, leaning far back on one end of the epistemological seesaw on whose other end sat Locke and Newton, in order simply to try to create a little movement.

Even the Socratic dialogue, that apparent epitome of rational discourse, was not intended to transmit information but to produce a certain psychic effect in the participants: first, inducing the awful realisation that they do not know what they are talking about, and then, after this uncomfortable dilation, helping to ease out, from the inside – from the womb of their unconscious, Socrates might have said – the birth of a new understanding.[18] Socrates was not conducting an academic seminar: he insisted on 'making it personal'. He described his process of knowledge induction as maieutic, the activity of a midwife. Or: 'like an indefatigable horsefly', says Hadot, 'Socrates harassed his inter-locutors with questions which put *themselves* into question, forcing them to pay attention to and take care of themselves.'[19] Philosophical thinking can be used therapeutically, as Wittgenstein said, 'to show the fly the way out of the fly-bottle',[20] though to do so it has to have the visceral effect which Socrates sought and pro-duced. Philosophy in a Romantic vein seeks clarity and vitality in living, not neat theorising. It is about escaping from prisons of conceptual cleverness, not about constructing them.

It may be odd to imply that the Senior Common Rooms of Oxford are 'prisons', but from the point of view of the Romantic sensibility they may indeed seem so. For the interest of the Romantics – whether classical, eighteenth century or contempo-rary – is in experience, emotion and imagination not as raw material for reason to work on, but as valuable ways of knowing in their own right. For them, dreams, mystical experience, poetry and art are portals to self-knowledge, the very essence of which is that they *cannot* be rendered into tidy propositions. Symbols such as the cross, or the dark landscape of the 'underworld', have their power precisely because they evoke in us multiple layers of resonance that are beyond explicit comprehension. They cut across the familiar, reasonable categories and oppositions of lan-guage, and hint at buried complexities to which the mundane patterns of speech have rendered people all but deaf. Carl Jung said: 'A word or an image is symbolic when it . . . has a wider 'unconscious' aspect that is never precisely defined or fully explained. Nor can one hope to define or explain it. As the mind explores the symbol, it is led to ideas that lie beyond the grasp of reason.'[21]

And, for the Romantics, nothing provokes these resonances more than Nature itself. Writing about some of the new develop-ments in landscape painting in *The Spectator* in 1712, Joseph Addison averred that: 'Our imagination loves to be filled with an object or to grasp at anything that is too big for its capacity. We are flung into a pleasing astonishment at such unbounded views, and feel a delightful stillness and amazement in the soul at the apprehension of them.' The essence of the 'sublime', which was shortly to follow, was to be found not in the cosy world of the garden or the still life, but in 'the hoary mountain and the solitary lake; the aged forest and the torrent falling over rock'.[22] In picturing vistas which dwarfed human beings, both in age and scale, artists such as Turner reminded their viewers of the power and grandeur of the natural world of which they themselves were a microcosm. Landscapes that are 'huge, obscure and terrible', said Edmund Burke, 'arouse feelings that invigorate and elevate the mind' (as opposed to the merely 'beautiful', which is 'smooth, unthreatening and pleasurable').[23]

There were explicit attempts, in the eighteenth and nineteenth centuries, to depict the unconscious as the subterranean passageway that led from the soul to the wider cosmos of which human beings were seen as an indissoluble part – whether you call it God or Nature. Reversing the traditional Christian orientation of seeking God Upward and Outward, away from the corrupt container of the body, the Romantics' favoured metaphor had them diving Down and In, seeking the Sublime in the deepest, most intimate depths of their own psyche: the dark place where nature and human nature were thought to meet and meld. One finds this version of the unconscious in many of the German Romantics, especially members of the mystical-scientific school of *Naturphilosophie* such as Goethe, Herder and Schelling.

For Schelling, for example, there is an unconscious 'formative principle', an implicit tendency in the whole of Nature, that makes itself manifest in human beings and their consciousness. As invisible water vapour in the air has the tendency to condense into visible clouds and tangible rain, so the unconscious 'life force' precipitates as, amongst many other forms, human thoughts and sensations. Everything in nature must be the product of the same organising principle, Schelling argued, so that our consciousness is representative of the selfsame underlying energy, itself a form of 'intelligence', that makes the clouds and the trees. There is 'soul' in everything, but until it congeals into a moment of consciousness, it is itself unconscious. 'The same activity which in free [human] actions is productive with consciousness, must, in producing the world, be productive without consciousness.'[24]

It was Carl Gustav Carus (1789–1869) who developed this quasi-biological, almost pantheistic version of the unconscious most fully (though his work was embellished and made more widely known by Edward von Hartmann in his precocious and monumental treatise *The Philosophy of the Unconscious*). Professor of Gynaecology in Dresden and Court Physician to the King of Saxony, Carus – like Aristotle before him – saw humankind, and human consciousness, as a marvellous manifestation of a more general, continual biological pulsing. This energetic groundswell moves continuously in human beings, so that 'although much that goes on in the organism never becomes conscious, everything that happens there has at least an indirect effect on consciousness'. Carus prefigured the later distinction between what Freud called the 'preconscious' and the 'subconscious'. The preconscious, or 'relative unconscious' is 'that region of the conscious life of the soul which may for a time become unconscious but returns to consciousness again and again'. The 'absolute unconscious', however, refers to 'a region of the soul which is inaccessible to the light of consciousness'.

For Carus and many of the Romantics, the unconscious thus took over some of the functions of the divine. It was neither wholly inner, nor completely outer, but, like the soul, connected the two. As the French philosopher Nicolas Malebranche had argued over a century earlier, unconsciously influenced phenomena, such as intuition or the 'sixth sense', are examples of God's thinking, not the individual's. Harking back to Homer, the oddities of experience are to be explained as the divine thinking *in* us, or *through* us; not as local, personal events at all.[25]

Carus was a major influence on Jung (with whom he shared his forenames), who read him during his student years. Their thought is similar in many ways, though Carus was less aware of the pathological side of the psyche than Jung was to become. They both stood on the shoulders of Kant and Goethe; both fascinated by the biological background to psychological phenomena; both medical men with a keen respect for empirical method. When Carus writes that 'our unconscious life is affected by all humanity, the life of the earth, the life of the world, because it definitely is a part of that totality', he is describing Jung's 'collective unconscious' in all but name.[26] And both Carus and Jung were fascinated by the ways in which art both represents and evokes unconscious patterns, Jung principally through his studies of Tibetan Buddhist mandala, and Carus through representations of nature. It is surely no coincidence, given what we have noted above, that Carus was an accomplished landscape painter whose work still hangs in more than half a dozen major German museums.

Carus added two lovely images to our collection of metaphors for the unconscious. In the first, he harks back, knowingly or unknowingly, to the daily passage of Ra over the subterranean sea. 'The life of the psyche may be compared to a great, continuously circling river which is illuminated in only one small area by the light of the sun.' In the second, he installs the unconscious not as an intermittent force, but as the permanent infrastructure of consciousness itself: 'All the finest qualities of the conscious life of the soul depend in countless ways on the unconscious soul. The cathedral spire will collapse if a single iron clamp breaks, or the cornerstone gives way. The most splendid products of the mind will also vanish if the smallest obstacle obstructs the unconscious activity of the soul.' This ceaseless, inexhaustible unconscious energy is responsible for the physiological functions of respiration, blood circulation and so on, but also for the processes that lie behind imagination and perception.[27] The cathedral spire image foreshadows the image of the iceberg and its tip which is usually attributed to Gustav Fechner, but was also a favourite image of both Freud and Jung.

Of the two iconic explorers of the twentieth century, Jung was of a much more 'Romantic' bent than Freud. Though, like Freud, Jung began by investigating the meaning of dreams, he soon came to believe that dreaming was not 'the royal road to the unconscious', as Freud put it, but just one amongst several starting points. 'One can reach the centre directly from any point of the compass', he said, and included, as entry points, free-associating to Cyrillic letters, meditating on a crystal ball, a mandala or a modern painting, 'or even from casual conversation about some quite trivial event'.[28] Through these portals of the unconscious, Jung believed he had discovered a layer of latent symbolism that had its root, not in individual life experiences but in the evolutionary history of humankind: his famous 'collective unconscious'.

> While the personal unconscious is made up essentially of contents which have at one time been conscious but which have disappeared from consciousness through having been forgotten or repressed, the contents of the collective unconscious have never been in consciousness, and therefore have never been individually acquired, but owe their existence exclusively to heredity. Whereas the personal unconscious consists for the most part of complexes [the tender spots of the psyche], the content of the collective unconscious is made up essentially of archetypes.[29]

The archetypes are 'mythological motifs' that Jung believed recurred in all cultures and in a variety of forms: dreams, legends, fairy tales, visual symbols and so on. These motifs underlie and shape the particular details of individual experience in their own cultures into archetypal forms. The lives and memories of Princess Diana, Saddam Hussein, Buzz Aldrin, Nelson Mandela and Michael Jackson attract the attention that they do because there is something universal in their character and situation – whether it be the sad, beautiful princess, the evil monster, the heroic explorer, the wise old man or the mercurial trickster that you can never quite pin down. You find characters drawn from the same cast-list in the most successful dramas and fairy tales: 'Little Red Riding Hood' is the innocent but nubile princess at risk, the essence of vulnerable femininity, the Anima. Obi-Wan Kenobi and Gandalf are Mandela, the Wise Old Man. Puck in *A Midsummer Night's Dream* and the Fool in *King Lear* are the Trickster, from whose mouths, as from a madman's, nonsense and truth come jumbling out together. Superman and Clarice Starling are the Hero and Heroine, whose unswerving moral clarity enables them to prevail. Frederick West and Hannibal Lecter are embodiments of Evil for our age, as are Saddam, Sauron and Darth Vader.

It's true that compulsive symbolisers can go way over the top, mistaking their own ingenious projections for archetypal discoveries. However, it is hard not to agree with Jung that the experiences of early childhood combine with our genetic inheritance to create a personalised portfolio of variations on a set of universal themes: dependency and disappointment; trust and betrayal; fear and rescue; affiliation and abandonment; frustration and overcoming; pleasure and disgust; justice and unfairness; reward and punishment; loss and reconciliation; error and forgiveness; anger and acceptance. There seems to be a primary 'palette' of basic human emotions, out of which each culture selects a subset of colours and combinations which it is going to legitimate, and another of which it disapproves. There are also prototypical relationships – parent–child, leader–follower – within which these basic emotions are evoked and resolved in either successful or unsatisfactory ways. All these factors form a perfectly rational basis, if one were needed, for something like the collective unconscious. You can interpret the idea, if you want, and as some people have, in an 'Outer' way, as an independently existing World Wide Web of universal wisdom to which we are unconsciously logged on throughout life, and which prints itself out in our minds as dreams and symbols. Jung himself moved in this direction later in his life, seeing the archetypes more as Platonic forms, existing separately from human minds, latent in all phenomena. But there is no need to take the outward turn.

The rise of new literary forms in the eighteenth and nineteenth centuries, with their expanded range of possibilities for what novels, plays and poems could be, fuelled the development of the Romantic unconscious in a number of ways. Though Descartes' conclusions seemed to reduce what was interesting about human experience to its most rational register, his reframing of the generic 'soul' as the individual 'mind', and his championing of introspection as a valid method for gaining self-knowledge, laid the foundation for a new kind of novel: one which explored the minutiae of experience. Prior to the eighteenth century, wrote Francis Jeffrey in the *Edinburgh Review* of 1804, writers and dramatists gave us access to their characters' interior worlds only 'in their dress of ceremony . . . We never see them except in those critical circumstances, and those moments of strong emotion, which are but of rare occurrence in real life.' But with the appearance of Richardson's *Pamela*, and later *Clarissa*, in the 1740s, 'we slip, invisible, into the domestic privacy of his characters, and hear and see everything that is said and done among them, whether it be interesting or otherwise.'[30]

In particular, Richardson developed the 'epistolary novel', in which intimate letter-writing (a practice which was itself becoming widespread at the time) was used as a way of opening a window onto the most private of reflections. And as these characters were given unprecedented freedom to look downwards into the recesses of their own minds, so they rapidly discovered that the Cartesian belief that minds were transparent to themselves did not match their experience at all. As Shakespeare had said a century and a half previously, more often than not the bottom of their feelings, desires and actions was not clear in the least. They had to 'infer' themselves, to replace what they could not see directly with tentative and unreliable inferences based on self-observation and pondering. Art began to approach Life more closely, and in doing so, Life, in the drawing-rooms of the emergent book-reading middle classes at least, began to imitate Art.

A forerunner of George Eliot's *Middlemarch* and Henry James's *Portrait of a Lady*, *Clarissa* reveals in excruciating detail the impossible disparity between the expectation and the reality, especially in matters sexual, which faces sensitive women in repressive societies. Such societies, Freud was to write, 'must incline their members to concealment of the truth, to euphemism, to self-deception, and to the deception of others', and Clarissa was indeed a prime case for psychoanalysis. Richardson shows her earnestly searching for truth and clarity, and equally vigorously denying it to herself. She catches glimpses of herself, as when she wonders 'what turn my mind has taken to dictate so oddly to my pen', but chooses to ignore her friend Anna's perceptive suggestion that the main reason why she is a mystery to herself is that she refuses to 'attend to the throbs of her heart'. Instead she retreats into bafflement: 'What strange imperfect being!' she muses. 'But self here, which is at the bottom of all we do, and of all we wish, is the grand misleader.'[31] Men are not to be trusted, Richardson tells us, but women cannot trust themselves. True or not, we find here, for the first time, literature depicting in great detail an unconscious which is *deliberately* created in order to solve the impossible equation of personal veracity and social acceptability (by obscuring the former), *and* a mind which cunningly covers its own tracks, so that both the fact and the method of self-deception are rendered invisible (to the heroine, but not to the reader), leaving Clarissa both confused, and confusing.

In *Pamela* and *Clarissa*, thwarted passion manages to make itself known to the reader, if not to the protagonist herself, disguised in the language of dream and symbol – and uncannily Freudian the symbolism is, too. Pamela's imagination has her pursuer transformed into a bull with bloodshot eyes. Clarissa, though consciously frightened of Lovelace, invites him several times to violate, even murder, her with scissors and daggers. 'Baring, with a still more frantic violence, part of her enchanting neck, Here, here, said the soul-harrowing beauty, let thy pointed mercy enter.' And after Lovelace has indeed raped her, she reveals her ambivalence in a delirious story about a lady who hand-rears a young lion which later 'resumed its nature; and on a sudden fell upon her, and tore her to pieces, And who was most to blame, I pray? The brute, or the lady? The lady, surely! For what *she* did was *out* of nature, *out* of character, at least; what *it* did was *in* its own nature.'[32]

Like a good Freudian, Richardson even plants clues in the text, in the form of the characters' names, which other characters can then decode, or at least, draw our attention to. 'Lovelace'/'loveless' is obvious, but so too is Clarissa's surname, Harlowe. In case the reader has missed the similarity of 'Harlowe' to 'harlot', Arabella writes to Clarissa: 'this is the celebrated, the blazing Clarissa – Clarissa *what*? *Harlowe*, no doubt! – and Harlowe it will be to the disgrace of us all.'[33]

Diderot wrote of Richardson that 'he carried the flame to the very back of the cavern. It was he who learnt to discern the subtle, dishonest motives which cloak themselves under the guise of the more respectable desires which pushed themselves forward. He blew away the good-looking ghost which presented itself at the mouth of the cave; and the hideous Moor which it had been concealing was revealed.' Rather unnecessarily, Watt explains to us that the 'hideous Moor is surely the frightening reality of the unconscious life which lies hidden in the most virtuous heart'.[34]

From such rich beginnings, many other literary explorations of the murky depths of the unconscious emerged throughout the eighteenth and nineteenth centuries. The Gothic novel, for example, which reached its apotheosis at the end of the eighteenth century, used pseudo-medieval settings to model the unconscious reaches of the mind, and to reclaim the darker side of human experience. Dracula and Dorian Gray were not to appear for another century, but Matthew Gregory Lewis's *The Monk* was published, relished and reviled in 1796. The lustful monk Ambrosio sells his soul to the Devil in order to avoid the Inquisition, murders his mother, rapes his sister, and is slowly devoured to death, over the course of a week, by birds and insects. Lewis suggests, heretically, that there is no clear dividing line between villainy and virtue, each being driven by the same unconscious forces that are symbolised by outer demons, but which have power over the protagonists only by virtue (*sic*) of their inner, buried desires and flaws. Such tales were often set in dark, dilapidated castles and ruined manor houses, full of secret passageways and underground tunnels, whose structures updated the spatial metaphors of the Greek and Egyptian underworlds, and served the same allegorical purposes.

The fascination with the interplay between inner and outer representations of the unconscious led, at the same time, to a spate of novels that used the device of the 'double'. Jean Paul's *Siebenkäs*, a study of the doppelgänger, was published in the same year as *The Monk*. Studies of other cultures were showing how common was the idea, for example, that a person's shadow constituted a parallel self or a second soul, that had to be taken seriously. (The inhabitants of the equatorial island of Uliase, it was said, would never walk outside at midday, because they would cast no shadow, and would thus lose their soul.)[35] Mirror images and reflections in water, too, were often endowed with 'alter ego' powers and properties. In German folklore, vain girls would see not their own but the Devil's face if they looked into a mirror at night. In one version of the legend, Narcissus took his own life after he fell in love with his reflection. And Dorian Gray's fear of ageing is symbolised by his infatuation with his youthful image. Only when he destroys the picture does he, instantly, re-own his aged face.

Edgar Allan Poe was one of many late eighteenth- and early twentieth-century authors to explore the literary possibilities of the doppelganger. This image of the eponymous William Wilson (first published in 1839) coming face to face with himself, by Arthur Rackham, comes from the 1935 edition of Poe's Tales of Mystery and Imagination.

At the same time, the emerging discipline of psychiatry was revealing that experiencing a disowned part of oneself as a projected 'other' was not uncommon. The doppelgänger syndrome, or *autoscopy* as it was officially dubbed, involved 'meeting' a compelling visual hallucination of oneself.[36] Such an experience was often taken as a harbinger of death or tragedy, an association not unconnected with the fact that, clinically, it was known to be triggered by intense stress. Many of those who used the device in their literary works had 'suffered', if that is the right word, from this phenomenon: Jean Paul, Kafka, Poe and, most notably, Dostoevsky. Shelley records that he was out walking near Pisa when he was approached by a hooded alter ego who asked him: 'Are you satisfied?', and scared him out of his wits.[37]

In literature, the dissociation into self and double is often caused by the attempt to get rid of unbearable emotion, such as guilt. Sometimes the double is the guilty figure; sometimes it is the reproachful conscience. An obvious reading of Dostoevsky's classic story *The Double*, published in 1846, for example, is that the creation of the double 'solves' the hero Golyadkin's problem of unbearable mental conflict at the high price of the fear of encountering the double itself. Where at first the idea of the double – of avoiding embarrassment by pretending to be 'another person who is confusingly similar to me' – is a voluntary ploy, poor Golyadkin's creation (like Frankenstein's monster) soon takes on a life of its own, invading his bedroom and impersonating him at work. The double functions as a kind of halfway house between Outer and Inner explanations of oddity, just as the idea of 'possession' does. When possessed, an aspect of the Outer has become Inner, and the inner is co-opted or subverted as a result. Conversely, the double is an aspect of the Inner that is detached and made into the Outer, where the neurotic conflict that results from ownership is traded for a clearer, but potentially madder, sense of dislocation, persecution, and lack of control.[38]

Dostoevsky himself was entirely clear that these projections are the progeny of self-deception. In 1864 he wrote:

> In every man's remembrances there are things he will not reveal
> to everybody, but only to his friends. There are other things he
> will not reveal even to his friends, but only to himself, and then
> only under a pledge of secrecy. Finally, there are some things that
> a man is afraid to reveal even to himself, and any honest man
> accumulates a fair number of such things . . . That is to say, the
> more respectable a man is, the more of them he has.[39]

The Romantic poets, especially in England, attempted to describe, express and evoke the prized feelings of depth and 'loss of self' in their work. They wrote verses *about* the unconscious. They wrote verses that attempted to express their own 'Romantic' feelings. And they saw, some of them, poems as devices that were deliberately constructed to induce in readers a state of mind in which they were more likely to experience some of those finer feelings for themselves. Keats's poem 'Sleep and Poetry', written in 1816, proclaims:

> A drainless shower
> Of light is poesy; 'tis the supreme of power;
> 'Tis might half-slumbering on its own right arm . . .

In a letter to his friend John Reynolds, two years after he wrote the poem, he recommended:

> Let [a man] on any certain day read a certain Page of full
> Poesy . . . and let him wander with it, and muse upon it, and
> reflect from it, and bring home to it, and prophesy upon it, and
> dream upon it . . . When Man has arrived at a certain ripeness in
> intellect, any one grand or spiritual passage serves him as a
> starting point towards all 'the two-and-thirty Pallaces.' How

happy is such a 'voyage of conception,' what delicious, diligent Indolence!

And a month later in another letter, this time to his brother and sister-in-law, he describes the conducive state that poetry induces as 'a delightful sensation, about three degrees this side of faint-ness ... In this state of effeminacy, the fibres of the brain are relaxed in common with the rest of the body ... this is a rare instance of the advantage of the body overpowering the mind.'[40] (We shall come back to the 'fibres of the brain', and their relation to poetry, in chapter 10.)

Keats captured one of the essential features of this poetic atti-tude in his famous concept of 'negative capability'. Musing over a boring evening in the company of a major league know-it-all, Charles Dilke ('who cannot feel he has a personal identity unless he has made his mind up about everything'), in another letter to his brothers, Keats exclaims:

At once it struck me what quality went to form a Man of Achievement, especially in Literature & which Shakespeare possessed so enormously – I mean *Negative Capability*, that is when man is capable of being in uncertainties, Mysteries, doubts, without any irritable reaching after fact & reason.

Negative capability lets go of the need to know and of the anxious need to control the processes of one's own mind; it welcomes con-fusion and the spontaneous swirling of ideas, and in this way, by daring to sink down towards the murky bottom of your mind, it allows you to get closer to the unconscious, and to experience the ineffable benefits of so doing.

Just as today, business guru Tom Peters tells his audiences: 'If you're not confused, you're not thinking clearly', so the Romantics believed there was a profound intelligence that could be accessed only through surrendering to one's own incomprehension, and creating space and time for the unconscious to speak at its own speed, and in its own imaginative, symbolic way. When Keats asks, in *Lamia*, 'Do not all charms fly/At the mere touch of cold philosophy?', you know that his answer is going to be the same as Blake's (in his derision of 'Newton's Sleep'), and Wordsworth's ('murdering to dissect'), and Hazlitt's ('the progress of knowledge . . . clips the wings of poetry'). To find something *beautiful* is to feel an emanation of satisfaction from the Romantic unconscious; to find it *awesome* is to feel an even deeper tremor, one which jolts the complacent little self out of its presumed position at the centre of its own world.

The Romantics' search for aesthetic methods by means of which the unconscious could be approached parallels that of a strand of mysticism, from ancient Egypt to the present day, that has had its own conception of the unconscious. Sometimes called in the Christian tradition the 'apophatic' mystics, they have consistently claimed experiences that are somewhat similar to the unity and awe of the Romantics, but of a yet more profound or 'spiritual' hue. For them, God is not any kind of transcendent 'being', humanlike or otherwise, that is Out There, nor even the kind of pantheistic Life Force, immanent in all of Nature, of which Carus and others wrote. Instead, 'God' is a misleading name for a radical transformation in the quality of experience, in which all sense of a knowing, questing, controlling, separate 'ego' or 'I', busily perceiving, planning and doing, drops away, and yet the up-rush of experienced life continues, miraculously, by itself. In such a state, you found that, at the core of your own being, there sits not an anxious little 'me', but a mighty gushing fountain that cannot be fathomed or tapped, but which seems to 'leave nothing undone'. This is the 'cloud of unknowing' that continually precipitates 'knowing': the Godhead itself that lives even upstream of 'God', and about which nothing can be said. (*Apophasis* was a Greek rhetorical ploy of passing over without direct comment what was in fact your main point.)

Jung knew of this mystical unconscious, which he described as 'simply the medium from which religious experience seems to flow. As to what the further cause of such experience may be, the answer to that lies beyond the range of human knowledge.'[41] But the theme of 'divine incomprehension' goes back at least to the fifth century AD Syrian monk Dionysius the Areopagite, who is reputed to have declared: 'the most godly knowledge of God is that which is known by unknowing.' The mystic is a person who, 'having renounced all knowledge, is united to the Unknowable in a better way, and knowing nothing, knows with a knowledge surpassing the intellect'. Meister Eckhart, the renowned fourteenth-century apophatic, said: 'there is only unity in the Godhead, and there is nothing to talk about.' Whilst in *The Cloud of Unknowing* itself, the anonymous author explains, as best he (or she) can:

> By 'darkness' I mean 'a lack of knowing' – just as anything you do not know or have forgotten may be said to be 'dark' to you, for you cannot see it with your inward eye. For this reason it is called a 'cloud', not of the sky of course, but of 'unknowing': a cloud of unknowing between you and your god . . . We are apt to think we are very far from God because of this cloud of unknowing between us and him, but surely it would be more correct to say that we are much farther from him if there is no cloud.

Johann Tauler, also of the fourteenth century, talked of 'the unseen depths of the spirit, wherein lies the image of God'. The Christian mystic Jakob Boehme said three hundred years later that 'the hidden man is God's own being', and described the shift in experiential quality as clearly as one can. 'In my inward man I saw it well, as in a great deep; for I saw right through into a chaos in which everything lay wrapped, but I could not unfold it. Yet from time to time it opened itself within me like a growing plant.' (Perhaps the apophatics and the Romantics are not so far apart.

Had Tennyson been reading Boehme, or even having such experiences for himself, when he wrote: 'Heaven opens inward, chasms yawn,/Vast images in glittering dawn/Half-shewn, are broken and withdrawn'?)[42]

Even more explicit in their association of some kind of 'spiritual breakthrough' with an enhanced access to, and acceptance of, the unconscious are some of the schools of Buddhism which began to become known to the Romantics from the beginning of the nineteenth century. (In 1800, Friedrich Schlegel, one of the leaders of the German Romantics, declared that it was 'in the Orient we must seek the highest Romanticism'. Schopenhauer's later philosophy was greatly influenced by his reading of the Buddhist *Diamond Sutra*.)[43] In the seventh century, Hui-neng, the Sixth Patriarch of Chinese Ch'an Buddhism, taught that 'enlightenment' (in the Buddhist, not the European, sense) inhered in accepting that this wider, impenetrable source was, and always had been, in charge. D. T. Suzuki explains that, for Hui-neng, 'the Unconscious is to "let they will be done", and not to assert my own.' Action, feeling, perception, thought: all continue to arise, but 'I' am neither 'doing' them nor 'having' them.

So who or what is the ultimate source? We just don't, and cannot, know, says this mystical literature. We can solve the riddle by taking a nothing and calling it a something, 'the Unconscious', but this unconscious is not at all like the 'locked ward' or the fetid jungle of Freud, nor even the Nature-resonator of the Romantic Sublime. It is simply the wellhead from which all form and motion bubbles forth. 'Psychologically we can call it the Unconscious,' says Suzuki, 'in the sense that all our conscious thoughts and feelings grow out of it.'[44] Normally, he says, 'the apperceiving mind is occupied too much with the outgoing attention, and forgets that at its back there is the unfathomable abyss of the Unconscious.' Simple though it sounds, the experience of nirvana is a matter of remembering, deeply, in the moment, that 'the Unconscious and the world of consciousness lie back to back'.[45]

Consciousness, on this view, becomes an extraordinary, and rather unpredictable, light-show that is generated by a complex system, a 'something', that is itself for ever dark (rather like those stage shows in which luminous puppets are being manipulated in a dimly lit theatre by puppeteers wearing black velvet suits that render them invisible. Imagine your thoughts as those luminous marionettes . . .).

The Romantic movement thus rekindled, developed and began to give explicit voice to several varieties of the unconscious that had been implicit in human culture from the dawn of history. The interest in the interpretation of dreams, and the decoding of symbols more generally, was nothing new. Even the idea that their cryptic counsel came not from the gods, but from buried sources of wisdom inside human beings themselves, had been kept alive, not least in the esoteric world of the mystics, for a millennium or more. But this aspect of the soul was becoming psychologised, and popularised, as the mass of people became interested in plumbing the depths of their own minds: in trying to see what actually was there, rather than selecting and interpreting their experiences through filters of hope and fear engendered by the religious moralism of the Middle Ages.

Of all the oddities of human nature, the Romantics were most interested in those that seemed to speak of mystery and depth: experiences such as dreams, feelings such as awe, and shifts in consciousness such as those that occurred in mystical moments and 'peak experiences', where the causes were hard to discern. If they were not to be attributed to the gods and spirits, there had to be some inner sources; hidden realms of the psyche or the soul that possessed reservoirs of creativity and wisdom, and where 'we are not what we thought we were'. Gaining access to those realms, and to the treasures that they contained, was thought to be a possibility, and methods were devised – from incubation in a 'sleep temple' through prayer and meditation, to the Keatsian contemplation of a poem – that might make the conscious and unconscious more permeable to each other. Let Harold Monro, early twentieth-century Romantic poet in a business suit, sum up the Romantic unconscious:

> Look downward in the silent pool:
> The weeds cling to the ground they love;
> They live so quietly, are so cool;
> They do not need to think, or move.
>
> Look down in the unconscious mind:
> There everything is quiet too
> And deep and cool, and you will find
> Calm growth and nothing hard to do,
> And nothing that need trouble you.[46]

But as introspection grew in popularity and sophistication, people discovered that, when you looked down into the deep pool of your own mind, you did not always find, as Harold Monro had promised, that 'everything is quiet and cool', nor that there was 'nothing that need trouble you'. On the contrary, there seemed to be a good deal down there that was perverse, frightening and self-destructive. Was that, too, coming from the same unconscious source? Or were there other regions of the catacombs of the mind that had rather different characteristics? If we could internalise the wisdom of the gods – even God himself – and the source of the sublime, could we also find an inner home for the convolutions of confused and painful emotion, and of madness itself?

6

The Beast in the Basement

If I cannot bend the gods above, then I will move the Infernal
Regions.

– Virgil (used by Freud as the epigraph for
The Interpretation of Dreams)[1]

In the deep shade, at the farther end of the room, a figure ran
backwards and forwards. What it was, whether beast or human
being, one could not, at first sight, tell: it grovelled, seemingly,
on all fours; it snatched and growled like some strange wild
animal: but it was covered with clothing, and a quantity of dark,
grizzled hair, wild as a mane, hid its head and face.

'Ah! Sir, she sees you!' exclaimed Grace . . .' – for God's sake,
take care!'

The maniac bellowed: she parted her shaggy locks from her
visage and gazed wildly at her visitors . . . Mr Rochester flung me
behind him; the lunatic sprang and grappled his throat viciously,
and laid her teeth to his cheek . . .

Thus, the prototype of madness, as recounted by Jane Eyre on first
confronting Mrs Rochester in her attic-prison.[2]

Madness is very scary. Mad people are akin to us, and yet they
behave or talk or feel in ways that are profoundly at odds with
'common sense'. They exhibit extremes of emotion – fear, lust,

rage, sadness, hilarity – that frighten us in their intensity and inappropriateness. They stand like stone, insensitive to speech or pain. They pierce our hearts, yet seem beyond our reach. Normal expectations do not apply; we feel adrift and inept in their company, uneasy, as we are with snakes and animals whose intentions we cannot read, uncertain as to what the next moment may bring, and therefore deprived of our usual reassuring ability to be prepared. We cannot come fully prepared into the presence of insanity. And because its meaning and its origins are so often obscure – the usual causal stories do not seem to apply – they make our hold on our own minds seem more tenuous. If we do not understand the provenance of our own nightmares, there is little we can do to stop them taking over. Normal dreams do not spill over into our waking lives, yet the possibility that they could is very real, and common sense lacks pre-emptive strategies. Madness is the prototypical oddity, and the need for 'explanations' correspondingly strong.

Throughout human history, and to the present day, our three familiar kinds of story have contested the explanatory ground: supernatural, physiological and psychological. In the supernatural, the immediate cause of madness is the direct influence of the gods or spirits. Your mind has been commandeered, either remotely, by an occult power acting at a distance, or through the occupation of an invasive being. 'Those whom the gods wish to destroy, they first send mad', the Greeks said. On this view, there are a number of possible therapeutic responses. If the demons have got trapped inside your skull, you can bore small holes in the top of your head to let them out. Skulls have been found, trepanned in this way, that are more than 5,000 years old.[3] You can try propitiation. You can attempt to butter up the malign spirit, to see if it can be persuaded to undo its curse and leave you in peace. You can try exorcism, and see if you can expel the invader through superior moral or spiritual force. Or, if all else fails, you can opt for fatalism, accept 'God's will', and see if you can concoct a secondary

Another epitome of female insanity is provided by Henry Fuseli's portrait of
Mad Kate, *painted in 1806–7.*

story in which value and meaning can be attributed to apparently undeserved and unavoidable suffering (though madness is doubly accursed, for it removes the ability to make sense of the suffering it brings). For Homer, 'there is no notion that mental disturbances arise from a disorder or derangement within a mental structure, since there is no notion of [such] a structure.'[4] The internalisation of forces and conflicts has yet to occur, and when it does begin, in the Lyric Age of the great Greek dramatists, the conflicts, such as Medea's, have nothing of the unconscious about them. Medea is mad with rage and jealousy – but all the causes and impulses are transparent to her.

The second strand sees madness as the upshot of some bodily imbalance or disorder, most commonly in the 'humours'. Just as psychiatry today translates hallucination and depression into changing levels of neurotransmitters and neuromodulators in the brain, so the ancients and the medievals saw an excess of 'black bile' as the cause of melancholy, of 'choler' as causing irascibility or rage, or of 'blood' as making the subject manic and over-confident, or 'sanguine'. When the mixture of blood and choler was especially viscous, warned Denis Fontanon of Montpellier, there would be 'brutal madness, and this is the most dangerous mania of all'.[5] Complex quasi-medical systems linked these (in most cases) hypothetical fluids (humour means fluid in Latin) to what were seen in those days as the four basic 'elements' of earth, air, fire and water. Being warm, moist and 'animated', blood was akin to air; choler was warm and dry like fire; phlegm, like water, was cold and wet; while black bile had the cold, dry nature of earth. Out of these categorisations were created fantastic rationales for all kinds of weird and wonderful 'cures', such as blood-letting, some of which, every so often, no doubt worked. The humours are hypothetical and internal – as the unconscious will be – but they are definitely somatic rather than psychological. One 'has' madness in just the same way that one has a headache, or measles. Phlegm does not have a mind of its own.

In practice, these two approaches and their allied therapies have often been combined. Gods and spirits may prey on those who are constitutionally unable to resist them; and they can achieve their effects through thoroughly somatic means. The Erinyes, spirits wreathed in snakes and dressed in black, explain how they sent Orestes mad: 'Over our victim we sing this song, maddening the brain, carrying away the sense . . .'[6] Sometimes supernaturally induced madness can be cured somatically. In the first century AD, Celsus, the so-called 'Roman Hippocrates', distinguished between madness due to being 'duped by phantoms' and that which was due to the malfunctioning of the mind itself. If it is phantoms that are to blame, then, paradoxically, herbal treatments will be effective: depression is to be cured by black hellebore, and 'hilarity' by white hellebore, 'and if the patient will not take the hellebore in a draught, it should be put into his bread to deceive him the more easily'. If however it is the mind itself that is at fault, then the madman is best treated by a variety of tortures. 'When he says or does anything wrong, he is to be coerced by starvation, fetters and flogging . . . Thus it will be brought about that, little by little, he will be forced by fear to reconsider what he is doing. To be terrified suddenly, and to be thoroughly frightened, is beneficial in this illness.'[7]

It is harder to trace the beginnings of the *psychological* approach to 'mental illness' back into antiquity. One of the seeds is already there in pre-Christian times, in Plato's equation of madness with the disinhibition of wild and destructive appetites, and in his argument that it is Reason and Knowledge that prevent those break-outs from occurring. Another is the idea of self-deception, which we first find clearly stated by Plato's contemporary Xenophon. It was Xenophon who developed Socrates' thinking to the point where it could offer the beginnings of a psychological account of insanity: 'Not to know oneself, *and to imagine that he knows things that he knows he does not know*, is the nearest thing to out-and-out madness' (emphasis added).[8]

However, a truly psychological approach begins much later with the recognition that human beings possess complex inner processes and mechanisms that are designed to aid survival and promote well-being – but which can, under certain conditions, malfunction, and in doing so turn on their owners and undermine, rather than support, their sanity. This requires the ability, that we encountered in chapter 4, to look at people's passions not through a moral lens, but through one that is simultaneously dispassionate and compassionate. John Locke, like Hobbes and Spinoza, was a pioneer in this regard, and one of the first to see madness as neither diabolical nor somatic but essentially delusional. He picked up Plato's association between madness and irrationality. 'Mad men', he explained, 'put wrong Ideas together, and so make wrong Propositions, but argue and reason right from them.' In this regard, madness is distinct from idiocy, for 'Idiots make very few or no Propositions, but argue and reason scarce at all.' A century later, Voltaire confirmed Locke's view in his *Philosophical Dictionary*: 'Madness is to have erroneous perceptions, and to reason correctly from them.'

But even Locke was not the first to take a psychological attitude to madness. Towards the end of the fifteenth century, the Italian Renaissance scholar Pico della Mirandola had disinterred Plato's model of the charioteer in order to explain that such emotional convolutions come about as a result of inner strife. Man's soul contains two dissonant centres of energy and operation, and it is their violent contentions and contortions that cause natural emotions to curdle and go sour. 'Two natures are planted in our souls,' he said; 'by the one nature we are lifted upward to the heavens, and by the other, shoved downward to the lower world.' Thus we are 'driven by strife and discord *like a madman* and banished from the gods. Indeed, fathers, there is multiple discord in us, and we have severe, intestine, and more than civil wars at home.'[9] Such strife, says Pico, is characteristic of us all – we are all, God save us, akin to the madman, though mercifully, not driven quite to his extremity.

Fifty years later, the Spanish scholar Luis Vives – a prime con-
tender for the title of the first modern psychologist – argued that
it was not propositions, nor perceptions, that lay at the root of
madness, but emotions. He saw that all the basic negative emotions – fear, anger, sadness and so on – were essentially useful: we
had them for good reason. But they could go wrong. For example,
'Fear has been given to man so that he can guard himself against
injurious things, before they reach him.' Vives observed that 'in
fear the voice is weak, because the heat has gone from the heart
and the upper parts . . . hence paleness and chills . . . while in
anger it is strong because the heat rises . . . The effect of fear on the
soul is to disturb it and confuse its thoughts. The consequences of
fear are dejection, self-degradation, flattery, suspicion and cau-
tion, which . . . in weak souls causes consternation, terror,
dispiritedness, as well as sluggishness, hopelessness, and prostra-
tion.'[10] Though based on the naïve physiology of the time, Vives'
understanding of depression and paranoia as reflections of natural
psychological processes 'gone wrong' was another early harbinger
of Freud.

It is worth noting that the Plato–Pico–Vives tradition anticipates Freud in reifying irrationality, and gives it its own centre
within the psyche from which to operate. It is an antagonistic
force to reason. For Locke, on the other hand, irrationality was
merely a weakness or absence of reason: a wavering, temporary or
permanent, in the power of the faculty of reason itself. It was this
Lockean tradition that was to shape psychiatry in the nineteenth
century into the profession whose core concern was the 'reanima-
tion of reason'.[11]

One important strand in the psychologisation of madness was
the realisation that insanity might have its uses: it could be seen as
strategic, though whether the sufferer was at all aware of this was
open to doubt. 'Though this be madness, yet there is method
in't', as Polonius observes. To be mad got you noticed, as being
'possessed' did, though whether the consequences of that attention

were nice or nasty depended very much on an accurate assessment of the social context. Being mad also enabled you to get away with things that normal, sane folk could not. An eighteenth-century visitor to Bedlam observed one of the inmates 'holding forth with much vehemence against Kingly government'. The visitor told him that he deserved to be hanged for such treasonable talk. But the madman replied that it was the visitor who was the fool, 'for we madmen have [the] privilege of speaking our minds . . . you may talk what you will and nobody will call you in question for it. Truth is persecuted everywhere abroad, and flies hither for sanctuary, where she sits as safe as a knave in a church, or a whore in a nunnery. I can use [truth] here as I please, and that's more than you dare to.'[12]

The idea that the mind could cope with its inherent tensions and dissonances by deliberately distracting itself from thoughts and feelings which it found worrisome (and that also 'that way madness lies') the possibility of repression, and of its psychopathological backlash, in other words – developed sporadically from the thirteenth century onwards. Dante in the *Purgatorio* claims to have forgotten his shameful mistreatment of Beatrice: 'I remember not that ever I estranged myself from thee.' In reply, Beatrice taunts him: 'As from the smoke the fire may be inferred, So thy forgetfulness doth clearly prove, Fault in thy will, that otherwise was bent.'[13] Shakespeare, as we have seen, was alive to the ever-present possibility of 'motivated forgetting'. And Richardson built *Clarissa* around a young woman's unconscious attempt to ignore her own sexual attractions and frustrations.

The idea that repressed sexuality is one of the main causes of mental and emotional disorders goes all the way back to antiquity. In *The Anatomy of Melancholy*, first published in 1621, Robert Burton summarises the history of ideas about the 'particular species of melancholy' that can afflict those whose natural sexual drives are denied expression. Yet, he notes, 'many of them cannot tell . . . what ails them'. In Burton's opinion, 'nuns, maids, virgins, widows [and] nice gentlewomen such as are solitary and idle' are particularly prone to both mania and depression resulting from unacknowledged sexual frustration, and he suggests that 'the best and surest remedy of all is to see them well placed and married to good husbands . . . to give them content to their desires.' The problem is not so much the frustration as the repression of it. 'They will by all means quench their neighbour's house if it be on fire, but that fire of lust which breaks out into such lamentable flames they will not take notice of, their own bowels oftentimes, flesh and blood shall so rage and burn, and they will not see it . . .'[14]

But it was Schopenhauer, at the beginning of the nineteenth century, who took the concept of repression to a new level of sophistication, and used it, as Freud was to do, as the lever for a more general reinstatement of the unconscious to a central place in the dynamics of the mind. In *The World as Will and Idea*, first published in 1819, Schopenhauer ruminates on the ways in which we avoid thinking about the things which may 'injure our interests, wound our pride, or interfere with our wishes'.[15] He notes how unwilling people are to face such things consciously, and how easily and '*unconsciously* we break away or sneak off from them'. Our attention slides away from them onto more neutral or agreeable subjects. But if this habit of avoidance becomes too strong, he suggests that the long-term cost may be considerable. For 'in that resistance of the will to allowing what is contrary to it to come under the examination of the intellect, lies the place at which madness can break in upon the mind.'

Schopenhauer argues that our psychological health depends on the willingness to overcome this resistance, and to integrate even that which frightens or displeases us into our 'intellect', a term he uses very much in the same way that Freud came to use the 'ego'. The intellect, he says, is not 'of the depth' of the mind, but 'merely serves the end of self-preservation by regulating the relations of the organism to the external world'. And it also acts as the editor of consciousness, hiding unpalatable things from us, but at the cost of leaving them buried, unintegrated and unrequited in the dark corners of the mind. If that integration is not carried out,

> then certain events or circumstances become for the intellect completely suppressed, because the will cannot endure the sight of them, and then, for the sake of the necessary connection, the gaps that thus arise are filled up at pleasure; thus madness appears. For the intellect has given up its nature to please the will: the man now imagines what does not exist. Yet the madness which has thus arisen is now the lethe of unendurable suffering; it was the last remedy of harassed nature . . . One may thus regard the origin of madness as violent casting out of the mind of anything, which, however, is only possible by taking into the head something else.[16]

It is interesting to note that Schopenhauer's emphasis is on the dynamics of repression – an active avoidance of aspects of experience that conflict with a more conscious, and more acceptable, image of oneself – rather than on the hypothetical unlit 'space' in the mind to which such contents are consigned. In this he is, as we shall see, even more modern than Freud. Note too that he is acutely aware of the fact that repression will only work, as a mechanism of self-deception, if its activities are themselves concealed. A crude army censor may black out critical lines of text from a soldier's letter home with a felt-tip pen, and not worry that the fact of his censorship is evident for the recipient to see. But the mind, if it is to sanitise its own experience effectively, must bleach out the offending content, and then write something anodyne in its place. The magician must deceive us, and must also draw our attention away from the deception, or we may become too inquisitive about the artifice, and will know where to look to uncover it. And so must the mind that wishes to exchange its integrity for a quiet life, says Schopenhauer.

Schopenhauer developed his ideas about repression into a general model of the mind as a whole that embraced both conscious and unconscious regions, and was meant to apply both to its sane and 'cognitive' as well as to its troubled and impassioned aspects. In this model he, like Carus, turned the conventional Cartesian image of the mind on its head, by placing its unconscious aspect at the centre, and representing consciousness as rather marginal, superficial and untrustworthy. For an image to capture this, he harked back to the 'geographical' mental metaphors of the ancient world, rather than the more familiar anthropomorphic skirmishing between two or three wilful, humanlike agents of Plato and Pico. He invited his readers to imagine the mind as a body of water, like a sea, that is in continual motion. Its inherent currents and forces add up to what he calls the 'will', which constitutes 'the inner, true and indestructible nature of man; *in itself, however, it is unconscious*'. This dark dynamic mental mass mingles with 'indistinct thoughts and feelings' and the 'after-sensations of perceptions and experience generally', and it is 'in the obscure depths of the mind that the rumination of [these] materials received from without takes place . . . and goes on almost as unconsciously as the conversion of nourishment into the humours and substance of the body'. Through these unconscious machinations our active desires and forgotten memories are 'worked up into thoughts', and these bubble up to the surface, which constitutes consciousness itself. 'What rise to the surface . . . are the clear pictures of the fancy or the distinct conscious thoughts expressed in words and the resolves of the will.' These represent only intermittent products of the unconscious, the spindrift of its inscrutable heaves and swells. 'The whole process of our thought and purpose seldom lies on the surface [or] consists in a combination of distinctly thought judgements'.

Schopenhauer suggests that these conscious products can misrepresent the actual state of mental affairs in two respects. First, as we have seen, they may be massaged and expurgated in order to avoid the conscious recognition of unpleasant truths. But second, we may imagine that the conscious stream of thoughts is more comprehensive, more 'joined up', and more logical than it is. 'We strive against this [bittiness]', says Schopenhauer, 'in order that we may be able to explain our thought to ourselves and others' – because, post-Descartes, we are brought up to think of ourselves as continuous, joined-up 'thinkers'. For Schopenhauer, the truth is that bits and pieces of clear conscious thoughts or perception bob up, and then we, *post hoc*, try to string them together (or to ignore the discontinuities) so as to perpetuate the illusion that complete trains of thought *originate*, and are *assembled*, in the well-lit workshop of consciousness, by ourselves, by 'me', because thought-construction is the central means, we have been led to believe, through which we know ourselves.

Schopenhauer is of his time, and there is little in the way of systematic evidence to underpin his theorising. He has only his own observations and intuitions to go on, and he knew, as well as we do, how fallible personal experience could be. Indeed, in a kind of Catch-22, the fact of the fallibility of consciousness is one of the central planks of his own model of the mind. Yet despite the fact that the science of psychology had still to emerge, it is extraordinary – as we shall see – just how prescient Schopenhauer's views would turn out to be. Indeed, some of the most recent views of the unconscious, which we shall meet later, leapfrog back over Freud to Schopenhauer, a century earlier.

The idea that repression, to be successful, requires you to cover up the gap which it has left by doing or thinking something else – something less threatening – gained currency throughout the nineteenth century. Though Shakespeare had already illustrated the self-deceptive tactic of projection, in which one judges in others what one is unwilling to acknowledge in oneself, he had little in the way of an explicit, coherent theory of the mind on which to hang his acute observations. But by the nineteenth century the idea of 'psychological defence mechanisms' was already being discussed. In 1831, an M. Ryan, for example, echoing Robert Burton, averred that sexual frustration may conceal itself in 'a total disrelish for the procreative act, even by well-informed, interesting and lovely women'. Instead, in his experience, 'all the subjects were excessively vain of their personal appearance, and fond of admiration'. So congealed and diverted had their sexuality become, said Ryan, that even if they did have sex, 'they would talk most ardently of dress during the conjugal act, and suffered it without the smallest enjoyment'.[17] (We might wonder, perhaps, how he knew, and what kind of remedy he was wont to offer.)

In the 1850s, the French writer Sainte-Beuve was recorded, in the scurrilous journal of the Goncourt brothers, explaining over dinner to the assembled company what Freud would later refer to as 'sublimation':

'I have in my head here, or here,' – he tapped his cranium – 'a drawer, a pigeonhole, that I have always been afraid to look squarely into. All my work, all that I do, the spate of articles that I send forth – all that is explained by my desire not to know what is in that pigeonhole. I have stopped it up, plugged it with books, so as not to have the leisure to think about it, not to be free to come and go through it.'[18]

In 1892, Charles W. Paige, Superintendent of the Danvers Lunatic Hospital in Massachusetts, published a paper entitled 'The adverse consequences of repression', in which he described 'repressed emotional sentiments', and – in very similar terms to Schopenhauer – the associated psychological dangers. 'Auditory hallucinations', he wrote, 'are exceedingly liable to voice ideas and suggestions which the subject of them has endeavoured to rule out of his mind and life . . . thus linking them the more closely to his personality and rendering them the most aggressive thoughts in his mind.'[19] In the 1880s, when Freud was a little boy, repression, and the concomitant idea of the unconscious as the pressurised container of these repressed memories and ideas, were common-places in informed society in both America and Europe.

In nineteenth-century Europe the idea of repression developed alongside another key notion; that of dissociation. If aspects of oneself could be kept out of awareness, perhaps they could, nevertheless, continue to live a life of their own. A person could become split into two – or maybe more than two – parts or 'sub-personalities', one of which operated with the benefit of consciousness, and the other(s) without. If the dominant, 'light' personality was continually, inextricably associated with self-awareness, the other, 'dark' ones could only operate in secret, making themselves known indirectly through madness or other strange powers or afflictions. But if the sub-characters could alternate, taking turns to occupy the limelight of consciousness, then we might see several, perhaps dramatically different, personalities in the same body, each of which is oblivious of the existence of the others.[20]

It is hardly surprising that 'dissociation' came to occupy a central place in the developing psychology of the later nineteenth century, for blatant dissociations of a very public kind were characteristic of the times. Abroad, the armies and the missionaries were bent on 'bringing civilisation to the world', and converting the heathen, yet their beneficence was regularly accompanied by wanton plunder, slaughter and the spread of disease. Moral purpose linked arms with material greed and cultural vandalism, and in public discourse, the former cloaked the latter. At home, society was splitting in two, with the rapid rise of the professional 'middle class', and its antithesis in the abject poverty to be seen, by anyone who cared to look, in the slums of the cities. Many did not care to do so – though they managed to lap up fiction such as Dickens's *Hard Times*, or Zola's *Germinal*, which chronicled their hypocrisy, without apparently realising that it was they who were the 'baddies'. Craftsmen turned wood into sexy table-legs that were then concealed with damask cloths, and the pater familias delivered homilies to his children before slipping out to be fellated by his mistress.[21]

Double standards and double lives were rife, but dissociation, like repression, only works if it covers its tracks, so direct talk was rare and tactical myopia was common. Outside clinical circles, little was being written explicitly about the hidden irrational reaches of personality. Yet indirectly, the phenomenon of dissociation was a source of fascination. It could be observed from the packed public galleries at lunatic asylums such as 'Bedlam' (the Bethlem Royal Hospital, then in Southwark), where inmates could be observed speaking rationally one minute, and howling the next. Exotic 'dissociative' phenomena such as hypnosis and mediumship excited much interest. And stories could be told and relished about werewolves and 'split personalities'. Provided dissociation was lightly disguised as freak-show or fiction, it could be acknowledged, albeit at arm's length.

The prototypical depiction of dissociation was, of course, Robert Louis Stevenson's *Dr Jekyll and Mr Hyde*, published in 1889. At one level, the transformation of respectable Jekyll into evil, violent Hyde is caused by drinking a chemical concoction (which Stevenson may well have wanted to stand for alcohol). At another, however, the reader gradually learns of Jekyll's earlier struggles with his dissipated urges, his fascination with 'low pleasures' and his violent streak, and his efforts to keep these separate from his upright, moral persona. As a child, we discover, he suffered no trauma, but simply learned the habit of dissembling to others, and then to himself, about the unacceptable side of his own nature. As an adult, up to a point, he succeeds in his strategy of denial and disowning. Hyde and his appetites appear as a distinct, dissociated personality.

But then the internal division begins to break down, the veil of mutual unconsciousness is torn apart, and Hyde's desires begin to haunt, and then invade, the hapless Jekyll. (It is, after all, Jekyll's name that chimes with 'jackal', and thus suggests the vicious nature of the wild animal, beside which the mere concealment of 'Hyde' sounds positively respectable.) In earlier times, Hyde would have been an invasive spirit, sent by the Devil to subvert Jekyll's probity through his wayward thoughts. But in Stevenson's story we are invited to see Hyde as a dissociated aspect of Jekyll's own psychology. More than that, he wants us to see that Hyde's power exists because of early internal conflicts which have been mismanaged – self-deception is self-destructive, he tells us – and, furthermore, that the internal mixture of dissociation and repression is explosive. It builds up pressure which may be released in moments of weakness or lack of vigilance – such as drunkenness. It is a thoroughly modern message, published in 1886, five years before Freud's first major publication.

Hypnosis was one of the oddities that excited much interest in the nineteenth century. In a hypnotic trance, people seemed able to do, feel and remember all kinds of things that they could not in their normal state of consciousness, and which they could not reproduce as a matter of conscious will. They convincingly recalled things from their early childhoods, or even from 'previous lives'. They could make their bodies so rigid that, with head on one chair and feet on another, and nothing in between, they could nevertheless support the full weight of a man sitting on their middle without any apparent sign of strain. They could enthusiastically eat a raw onion that they had been told was an apple, could make themselves deaf, so that they did not flinch at loud, unexpected noises, and were impervious to the pain of holding their hand in a bucket of icy water. Uncannily, normal consciousness seemed to be the *object* of these effects, not the *instrument* of them, as the 'official doctrine' of the mind would have us believe. The conscious mind was being altered, but it could not be the mind that was doing the altering. What was going on?

Well, if it was not the 'mind' that was doing the work, it looked, at first, as if it had to be matter – the body. What else was there? So Franz Anton Mesmer, eighteenth-century hypnotist extraordinaire, invented an ethereal, but definitely physical force which, he said, flowed from the hypnotist into the subject, and gave them unusual capabilities. Only certain hypnotists – such as himself, naturally – possessed sufficient reserves of this 'animal magnetism' to enable this discharge to take place. (Mesmer was extrapolating from his doctoral thesis, in which he argued that the movements of the heavenly bodies affected human physiology through an analogous kind of physical magnetism or 'celestial gravity'.)[22] Mesmer applied his methods to a variety of physical and psychological problems, at first claiming dramatic, and scientifically validated, cures for his novel form of 'treatment'. He was certainly a consummate showman, and was lionised in Paris for a while in the late 1770s, where, as Jonathan Miller puts it, 'an educated public was almost frivolously susceptible to scientific novelty', and where, in consequence, 'a medical treatment based on a previously unacknowledged force of nature proved irresistibly attractive'.[23] However, in 1785 an official commission, which included Benjamin Franklin and the renowned chemist Antoine-Laurent Lavoisier, found that there was no evidence whatsoever for 'animal magnetism'. After carrying out their own tests, they concluded that: 'Imagination, apart from magnetism, produces convulsions [while] magnetism without imagination produces nothing.'[24] Though Mesmer continued to attract popular audiences – many of the Romantics, not surprisingly, were great fans – his scientific credibility was shot. (It was suspected that he 'cheated' by strapping magnets to his body in order to augment his own powers.) The search was on for an alternative explanation for what were, still, enormously perplexing phenomena.

There were false starts, of course. In 1841 James Braid, a Scottish surgeon resident in Manchester, thought he had the answer. He noted that the induction of a hypnotic trance was often accomplished by getting the subject to stare fixedly at a point above eye-level, and Braid became convinced that this rapidly exhausted the eye muscles, causing the subject to fall into a 'nervous sleep'. Braid devised an ingenious neurological theory to account for the heightened suggestibility that occurred in this 'sleep', but, though this was a distinct improvement on Mesmer, he unfortunately tried to tie hypnosis (it was Braid who actually coined the term) to the then fashionable phrenology – the reading of brain function from the shape of people's heads. Thus, Braid claimed that touching the 'organ of veneration' in a hypnotised patient made her sink to her knees in an attitude of pious adoration, while 'a touch on the organ of self-esteem, and she flounced about the room with the utmost self-importance'.[25]

Though these excesses led him nowhere, Braid did instigate the systematic investigation of hypnosis, and drew attention to the curious effects of suspending conscious will and intention. On the Cartesian model, Conscious Volition was needed to instigate Intelligent Action: no intention, no action, or at least nothing beyond menial physiological housekeeping. Yet here were a whole variety of intricate actions apparently unwilled – or willed more by the hypnotist than the subject. The challenge remained: who or what was behind them?

In Britain the challenge was taken up by a philosopher, Sir William Hamilton, and three physiologists, Benjamin Carpenter, Thomas Huxley and Thomas Laycock, who argued, in effect, for a different model of the causation of action, one not unlike Schopenhauer's. It was not that Thought caused Action, but that both Thought and Action were the products – sometimes correlated and sometimes not – of an Unconscious Intelligence that underlay them both. Hamilton, for example, declared, in 1842, that: 'What we are conscious of is constructed out of what we are not conscious of . . . there are many things which we neither know nor can know in themselves, but which manifest themselves indirectly through the medium of their cognitive effects.' The significance of hypnosis was that, by taking the subject's own thoughts and intentions out of the way, these underlying, unconscious processes were made more visible. Huxley dared to put this

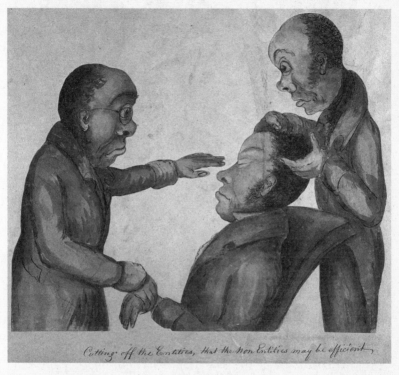

Cutting off the Entities, that the Non Entities may be efficient

This nineteenth-century watercolour pokes gentle fun at the founders of 'phrenology', Joseph Gall and Caspar Spurzheim, as they earnestly 'treat' a patient by both feeling his bumps and adjusting the 'animal spirits'. The lettering reads, cryptically: 'Cutting off the entities, that the non entities may be efficient'.

Bumpology

"Pores o'er the Cranial map with learned eyes,
Each rising hill and bumpy knoll descries,
Here secret fires, and there deep mines of sense
His touch detects beneath each prominence."

Another caricature, by George Cruikshank (1826), shows a 'bumpologist' as he 'pores
o'er the Cranial Map with learned eyes . . .' and dictates his findings to his assistant.
The woman, perhaps the patient's mother, gives nothing away as she observes the
proceedings.

heretical idea even more plainly: 'The feeling we call volition', he said, 'is not the *cause* of the voluntary act, but simply the symbol in consciousness of that stage of [the underlying activity] which *is* the immediate cause.'[26] In a famous metaphor, Huxley claimed that our conscious sense of being in charge bears the same relation to what we actually do as the locomotive's whistle does to the turning of its wheels: it signals it, but does not cause it.

While hypnosis provides a short-term, readily reversible and quite benign – not to say entertaining – demonstration of the 'power behind the throne' of consciousness, those who worked in mental hospitals daily encountered an altogether darker side of dissociation. They saw how cut-off unconscious forces served, all too often, to subvert and pervert people's lives, making them miserable and undermining their ability to function. At the Salpêtrière Hospital in Paris, the great neurologist Jean-Martin Charcot, and later Pierre Janet, developed the idea that a range of psychiatric disorders, especially the hysterias, resulted from traumatic ideas becoming split off from the main, conscious personality, and buried in the unconscious, from where they manipulated action, thought and feeling. Just as the hypnotist could implant in the unconscious of a willing subject the idea that they would be deaf to all sounds until a releasing signal was given, so a repressed traumatic memory could plant the same kind of idea, resulting in apparent blindness or paralysis, or in the numbing or the exaggeration of feelings such as sadness or delight. The healthy coherence of consciousness was ruptured, with a depleted part of the stream continuing to flow on the surface of consciousness, and another – or, in the case of 'multiple personality disorders', others – going underground and taking on a dissociated, and disruptive, life of their own.[27]

A hysterical paralysis is the inability to move a leg, for example, in a person without any apparent neurological damage. Towards the end of the nineteenth century, such quasi-physiological afflictions were not uncommon (though, like many psychiatric ailments, they go in fashions, and are relatively rare now, having been replaced by such contemporary enigmas as anorexia and 'chronic fatigue syndrome'). Charcot reasoned that, if such states can be reproduced by hypnotism, then hypnotism could function as a cure, bringing to light the repressed memory, in the same way that a buried 'post-hypnotic suggestion' can be recovered, and, simply by being exposed to consciousness, lose its hold and release the patient from their disorder. However, the story of hypnosis as a psychological cure is a depressingly familiar one. Charcot, the 'Napoleon of neuroses' as he was dubbed, gave dramatic demonstrations of his powers, and made dramatic claims for their efficacy, which were not sustained, and could not be replicated by others. Freud, a few years later, impressed by Charcot's work on hysteria and hypnosis – he spent four months at the Salpêtrière in 1885/6 – collaborated with Joseph Breuer on several studies of hypnosis, but soon grew disappointed with it, and moved quickly on to develop 'free association' as the key technique of his famous psychoanalytic 'talking cure' (which itself proved disappointing, as Freud himself admitted towards the end of his career).[28]

The widespread interest in hypnotism in the nineteenth century spawned other attempts to gain access to the mysterious depths – and apparent capabilities – of the unconscious. Many of these were taken up uncritically by the Romantics and the adherents of spiritualism. Mediums presented their work in supernatural terms, claiming to channel communications 'from the other side'. In the gullible Paris of 1853, Baron de Guldenstubbe claimed to have taken dictation directly from Plato and Cicero. But by the 1880s, informed opinion came to see spiritualist techniques such as 'automatic writing' in more psychological terms, as ways of tapping into personal unconscious reservoirs by bypassing the controlling, and censoring, influence of conscious reason. The Society for Psychical Research concluded in the late 1880s that it was safer to interpret such methods psychologically, in terms of the unconscious, rather than as the voices of gods, spirits or the deceased. And psychiatric opinion routinely translated symptoms of 'possession' into the language of dissociation.

Claims that seemed incompatible with this translation – for example, knowledge of previous lives, or of information or languages that the person could not have come by in the normal way – were popular, but many scientists were cautious, as they are today. In one of the most detailed cases, Theodore Flournoy, professor of psychology – one of the first – at the University of Geneva, and close friend of William James, studied the remarkable memories and linguistic capabilities of the renowned medium 'Helen Smith'. Scrupulously open-minded, though guided by Laplace's Principle that 'the weight of evidence must be in proportion to the strangeness of the fact', Flournoy traced her early history, and demonstrated that the knowledge she displayed from her 'previous life' as a fifteenth-century Indian princess could well have been picked up from her childhood reading, consciously forgotten, but remembered and reproduced, as it were, 'spontaneously'. Likewise, the 'Martian' language that Helen sometimes spoke showed strong resemblances to the Hungarian which was her father's native tongue. If we allow for what today is called 'implicit memory' – memories that influence thought and behaviour without themselves being capable of being recalled – many, though not all, of the spiritualists' claims become easier to read in a psychological light.[29]

The British psychiatrist Henry Maudsley contributed to developing notions of the unconscious in many ways, not least in his recognition that unconscious forces reflected a person's personal life history, especially their early years. In his 1867 book *The Physiology and Pathology of the Mind*, Maudsley observed: 'how necessary to a complete psychology of the individual is the consideration of the circumstances in which he has lived, and in relation to which he has developed.'[30] He even hints (in his impenetrable prose) at the therapeutic value of unravelling these antecedents of current problems. 'If the particular volition were to be resolved by a retrograde metamorphosis into its component elements, there would be an explication or unfolding of all the ideas and desires which had gone to form it; and, going back still further in the analysis, there would be a revelation even of those particular relations in life which the individual's . . . ego implies.'[31] He particularly notes the importance of children's sexuality, asserting that 'there are frequent manifestations of its existence throughout early life, both in animals and in children, without there being any consciousness of the aim or design of the blind impulse.' And – again anticipating Freud – he warns: 'Whosoever avers otherwise must . . . be strangely or hypocritically oblivious of the events of his own early life.'[32]

Maudsley, incidentally, was well aware of the challenge that madness posed to the tidy Cartesian view of the mind. Delusions and hallucinations, he pointed out, are 'sufficient to excite profound distrust not only in the objective truth, but also in the subjective worth, of an individual's self-consciousness. Descartes laid it down as the fundamental proposition of philosophy that whatever the mind could clearly and distinctly conceive, was true: 'if there is one thing more clearly and distinctly conceived than another [however] it is commonly the madman's delusion.' He concluded that self-consciousness is not only unreliable, but that 'it does not give any account of a large and important part of our mental activity.'[33]

Time to state baldly what I have been hinting at all along. Knowingly or not, Sigmund Freud's conception of the unconscious incorporates many of the historical themes which I have been tracing. Far from being 'the discoverer of the unconscious', he belongs to a long and honourable lineage. Like those of the ancients, Freud's attempts to account for the oddities of human action and experience draw on the metaphors of place and space, on the one hand, and of invisible, humanlike agents, on the other.

Except now the Underworld, with its forces of destruction and regeneration, is enfolded within the psyche; and the gods and spirits, both good and evil, are also tucked inside, and hidden away like Morlocks in the dark recesses of the mind.

Both these metaphors pervade Freud's writings. On the one hand, the unconscious is a 'realm' of mental activity positioned somewhere between the conscious mind and the body. Just like the 'inner Africa' – the Dark Continent – this realm is the same *kind* of place as consciousness – similar sorts of things go on there, and the same vocabulary applies – but they proceed out of sight of one's own introspection. And just as I think of 'myself' as having thoughts and desires, experiencing conflicts, formulating intentions and initiating actions, so does the internal bit of me that is *not me*. And in order to make this puzzling idea more tangible, Freud attributed these psychological dynamics – and shenanigans – to the three agents that were his more scientific equivalents of Plato's two horses and a charioteer: the white horse of the superego, the black horse of the id, and the charioteer of the ego, struggling to reconcile the competing demands of conscience and libido, and the constraints and opportunities of the outside world.[34] Or, to put it back into the vernacular, Freud's anthropomorphic model envisaged the mind as a continual fight between a puritan priest and a sex-crazed monkey, refereed by a rather nervous bank-clerk.[35] Except that most of this contest took place in the dark.

It is interesting to contrast a poem by the early twentieth-century English poet Barrington Gates, much influenced by such Freudian thinking, with its Romantic counterpart by Harold Monro with which I concluded the previous chapter. Both use the image of a pool – but to very different effect. Gates's poem, called, significantly, 'Abnormal psychology', begins:

> I am, they say, a darkling pool
> Where huge and cunning lurks a fool

Childish and monstrous, untaught of time,
Still wallowing in primaeval slime . . .

He is most merciless, lone, and proud,
There in the scaly darkness bowed,
And sleeps, and eats, and lusts, and cries,
And never lives, and never dies.[36]

By separating out the good and bad bits of the psyche, as many
had done before him, Freud was, in a way, trying to save the rep-
utation of the 'soul'. He took all the odd and dodgy bits of human
nature out of the soul or 'ego', and put them somewhere else. But
instead of throwing them away, and making them the Devil's
work, he locked them in the basement of the mind itself. Since the
Greeks, theologians had argued about whether the 'black horse'
was to be included within the soul – in which case the soul's sup-
posedly divine nature was in danger of being compromised – or
whether to exclude it, in which case there had to be a 'something'
or a 'somewhere' – either internal or external – where it had to live.
Freud's preferred option was to locate the source of the trouble
inside, but to place this source outside the bounds of 'the real
me' – hence 'das Id', the It, the part of me which is other than me.
In this way, he could adapt the sanitised Cartesian model of the
psyche, supplementing it so that it could offer an account of the
oddities (as well as the ideal of rationality), but retaining the core
conception of the conscious mind as essentially Me, and essentially
Intelligent. The unconscious – unlike the menial mechanics of the
body – could be credited with a kind of low cunning, capable of
disguising its true, base, selfish motives; but 'rational' it most certainly was not. Descartes said, in effect, that the unconscious was
Not Me, Not Intelligent, and Not There. By casting it in the way
he did, Freud was able to hold on to two out of the three, and thus
preserve intact the moral dualism of Plato, and of the entire Judeo-
Christian tradition.[37]

Freud's tripartite model obviously harks back to Plato's charioteer and his struggle to reconcile the conflicting temperaments of his two horses. Structurally, they are very similar. However there is much more subterfuge in Freud's world. For Plato, each of the three actors knows perfectly well what the others are about. There seems to be no difference between them in terms of their conscious knowledge of each other. Plato's black horse has libido but no guile, while Freud's does not gallop wildly towards the object of its desire, but dissembles and prevaricates. Plato missed the opportunity to point out that the black horse is black precisely because it is hard to see and hard to read. Even the 'white horse', the super-ego, in Freud's hands will become not pure white but piebald; it too is partly unconscious, and operates in ways that are not fully understood by or evident to the charioteer. As I noted in chapter 3, Plato's chariot seems only to be wheeled out to account for the conspicuous oddities of human life. When things are going according to plan, it stays safely in the garage, unlike the Freudian trinity, which purports to be a general model of psychic life, potentially as applicable to a normal day at the office as to the most bizarre of neurotic symptoms.

In terms of therapy, Freud agrees completely with Descartes that consciousness is good, and that the more conscious we are of our psychological ideas and dynamics the happier and healthier we shall be. The mantra of his remedial process is: 'Where Id was, there shall Ego be', and one of his dominant metaphors for therapy is archaeology. Freud himself had a passion for archaeology, and his consulting room, stuffed with relics, looked more like a museum than a relaxing sanctum. He often explicitly likened psychoanalysis to excavation, or sometimes to land-reclamation. He saw the ego as 'like a land mass threatened by the rising waters of the id', and argued that 'in the same way that the Dutch reclaimed the Zuider Zee, so must the psychoanalyst win back parts of the mind that have succumbed to the unconscious.'[38] Unlike Jung and the Romantics, who respected and gloried in the language and imagery of the unconscious, Freud was always impatient to unpack and interpret it, and to convert its poetry into the prose of 'insight'.

In fact, his whole approach can be seen as an attempt to swaddle the seamy, irrational side of human life in the neutralising language of rationality – of 'science' – itself. The Romantics and the Gothic novelists had forcefully reminded European culture, in the eighteenth century, of all the awkward bits of human nature that Descartes had tried to ignore, but they had done so through the media of poetry, fiction and visual art: media which, however, had already, in Freud's time, lost epistemological status in the face of the rapid, aggressive rise of scientific rationality. Artists' comments on human nature were increasingly treated as aesthetic accessories to the essentially rational, proto-scientific models of mind that were being hotly contested in European, and increasingly American, philosophy and psychology. What was needed, if the darker corners of the psyche were to be taken seriously, was an account of them in the language not of poetry but of sober, scientific-sounding prose. During the nineteenth century, this language was being shaped. The idea of 'the unconscious' as an identifiable region of the mind came to be accepted as a valid technical term.

But it was left to Freud to offer something that had the form, at least, of a well-worked-out scientific theory. And though many of his theories turned out to be highly fanciful, his evidence weak and his reasoning flawed, nevertheless the empirical enterprise which he launched has continued, and is at last making, as we shall see, sound and significant progress. Like hundreds of narcissistic scientists since, Freud fell in love with his own ideas, saw their reflections all around him, and mistook his projections for discoveries.[39] All dreams had to be forced to fit the theory of wish-fulfilment; all childhood problems had to be manifestations of unresolved Oedipal desires. And his formidable ingenuity enabled him to find what he needed to. (His former collaborator Breuer noted that Freud seemed driven by a 'psychical need for excessive generalisation'.)[40] So much is well known. But the *impulse* to see how far one could find causes for the oddities of human experience within the psyche itself, and to try to stretch the model of the mind to generate such explanations: that was sound, honourable and, in its scope and breadth, novel.

We have already had cause to cast a quizzical look at those who claim to discover symbolic meaning in everything, and to accuse Sigmund Freud of being guilty in this regard. Here we might note just one particularly apposite instance, in which Freud was obliging enough to offer a psychoanalytic interpretation of a seventeenth-century case of possession. As you might expect, he confidently translates the demons and devils into 'bad and reprehensible wishes, derivatives of instinctual impulses that have been repudiated and repressed. We merely eliminate the projection of these mental entities into the external world, which the Middle Ages carried out; instead, we regard them as having arisen in the patient's internal life, where they have their abode.' However, this is not nearly detailed enough for Freud. Let us see how he proceeds.[41]

The case concerns one Christoph Haizmann, a Bavarian painter, who, in 1677, had suffered convulsions which were 'revealed' by the local priest to have been caused by Haizmann having sold his soul to the Devil some nine years previously. From the contemporary accounts, Freud diagnoses depression caused by the death of Haizmann's father, and interprets the Devil as a father-substitute. Why is the lamented father demonised (when all the historical evidence shows that he was much loved)? Because, says Freud, we know 'from the secret life of the individual which analysis uncovers, that his relation to his father was perhaps ambivalent from the outset, or, at any rate, soon to become so'. The tell-tale 'perhaps', however, is soon forgotten in Freud's account, and we are confidently assured that the father is 'the individual prototype of both God and the Devil'. The fact that Haizmann's mourning is 'melancholic' is further 'proof' of his ambivalence. What's more, his ambivalence is sexual, because the nine years of the pact 'stands for' the nine months of pregnancy. (Freud reassures us that there is no need to be 'disconcerted by the change from nine months to nine years', because we know – that authoritative 'know' again – 'what liberties unconscious mental activity takes with numbers'. It is not clear what purpose has been served by this imaginative (and entirely gratuitous) reconstruction.[42]

Freud's model of the mind, and of the place and role of its unconscious regions, changed and developed over the course of his long and prolific writing career, and we cannot blame him for that. Crudely, he first divided the unconscious into two functionally distinct layers: the preconscious, which contains ideas that could perfectly well be conscious but happen not to be at the moment, and the subconscious, which is the home of ideas that can be made conscious only with difficulty, if at all, because they have been repressed, and thus actively resist being brought to light. This way of characterising the unconscious relies on the metaphor of 'place'. The preconscious is the anteroom of consciousness, a kind of buffer-zone between it and the subconscious, which is the locked and inaccessible cellar of the mind, containing unacceptable impulses, and memories too frightful to be acknowledged. In the preconscious lives one of Freud's earlier kinds of hypothetical inner agents, the censor, whose job it is to take those aspects of the subconscious that are demanding expression, and kit them out in disguises – dream symbols, or neurotic symptoms – which will prevent them from frightening the ego too badly. He described the censor as 'the guardian of our psychic health'.[43] Through this safety-valve, the psyche was able to prevent the build-up of excessive pressure in the subconscious, which, if unreleased, could cause real madness.

Later on, however, in *The Ego and the Id* (1923), Freud peopled the mind with more human-like sub-personalities. The new metaphor was more like Plato's 'chariot' than his 'underworld', and it enables him to attribute humanlike stratagems and intentions to different bits of the mind: the ego, super-ego and id.[44] He would speak of these quite anthropomorphically. 'The poor ego serves three tyrannical masters . . . the external world, the super-ego and the id.' Or: 'during a melancholic attack the super-ego becomes over-severe, abuses the poor ego, humiliates it and ill-treats it.'[45] The unconscious and the id think differently from consciousness and the ego. They are less concerned about clarity and consistency, but they are the kinds of things that 'think', and have ideas and motives. The more intense these conflicts become, the more tired and stressed 'the poor ego' becomes, and therefore the less able it is to keep the repressed thoughts in their place, and the more likely they are to break through as neurotic 'symptoms' or nightmares.

I cannot resist an aside. The compulsive Freudian penchant for attributing unconscious motives to other people reaches its *reductio ad absurdum* in the suggestion by the psychoanalyst Bennett Simon, in his review of 'the classical roots of modern psychiatry', that Plato's entire philosophy stemmed from his having, as a small boy, caught his parents having sex.[46] It is true that Plato (like Freud himself) grouped sexuality together with the other 'basic instincts' as aspects of the baser part of the mind or soul – the black horse – and saw health and morality in terms of balance and restraint. For Plato, madness, like dreaming, was associated with wildness and lack of inhibition. And why did he see the world this way? Because, says Simon, 'the core unconscious meaning of madness in the Platonic dialogues is the wild, confused and combative scene of parental intercourse as perceived by the child.' Thus – obviously – Plato's conscious philosophical and political desire to constrain such powerful emotions 'is a reflection of an unconscious preoccupation with the primal scene', and his design for the ideal state likewise reflects 'the unconscious wish to protect the elite and the guardians from the primal scene trauma and its consequences'. The banality of such theorising stems not so much from its evident falsity as from its complete gratuitousness. Simon's attempts to drum up supporting 'evidence' are really funny. Even Plato's famous 'cave' metaphor for reality and appearance – in which the men in the cave see only the shadows cast on the wall before them of unseen activity behind them – 'can be understood as a primal scene fantasy: children in the darkness of the bedroom, seeing the shadows and hearing the echoes of parental intercourse'. It's OK as a party game, but you don't want to keep on playing Musical Chairs on the drive home.[47]

Freud's acknowledgement of the antecedents of his views of the unconscious is, to put it mildly, rather patchy. He was happy to give credit to some of his more remote forerunners, such as 'the divine Plato', and to classical dramatists such as Sophocles, from whom he borrowed the myth of Oedipus to form a cornerstone of the theory of infantile sexuality. As we have just seen, he saw a direct link between some of his own early ideas and existing theorising about 'possession'. In a letter to his friend and mentor Wilhelm Fleiss in 1897, for example, he noted that 'the whole of my brand-new theory of hysteria is already published a hundred times over centuries ago . . . the medieval theory of possession is identical with our theory of a foreign body and a splitting of consciousness.'[48] And he did eventually acknowledge Nietzsche as an influence, especially on his developing conception of repression, quoting Nietzsche's famous summary: '"I did that", says my memory. "I could not have done", says my pride, and remains inexorable. Eventually – the memory yields.'[49]

However Freud was generally niggardly in his recognition of his more recent influences. Though it eventually became clear that he knew of Schopenhauer's work, for example, he continued to claim, until quite late in his career, that 'the doctrine of repression quite certainly came to me independently of any other source; I know of no outside impression that might have suggested it to me.' Though no one was more conscious than Freud of the fact that writers often assimilate ideas from other writers and forget that they have done so, in his own autobiography he strenuously denied that this insight applied to himself![50] He claimed to have deliberately resisted reading other people's work, in order to 'preserve my impartiality', and this may have been true.

Nevertheless, his world would have been buzzing with ideas about the unconscious, many of which he must have assimilated. The year that Freud began his studies at the University of Vienna, 1874, Professor Franz Brentano published a detailed examination of the views of Henry Maudsley. Brentano was one of Freud's lecturers for two years. Another of Freud's tutors was Theodore Meynert, professor of neurology and psychiatry in Vienna, whose own theorising about the mind was much influenced by two champions of the unconscious. One was Johann Friedrich Herbart, who first developed the idea of repression as a dynamic process, with more 'powerful' ideas actively struggling to keep the less powerful down below the 'threshold of consciousness'. The other was the German psychiatrist Wilhelm Griesinger, who had been publishing ideas about the unconscious roots of insanity as far back as 1845. In fact, Freud had encountered the ideas of Herbart even earlier, in his senior year at the Gymnasium, where he studied Gustaf Lindner's *Textbook on Empirical Psychology*, an introduction to Herbartian ideas. Yet neither Herbart nor Griesinger was properly acknowledged by Freud.[51]

In 1889, at the International Congress for Experimental and Therapeutic Hypnotism, Freud sat in the audience while Pierre Janet argued that hysteria resulted from part of the mind having become 'detached' from the main stream of consciousness. Throughout his career, Freud was well aware that Janet had pipped him to several important posts. But he, likewise, was never acknowledged, and Freud took every opportunity to disparage him. When Janet suggested a meeting as he was passing through Vienna in 1937, Freud sent a rude note and refused to see him.[52]

Lancelot Law Whyte has demonstrated beyond doubt that 'by 1870–1880 the general conception of the unconscious mind was a European commonplace, and many special applications of this general idea had been vigorously discussed for several decades.'[53] Fifty thousand copies of von Hartmann's book on the unconscious were sold in Europe in the 1870s, and it was as widely discussed as, say, the works of Richard Dawkins or Stephen Jay Gould are today. During the two hundred years before Freud dozens of thinkers, possibly as many as a hundred, had published a wide variety of ideas about unconscious processes. Yet shortly before his seventieth birthday, Freud was still insisting that 'the overwhelming majority of philosophers regard as mental only the phenomena of consciousness'.[54] Whether his amnesia for all the sources that were saying otherwise was feigned, deliberate or itself unconscious, we can only surmise.

Though Freud, in the end, may have added few if any truly novel ingredients to our understanding of the unconscious, he drew a number of strands of thought together, and packaged them in a way that was at once accessible, salacious and seemingly scientific. He appealed to people with tabloid interests and broadsheet intellects, and gave a repressed European society an impersonal language with which to talk about the desires and failings which their upbringings had taught them to hide. His perpetual insistence on using the quasi-archaeological language of discovery – of having dug up, by his careful methods, another buried treasure of the psyche to wonder at – rather than acknowledging that much of his work was invention and imagination, wore away at many people's scepticism, and won them over. They believed Freud's claim that psychoanalysis 'has put us in a position to establish psychology on foundations similar to those of any other science, such, for instance, as physics'.[55] Yet even many analysts now agree that the veneer of scientific objectivity and 'discovery' was only that. Freud's contentions cannot be found true or false; they 'can only be more or less inspiring, more or less interesting', said the psychoanalyst Adam Phillips recently (echoing the judgement of R. S. Woodworth, one of the founders of

American psychology, who concluded in 1917 that psychoanalytic ideas 'are to be regarded as products of the decorative art'.[56]

Richard Webster's judgement, in his book *Why Freud Was Wrong*, is harsh. 'The wisdom [already] contained in a diverse collection of fluid and metaphorical insights was . . . displaced by the scientifically spurious notion that there was actually a mental entity called the Unconscious – a biologically circumscribed area of the mind with pathogenic power. Freud . . . did not invent the idea of 'unconscious motivation'. He did, however, empty it of many of the subtleties it had formerly contained.'[57] Many of Freud's excesses – his over-interpretations and over-emphases, on, for example, the ubiquity of the Oedipus Complex, and his ignoring of female psychology, have now been corrected. Yet Webster's challenge still hangs in the air.

If, after all, there is no mental entity called the unconscious, if the whole apparatus of interior infernal regions and subversive agencies is misconceived, on what can we begin to build an account of the most puzzling aspects of human experience? They clearly do not arise from the workings of conscious reason. If they did, they would not be 'odd'. And yet many people equally have difficulty in recapturing a whole-hearted belief in the supernatural. There is only one other possibility. We shall have to look again at the capabilities of the physical body. Could it be that we are now in a position to begin to assimilate at least some of the oddities of dreams and neurosis, hypnosis and the sublime, to the workings of the physical brain? We are almost ready to explore this possibility. But before we do so, there is one other version of the unconscious, as powerful in history as the Romantic and the pathological, which we have to discuss – what has come these days to be called the *cognitive* unconscious.

7

The Intelligent Incubator: Cognition and Creativity

> In the dark recesses of memory, in unbidden suggestions, in trains of thought unwittingly pursued, in multiplied waves and currents . . . in dreams that cannot be laid, in the forces of instinct . . . we have glimpses of a great tide of life, ebbing and flowing, rippling and rolling, and beating about where we cannot see it.
>
> – E. S. Dallas, *Gay Science*, 1866

Sigmund Freud came to be associated with just one version of the unconscious: the beast in the basement that twists our tongues and tangles our emotions. But it was Freud's original dream to develop an overview of the unconscious that was much more comprehensive – pervasive rather than merely pathological. Like his predecessor Sir William Hamilton, he first envisaged an unconscious that was not an intermittent antagonist to consciousness and reason, but rather their continual background. Some forty years before Freud's first publication, Hamilton had suggested that 'the sphere of our conscious modifications is only a small circle in the centre of a far wider sphere of action and passion, of which we are only conscious through its effects.' Using strikingly similar language, Freud, in 1900, introduced his original concept of the unconscious like this:

The unconscious is the larger sphere, which includes within it
the smaller sphere of consciousness. Everything conscious has an
unconscious preliminary stage; whereas what is unconscious may
remain at that stage and nevertheless claim to be regarded as
having the full value of a psychical process. The unconscious is
the true psychical reality; in its innermost nature it is as much
unknown to us as the reality of the external world, and it is as
incompletely presented by the data of consciousness as is the
external world by the communication of our sense organs.[1]

Here his vision of the unconscious is not the seething stew of
repressed memories and desires that it was to become: it is ubiquitous, cognitive, epistemological, even. In this very different
image, the unconscious is to consciousness not as mad monkey to
nervous bank-clerk, but, to repeat an earlier image, as the ocean is
to the white caps of waves – or, to update the metaphor, as the
motherboard to the computer screen.

Unable to move beyond metaphor, and produce a satisfactory
biological basis for this view, however, Freud abandoned it, and
concentrated his efforts, as we have seen, on trying to explain the
causes and consequences of repression, and to develop methods for
the alleviation of psychological distress. Perhaps unwisely, he then
tried to install *this* model of the unconscious – one designed to
account for some of the odder oddities of the mind's operation –
right at the centre of his view of the mind as a whole. No wonder
people were simultaneously intrigued, bemused and repelled.
What was needed was a more balanced model: one which
explained more of the mind's smooth, everyday functioning, as
well as the causes of its more spectacular breakdowns. And what
was needed, too, was more systematic and dispassionate investigation – better methods and sounder evidence – than Freud, for all
his protestations, and the Romantics, for all their passion, had
been able to muster.

Luckily, the exploration of what has now come to be known as the 'cognitive' unconscious was already well under way in the nine-teenth century, and had been for nearly two thousand years. People with the inclination to observe and wonder about their own actions, urges, thoughts and perceptions have always found plenty to puzzle them. If you look carefully, the oddities of human experience are not just the big, in-your-face things, like madness, religious experiences and dreams. There are dozens of small, everyday mysteries as well. Three particular areas of mental activity stood out. The first was memory. The second was perception. And the third was creativity.

If the 'mind' or the 'soul' are associated with consciousness, and if the 'body', including the brain, doesn't have anything to do with 'mind stuff', then where do all the things I know go when I am not thinking about them? We saw in chapter 4 that St Augustine puzzled about this, and conceived of memory as a vast interior storehouse, from which particular memories had to be more or less laboriously retrieved into consciousness.

Plato before him had also tried to understand memory, and had produced two metaphors to try to explain some of its strange ways. Why do some people learn more quickly than others? And why do some forget more readily? Perhaps, he argued in the *Theatetus*, memory is like a wax tablet, on which events impress themselves like seals. He conjectured that some people – the less 'intelligent' – are born with very hard wax, so it takes a lot of experience before a good impression can be formed. Others might have very soft wax: they learn quickly, but the memory impression might fade equally fast, or be easily overwritten by subsequent impressions, so they are forgetful.

But then Plato wondered how it is, when you are trying to remember something, a person's name, for example, that another name, which you know is wrong, keeps popping into your mind. The wax-tablet model didn't seem to be very helpful here, so Plato introduced his second image, that of memory as an aviary, or a dovecote, divided into different sections or 'pigeonholes'. I'll let him explain this in more detail:

Let us now, as it were, frame in each man's soul a dovecote of all manner of birds, some in flocks apart from the others, and some in small detachments, and some flying about anywhere and everywhere by themselves . . . When we are children, we must suppose that the receptacle is empty – and by the birds we must understand knowledges; and whatever knowledge is acquired and shut up in the enclosure we must say that the child has learned . . . Now, shall we not compare [remembering] with the possession and recapture of the doves, and say that there was a double chase; one before the acquisition in order to acquire it, and the other after possession, for the purpose of having in his hand again what was already long acquired? . . . It is possible for someone to have in his hand not the knowledge of the thing he wants, but some other knowledge instead, if, when he is hunting up some particular knowledge from his stock, others fly in the way, and he takes one by mistake for another – as it were, a ringdove instead of a pigeon.[2]

Having a bird in your hand is, on this model, being conscious of it. Birds that are in the aviary somewhere, but not currently being held, are unconscious – or what Freud would have called preconscious. Sometimes, when you are groping in the dark cage for a pigeon, the stupid ringdove keeps flying into your hand instead. So the idea that 'we know much more than we know we know' (as the more recent philosopher Michael Polanyi put it) and that somewhere inside us there has to be a dark repository for all this 'more', has been self-evident for more than two millennia.

The difference between Plato's two images is instructive. On the wax tablet model, the records themselves are inert. When they are not being attended to, they just sit there. They may be eroded by the passage of time, or by the superimposition of later impressions, but memories do not have a life of their own – as birds do. On the second image, although at any moment the vast majority of the complex aviary is pitch-black, nevertheless, there may be a good deal going on. Birds can still be moving about, fighting, mating, laying eggs and building nests even though 'you' – consciousness – is not watching. Which of these two images better captures the true nature of the unconscious mind?

Up to and throughout the Middle Ages, the metaphors for memory were more of the passive type. The 'wax tablet' model was updated in line with developing bibliographic technology – first to the scroll, then the codex, and finally the book and the library. Memory 'contains' knowledge, as a book contains words. Chaucer, for example, makes frequent use of this image of memory as a container. His memory is called the *male* or the *mail*, literally a leather travelling bag or pack. Thus, in the *Canterbury Tales*, when it is his turn to speak, the Parson is invited to 'unbokele and shew us what is in they male'.

All of these images leave the intelligent *exploitation* of memory in the hands of the 'person' themselves: the 'librarian' who was quite separate from the memory-store. In these models, all the 'work' is done by the librarian: it is his or her job to design an effective category system and 'index' for their own library, and to develop the skills of memory retrieval. From Aristotle on, a dominant image for recollection was of the skilled angler or the hunter 'fishing for' or 'tracking down' the sought-after memory, and much store was set by these mnemonic tracking skills. The Roman orator Quintilian likened 'the skilful orator to a huntsman or fisherman who knows exactly the habits and haunts of his game', and fish of different kinds were frequently drawn in the margins of medieval manuscripts as mnemonic aids.[3] Likewise, learning was often likened to deliberate construction of, for example, an intricate building. Hugh of St Victor represented learning as building an elaborate multi-storey 'Noah's Ark', the *arca sapientiae*, in memory, 'like an apothecary's shop, filled with a variety of all delights', and in which, if it has been properly structured, 'you will seek nothing in it which you will not find'.[4] Through effort and craft, Hugh is saying, you can create a memory that is comprehensive, and in which retrieval will not fail. But memory does not build or organise itself: that is 'your' responsibility.

However, when, from the seventeenth century, people began to take a renewed interest in how their minds *actually* worked (as opposed to how some theory said they *should* work), they began to notice that all was not as tidy and controlled as these models would have it, and models of the 'aviary' type began to come back into fashion. For Freud, as we have seen, unconscious memory was definitely more like the dovecote – though the 'birds', in his case, were malevolent ravens and vultures rather than sweet little budgerigars. In the quotation from Freud above he calls the unconscious a 'psychical process', of the same status as conscious thought. Hamilton talked of unconscious 'action and passion' that we only become aware of through their effects. And indeed, since the seventeenth century, a great many people have opted for the idea that memory can have an unconscious life of its own.

To give just a couple of examples: Immanuel Kant, in the eighteenth century, declared:

Innumerable are the sensations and perceptions whereof we are not conscious, although we may undoubtedly conclude that we have them, obscure ideas, as they may be called . . . The clear ideas, indeed, are but an infinitely small fraction of these same exposed to consciousness. That only a few spots on the great chart of our minds are illuminated may well fill us with amazement in contemplating this nature of ours.[5]

To talk of unconscious sensations and perceptions is to speak not just of the inert *contents* of the unconscious, but of its current *activities*.

In 1880, Samuel Butler wrote an entire book called *Unconscious Memory*, in which he made use of another venerable image: that of memory as an active ocean within. For instance:

Memory is a faculty not only of our conscious states but also, and much more so, of our unconscious ones. I was conscious of this or that yesterday, and am again conscious of it today. Where has it been meanwhile? . . . Who can hope to disentangle the infinite intricacy of our inner lives? For we can only follow its threads so far as they have strayed over within the bounds of consciousness. We might as well hope to familiarise ourselves with the world of forms that teem within the bosom of the sea by observing the few that now and again come to the surface and soon return to the deep.[6]

The ocean does not just *contain* objects; it *teems* with life.

By and large, these general metaphors for the mind were developed by investigators who approached the unconscious in a more sober and inquisitive way than did either the Romantics or the psychiatrists. The Romantics were not interested in the details of processes – they rejected that whole mechanistic way of approaching something as delicate and profound as their version of the unconscious. For them, such a crude analysis was like tearing a flower apart to see how it was made – an unconscionable violation. Their prime interest, after all, was in the richness and ineffability of experience itself. The clinicians, on the other hand, were, for the most part, interested in the possibilities of treatment, and their theories of the unconscious were therefore driven by more pragmatic concerns. If it's devils, we can try to cast them out. If it's an imbalance in the humours, we can lace their bread with hellebore. If it's repressed memories, we can try to bring them to the surface and hope that (rather like vampires) their power withers away in the conscious light of day. But the philosophers, and more latterly, of course, the experimental psychologists, were bent on developing increasingly general and powerful models that could make sense of a range of more mundane oddities. They were less interested in 'curing' or 'experiencing' than in intellectual understanding. And this led them to develop more refined, reliable and systematic methods of observation, capable of revealing the psychological complexities that underlie even the most ordinary processes of human nature (though when more dramatic oddities and malfunctions came their way, they would happily seize on those too).

Memory was a prime site for exploring unconscious processes and effects, not only because so much of it *had* to be unconscious, much of the time, but – as the 'dynamic' lobby had noticed – because it often seemed to have a mind of its own. Sometimes it throws up all kinds of thoughts and ideas that are unwanted and inappropriate, to the puzzlement of its owner. In a lovely poem called 'The Flightiness of Thought', for example, a tenth-century Irish monk complains how unruly and irreverent his own mind can be:

> Shame to my thoughts, how they stray from me.
> I fear great danger from it on the day of eternal doom.
> During the psalms they wander on a path that is not right:
> They fash, they fret, they misbehave before the eyes of great
>   God.
> Through eager crowds, through companies of wanton
>   women,
> Through woods, through cities – swifter they are than the
>   wind . . .
> Though one should try to bind them or put shackles on their
>   feet,
> They are neither constant nor mindful to take a spell of
>   rest . . .
> As slippery as an eel's tail they glide out of my grasp . . .[7]

In similar vein, a certain fifteenth-century French nobleman, Chevalier de la Tour Landry, was moved to write a booklet on the waywardness of thought for the edification of his lusty daughters. 'Many women say, who were in love in their youth, when they were in church, that their thoughts and fancies made them dwell more on those nimble imaginations and delights of their love affairs than on the service of God, and . . . just at the holiest moments of the service . . . the most of these little thoughts would come to them.'[8]

At other times, familiar words or names stubbornly refuse to come to mind, and memory contrarily and consistently serves up some conspicuous impostor in its place. Then, when you are thinking about something completely different – Bingo! The lost word pops up spontaneously into consciousness like a piece of toast from a toaster. No mere 'library' could do that by itself. Disconcertingly, if 'I' consider myself to be the 'librarian' of my own mind, and 'I', in these 'tip of the tongue' situations, seem unable to take control of my own remembering, then something must be going on down there by itself.

Many people (especially as they get older!) have had the experience of reading a 'new' book, or watching a 'new' video, and then having the creepy feeling that they know what is going to happen next. You have no idea how you know, but you just *know* that a man in a blue denim shirt and a scraggly beard is going to come round that corner. And sure enough he does. Then, gradually, it may dawn on you that you *have* seen the movie or read the book before, but you had no 'memory' of having done so. There is no need to reach for the supernatural to explain such commonplace oddities: the phenomenon is now very well researched, and cognitive scientists refer to it as 'implicit memory'. It is clear that memories are able to affect what *else* pops up into your mind, or to influence your feeling or your action, without being able to come to mind themselves. They can work behind the scenes.

It is easy to underestimate how prevalent such effects are, simply because consciousness is usually busy noticing something else at the time. But they can be observed very clearly in people who have suffered certain kinds of head injury. In a celebrated case recorded in the early years of the twentieth century, the French physician Edouard Claparède had a patient who seemed to lack all ability to form new memories. Week after week she would greet him each morning as though he were a total stranger. Even if Claparède left the room for a few minutes, she would show no memory of his previous visit on his return. However, Claparède had an inkling that, though she completely lacked any *conscious* recollection, nevertheless she might have some 'implicit memory', and in order to test this idea, one morning he concealed a pin in his hand as they were 'introduced' (yet again), so that their handshake resulted in her being pricked. On the following morning, though she still greeted him as if it were for the first time, she exhibited a curious reluctance to shake his hand. When pressed as to why this might be so, she professed herself puzzled by her own reluctance, but ventured that 'sometimes doctors play tricks'.[9] (The neurologist Antonio Damasio has recently demonstrated the same effect with a patient called David, who, despite showing the same complete absence of conscious recognition, spontaneously chooses the photograph of someone who has been kind to him out of an array, and avoids a person who had been brusque and boring, if he is asked to choose 'who he would go to if he needed help'. If he is asked to pick out any face that he consciously recognises, however, he fails to do so.)[10]

These demonstrations are vivid, but implicit memory does not just occur in the damaged brain. You can see the same processes at work in people with uninjured brains, provided you rig the situation so as to keep consciousness out of the way. It is through devising these give-away situations, and in taking precise and systematic observations, that the discipline of scientific psychology has enabled us, in the twentieth and now the twenty-first centuries, to build on the intuitions and inspired guesses of the earlier centuries.

For example: flash a list of words at an attentive guinea pig at an exposure that is too fast for them to report seeing anything. Ask them to recall the words, and they naturally look at you as if you are mad. But invite their memories to speak in a different, more indirect way, and you will see that the information has in fact gone in and been retained. Suppose that one of the flashed words was BRUNT – a relatively rare word in English. A little while later, you ask your informant to play a game with you – which she thinks has nothing to do with the original subliminal flash – which involves saying the first word that comes to mind that can correctly complete a word 'frame' which you give her, such as BR____. Other people who have not had the subliminal exposure produce common words such as BRUSH or BRAND. But your original subject is much more likely spontaneously to come up with BRUNT. Likewise, if you briefly show (non-Chinese) people images that look like Chinese characters, they are unable to pick them out of a larger array a little while later. But if, instead, you later show them a string of characters and ask them, not which ones they *remember*, but which they *prefer*, they will reliably choose the ones that were in the original display. Memory is there, but it only shows itself indirectly. Events can change our memories without our being conscious of them; and those changes can change what we do (or think, or prefer) without our realising it. There is no question but that contemporary science has confirmed the active 'aviary' view of the cognitive unconscious.[11]

Memory does not just make itself known in acts of remembering. It is obviously at work – largely behind the scenes, again – as we think and feel and make sense of what is going on around us. Take perception. As I sit here at my desk, I see – I don't just think, I actually perceive – in terms of familiar categories that have meaning for me. I do not see patches of light and shade. I could not even if I tried. I see a 'computer screen', a 'mouse-mat', a 'cup of coffee', a 'pink telephone', and so on. Somewhere between patches of light falling on my retinae, and a picture of the world consciously appearing to me, a tremendous amount of 'looking up' and 'filling in' must have already happened – yet I am hardly aware of any of that backroom activity. I just know that the mouse-mat continues underneath the mouse and that there is a dribble of cold coffee that I cannot see at the bottom of the mug, I know that I 'know' these things because I unreflectingly act on the (unconscious) assumption that they are true – I move the mouse, I reach out for the coffee mug – and occasionally, when I am wrong, I feel surprised – if, suddenly, the mouse-mat does, against all the odds, turn out to have a concealed, mouse-shaped hole in it, or if the cold brown liquid that I absentmindedly sip turns out to be yesterday's tea. I could not have been surprised unless I had some expectations – most of which I am not even aware of having. My world shows up to me pre-saturated with my own beliefs, memories and desires – yet how they got in there, I haven't a clue. Such trains of thought no longer refer only to sporadic, exotic events like dreams or mystical moments: they impact on my understanding of the mundane, moment-to-moment heart of how I function. It's worse than experiencing occasional oddities: I am, it turns out, not just intermittently but *essentially* odd. If 'I' am conscious, how come so much of me – much, much more than I thought – is happily going on behind my back? Do I have to expand my mind to include the unconscious *always*?

The role of unconscious processes in perception intrigued many people from the seventeenth century onwards. The French philosopher Ignace Gaston Pardies published a book entitled *Concerning the Knowledge of Beasts* in 1672, in which he developed a slightly different argument that nevertheless arrives at the same conclusion.

> We sometimes also have perceptions . . . in which we perceive without being aware that we are perceiving . . . To become fully convinced of this, we need only reflect on what happens to us every day when we are reading a book with some application. We are attentive to the meaning of the words, and we have no attention for thinking about the letters which, by their various shapes and arrangement, make up the whole tenor of the discourse . . . In this case we do not perceive the letters and the

words with that perceptive reflection which would allow us to give an account to ourselves of what we are perceiving, and which would make us aware that we are perceiving. Yet it is clear that we have seen all these letters . . . and that without this, we would never have been able to penetrate the meaning which, nevertheless, we have well understood.[12]

On the basis of arguments like this, Pardies, a mere thirty years after Descartes' *Meditations*, declared: 'I do not think that anyone will any longer contest that we have certain perceptions of which we are unaware.'

The first theorising about 'unconscious perception' is usually credited to Gottfried Leibniz, but Pardies anticipated by another thirty years the completion of Leibniz's *New Essays Concerning Human Understanding*, and it is certain that the two men, who shared what Leibniz called 'an uncommon friendship' during the early 1670s, developed their ideas together, and likely that Pardies more than pulled his intellectual weight. For reading, Leibniz was wont to substitute the example of listening to the sea, to make the same point. What we hear is a single sound: the roar of the waves. Yet we would not be able to hear it unless we were also 'hearing', at an unconscious level, all the tiny individual sounds – what he called '*petites perceptions*' – of which the overall 'roar' is composed. He also pointed out that our unconscious perception is demonstrated when we are alerted to something that has just occurred, but which we did not notice immediately. 'Some of our own present perceptions we allow . . . to pass without reflection, and even without being noticed; but if anyone . . . makes us notice, for example, some noise which was just heard, we remember it, and are conscious of having had at the time some feeling of it.'[13]

So the 'official doctrine' of Descartes and Locke was quickly being disputed not on one but on two fronts. The pre-Romantics complained about the exclusion of some of their most prized sensibilities; but at the same time, philosophers like Leibniz and

Pardies were insisting that *all* experience, carefully observed, demanded a recognition of unconscious processes and contributions. There were cooler, more scientific grounds for doubting the contention that the mind was in principle completely transparent to itself. And there were soon many voices raised in philosophical protest. Nicolas Malebranche protested in 1675 that 'the awareness we have of ourselves does not perhaps reveal to us more than the smaller part of our being.' And many counter-arguments to the 'official doctrine' were mustered by the Cambridge philosopher Ralph Cudworth. The Cartesian implication that, if you cease to think, you cease to be, is just plain silly, he pointed out. He noted that many actions are performed without consciousness, on 'automatic pilot'. And we are not even conscious of the processes whereby our conscious thoughts themselves are formed. 'There is also a more interior kind of plastic power in the soul . . . whereby it is formative of its own cogitations, which itself is not always conscious of.' And Malebranche's disciple, the English Platonist John Norris, stated baldly in 1690: 'There are infinitely more ideas impressed on our minds than we can possibly attend to or perceive.'[14]

However it was Leibniz's riposte to Locke which attracted the most attention, and it is he who is often credited with originating the modern investigation of the 'cognitive unconscious'. His view of the mind was a distinctly modern one. He saw it not as a passive, more or less straightforward recorder of impressions and perceptions, but as a complex, difficult-to-comprehend inner mechanism, possessing both structures and processes that, largely behind the scenes of consciousness, transformed sensations into conscious perceptions: the view that cognitive scientists still hold today. He also inaugurated the modern approach to the vexed nature–nurture issue. The mind, he said, is not like a blank slate – Locke's *tabula rasa* – on which experience can write anything at all, but like a block of marble, whose internal faults and structures limit and channel the ways in which it can be sculpted by experience. The resulting mental structures and processes are thus the indissociable resultants of both innate and experiential factors.[15]

It was certainly Leibniz who popularised two key ideas that were to play a large role in shaping the developing image of the unconscious. The first was the idea of a continuum of consciousness that extended from bright, clear percepts at one end, through the more hazy or indistinct, to those that remained entirely unconscious. And the second was the idea of a threshold between conscious and unconscious: a critical level of 'energy' that an idea had to have before it was 'strong enough' to rise up from the unconscious into consciousness. To reconcile these two ideas, he coined one of the most enduring images of the relationship between conscious and unconscious: the 'island' or 'iceberg' model. 'Our clear concepts are like islands that rise above the ocean of the obscure ones.'[16] At the summit of the island are the clearest percepts; lower down are those that are shrouded in mist, and below the waterline lies the truly unconscious.

Actually, the idea of a continuum of consciousness was not entirely new. At the end of the thirteenth century Duns Scotus had observed that 'in the field of vision there is one point of distinct vision and many indistinct elements.' He argued that, if this is possible in the field of perception, it must be all the more true of thinking. 'Beneath those thoughts which the will makes clear there may be many indistinct or incompletely actualised thoughts; the will turns to these and exerts itself to raise one of them to clearness. Conversely, with the cessation of the act of will, the idea tends to lapse from distinctness.'[17]

Though he disputed Descartes' conclusions about the mind, Leibniz was respectful of his careful observational, quantitative methods, and part of his appeal derived from the way in which he developed these ideas in quasi-mathematical language. This quantitative, experimental approach to the unconscious was, in fact, to form one of the foundation stones, in the nineteenth century, of the fledgling science of psychology. The first true experimentalists such as Weber and Fechner were to spend a good deal of time trying to locate the 'threshold' of consciousness, for example by identifying the amount of physical energy in the weakest flash of light, or faintest sound, that could be consciously detected. Only recently, Anthony Marcel at Cambridge, working in this tradition, has shown that this apparent threshold varies, depending on how you ask your informants to respond. If they have to say 'Yes' when they detect the faint stimulus, they need a higher level of energy than if they press a button with their finger, or even just blink.[18]

Leibniz also attempted to derive from his view of the mind a mechanism for making choices and decisions that did not depend on the ghostly hand of the soul. Like Hobbes and Spinoza, he believed that we think we decide 'freely' only because we are not conscious of the many influences – the *petites perceptions* – that are being weighed up unconsciously. These unconscious *petites perceptions*, he suggested,

> resemble so many little springs trying to unwind and so driving
> our machines along . . . That is why we are never indifferent,
> even when we appear to be most so, as for instance whether to
> turn left or right at the end of a lane. For the choice that we
> make arises from these insensible stimuli which, mingled with
> the actions of objects and our bodily interiors, make us find one
> direction of movement more comfortable than the other.[19]

Of course, Leibniz's metaphor of the 'little springs' has not stood the test of time, but the thinking behind it most certainly has. In his 1906 *Devil's Dictionary*, Ambrose Bierce wryly defined 'to decide' as 'to succumb to the preponderance of one set of influences over another', and Daniel Wegner, in his recent book *The Illusion of Conscious Will*, takes a similar position on the basis of a good deal of solid research evidence.[20]

The idea that perception involves a good deal of preconscious processing, and that what gets served up to consciousness is a 'plausible fabrication of our own minds', rather than a (sometimes slightly degraded) copy of 'what's out there' was strengthened by the study, particularly in the nineteenth century, of various kinds of visual illusion. For example, page 207 shows three different views of a cube, partially obscured by diagonal bars. In (a), the bars are directly shown, and there is no ambiguity, while in (b), the mind 'invents' the bars, in order to create a coherent, plausible interpretation for the odd collection of outline shapes which is all that is actually given. In order to support this interpretation, the mind actually 'massages' the data, in line with the 'conclusion' which it has already reached, about the interpretation which it is going to present to consciousness. It adds in the sense of edges of the bars, though they are not there. It makes the bars look a bit 'whiter' or brighter than the background, though they are not. And it even, for many people, creates a little illusion of depth, in which the illusory bars actually look as if they are nearer to the viewer than the cube. If you now compare (b) and (c), you will see how subtle this interpretation is. Simply by completing the shapes, by putting ends on them, the hypothesis that these are 'really' K- and Y-like shapes in their own right is strengthened, while the hypothesis that they are bits of a cube is weakened. And this shift comes through not as an idea, but as the perception itself. In (c), it is much harder to see the cube – though people often can if they try.

The nineteenth-century German physiologist Hermann von Helmholtz was one of the first to follow this train of thought. In his 1867 book *A Treatise on Physiological Optics*, he developed the idea of perceptions as 'conclusions' or 'inferences', not worked out by the conscious mind but delivered directly to us in the form of perceptions: 'The psychic activities that lead us to infer that there in front of us at a certain place there is a certain object of a certain character, are generally not conscious activities, but unconscious ones. In their result they are equivalent to a *conclusion*.' In

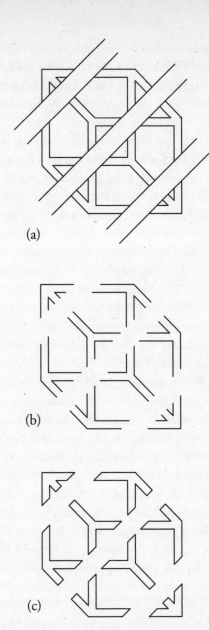

(a)

(b)

(c)

The obscured cube illusion created by the eminent psychologist Professor Richard Gregory FRS.

other words, *perception* is actually much more akin to *imagination* than we commonly think, and 'such objects are always imagined as being present in the field of vision as would have to be there in order to produce the same impression on the nervous mechanism.'[21]

As with memory, questions about unconscious perception are stimulated by certain kinds of brain injury. Damage to the rear portion of the brain, the occipital lobe, for example, can lead to a strange kind of blindness in which people's *conscious* sight is removed without leaving them entirely unable to respond to visual events. Some kind of unconscious seeing is left behind – though sufferers are so unused to such an idea that they are very reluctant to make use of it. This 'blindsight', as it has come to be known, was first detected when an inquisitive neurologist, Elizabeth Warrington, asked one of her patients to 'guess' where a spot of light had been flashed, even though he hadn't consciously 'seen' it – and was amazed (as was the patient himself) when he pointed unerringly in the correct direction.[22]

Other examples, occurring to people with normal vision, can be so dramatic that one's first reflex is to wonder whether something genuinely supernatural is going on. Such an event happened to the World Motor Racing Champion, the legendary Argentinian Juan Fangio, in the 1957 Grand Prix race in Monaco. Approaching a blind corner, Fangio braked unnaturally hard – so much so that, as he rounded the bend, he was able to avoid the multiple pile-up that had just occurred ahead of him, which he could not possibly have seen. Weaving delicately between the crashed cars, Fangio went on to win the race. For months he believed that God had smiled on him, and benignly exaggerated the pressure in his right foot. But then, as he was waking up one morning, he saw in his mind's eye what had actually happened. As he was approaching the bend, there was a stand of spectators ahead of him. The great Fangio would normally (but unconsciously) have expected them all to be looking at him – but instead, as he saw in his waking reverie, they were all facing sideways, their attention drawn by the crash. It must have been Fangio's unconscious registration of this deviation from expectations that alerted him to the fact that 'something was wrong', and, in an instant, great driver that he was, to take precautions.

Things that we do not see consciously, but which are registered nevertheless, have been shown to be capable of influencing 'what happens next' in a variety of ways. As in the classic demonstrations of 'subliminal perception', our pre-existing desires can be activated – and we may be all the more likely to act on them, because we do not know that we have been influenced. If, for example, we have a higher-level desire, which under normal circumstances would override urges that we might want to suppress, that 'control system' may not get activated if the triggering event sneaks into us subliminally. So, if you are thirsty, because you are in a hot cinema, you might have the urge to buy a soft drink. But that urge could be held in check by other, more conscious, considerations, such as expense, being on a diet, or setting an example to the kids – provided the impulse to 'Drink Coke' or 'Eat popcorn' is triggered consciously. But when these messages were displayed subliminally in a New Jersey cinema in the 1950s, they did indeed increase sales: Coca-Cola by 18 per cent and popcorn by an alarming 58 per cent. Or so it was originally claimed. In the midst of the subsequent furore, however, those involved in the study changed their tune and announced that the whole thing had been nothing more than an elaborate hoax. Fifty years on, the truth of the matter is still not clear.[23]

Whatever the status of subliminal advertising, the fact that unconscious perception can release tendencies which are usually held in check by more conscious controls has now been demonstrated in laboratory studies on many occasions.[24] A particularly vivid example is provided by C. J. Patton in her research on the relationship between subliminal stimulation and binge eating. She studied two groups of female college students, one composed of women whose scores on a questionnaire concerning eating disorders were like those of women suffering from bulimia, and a control group whose scores were average. All the subjects were first given what they thought was a preliminary 'eye-test', during which one of two different messages was flashed to them, either long enough to be visible, or subliminally. One message was 'Mummy is leaving me', which had been shown previously to be capable of affecting physiological indices of anxiety. The other was a control message, 'Mummy is loaning it'. After the eye-test, the women were introduced to 'the experiment proper', which they were told was a consumer test about the relative merits of three different types of crackers. After the test had been explained, each of the women was left alone in the room with the three bowls of crackers. The question was not how good their taste was, but how many crackers would they eat? Only one group differed from all the others: the bulimic-like women who had had the 'threatening' message flashed to them subliminally. They ate twice as many biscuits as any of the others. It seemed that the anxiety-provoking message triggered their tendency to 'comfort eat' – but only when the message was processed unconsciously, and they were therefore unable to consciously guard against their own 'bad habit'.[25]

The view of the cognitive unconscious that is developing suggests that people may sometimes operate at two different levels, conscious and unconscious, and that different parts of their memories and beliefs may underlie different aspects of what they say and do. One part of us manifests 'implicitly', in our spontaneous, unreflective, acting and feeling, while another part is in control of what we are consciously thinking and perceiving. We are, in other words, capable of giving 'mixed messages', saying one thing non-verbally, for example, and another verbally. Sometimes the conscious part may be capable of suppressing the unconscious part; other times, especially when consciousness is not put on the alert, or is unable to 'stand guard', it might not. I'm angry, but I don't even know it. You ask if anything is wrong, and I tell you I'm fine – and, on this occasion, I genuinely believe it. But you know otherwise, because you can see that vein throbbing in my temple, which you know is a sign of tension . . .

John Dovidio in the USA has investigated this effect in terms of what he calls 'subtle racism'. He has found many people who give all the right (non-racist) answers on a questionnaire, believe themselves to be equitable in their dealings with black and white people, but still emit behavioural signs of prejudice. Dovidio has tried to assess non-conscious racism not through the use of subliminal stimuli, but by using a test that requires people to answer too fast for conscious checking to occur, so that their less conscious attitudes become more visible. For example, his subjects might be asked to take part in a test of how well they can do two things at once – memorise faces, and judge the meanings of words, say. They have to push one button if a word has a generally positive meaning ('likeable', 'wonderful') and another if it is negative ('dirty', 'annoying'). Words come at them on a screen thick and fast, and they have to respond as fast as they can; meanwhile, there are pictures of faces being flashed up too for them to remember. It just so happens that some of the faces are white and some black. Most white people, regardless of their scores on a racism questionnaire, respond to positive words slower, and negative words faster, after just having seen a black face, and vice versa after a white face. Does this 'subtle racism' make any practical difference in real life? Well, yes it does. When the same white students were interviewed by both an African-American and a white interviewer, they showed varying degrees of non-verbal discomfort – lack of eye contact, more withdrawn body language – with the black as opposed to the white person. Again, how much discomfort they showed bore no relationship at all to their self-rated racism, but was directly related to the amount of bias they had shown in the previous picture/word meaning test.[26]

From studies such as this, authors like Timothy Wilson of the

University of Virginia have concluded that our minds really do consist of two separate systems, one conscious and the other which he calls the 'adaptive unconscious' (though without meaning to imply, I'm sure, that the conscious system is 'maladaptive'). The two systems have a somewhat uneasy, somewhat symbiotic relationship. The unconscious system is more emotional and evolutionarily more primitive, and it can be prone to stereotyping and bias, but it is faster and in some ways more accurate. The conscious system is slower and more deliberate, but it helps us to live up to our higher ideals, and to control our baser instincts. Though this division is neither as dramatic nor as antagonistic as Freud's, nevertheless it is similar in structure: two distinct systems in the mind that can both talk to, and ignore, each other, and which sometimes come into conflict. It does look as if experimental psychology is uncovering a more sober version of the ego and the id.[27]

One of the things that scientific studies have revealed is just how rapidly the effects of unconscious perception can ripple through the memory system. For example, what you hear unconsciously through one ear can affect how you interpret what you are consciously hearing through the other ear, within a few hundredths of a second. Imagine that you are wearing a set of stereo headphones, with different sentences being played to each ear. Your task is to attend only to what is happening through the right-hand channel, and totally ignore anything that comes through the left-hand channel. If you having been following instructions carefully, when you are asked subsequently what you heard through your left ear, all you can say is whether it was a male or female voice: nothing more. You have no idea what was being said. However, there is a relationship between the two channels. In the attended ear, some of the sentences you heard were ambiguous, such as 'He put out the lantern to signal the attack.' Did he *extinguish* the lantern, or did he *display* it? If you were simultaneously played a sentence on the unattended channel which suggested one meaning rather than the other ('He extinguished the lamp', say), even though you did not 'hear' this input, you are neverthe-less much more likely to interpret the ambiguous sentence that way – without even realising that it could be understood differ-ently.[28]

The same kind of process can subliminally activate an emo-tional response. In a slightly different version of the experiment, neutral words that had previously been associated with a mildly painful electric shock were inserted every so often in the unat-tended channel, as well as other words that were related in meaning to the 'shock' words. Subjects did not consciously hear these words, nor did their attention to the other channel waver, yet a measure of their physiological arousal showed a clear jump every time one of the words – or one similar in meaning – was played.[29]

A similar kind of fast ripple effect occurs with words arriving through vision rather than hearing. Your job this time is simply to indicate by pressing a button, as fast as you can, if a string of let-ters that pops up on a screen is a real English word or not. Unbeknownst to you, a few hundredths of a second before the test letters appear, you might be given a subliminal flash of another word which is either related to the upcoming word or not. So your subliminal prime might be OCEAN and your test word might be SHIP, say. If their meanings *are* related, you are faster at telling that SHIP is a real word. In a flash, you must have unconsciously reg-istered not just the first, subliminal word, but also its meaning.[30]

Unconscious perception does not always speed things up, how-ever. Sometimes it can slow your mind down – if the subliminal message is something you don't want to know about, for example. This phenomenon has been thoroughly investigated since the 1940s, and it is called 'perceptual defence'. In one version of the experiment, I flash you a word – FORK, say – too fast for you to say what it is, and then I gradually increase the duration of subse-quent exposures until you can just make out what the word is. We do this for a number of words, and then I slip in a word that is taboo or threatening – FUCK or DEAD, say. What I find is that it takes you roughly three times as long to recognise one of these loaded words as it does to recognise the neutral ones. And this is not just because you are reluctant to report it; you genuinely don't register the word in consciousness. Yet you must have recognised it at some level, in order to selectively raise the conscious 'threshold', and so protect yourself from seeing it! The mind is able to work like the peephole that you find in a hotel bedroom door – you can take an (unconscious) peek out at the world, and then, if you don't like what you see, you can put the chain on, your earplugs in, and go back to bed! Despite the last-ditch efforts of a few Cartesian diehards, the fact that unconscious perception can do some pretty smart things is almost universally accepted in psychology now.[31]

As I mentioned earlier, this idea of a threshold between conscious and unconscious was developed in the early nineteenth century by the German philosopher Johann Friedrich Herbart, in a way that almost certainly contributed to psychoanalytic as well as to cognitive thinking. By Herbart's time, the idea of layers within the mind, some of which were unconscious, was unexceptionable. But he added the speculation that ideas themselves were active, almost 'alive' forces within the mind, and the threshold or 'limen' was the location at which these ideas jostled with each other for access to consciousness. The strongest scramble up into consciousness on the shoulders of the weaker, in the process pushing the latter more firmly down into the unconscious. Below what he called the mechanical threshold, the temporarily vanquished ideas do not take their treatment lying down, and may continue the struggle for conscious recognition, sometimes successfully displacing the previously winners in their turn. However, there is an even deeper threshold, the 'static' one, below which ideas are completely robbed of their activity and become effectively 'dead' to the mind (though if repression itself disappears, resurrection can occur).

Herbart's approach was in some ways quite scientific, and he tried to make rigorous deductions about the characteristics of the unconscious. 'Science knows more than what is actually experienced in consciousness', he wrote, 'because what is experienced is unthinkable without examining what is concealed. One must be able to recognise from what is experienced, what is stirring and acting "behind the curtain".' Although Herbart tried to turn these ideas into a mathematical system, it is actually a highly fanciful, even anthropomorphic one, similar to that which Shakespeare gave to King Richard II, in which, you recall, the mind is likened to a dynamic society in which individuals compete for supremacy. Like Leibniz, Herbart tried to quantify the 'strength' of individual ideas, but his attempt was unconvincing. His theory seems to offer a kind of explanation as to how and why ideas come and go in consciousness, but little else.

The application of systematic scientific method to the study of the mind was taken up in the late nineteenth century by Wilhelm Wundt, who is usually credited with being the 'father' of modern experimental psychology. It was Wundt's appreciation of the existence of unconscious processes in perception that convinced him that objective, scientific, methods must be used if intuition, opinion and rhetoric were to give way to solid, cumulative progress. If our conscious experience – and *a fortiori*, our conscious experience of ourselves – arrived pre-saturated with desire and belief, then introspection, no matter how logically treated, had to be an unreliable guide to mental process. 'Self-observation cannot go beyond the facts of consciousness,' he said, 'and the phenomena of consciousness are composite products of the unconscious psyche.'[32] The mind's eye does not – indeed cannot – look inward on the workings of the mind, like a besuited visitor on a gantry, high above the bustling factory floor. On the contrary, we can only observe what comes out of the factory gates, and try to infer its method of manufacture *post hoc*.

Many people had noted that unconscious mental processes often seem to underlie our actions, especially when we are functioning on 'automatic pilot'. Everyone is familiar with the experience of 'coming to', and realising that some skilled activity, like driving or washing the dishes, has been carrying on smoothly and efficiently while their conscious mind has been otherwise employed. So was Claude Perrault, who commented, as far back as 1680, that 'we think in two different ways. [one] distinct and explicit, for those matters to which we apply ourselves with care, and a kind of thinking which is confused and negligent, for things which long practice has rendered so easy that exact and explicit thinking is not necessary.'[33]

In opposition to Descartes, Perrault was the first person explicitly to associate the soul with the unconscious, an idea which, as we saw in our discussion of the Romantics, took on great appeal towards the end of the nineteenth century. However, the Romantic and the cognitive camps held each other in great suspicion, and several authors were at great pains to distinguish their version of the unconscious from others which they considered inferior. Romantics saw attempts to subject the unconscious to mathematical treatment as entirely missing the point, while the more logically-minded saw the Romantic formulations as hopelessly woolly and uninterpretable. Having expounded his cognitive model of 'unconscious memory', Samuel Butler, for example, went on to pour scorn on the work of Hartmann. He archly introduces a translation of a chapter from Hartmann's *Philosophy of the Unconscious* by apologising to his readers 'who will find [this chapter] as distasteful to read as I did to translate, and would gladly have spared it them if I could.'

He is particularly scathing about Hartmann's 'unconscious clairvoyance', the idea, ahead of Jung, that there is some kind of universal reservoir of wisdom to which we have access only unconsciously, and which 'is supposed to take possession of living beings so fully as to be the very essence of their nature'. This is not an unfair depiction of Hartmann. Like Carus, from whom he got the idea, he contends, for example, that 'heredity is only possible under the circumstances of a constant superintendence of the embryonic development by a purposive unconscious activity of growth.' And 'when swallows and storks find their way back to their native places over distances of hundreds of miles ... we can say no more than that the clairvoyance of the unconscious has allowed them to conjecture their way.' Butler sharply points out that it is quite unnecessary to infer, from the fact that we do not know how something happens, that there must therefore be an 'unconscious power' that makes it happen. He quotes his friend James Sully writing in the *Westminster Review* for 1878: 'What, in fact, is this "unconscious" but a high-sounding name to veil our own ignorance?'[34]

Yet not all explorers of the unconscious take quite such a stark and polarised tone. Ten years before Butler's *Unconscious Memory* was published, the American anatomist, essayist and poet Oliver Wendell Holmes had read a paper on 'Mechanism in thought and morals' to the Harvard Phi Beta Kappa Society, in which he begins by inferring a cognitive version of the unconscious from his own self-observation: 'The more we examine the mechanism of thought, the more we shall see that the automatic, unconscious action of the mind enters largely into all its processes.' He noted, as did William James, with his famous metaphor of thought 'flying and perching' like birds, that the clear thoughts and impressions we have are not continuous, but are like temporary stopping points, or stepping stones, and 'how we get from one to the other, we do not know'.

However he immediately goes on, from this rather careful introspection, to identify the 'unknown' that ties our thoughts together behind the scenes with 'a creating and informing spirit which is with us, and not of us', and which 'is recognised everywhere in real and in storied life'. In a passage that rather uncannily parallels the structure and the argument of the present book, he grandly declares that the unconscious:

is the Zeus that kindles the rage of Achilles; it is the Muse of Homer; it is the Daimon of Socrates; it is the inspiration of the seer; it is the mocking devil that whispers to Margaret as she kneels at the altar; and the hobgoblin that cried, 'Sell him, sell him!' in the ear of John Bunyan; it shaped the forms that filled the soul of Michael Angelo when he saw the figure of the great Lawgiver in the yet unhewn marble; . . . it comes to the least of us . . . it frames our sentences; it lends a sudden gleam of sense or eloquence to the dullest of us all, so that . . . we wonder at ourselves, or rather, not at ourselves, but at this divine visitor, who chooses our brain as his dwelling place.[35]

Holmes alludes to one obvious strand in the history of the unconscious that we have not noted explicitly so far, though its presence has been felt, and that is creativity. Throughout history, the fact that wise thoughts and fruitful metaphors can pop, unheralded, into someone's mind has been one of the great oddities of human nature. Where do such insights and inspirations come *from*? And how are they 'made', and by whom? Perhaps more than any other form of experience, they give the lie to the idea that conscious rationality does all the interesting mental work itself. On the contrary, in creativity, consciousness functions as the grateful, bemused beneficiary of a high form of intelligence that, self-evidently, is operating unseen by the mind's eye.

The supernatural kind of account is the easiest to reach for. Even the arch-rationalist Descartes called on the divine to get him out of this particular difficulty. But, as Holmes says, we can trace this strand back at least to the Homeric Muses, seen at the time not as psychological entities projected outward, but as genuine, albeit invisible, mediators between individuals and sources of knowledge and inspiration to which they would otherwise not have had access. However, the Muses themselves were not originally creative: they stood by the side of the sleeping or drowsy person and conveyed information about distant events which they, the Muses, had personally witnessed. They did not make things up, they reported what they had seen, and the 'creativity' of the human recipient lay in rehearsing these fragments of passed-on eyewitness testimony, which were often held to be prophetic. The dream or the vision is seen as being 'true' – in some world or other (though the Muses did once confess to Hesiod that they 'could, on occasion, tell a pack of lies that counterfeited truth'!).[36] Homer himself distinguishes between the two 'professions' of poet and seer, but both before and after Homer they have been seen as strongly akin.

By the time of Plato and Aristotle, the inner person was beginning to make some contribution to creativity. Dionysus came to be seen as the god who, for a short time, enabled you to stop being yourself, and thus to open up to other influences and possibilities. For Socrates, 'poetic madness' was one of the four forms of divine madness which 'worked' by inflaming the person's wits and the imagination. Aristotle, though he originally subscribed to the God theory, later preferred a somatic explanation: creativity reflected a mild excess of black bile (a more extreme superabundance leading to melancholy – thus making the first link, that survives to this day, between creativity and depression). The 'incubation' tradition of Empedocles and others, of withdrawing from the world into a sleeping–waking state of reverie, was originally employed for the purposes of healing, but also came to be associated with the encouragement of creativity. The gods and daemons still had a role, but through these spiritual practices one could make oneself more 'god-prone', and thus stimulate one's own creative muse.

The link between creativity and relaxation – giving up of conscious striving, and allowing a different source of intelligence a quiet mental space in which to shine – was strengthened by Virgil's invention of the mythic region of Arcadia in around 39 BC. The rural idyll is especially conducive to those moods in which the delicate seeds of poetry and song have their germination. The quality of the person, no longer seen as merely a sensitivity to the divine, is now of paramount importance. The Virgilian poet deliberately tenderises his soul, so that his own imagination can take wing. He becomes, for the first time, the origin of creativity, and the source is buried in the inaccessible depths of his own being.[37]

As had *psyche* for the later Greeks, so for the Romans the concept of *genius* held many of the properties of the modern unconscious, not least as being the mysterious source of creativity. In general *genius*, like *psyche*, was the generative life-spirit, associated with the head rather than the torso, that underpinned the more narrow sphere of consciousness and reason. For Plautus, for example, a person's *genius* enjoyed access to sources of knowledge that were inaccessible to the conscious self.

In the 'Dark Ages', the rural motif reappears in Bede's eighth-century account of the creativity of the illiterate herdsman Caedmon. Ashamed of his inability to take part in what must have been the seventh-century equivalent of an after-dinner rap contest, Caedmon went to bed and dreamed of a stranger who commanded him to sing 'of the beginning of things', whereupon he found himself uttering 'verses which he had never heard'. Note that the stranger is not a Muse in the classical sense; she does not dictate the answers to him, but only unlocks and encourages his own creativity. When his gift became known to the abbess of the nearby monastery at Whitby, Caedmon was invited to become the resident 'rap-artist', spontaneously converting passages of learned scripture, explained to him by the monks, into vernacular poetry and song.

For Bede, it was no coincidence that Caedmon was both illiterate and a cowman. The illiteracy kept his mind free of learned notions, while his affinity with cows led him to pick up the 'ruminative disposition' of his beasts, and provided a metaphor for creativity that was to last through the Middle Ages and on to the present day. The relationship between stomach and mouth offered a fruitful parallel to the unconscious and consciousness. In the *Regula Monachorum*, an anonymous twelfth-century writer develops it in perhaps too much detail:

Wherefore, as a belch bursts forth from the stomach according
to the quality of the food, and the significance to health of a fart
is according either to the sweetness or stench of its odour, so the
cogitations of the inner man bring forth words, and from the
abundance of the heart the mouth speaks. The just man, eating,
fills his soul. And when he is replete with sacred doctrine, from
the good treasury of his memory he brings forth those things
which are good.[38]

(In the spirit of the times, such metaphors were often taken literally, leading people to link the quality of thought with their diet.
'A diet of fatty meats, strong wine, vinegar and all sour things,
legumes such as beans, and especially garlic, onions and leeks, are
very bad for memory', says Chaucer's physician Arnold of Newe-
Town. Later, John Milton would complain, if his secretary was
late, that he was distended with ideas, and needed to be
'milked'.[39])

The medieval monks developed a rather sophisticated model of
creativity that relied on this interplay between 'rumination' (*cogitatio*) and 'concentration' (*intentio*). *Intentio* involves following a
single, disciplined train of thought, while *cogitatio* is lateral, allowing ideas from different compartments of memory to be woven
together into new patterns and connections. The de-focused frame
of mind required for *cogitatio*, similar to that induced in the 'incubation temples' of old Greece, was taught in the monasteries
through meditation, and captured through the strategic use of
sleep. Thomas Aquinas, for instance, would have himself roused
after a short sleep, and while still in that muzzy, in-between mode
that modern psychologists call 'hypnagogia', would lie prone on
the ground to pray, and it would come to him what he was to
write or dictate the following day. (The contemporary choreogra-
pher Ghislaine Boddington, too, if the creative juices are not
flowing well, will nap in her studio and by starting to dance immediately on waking, often finds renewed inspiration.) As today,

however, not everyone was comfortable with the uncontrolled mind-set required for *cogitatio*. At the end of the eleventh century, St Anselm thought that such mental wool-gathering and idea-weaving was the work of the Devil, and he tried to banish it – though he discovered that the more vehemently he tried to suppress it, the more distracted he became!

Shakespeare, as we saw in chapter 4, had a characteristically eloquent way of presenting the creative process as an interaction between the unconscious forces of imagination and the consciously controlled craft of the artist. 'And as imagination bodies forth/The forms of things unknown, the poet's pen/Turns them to shapes, and gives to airy nothing/A local habitation and a name', says Theseus in *A Midsummer Night's Dream*. In *Paradise Lost*, Milton borrowed Shakespeare's expressions, and even named the unconscious source of imagination. The faculty of Fancy, he said, 'forms imagination, aery shapes, which Reason, joining or disjoining, frames [into] our knowledge or opinion, [and Fancy] then retires into her private cell, where Nature rests.' Isaac Newton, when he could not be bothered to spell out the proof for one of his mathematic conclusions, would simply say: 'it is plain to me by the fountain I draw it from.'[40]

Since the seventeenth century, any number of creative people, scientists as well as artists, have commented on the fact that it is not usually the conscious, systematic 'I' that comes up with the creative goods. Many of these stories have become apocryphal, such as that of Kékulé, dozing at his fireside, discovering the cyclical structure of the benzene molecule by seeing flames turn into snakes and curl round to bite their own tails. Or A. E. Housman recalling, of one of his poems, that 'two of the stanzas came into my head, just as they are printed, while I was crossing the corner of Hampstead Heath between Spaniard's Inn and the footpath to Temple Fortune. A third came with a little coaxing after tea.'[41]

Perhaps slightly less well known is this passage from a letter from Goethe to Baron Wilhelm von Humboldt, written in 1832, just five days before Goethe's death at the age of eighty-three. In the letter he tries to convince his friend that the fluid balance between conscious and unconscious processes is essential to creativity, and is capable of being manipulated to one's own creative advantage:

> Take for instance a talented musician, composing an important score: consciousness and unconsciousness will be like warp and weft, a simile I am fond of using. Through practice, teaching, reflection, success, failure, furtherance and resistance, and again and again reflection, man's organs unconsciously . . . link what he has acquired with his innate gifts, so that a unity results which leaves the world amazed . . . The earlier man becomes aware that there exists a craft, an art that can help him towards a controlled heightening of his natural abilities, the happier he is.[42]

Many creative people have developed their own 'craft'. Thomas Edison would try to catch himself in the creative, sleepy state by holding some steel balls in his hand, which he rested over the arm of his chair, above a metal tray on the floor, so that, if he actually fell asleep, the balls would drop into the tray and the noise would bring him back. The present Poet Laureate, Andrew Motion, tries to trick his mind into feeling muzzy by taking a Beecham's Powder, in the hope that by doing so, his body will be fooled into simulating the symptoms of having a cold. Composer Brian Eno holes up in a strange place with no stimulation and nothing to rely on except 'the horror of my own company'. Eventually, out of nowhere, the creative spark crackles. 'It's like jumping into the abyss and discovering that you can just drift dreamily on air currents', he says.[43]

Recent research seems to confirm the general approach to creativity, and the role of the unconscious, which these earlier thinkers arrived at through intuition and speculation.

Incubation – putting a problem on the 'back burner', as well as earnestly trying to figure it out – has been shown to aid creative problem-solving in a number of ways. It enables you to get out of a rut in which your more deliberate thinking might have been unwittingly trapped, and come at the problem from a fresh perspective.[44] It also allows *cogitatio* to occur, reducing the strongly focused 'magnetic attraction' of the desire for a solution, and replacing it with a broader, weaker kind of 'force field' in the mind that has the capacity to attract a wider range of less obvious material into its sphere of influence. Thus casual conversation or observation, while going about your business, can throw up possible analogies and associations that sometimes offer a different, potentially more productive 'angle' on the problem.

The historian John Livingston Lowe captured this process nicely in his study of the processes that resulted in Coleridge's *Rime of the Ancient Mariner*:

> Facts which sank at intervals out of conscious recollection drew
> together beneath the surface . . . And there in Coleridge's
> unconscious mind, while his consciousness was busy with the
> toothache, or Hartley's infant ills, or pleasant strollings with the
> Wordsworths between Nether Stowey and Alfoxden, or what is
> dreamt in this or that philosophy – there in the dark moved the
> phantasms of the fishes and animalculae, and serpentine forms
> of his various voyagings, thrusting out tentacles of association,
> and interweaving beyond disengagement.[45]

The painter Max Ernst described his working method as 'the exploitation of the chance meeting of two remote realities on a plane unsuitable to either of them'.[46]

Experiments have also shown that 'thinking too hard' can get in the way of creativity, by restricting the 'search space' for a solution to the conventionally 'thinkable'. When people are asked to solve problems that require a leap of insight, rather than methodical

This watercolour appeared in the Boxing Day edition of the Illustrated London News *in 1874. As she sits snugly by the fire, hovering on the brink of sleep, the girl's mind conjures up a teeming world of fairies, baubles and mishaps. It is this state of receptive reverie that lies at the heart of the creative process.*

reasoning, their chances of success are increased if they can allow themselves to have the experience of 'going blank'. As in a poem, sometimes words and thoughts need to be put together in a way that sounds, at first sight, strange or nonsensical. Only after the event does it become clear that there is something of value in this novel way of looking at things. That is why the sculptor Henry Moore advised other artists not to think about their work too much; for 'by trying to express his aims with rounded-off logical exactness, he can easily become a theorist whose actual work is only a caged-in exposition of concepts evolved in terms of logic and words'.[47]

The wealth of well-conducted research on unconscious processes in human cognition, which I have had only begun to illustrate, has given the lie to the Official Doctrine. As Julian Jaynes said, summarising his own review:

> Consciousness is not what we generally think it is . . . It is not involved in a host of perceptual phenomena. It is not involved in the performance of skills, and often hinders their execution. It need not be involved in speaking, writing, listening, or reading. It does not copy down experience, as most people think. Consciousness need not be involved in the learning of skills or solutions . . . it is not necessary for making judgments or in simple thinking. It is not the seat of reason, and indeed some of the most difficult instances of creative reasoning go on without any attending consciousness.[48]

More recently, the American researcher John Kihlstrom hammers the last nail into the Cartesian coffin when he succinctly concludes that 'conscious awareness . . . is not necessary for complex functioning'.[49]

Let us take stock. Over the last three chapters we have encountered not one but a wide variety of images and expressions of 'the unconscious', designed to do a variety of jobs. I have grouped these roughly into three families: the Romantic and mystical; the psychopathological; and the cognitive. For the Romantics, the unconscious was a supra-personal 'life force', a source of energy and wisdom that connected the personal to the Universal, and in that way it took over many of the functions of the 'soul'. For many in the nineteenth century, the soul *became* the unconscious, and that image was developed in the twentieth century by Carl Jung and his followers. This unconscious made itself known in – or, to put it more neutrally, was used to explain – otherwise unaccountable depths of human knowledge and experience: dreams pregnant with profundity, awe in the face of the might of Nature, religious experiences of selflessness and universal love.

Then there was the pathological unconscious, the 'beast in the basement', there to explain the destructive, and self-destructive, extremes of madness, depression and perversity. Where once these were sent by the gods, or arose from physical imbalances in the hypothetical humours, these too became psychologised and tucked inside the individual. Instead of being possessed by an intrusive spirit, people became possessed by psychological demons such as memories, ideas and desires. These invisible weevils were either intrinsically too scary, or too at odds with conscious images of self, to contemplate, and therefore had to be kept out of sight by the use, if necessary, of psychic force; or they just were, inherently, creatures of the night. Either way, there had to be a dark place in the mind where they lived, or in which they were incarcerated.

Finally, there was a raft of more mundane oddities in need of explanation. People acquire sophisticated skills often without knowing what they have learned, or how they learned it. Things pop into their minds unbidden, or stubbornly refuse to be winkled out when they are needed. Creative ideas, especially, explode into consciousness as insights, or sidle in as glimmerings and hunches, yet their 'feeling of rightness' cannot be justified by any conscious process. A little thought reveals that perception cannot be a straightforward 'video' of reality, but is already highly interpreted, and arrives saturated with our own experience and desire, yet we have no inkling of how that lightning infiltration occurs. We notice something unusual, yet we do not notice what caused us to swivel the spotlight of awareness towards it so it could be 'noticed'. In many ways, the mind seems to have a mind of its own, to which we, as conscious observers, have little or no access. This inaccessible source of cool intelligence is what has been dubbed the cognitive unconscious.

Each of these three, very different, images of the mind's dark basement is alive and well – though they still jockey for position in popular culture. In the eighteenth and up till the mid-nineteenth century, it was the Romantic and the cognitive versions of the unconscious that were most visible. Art, poetry and the rise of spiritualism made people aware of the trembling foundation of their finer sensibilities, while the many psychological and philosophical writings that we have sampled aroused a general interest in the cognitive side. But it was the development of psychiatry and psychotherapy, towards the end of the nineteenth century, culminating in the primitive, cunning, churning subconscious of Sigmund Freud, that was to capture the popular imagination most strongly, and embed itself, albeit equivocally, in the collective psyche's impression of itself.

The ambivalence was everywhere. In 1925 the *Daily Mirror*, alarmed by news that Freud was working on a film to be called *Secrets of the Soul*, warned: 'If we are to believe our psycho-analysts, the Subconscious is much worse than any of Mr Noel Coward's fallen angels. If so dreadful a person were made visible, even for a moment, he, she or it – we don't know what gender to give them – would frighten the most hardened lover of cinema horrors out of the dark into the light of the street.' Virginia Woolf once took tea with Freud, and read his work voraciously, though she attended 'a great Psycho Analysts' dinner on a wild wet night', 11 March 1939, and tersely noted in her diary: 'Speeches of a vacancy and verbosity incredible.' In the same year W. H. Auden's poem 'In Memory of Sigmund Freud' noted: 'if often he was wrong and, at times, absurd,/to us he is no more a person/now but a whole climate of opinion/under whom we conduct our different lives'. It is only in the last few years that experimental psychological research has begun to force the less exotic, but more pervasive, and ultimately more unsettling, claims of the cognitive unconscious back into people's consciousness.[50]

All these images, though, continue to coexist with the various kinds of supernatural interpretation which the 'unconscious' was designed to supersede. It seems as if we have accreted a heap of explanations for the various oddities of human nature, rather than tidying up and replacing them as we have gone along. In religious and 'new age' circles, particularly, the supernatural lives on. However much Christian theologians argue about the true nature of God, the image of a personlike Other with superhuman insight and ability still holds enormous power, and many resist the attempt to 'de-literalise' this image and turn it back into poetry. Heaven remains a sort-of place, though Hell is something of an embarrassment nowadays. The US president confidently refers to 'evil' as a real force that must be fought using real weapons in reply. Followers of the New Age delight in the 'scientifically inexplicable', and in postulating occult, quasi-physical forces and 'visitors from Space' to account for anything from crop circles to a lucky bet to the hallucinated voice of a dead relative. Millions read their horoscopes every day and believe 'there must be something in it'.

We play with the inner–outer polarity in sophisticated ways, but 'outer' attributions for human fate are still very much in evidence. Movies externalise for us the brain-mind of actor John Malkovich and reassure us that 'the force is with us'. Instead of *Annie Get Your Gun*, Stephen Sondheim gives us darker musicals like *Into the Woods* that knowingly play with the unconscious motives and feelings that animated the classic fairy tales of Cinderella, Jack and the Beanstalk, and so on. 'Into the woods/to get our wish' they sing, as they enter the 'large forest that separates them from the rest of the kingdom' in pursuit of their fantasies. 'The way is clear/The light is good/I have no fear/Nor no one should', they lie to themselves, as they set out, wilfully, disastrously ignorant of the impending traps set by their own unconsciouses.[51] The surrealist artists, now enjoying a resurgence of interest, explored 'desire' as 'the authentic voice of the inner self', said Sir Nicholas Serota in his introduction to a major 2001 exhibition at Tate Modern. 'The surrealists took from Freud confirmation of the existence of a deep reservoir of unknown and scarcely tapped energies within the psyche.'[52]

In New Zealand in November 2002, building of a new road was halted because a local swamp spirit, the *taniwha*, had been disturbed. Why was there a *taniwha* living alongside that stretch of road? Perhaps because there had been an *inexplicable* number of accidents there in recent years. Is the *taniwha really* real? Definitely Yes, said Remi Herbert, manager of the local Ngati Naho Cooperative Society. 'It's part of our historical belief that *taniwha* do exist all along the Waikato river.' Dr Ranginui Walker, former professor of Maori Studies at Auckland University, however, took a more 'postmodern' line. 'People who haven't got much power . . . reach back in time to these mythical creatures to stop so-called progress,' he said. 'It's a valid reaction on their part.'[53]

Through letter-boxes in North London in May 2003 came a small green card: 'Sheik Imam, Godgifted Marabout, he work with very powerful spirits can help for all your problems regarding love, lucky, work, exams, business, black sickness, protection against evils spirits, future regarding sexual impotency etc.' And it is not just freelance healers who trade in spirits. In the main, the UK Royal College of Psychiatrists continues the fine tradition of somatising madness, replacing imbalances in the hypothetical humours with better-researched, but still mysterious, imbalances in neurotransmitters and neuromodulators such as acetylcholine and serotonin, and prescribing Prozac in place of St John's Wort.

However, some Fellows of the College have set up the British Association for Spirit Release, which is exorcism by another name, and others offer 'soul therapy', in which the therapist 'helps the patient to discover . . . that while the soul may have been obscured, it cannot be destroyed. The therapist's task is to guide this process of enabling the patient to make contact once again with the enduring nature of his [sic] own soul, and [to feel] the joy of union with . . . the supreme soul, the Godhead.'[54] Whether God and the soul are dead or not, they are certainly refusing to lie down.

We still say 'I don't know what *possessed* me', when we act out of character. Yet we also talk easily of the sixth sense, subliminal perception and inferiority complexes, and attribute unconscious motives to each other without a second thought. The unconscious is embedded in our culture, though it is, on reflection, a multiple and incoherent notion, and sits alongside other, older, agencies and forces that are projected into the world around us. Do we need gods and daemons as well as the unconscious? And how many unconsciouses are there? Is the unconscious that fabricates my dreams the same as the one that makes me check that the lights are off a dozen times before I can leave the house? Is the wellspring of our best ideas the same source as the one that senses sights and sounds without our knowing? Does a moment of mystical grace depend upon the same underlying processes that prevent me from recalling the name of my old head teacher? Can we tidy up this psychological scrapheap, and replace it with something more elegant and comprehensive? And if we can, where shall we begin?

There are clear precedents for science's replacement of 'explanatory fictions' with other notions that are better informed. We used to think that there had to be some explanation for life itself, for example: the 'life force', 'vital spirit' or '*élan vital*'. From the Greeks to the Renaissance, it seemed inconceivable that bodies could 'come alive' all by themselves. There had to be an additional 'something' that breathed life into them. For the Greeks, as we saw in chapter 2, this 'something', *psyche*, was itself the seed of what was to become their equivalent of 'the unconscious'. But now we know that this magic ingredient is superfluous. When various chemicals twine themselves into self-replicating molecules; and such molecules band together with others and develop the ability to keep their milieu steady by building a semi-permeable membrane around them-selves; and such tiny enclaves begin to split, and their daughter cells to stick together; and different cells take on different functions and forms within the collective . . . when all that and more begins to happen, over evolutionary time, then what you have *is* what we call life. Simple ingredients, put together in intricate ways, develop the ability to self-organise, self-replicate and self-repair, and we now know a fair bit about how that happens. Nothing else, so far as we now know, is required.[55]

There are, it seems, only three places to look for explanations of human oddity: the outside world, in the form of occult spirits and forces; the 'unconscious', conceived of as an internal demi-monde, and the body. We have had a good look at the first two and, so far, have passed over the body as a rather unpromising source of dreams and intuitions and religious visions. Since the start of his-tory, it has seemed inconceivable that the body could be smart enough to come up with such extraordinary phenomena. How could a dream, or the heart-stopping appreciation of beauty, issue from an unholy confection of gristle, guts and sweat – however complicated this confection might be? Indeed. But that was before we began to understand just what an incredible organ occupied the space between our ears. The place to start, if we are to investi-gate the body's ability to generate odd experience by itself, without a helping hand from a ghostly god – or even an equally ghostly 'unconscious' – has to be the brain.

8

Putting Humpty Together Again:
Neural Networks to the Rescue

But who is it speaks in me now?
Who is it speaks?
Is it my brain?
Who was it talking within me and to me at once?

Silence replies,
And no one can tell
The voice from the silence, or knows when the Voice shall begin.
                                                    – Harold Monro[1]

If we are to do away with both occult forces, on the one hand, *and* the *éminences grises* of the 'soul' and the psychologised 'unconscious' on the other, we are left in the unenviable position of having to believe at least two impossible things before breakfast. First, we have to entertain the possibility that a lump of live meat, even one that contains as intricately constructed an organ as we now know the brain to be, is capable of generating consciousness. And second, we have to swallow the idea that it can generate not only normal kinds of consciousness, but also the weird kinds that we have been referring to collectively as the oddities. Can either of these things possibly be true? It certainly has not seemed so, at least until quite recently.

Brains are silent. They do not heave or grind as they work – or not if they are in good working order. As Henry Maudsley said back in 1867, 'he whose brain makes him conscious that he has a brain is not well, but ill.' The ancient Egyptians thought the brain had no function, on the grounds that it was cold, bloodless and insensible to pain, that small animals seemed to manage perfectly well without one, and that it was not connected to the senses (the optic nerve, in their view, being only a channel for moisture). Aristotle agreed. So it is not surprising that the ancients would have located the soul in parts of the body where there are tangible signs that something is going on: the pounding heart, the sinking stomach, the tightening diaphragm – the *phrenes* and *thymos* of Homeric man. Aristotle placed the soul in the heart, and the book of Genesis concurred, recording that, when God looked down on his human creations, he saw that their hearts – not their heads – were 'full of evil imaginings'.[2]

Not everyone in fifth-century BC Athens agreed with Aristotle, however. Hippocrates was one of the first vehemently to insist that it was the brain that ran the show. 'Some say that we think with the heart, and that this is the part that is grieved, and experiences care. But it is not so,' he said. 'The heart and the diaphragm . . . have nothing to do with operations of the understanding, but of all these the brain is the cause.' Without the benefit of any but the crudest anatomical knowledge, he was able to get the function of the brain right – more or less:

From the brain and the brain alone arise our pleasures, joys, laughter and jests, as well as our sorrows, pains, griefs and tears. Through it in particular we think, see, hear and distinguish the ugly from the beautiful, the bad from the good, the pleasant from the unpleasant, in some cases using custom as a test, in others perceiving them from their utility. It is the same thing which makes us mad or delirious, inspires us with dread and fear, whether by night or by day, brings sleeplessness, inopportune mistakes, aimless anxieties, absentmindedness, and acts that are contrary to habit. These things that we suffer all come from the brain, when it is not healthy, but becomes abnormally hot, cold, moist or dry, or suffers any other unnatural affection to which it is not accustomed. Madness comes from moistness.[3]

However, it was not the brain itself that was at work. When the first rough autopsies were performed, it was obvious to the Alexandrian physicians Herophilus and Erasistratus at the beginning of the third century BC that the brain could do all these things only because it housed the soul. It was clear that the airy soul must live in the apparently empty chambers within the brain, the ventricles. Nature spirits don't live in the rock, after all; they live in caves, so it was fairly self-evident that the soul should dwell in the caves of the brain.

In one popular version, the various faculties of the soul inhabited different ventricles, like tenants in an apartment block. 'Common sense' lived in the first ventricle, 'imagination' in the second, 'reasoning' in the third and 'memory' and 'motion' in the fourth (though, as we have seen, the heart continued to be a popular rival for the seat of memory). Even Shakespeare spoke of our thoughts being 'begot in the ventricle of memory'.[4] It may be that the driving analogy behind these assignments of functions was the common architecture of the temple, one of whose functions was as a court. It was divided into areas, such as the *vestibulum*, *consistorium* and *apotheka*, where different aspects of the legal process were carried out, and these were often mapped straight onto the chambers within the brain.[5]

Herophilus and Erasistratus were also the first to trace the 'central nervous system': the collection of nerves that bring sensory information to the brain, and organise the control of the muscles that issue forth from it. And in the second century AD the influential idea of 'animal spirits', first originated by Theophrastus, was being developed by Galen. Animal spirits were conceived of as a kind of vaporous substance that was created in the ventricles of the brain from a mixture of air and an equally mysterious ingredient called 'vital pneuma' which was a constituent of the blood. From the ventricles, this gas flowed out into the nervous system, which was imagined to be a network of fine tubing, and thence to the muscles and organs of the body, which were 'inflated', and thereby caused to move.[6]

This ingenious hydraulic model persisted right up to the seventeenth century. Descartes himself relied upon it, though he supplemented it with a system of tiny threads that ran up to the brain from the sensory organs. When the senses were stimulated – for example, when you inadvertently burned your hand – these filaments contracted and pulled on tiny valves in the brain which then released animal spirits that could run to the appropriate muscles, and pull the hand away from the source of the heat. For Descartes, the machine of the body was 'worked' by such small physical movements. He could not imagine, however, that thoughts could ever arise in this way: they had to be generated in an entirely different way, by the soul-mind. The mental and spiritual activities of the soul were able to reach down into the physical mechanism of the body, and influence its processes, through the brain's pineal gland, which, he wrote to Mersenne in 1640, 'is the principal seat of the soul and the place where all thoughts originate. The reason from which I derive this belief is that I find no part in all the brain, save this alone, which is not double . . . Further, it is situated the most suitably possible for this purpose, to wit, in the middle, between the cavities.'[7]

Though Descartes' imagination was restricted by his lack of knowledge of the brain, his intuitions about its functioning were often acute. Despite his denial of the unconscious mind, he seemed to acknowledge the role of unconscious perception in selective attention, for example. When we suddenly zero in on an unusual sight or sound, what is it that tells our conscious minds to do so? Descartes suggested that it is the brain that makes the

From the 1677 edition of Rene Descartes' De Homine, *this woodcut illustrates his conception of a rudimentary nervous system. The heat from the fire activates what we would now call a series of afferent nerves running to the brain, where efferent signals to withdraw his toes are initiated.*

preliminary decision that something strange has occurred, and alerts the 'soul' that something worthy of its attention is present. Two and a half centuries later, the great Russian physiologist A. N. Sokolov would refer to this preconscious alerting as the 'orienting reaction', but Descartes called it 'admiration':

> Admiration is a sudden surprise to the Soul which causeth in her an inclination to consider with attention the objects which seem rare and extraordinary to her. It is caused first by an impression in the brain that represents the object as rare, and consequently worthy to be seriously considered; after that by the motion of the spirits, which are disposed by this impression to tend with might and main, towards that place of the brain where it is, to fortifie, and conserve it there; as also they are thereby disposed to passe from thence into the muscles which serve to hold the organs of the sense in the same situation as they are, that it may be fomented by them.[8]

Though he balked at allowing the brain to underwrite the functions of the soul entirely, nevertheless Descartes was obviously quite willing to involve the brain in 'behind-the-scenes' manoeuvres of quite a sophisticated, psychological kind, and in doing so contributed significantly, if perhaps inadvertently, to opening up ways of thinking about the brain that were eventually to lead to the soul's dethronement. The brain was to become, not the soul's lodging house, but the very engine of consciousness. Without Descartes, it would have been impossible, for example, for David Hartley, a century later, to propose that 'the white medullary substance of the Brain is also the immediate instrument by which Ideas are presented to the Mind; or, in other words, whatever Changes are made in this Substance, corresponding Changes are made in our Ideas; and vice versa.'[9] Hartley also proposed that memories have a physical basis in the brain; they live on as minute vibrations, 'vibratiuncles', that are faint copies of the patterns of sensory vibration through which they originally arrived.

As the science of anatomy developed, from the seventeenth century onwards, so the modus operandi of the central nervous system came to be understood more clearly, and attention shifted from the empty ventricles of the brain to the intricate organisation of the matter of which it was composed. In 1729 Isaac Newton replaced the hydraulic model with a harmonic one, likening the nerves to violin strings along which vibrations could be conducted. He acknowledged that he could not explain 'the laws by which this electric and elastick spirit operates', and it took another sixty years before Luigi Galvani was able to develop the idea of nerves as conductors, neither of vapour nor of vibrations, but of electric current. By the risky operation of prodding a frog's exposed nerves with a pair of scissors during an electrical storm, Galvani found that electrical stimulation itself – without any intervention by conscious will, or assistance from the soul – could cause muscular contraction.

Such glimmerings of the modern understanding of the brain as an electrochemical device, capable of considerable autonomy and intelligence, put the soul ever more firmly on the back foot, and its appearances in theory came to appear more and more implausible and gratuitous. However, it was a brave man (or, more rarely, woman) who dared dispense with it entirely. In the eighteenth and nineteenth centuries, the idea that the 'body' could take over not just some but all the functions of the soul was talked about, but only amongst friends, or after a few drinks. It was still dangerous to question the existence of the soul, and its divine provenance, in public. Between 1815 and 1830, informers and highly active secret police were employed throughout Europe to crush any questioning of the religious, as well as the political, status quo.[10]

The eighteenth-century Scottish physician Robert Whytt, for example, discovered that even a frog without a brain could do some quite clever things – but he felt forced to save the soul by allowing it to leave its Cartesian headquarters in the brain's pineal gland and percolate down into the body itself (thus, of course, raising more questions than he solved). A century later, John Bovee Dods was invited to summarise the considerable developments in 'electrical psychology' for the benefit of the US Hall of Representatives, but was at pains to reassure his audience that, despite these advances in understanding, 'the brain is invested with a living spirit which, like an enthroned deity, presides over and governs all the voluntary motions . . .'[11]

Several thinkers found it safer to explore the possible reduction of mind to matter through fiction, rather than directly through philosophy or science. In 1822, E. T. A. Hoffmann published in Berlin a novella called *Master Flea*, which took its ideas straight from the bolder – and therefore more thoroughly persecuted – Erasmus Darwin. In the story, Master Flea has built a microscope so fine that it enables the hero, Peregrinus Tyss, to see into people's brains and read their thoughts directly from the activity of their neurons. Hoffmann used this device to create playful explanations for some of the apparent oddities of human thought. For example, while Peregrinus was studying this 'strange network of veins and nerves', he observed 'that when people talked with exceptional eloquence about art and learning . . . their veins and nerves did not penetrate into the recesses of their brains, but curved back, so that it was impossible to discern their thoughts with any clarity.' He communicated this observation to Master Flea, who remarked that 'what Peregrinus had mistaken for thoughts were nothing more than words, vainly endeavouring to become thoughts.'[12]

By the 1850s, in France at least, it was becoming somewhat safer to air one's doubts about the soul in public. The Goncourt brothers report that Sainte-Beuve, albeit drunk, harangued Baudelaire in a bar on the non-existence of the soul 'so fiercely as to bring every game of dominoes in the café to a stop'. Philosophers 'talk of nothing but God and the immortality of the soul', Sainte-Beuve spluttered. But 'they know perfectly well the immortality of the soul doesn't exist any more than God does. It's disgusting!'[13]

But it was in England, in the same decade, that the decisive break with *any* 'ghost in the machine' – be it 'the soul' *or* 'the unconscious' – was first mooted by the naturalist and physician William Carpenter. Carpenter coined the term 'unconscious cerebration' – later to be popularised by Henry James, in *The Aspern Papers*, as 'the deep well of unconscious cerebration' – to refer to the 'unconscious operation of the brain in balancing for itself all . . . considerations, in putting all in order, so to speak'.[14] It is the words 'for itself', and 'all', that are telling. In Carpenter's brain, both the soul and 'the' unconscious, conceived of as invisible and incorporeal centres of intelligence, are rendered superfluous, and pensioned off. The 'brains' behind consciousness is nothing other than the brain itself. As DNA pioneer Francis Crick was to put it, rather more forcefully 150 years later, 'You're nothing but a pack of neurons!'[15]

The resistance to such a preposterous idea, then as now, was considerable. After all, if there's no ghost, where does that leave 'me'? But before we consider the implications of the double assassination of the soul and the unconscious for human identity, we should look more closely at the evidence. How could the soul, that seems to underlie conscious reason and volition, and the unconscious, that complements the soul by underwriting the other, odd forms of experience which the soul has difficulty in explaining, both be incorporated into the working of the physical brain?

Today we know much more about the brain than we did a century ago, and one of the things we know is just how much we don't know. Modern neuroscience tells us that the brain is composed of around 100 billion tiny tree-like filaments, the nerves or neurons, each of which can develop functional connections with up to 10,000 of its neighbours. In one tiny cubic millimetre of the brain's cortex, you will find about 100,000 neurons and 10 million synaptic connections between them. Through this vast, delicate filigree of electrically and chemically responsive tissue flow continual patterns of activity, with the state of activation of each minuscule site capable of influencing the actual or potential activation of a host of others in a wide variety of ways. The activity at the branch-tips of one neuron may contribute to the triggering of activity in the branch-tips of its neighbours directly. But it may also change the excitability of areas of the network more indirectly by, for instance, changing the consistency of the chemical soup in which the whole network is continually bathed.

A good start has been made at discovering how some of these reactions work, and how they can be changed by experience. For example, when one clump of neurons is involved in triggering activity in another clump, the two tend to grow more tightly together, so that the second tends to fire more readily whenever the first is activated. We also know that experience modifies the activity within the network as a whole, very fast, in very complicated ways, and that the whole network is intrinsically active, all the time. Stimuli do not 'switch on' inert bits of the network, like a light-bulb going on in a dark room. Their effect is more like that on the water of one child jumping into an already crowded swimming-pool. Within a small fraction of a second, that input of activity has rippled out and affected what is going on throughout the network in a million ways, both large and small.

Scientists have also started identifying bits of the brain that seem to be dedicated to particular jobs. And slowly, they are beginning to understand the design specification of the brain as a whole. It is at this high-level conceptualisation of the brain's functions and purposes that we need to start, in trying to decide whether, and if so how, the physical brain can underpin our unconscious lives.

A great deal hangs on what we imagine the brain to be like: what key metaphors underlie the way we think about it. For these metaphors, especially if they are buried and unacknowledged, can smuggle into our thinking the very assumptions that we might be

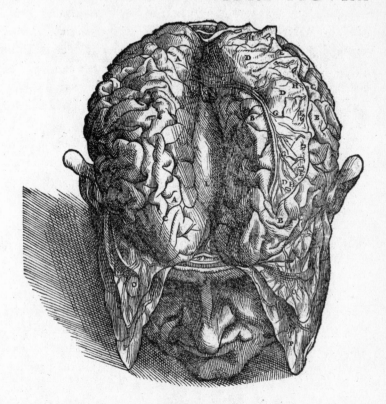

Andreas Vesalius's great work On the Structure of the Human Body, *published in 1543, set new standards of clarity and accuracy in the study of anatomy. His drawing of the exposed human brain represents a triumph of dispassionate observation over reflex disgust.*

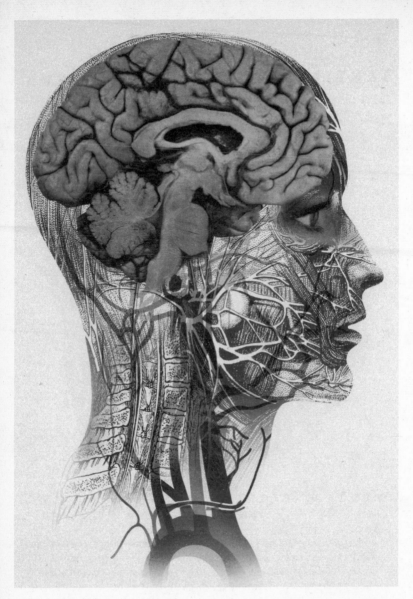

A modern representation of the brain, together with its supporting trellis-work of muscles and blood vessels, adds detail to Vesalius's image. Here the brain is shown chopped vertically through the middle, exposing the inside face of the left hemisphere.

trying to question. For example: Plato's wax-tablet model of memory requires a writer and a reader to bring it alive. His aviary model, though intrinsically active, has little internal organisation, and still needs the keeper to make decisions and catch the birds. A library needs a librarian. A computer needs a programmer. Each of these models of the mind has to be accompanied by a mysterious manager to make it work, and they therefore allow (almost *require*) the soul or the unconscious to slip back in. Books do not quietly reshelve themselves after the staff have gone home. But from what we now know about the brain, it appears increasingly unlikely that there is any such manikin at the controls at all.

Most of the traditional metaphors also assume that the mind is a collection of little bits of independent knowledge (books, birds, computer files), organised in some more or less tidy and methodical way, whereas we know that knowledge is represented in real people's heads by vast chains of associations that connect up far-flung corners of the brain, and which interact and intermingle over time in a way that books and files can never do. If we are going to explore how the brain really works, we therefore need to approach it without any of these inaccurate metaphorical presuppositions.

It might help, instead of asking what is the brain *like*, to start by asking what it is *for*. And to do that, we need to take a perspective that sees human consciousness and capability as the outcome of the slow, tortuous unfolding of evolution. If we can get an overview of what the brain's original jobs were – and, to a large extent still are, beneath our sophistication – we will be better placed to see how its functioning might become stretched, and even break down, in ways that could give rise to the oddities of human experience that have previously required the invention of mysterious explanatory fictions. So what is the 'design specification' of the human brain?

From the evolutionary perspective, our modern, complicated, conscious lives are recent, rather curious products of brains that

have been evolving for a long time: brains which were not originally designed to master *Tetris*, appreciate *Swan Lake*, or have
deep and meaningful conversations about the state of their owners'
relationships. On the contrary, brains originally evolved in order to
aid survival in two ways. First, they enabled animals' increasingly
sophisticated internal repertoires of needs, capabilities and sensory
detectors to be better coordinated. A central nervous system
enables you to coordinate the running capability of your legs with
the grasping capability of your hands and the grinding capability
of your teeth, to link these action possibilities with the current
agenda of needs, and to coordinate these 'desirable action pack-
ages' with the range of possibilities that your situation, as revealed
by the sensory systems, currently affords. And the second clever
thing brains do is learn. They pick out recurring patterns and
contingencies in the world, and turn them into useful expertise
that guides the ways in which actions are targeted and needs
expressed. A flexible, modifiable brain enables you to improve the
ways in which needs, actions and senses are coordinated on the
basis of stored knowledge about what has happened previously, in
apparently similar circumstances.

There is absolutely no reason to suppose that any of this
requires consciousness. Animals very much simpler than us, as
well as robots, can do the same kind of thing, though their repertoires are smaller. In essence, then, the brain started evolutionary
life as an unconscious on-board biocomputer whose fundamental,
built-in goal is to prolong an organism's life, and enhance its quality, by avoiding or neutralising threats and satisfying needs. It
makes sure that you don't run towards the banana that is behind
the tiger, try to crawl out on the ice that you have just seen someone else fall through, or take the last piece of cake while granny is
looking.

For an amoeba, the coordination problem is not too hard, but
for modern human beings it has become immensely complicated.
Needs, actions and perceptual discriminations have all proliferated

enormously. Let's illustrate each of these in turn. The basic array of needs starts out, for us as for other animals, with what psychologists have traditionally, and rather coyly, referred to as the six Fs:

- avoiding harm through *flight* from danger, or
- through *flocking* together with your relatives;
- minimising detection and maximising information by *freezing*;
- maintaining body systems through *feeding*, drinking and so on;
- protecting territory and young through *fight*;
- fulfilling reproductive destiny through *copulation*.

To these we might add:

- repairing physical damage, or adjusting to the loss of a core reference point in your 'predict and control' system (such as your mate), through *withdrawal* and 'licking your wounds', both literally and metaphorically; and
- protecting yourself against toxic inputs (such as poisons or – for most of us – violent pornography) by *closing* up the sensory channels, and, if necessary, *throwing up* (or *out*) the hazardous material.

On top of these come the social needs for:

- protection and *acceptance* (originally as a child, but rarely fully outgrown), and for
- more mature forms of *affiliation* and *affection*.

And finally we need to add on:

- all the idiosyncratic portfolio of acquired goals, values, interests, worries and neuroses that we all pick up along the way.

With such a vast and incessant agenda, every situation, however apparently simple, can teem with a complex pond-life of risks and possibilities, many of which may be at odds with each other. (I want to promote my self-respect by being honest, *and* to promote my affiliation by being liked [which may involve dissembling]; to seek an analogue of maternal affection, *and* to minimise the risk of being thought 'needy', and so on, *ad infinitum*.)

Then there is the repertoire of action systems, which include:

- the one that manages my senses, orienting towards what is interesting or threatening;
- the one that regulates my internal environment;
- the one that organises the intake of air, water and nutrition;
- the one that disposes of waste;
- the one that enables me to travel through space;
- the one that controls grasping and manipulating objects;
- the one that organises the fine, non-verbal details of my interactions with other members of my species – voice quality, eye contact, pupil size, facial musculature, breathing rate, shoulder position, etc. (through which we communicate so much); and
- the ones that exercise the fine motor control necessary for speech and writing.

It is not just actors, confidence tricksters and swimmers who have to learn how to manage and integrate these potentially conflicting systems as they are interwoven and elaborated by experience and practice.[16]

The various sensory systems that have to be managed and co-ordinated are perhaps more well known, though no less complex. There is

- the system that monitors the state of internal reserves and resources;

- the one that keeps track of where limbs, joints and eyes are, so that motor commands can appropriately get your hand or your head from here to there;
- the skin system;
- the speech recognition system;
- the threat detection systems;
- the smell and taste system;
- the 'where I am in space' system;

and so on. Again, developing and integrating these, both with each other and with the action and need systems, requires a good deal of brain power.

Although they are not actually separate from Need, Action and the sense of perceptual Possibility, we can bind *emotions* into the story at this point as well. As far as evolution is concerned, emotions are not divided into Nice and Nasty ('happiness' which we like and 'revulsion' which we don't, for example). On the contrary, they are, all of them, useful indicators of different overall survival 'modes' that the organism as a whole can be in. They are symptoms or concomitants of recurrent, general, combined states of need, perceived possibility and readiness for action.

For instance, to put it crudely, Physical Threat to Self (need) plus Perceived Escape Route (possibility) plus Readiness to Run (action) corresponds to Fear. Fear is not something extra, and certainly not optional. Fear is the name we give to the whole package of altered adrenalin levels, blood flow (away from digestion and towards muscles), breathing pattern, attention, and so on, that get us looking for bolt-holes and ready to flee. Likewise, Threat to Offspring, Home or other Cherished Position, plus Perceived Possibility of Overpowering the Threat, plus Readiness for Confrontation and Combat adds up to Anger. Threat to Security through Loss of Core 'Certainty', plus Perceived Inability to Regain Control, plus Readiness to Withdraw and Reappraise, adds up to Sorrow and Grief. And so on. When we experience one of these emotions – or Disgust or Desire or Happiness or Love or Shame or Fascination – we are experiencing our overall system being in one or other of these well-being-maintaining 'modes'.

And it is the brain that has to sum up the situation and decide which mode is most likely to ensure survival and enhance well-being. Sometimes the brain misjudges and gets it wrong (as when we experience love as threatening, for instance), and often it changes its mind, as the situation unfolds, so we swing between fear, anger, sadness and guilt at the death of a loved one. But emotions are, according to current thinking, an essential aspect of the brain's intelligent functioning, not puffs of (often unpleasant) smoke from some alternative centre of psychic operations in the mind, bent on pursuing its own selfish agendas and to hell with reason and decorum. In other words, the 'ego' and the 'id' aren't clearly-defined antagonists; they aren't even structurally separated in the brain. The spatial metaphor that carves Emotion away from Reason, and installs them in different locations, doesn't square with what evolutionary psychology seems to be telling us. Sure, different motives sometimes pull us in different directions: it was ever thus. You don't need inadequate potty-training to set up such moments of internal dissonance. All God's creatures have times when their needs conflict and they don't immediately know what to do for the best. Sorting them out is precisely what the brain evolved to do.

Nor is there any obvious reason why the room where Emotion operates should be dark and the salon of Reason brightly lit. Both trains of conscious thought and shifting currents of feeling seem to be better understood as intermittent conscious corollaries of complex negotiations and computations that are essentially unconscious. Conscious emotions are not signals from a grimy Engine Room to the immaculately turned-out Captain on the bridge: packets of data to inform his decisions. Our working assumption is that there is no captain, so we must not try to sneak him back in. Conscious feelings are emanations of complex decisions already made and being acted on.[17]

So although one can talk about 'needs', 'capabilities', 'perceptions', 'emotions' and so on *as if* they were separable, in reality they are all bundled up together in the brain. To break people down into a set of psychology textbook chapter headings is already to have badly misconstrued them. What we *don't* do is collect a set of neutral impressions about the state of the world; then look them up in memory and colour them in according to our previous knowledge; then compare them with what we want to do; and then decide which action to select and tell the muscles to do it – like this:

PERCEPTION → INTERPRETATION → EVALUATION → SELECTION → ACTION

Our ancestors would have become somebody else's lunch while such a cumbersome, sequential process was going on, and we would not be here. Though there are anatomical regions of the brain that are specialised for detecting thirst, or assigning 'fear', or organising the direction and focus of the eyes, they are all designed to work as a tightly integrated team. The bundles of nerves going *from* the motor and motivational areas of the brain *to* the sensory ones are at least as large as those going in the opposite direction, and the networks that do the sensing and moving, except for the most peripheral ones, are the selfsame networks that are continually being modified by experience. The way we see is saturated from the word Go with our experience, our personal agendas, and our intuitive sense of what is achievable.

I literally do not live in the same world as my cat. Where I see 'to read', he sees 'to sleep'. Where I hear all barking as 'to annoy', he hears some as 'to fear' and some as 'to ignore', and his differential response is an immediate consequence of his stored experience with different dogs. The same stuff in tins is for him 'to enjoy' and for me 'to repulse'. Neither of us smells the cat-food 'as it is'. Both of us, in our different ways, make what psychologists call a quick 'bottom-up' sketch of the world, and from then on, the very process of perception is infused – saturated – with what we expect, or want, or imagine, or dread to be there. And in the very process of seeing we are also readying ourselves to respond. My cat does not hear, and then raise his hackles. Hackle-raising, growling, eye-widening and hearing are integral parts of the same event. That's how his forebears, and mine, were able to beat the world to the draw, and stay alive long enough to breed. Neither his brain nor mine was designed to deliberate, though mine has different potentialities, and having been immersed from birth in a rather particular kind of environment, it has (up to a point) realised the 'deliberation' potential, and mastered the trick of thought.

Both evolutionary psychology and neuroscience are revealing that earlier conceptions of and metaphors for the brain have been wildly oversimplified. It cannot be neatly dismantled into different parts that can be understood separately, in the hope that one day, when we have figured out each bit, we will be able to put them back together again. The brain is not like a clock, or any kind of mechanism; it is a *system*, that evolved, and now functions, second by second, all of a piece. It is like a football team. 'Manchester United' cannot be boiled down to eleven individuals. Nor do they wait patiently to see where the ball is going before they start to move. They are continually anticipating. Every pass of the ball affects every player's position, direction and expectations, and players are immediately aware of and responsive to each other's movements. They respond not just to where each other is, but where they think they are heading. If you see the game as a collection of individual players and movements, rather than as a whole interlocking pattern unfolding, you don't understand football. And likewise with the brain.[18]

Because of this, doing good neuroscience is very, very hard, and progress is painstaking and slow. For example, there was a time, not long ago, when people thought they had the modus operandi of the individual neuron fairly well figured out. Basically, it worked by integrating all the stimulation that it was receiving at its branch-ends, the dendrites, through its synaptic connections with other active cells, and if the sum was big enough, it 'fired', and sent a wave of excitation down its trunk, the axon, to stimulate its downstream neighbours. Now we know that this one-way traffic model is itself far too simple. Activation continually travels back down from the cell body to the dendrites, adjusting their sensitivity in the light of what is happening downstream. Even at this micro-level, the brain is working as a complex, context-sensitive system rather than as a neat sequence of little causes and effects.[19]

Fortunately, for present purposes, we do not need to wait for all the details to be worked out. In order to see if the brain can do the job of the unconscious, we need to begin with a clearer sense of how, in general, it goes about doing its jobs of coordinating and learning. And for this purpose, despite the frenzied research activity of the last century, it is still hard to better William James's 1890 image of a kaleidoscope:

> The brain is an organ whose equilibrium is always in a state of change – the change affecting every part. The pulses of change are doubtless more violent in one place than another, their rhythm more rapid at this time than that. As in a kaleidoscope revolving at a uniform rate, although the figures are always rearranging themselves, there are instants during which the transformation seems minute and interstitial and almost absent, followed by others when it shoots with magical rapidity, relatively stable forms thus alternating with forms we should not distinguish if seen again; so in the brain the perpetual rearrangement must result in some forms of tension lingering relatively long, whilst others come and pass . . . As the brain changes are continuous, so do all these consciousnesses melt into each other like dissolving views.[20]

Let me build on James's image a little. If the brain were literally dark, and the momentary patterns of activation within it like flickering chains of fairy lights, and if you were able to slow it down, you would see a continuous unfolding of one pattern into the next. All of these shimmering patterns are temporary, but every so often one lasts a little longer, and perhaps glows rather brighter, than the others. Now if you speed the brain up again, and maybe turn up the house-lights a little so the background is not quite so dark, most of the evanescent activity becomes invisible to you, and all that stands out are the occasional patterns that are stronger and more stable.

The now-invisible background shimmer is the unconscious activity of the brain, while the stronger, bolder patterns correspond to consciousness.

In between may be a layer of borderline activity, strong enough to create some kind of hazy halo surrounding the bright moments of full consciousness, but not strong enough to stand out sharply in their own right. One part of this halo, as James noted, comprises an echo of the past – to shift metaphors, the pull of the dying wave that has just broken on the forming of the next. And another part reflects the anticipation of what is likely to happen next – the gathering undertow of the wave after this one that is already being formed. Thus each moment of consciousness is conditioned by the moments that surround it in time, as well as by the complex momentary pattern of underlying currents that never 'break' in their own right. This, in essence, is James's image of the relationship between unconscious brain and conscious mind, and it will serve us fine for the moment.[21]

James gives us an image of the relationship between conscious and unconscious which is very different from the 'place' and 'person' metaphors of history. His unconscious is not a separate compartment of the mind, 'just like consciousness but with the lights off'; nor is it a devious little sub-person who schemes and manipulates from behind the scenes. This unconscious does not have 'thoughts', 'beliefs' and 'desires' of the same kind that consciousness does: all it has are shimmering, ephemeral patterns of activity. True, such patterns have a motivational slant to them, but it is likely that these valencies and biases are enormously more complicated and interwoven than we can even conceive of, and only a crude caricature of them can ever be captured in words. We know that we often have the experience of acting for reasons that we did not foresee, and have difficulty articulating what it is we 'really, really want'. As Shakespeare said, 'we have much ado to know ourselves.' For James, this is simply because the brain's activity is infinitely more intricate and subtle than its conscious print-out can ever be.

Let me illustrate the different levels of complexity of consciousness on the one hand and the dynamic brain on the other, with a couple of recent experiments. First, one on memory for faces. People were shown a grid of mug shots of unfamiliar faces and asked to remember them. Half, they were asked just to look at; the other half, they had to try to describe as well as they could. A while later, the faces were re-presented, muddled up with some new ones. People turned out to be better at picking out the faces that they had *not* described than those they had. Jonathan Schooler of the University of Pittsburgh, who devised the test, points out that there is an enormous amount of information in a face that we can see, but simply cannot put into words. How can I capture the *relationship* between the curve of the nose and the wave of the hair? There is no word for it. So when I am told to be articulate, that is tantamount to saying: 'Please restrict your attention to those aspects of the face for which you have words' – and ignore the rest. And the 'rest' consists of the subtle patterns and relationships that our brains actually make great use of in deciding whether someone is familiar or not.[22]

The second is an experiment on unconscious learning by Pawel Lewicki and his colleagues at the University of Tulsa. People were shown a succession of displays on a computer screen, and they had to press one of four keys as fast as they could to indicate in which quadrant of the screen a predesignated target had appeared. Unbeknownst to them, the positions on each trial were not entirely random. On every seventh trial, the location of the target was a very subtle function of its locations over the previous six. Sure enough, people got progressively faster on the seventh trials – and were then very puzzled, when the contingencies were replaced with genuine randomness, to find that their performance every so often seemed uncannily slow! What is more, says Lewicki, 'the entire sample [of volunteers] consisted of professors from a university psychology department who knew that the experimenters investigated unconscious processes. These subjects tried very hard to "figure out" . . . what caused their performance to suddenly deteriorate at one point during the task. However, none of [them] came even close . . . Most subjects suspected that the experimenters were using subliminal stimuli.'[23] Here, the person's brain is clearly picking up the information that enables them to respond extra-fast on the seventh trials, but without being able, apparently, to boil this information down into a form that could be presented to conscious reason as a nicely articulated conclusion or 'insight'. Again, the brain is doing things 'by itself' that are more subtle – smarter – than the conscious mind can apprehend.

Just how smart the brain is at this kind of pattern detection has been revealed by the study of 'neural nets' – small brainlike networks of dramatically simplified 'neurons', the properties of which can be explored through computer simulations. One such 'minesweeper' neural net has learned how to recognise mines in the sea from the sonar 'echo' they reflect, and it does so even better than trained, experienced human operators can. Another has developed the ability to assess people's credit-worthiness better than experienced bank managers. A third has learned to recognise familiar people, correctly identify expressions (such as 'sad' or 'angry') which that person has never shown before, and to tell unfamiliar men from women, with impressive levels of accuracy. They don't do these things by applying 'rules' which they have been taught. They do them by distilling their own 'knowledge' out of a range of previous experiences – just as brains do. Interestingly, the knowledge that neural nets extract may look nothing like the knowledge that human beings have 'packaged' in language. Face recognition nets, for example, do not home in on 'noses', 'mouths', 'hair-lines', 'eye colour' and so on; they distil a set of much more hazy, holistic templates that embody *patterns* and *relationships*, not selected *features*. If this is the way real brains work, as we have reason to believe, then Schooler's results become all the more obvious. The way our brains work does not necessarily match the way we think and talk.[24]

This view of the brain turns the mind on its head. Unconscious activity has become primary; the brain's knowledge, experience and intelligence reside in the specific ways that one momentary pattern of activity segues into the next. Sometimes this electrical activity leads to a tangible outcome – a feeling of apprehension; the unwitting scratching of an ear; a naughty fantasy during the sermon; a dream. And sometimes it does not. Conscious experience is just one kind of manifestation of unconscious brain activity, and it may be well suited to the moment, or it may not. It may prefigure the next action ('I'm going to get up, right now'), or it may not ('I changed my mind!'). Why some states of the brain lead to consciousness, and why some of those conscious experiences seem to be accurate and helpful, and others misguided or inopportune, we don't yet know. But the primacy of the unconscious brain, as we get to know more about it, is becoming increasingly evident.

It even looks as if the brain has made up its mind what it is going to do next *before* it tells 'you'. In some celebrated studies, the Californian neuroscientist Benjamin Libet rigged students up with EEG equipment that would show what was happening in their brains, and then asked them to make a voluntary movement, like moving a finger, when they wanted to. He also asked them to record the moment when they first experienced the intention to move. He discovered that the intention to move appeared about a fifth of a second before the movement began – but that a surge of activity in the brain reliably appeared around a third of a second before the intention! Back in the 1960s, the British neurosurgeon Grey Walter had relied on the same effect to create a most disconcerting experience. Some of his patients, for clinical reasons, had electrodes implanted in the motor cortex of their brains. Grey Walter invited them to view a sequence of slides, at their own pace, by pressing a control button to advance the carousel to the next slide when they were ready. Unbeknownst to them, however, Grey Walter had rigged the projector so that it was triggered not by the push on the button, but by their own anticipatory brain waves, so the slide began to change just as they were about to change it! The technology worked faster than the brain's ability to concoct a corollary conscious 'intention', and the effect, according to his patients, felt very weird.[25]

The evidence that the brain responds to events that do not appear in consciousness is overwhelming. Patients in a deep coma – the 'persistent vegetative state', PVS – show no sign of awareness when a familiar face appears in front of them. Yet the face-recognition areas of their brains show increased activity that is almost indistinguishable from that of 'normal' people.[26] When fearful stimuli are flashed subliminally to normal people, the emotional centres of the brain, especially the limbic structures called the amygdala, respond in their characteristic 'fearful' way, though no conscious reason for the reaction is generated.[27] In a phenomenon called 'binocular rivalry', different images are shown to the two eyes. What typically happens is that conscious perception flips between the two images. Scans of the brain, however, show that patterns of activity corresponding to both images are continually represented. As the conscious percept flips, so the activity in the now unconscious stimulus is suppressed a little, but it still keeps firing. It is still being perceived unconsciously – so that, for example, if the unconscious stimulus is changed in some way, this change is detected by the brain, which immediately 'boosts' that percept back into consciousness.[28]

When one area of the brain is activated – as when I suddenly say the word 'rat' to you – it appears that activation automatically spreads outwards into other areas with which that concept area has become associated, like the ripples from a pebble thrown into a pond (though remember that this 'ripple effect' may not be easy to follow: imagine the stone dropped into an already choppy pond, rather than a still one). Experiments show that these ripples occur unconsciously, and they do so even if the original epicentre itself is only activated unconsciously. Thus, a subliminally presented happy or angry face will influence how much people like or dislike a neutral face that they consciously see a few seconds later.[29] Indeed, as we saw in the previous chapter, often these kinds of effects are *greater* when the first, 'priming' stimulus is presented subliminally than when it can be consciously identified. And conscious priming also seems to lead to a rather narrower spread of activation, with only the most usual, or the most 'relevant' associates being primed, whereas unconscious priming seems to lead to a wider, more 'neutral', and less stereotyped range of ripples.[30]

Results such as these confirm William James's idea that what becomes conscious, in any moment, emerges from a broader, unconscious appraisal of the situation. We begin, as it were, by sweeping the whole gamut of our sensory input with a low-level, preconscious level of activation, and then immediately start to knock out everything that fits so neatly with expectations that it can be safely ignored, or dealt with by a well-oiled, automated routine. This takes around a fifth of a second. As these aspects are then 'subtracted' from the initial sweep, so what remains begins to stand out from the background and become more strongly activated – sometimes, strongly enough for 'consciousness' of those aspects to appear. (The emergence of consciousness, therefore, is like a speeded-up version of the process whereby the morning's string of emails is rapidly winnowed down, through a process of deleting the spam, forwarding some for others to deal with, and sending some one-word replies, until only a few remain that require more attention.)

What stands out is, fairly obviously, a mixture of those things we are currently looking for – things that relate to current needs and interests – and things that do not fit with expectations: potential shocks, surprises and disappointments. In the front part of the brain, these significant aspects, at the same time as they are emerging, are beginning to be transformed into intentions, and these then get firmed up into plans for action. Meanwhile, in the structure called the hippocampus, this 'sketch of significance' is quickly captured and fixed, like a digital photo, so that it can be reactivated later, and used as a template on the basis of which the brain's lines of habit and prediction can be appropriately re-etched. [31]

The most basic form of activation in the brain is excitation. When one centre or pattern of connections becomes active, it tends to positively affect other centres and patterns with which it is associated. Some of those centres receive enough activation to become fully active in their own right, and they become the next runners in the relay, before handing on their batons of activation to still other centres. And some receive smaller levels of activation that do not fire them off immediately, but which prime them, so that they become more likely to fire, depending on what other contributions they may receive.

But not all the reciprocal influences in the brain are of this excitatory type. Many are inhibitory; they make their downstream neighbours not more but less likely to become active, and thus they become effectively muzzled or suppressed. Being able to deploy patterns of inhibition as well as excitation confers on the human brain a good deal of its recent evolutionary power. Why is inhibition so useful? In general, because it acts like the brake on a car. If you have a brake as well as an accelerator, you have much finer control over your speed and your steering. If the brain can inhibit as well as excite, it has much finer control over both the spreading and the sequencing of its own activation. Rather than activation just spreading out across the brain, like a blob of ink on a piece of blotting paper, it can be corralled and channelled much more precisely.

The importance of inhibition has been recognised for nearly 150 years. In 1863 the Russian physiologist Ivan Sechenov discovered that stimulation of certain regions of the frog's brain could override reflexes that were normally involuntary, and he linked this to the human ability to inhibit our own movements, as when we 'suffer in silence' at the dentist. He observed that inhibition also gave rise to greater motor control – 'one finger can be moved separately only if the movement of the other fingers is inhibited' – and that the balance of activation and inhibition thus vastly increased the range and precision of all kinds of physical skill. 'Releasing forces acting on the brain from moment to moment shut out from activity whole regions of the nervous system, as they conversely call other vast regions into play', Sechenov observed.

But he went further than this, and argued that it was inhibition that enables the brain to decouple 'thinking' from 'action', and thus allow us to muse, meditate and consider options free of the natural tendency to transform fear or desire immediately into behaviour. 'What, actually, is the process of thinking?' he asked. 'It is the series of interconnected notions and concepts which exists in man's consciousness at a given time, *and which is not expressed in external manifestations.*' Sechenov's contemporary, the British neurologist David Ferrier, spotted a further implication. In 1876 he concluded: 'By checking the tendency to outward diffusion in actual motion, we thereby increase the internal diffusion, and concentrate consciousness. For the degree of consciousness is inversely proportional to the amount of external diffusion in action.' In other words, if the natural outflow of activation is dammed, it can build up behind the dam, creating stiller pools in which more conscious kinds of fish may begin to breed.

Ferrier also foresaw what present-day neuroscience has

confirmed: that the degree of inhibition, and the benefits that it
bestows, develop throughout childhood. In adults,

> present impulses or feelings, *instead of at once exciting action, as*
> *in the infant,* stimulate the centres of inhibition simultaneously,
> and suspend action until, under the influence of attention, the
> associations engendered by past experience between actions and
> their pleasurable or painful consequences, near and remote, have
> arisen in consciousness . . . The centres of inhibition thus . . .
> constitute the organic base of all the higher intellectual
> faculties.[32]

Thus the brain, though it is designed to combine sensing, wanting
and doing into a seamless unfolding of appropriate, purposeful
action, has developed the secondary ability to partially decouple
these components, and to allow its internal machinations to
become more protracted, and therefore more enriched, exploring
a greater range of considerations and possibilities than would be
practical under more urgent circumstances. Through inhibition
the brain can arrest and attenuate its own natural outflow, and
thus allow its *internal* pools of activation to deepen and widen.

As a result, the private activities of consciousness become slower
and more richly elaborated. Speech, dampened, becomes *sotto*
voce, and this enables us to engage in that kind of talking to ourselves that we call thinking. Action, dampened, becomes the
internalised, mental rehearsal of action, while perception, dampened, becomes the internal visualising, hearing and feeling that are
the embodiments of imagination. Neuroimaging studies show
that imagining an object creates a pattern of cortical activation
that is very like directly perceiving it. Mental rehearsal of an
action – a golf swing, let's say – produces attenuated electrical
activity in the relevant muscles, but a level and pattern of activation in the brain that is very similar to that which accompanies the
full-blown action.[33] Indeed, such mental rehearsal has been shown

to contribute significantly to the development of the skill. As Jack Nicklaus famously wrote in the introduction to his classic coaching manual, 'Before every shot I go to the movies in my head.'[34]

David Ferrier was one of the first to localise this power of inhibition in the frontal lobes – the part of the brain that is massively developed in human beings as compared with any other animal. He observed, for example, that injury to the frontal lobes does not lead to any obvious impairment of skill. However, the consequent loss of fine inhibitory control 'causes a form of mental degradation, which may be reduced in ultimate analysis to loss of the faculty of attention'. Focused attention relies upon inhibition, for it involves prioritising and excluding, saying 'Not now!' to competing needs and stimulation. Without that ability, a person falls prey to all kinds of distractions, and in particular, their longer-term goals and deeper values may never surface, being constantly drowned out by the incessant clamour of more immediate calls on attention. Unfortunately, with the wisdom of hindsight, Ferrier rather spoiled his insights by falling under the spell of the then fashionable Phrenological Fallacy. For a while he assumed that a person's intellectual power could be simply inferred from the bulging forehead that must be required to accommodate their enlarged frontal lobes, but on discovering later that this correlation simply did not hold, he impulsively (ironically) abandoned the entire notion of neural inhibition.

An elegant experiment recently conducted by the British psychologist David Westley shows just how quickly and elegantly the brain deploys its patterns of inhibition and excitation. The test he used involved a party game, with a twist. The game is to see if you can think of a single word that is associated with *each* of three other words. So you might be shown RABBIT, HOUSE and CHRISTMAS, and given a short time to see if your brain can come up with WHITE. Immediately after this, whether you have come up with a solution or not, you are given another test. A string of letters is flashed on a screen, and your job is simply to indicate, by pressing one of two buttons as fast as you can, whether these letters make a proper English word or not. The string of letters can be one of four types. It might be a non-word, such as WOMIX, to which you say No. Or it could be one of three types of Yes: a 'neutral' word, such as WRIST, which has no relation to the previous 'associations game'; a word such as WARREN, which is an associate to *one* of the cluster of three, but not to all of them (and therefore not an answer to the puzzle); and the solution word, WHITE. The question is: how do the reaction times to these different types of stimulus vary?

The benchmark is provided by the neutral words: WRIST takes on average 900 milliseconds (ms) to recognise as being a proper word. The 'solution' word, WHITE, is recognised faster. If you have previously retrieved it – if you solved the puzzle – your reaction time is reduced significantly, to around 650 ms. This is not very surprising. The memory pattern for a word you have recently had consciously in mind is quite likely to still have some lingering excitation that enables you to detect it faster than the control word. But when it comes to the reaction times to solution words that you did *not* manage to dig up, you may well be surprised to know that these too are identified faster than the novel, neutral words – not just a little faster, but another 40 ms faster even than the solution words which you *did* get! Excitation has spilled over from the three puzzle words into their common associate (which thus gets three separate dollops of priming), even though – for reasons we don't know – that level of excitation was still insufficient, on this occasion, for the word itself to exceed its 'consciousness threshold' and pop into your head. Excitation has been sloshing around in your unconscious brain in a way that has influenced how fast you recognised a word, without enabling you to retrieve the word itself.

So far so good, but what about the words like WARREN that are single, rather than the required triple, associates? The reaction time to them turns out to depend hugely on whether you solved the original puzzle or not. If you didn't, then the recognition of WARREN is faster than the neutral words, as you might expect. It will, after all, have received its corollary dollop of activation from RABBIT, and, on the same logic as before, this should help to short-circuit the recognition process. However – here comes the second surprise – if the problem *has* been solved, the response to WARREN is *slower* even than the response to the neutral words. What appears to have happened is that, once the 'correct' word has been retrieved, all the other candidates that had received some preconscious activation are immediately suppressed. As WHITE becomes conscious, and is accepted as 'the right answer', so it sends a burst of lateral inhibition to 'clear the decks' by turning off all its previous rivals, such as WARREN. This study (and dozens like it) show how excitation and inhibition work together in a fast, intricate dance – and normally, we are not aware of it at all.[35] As we have seen, it may well be that consciousness itself is intimately bound up with this wave of suppression that boosts the 'winner' and temporarily suppresses the 'losers'. Its nature seems to be to pick out what is most interesting and treat it as 'foreground', dampen some other aspects that are now to function as background, and completely silence others.

Thus excitation and inhibition may spread at different rates. First, quick, rather indiscriminate waves of excitation ripple out from the epicentres that have been activated by the senses; and then, as their significance is weighed up, the duller ones get suppressed until a central core remains, and if this is then strong or significant enough to become conscious, a general wave of inhibition goes out to 'clean the blackboard' of all the accumulated provisional jottings and impressions, so that the next event can be inscribed on a background of relevant, as opposed to irrelevant, detail.[36]

If this is true, then it makes sense of some otherwise rather puzzling findings. When people are asked to respond with a button-press to very faint flickers of light as fast as they can, they sometimes make a very quick correct response – and then apologise for having made a mistake. The unconscious excitation initiated the response, but a burst of inhibition then wiped the trace, making it look like an error. Daniel Robinson sums up: 'the neural processing associated with [non-verbal] reaction time is different from (and more efficient than) the processing associated with verbal (conscious) reports.'[37]

So inhibition is used not only to dam the outflow of the brain; it is also employed to accentuate, or attenuate, areas of its own internal workings. But it does not do so 'mindlessly' or mechanically. Where and how and how fast it does it depends on what the brain as a whole is up to. It also depends, as we shall see in a moment, on whose brain it is. In unpicking some of the clever ways in which the frontal lobes of the brain control the use of inhibition, we can begin to see how some of the conundrums of the unconscious may be accounted for in a new kind of way: not in terms of a mysterious sub-compartment of the mind, or a ghost in the machine, but as reflections of the brain's intrinsic – but unconscious – inhibitory intelligence.

Take creativity, for example. There are many interesting and puzzling aspects to creativity, of which I shall try to explain just two: how is it that creative ideas so often just pop into our (conscious) minds 'out of the blue'; and why is it that some people are more creative than others? Research by Colin Martindale, at the University of Maine, suggests that variations in the inhibitory activity of the brain can account for both. Martindale selected two groups of volunteers for his study: one composed of those who scored well on tests of general creativity ('How many uses can you think of for the little plastic cans that camera film comes in?'), and the other of those who scored poorly. He wired all of them up to an EEG machine, and then asked them to do two things: first, to dream up a novel 'bedtime story' for a child; and then, after a few minutes, to take what they had come up with and start refining and improving it. Let's call the two groups the

Creative and Uncreative people, and the two phases of the task the Inspiration phase and the Elaboration phase.

The thinking behind the experiment was this. Creativity consists of both inspiration and elaboration phases, but the kind of thinking that each requires is different. When looking for inspiration, people need to let the excitation in their brains preponderate over the inhibition, so that a variety of ideas can be concurrently active, and their ripples can spread out more widely, overlap and thus bring to light new connections. You want to encourage a state of mind which is not the 'winner takes all' mode of focused, purposeful attention, but one which delays foreclosure, and permits wider exploration of a priori less likely – i.e. less stereotyped or conventional – associations. Instead of progressing logically and consciously down a well-worn path in the brain, different currents of activation are allowed to mingle unconsciously, and then, when something 'gels', to concentrate around a new pattern until it is strong enough to 'pop up' into consciousness. This kind of low-inhibition brain activity shows up on the EEG as what are called 'alpha waves'.

When you move into the elaboration phase of creativity, however, you want your brain to behave differently. You want it to be more selective, critical and purposeful. In other words, you now want to deploy more inhibition, to suppress ideas other than the one you are working up, and to keep your thought processes more in order and on track. You want the centre of activation to be corralled by an inhibitory stockade that stops it leaking away. This kind of thinking shows up on the EEG as 'beta waves'. Martindale's question was: would the pattern of their brain-waves differ between the two groups and the two phases?

He found that they did, in exactly the way you might expect, given his reasoning. In the elaboration phase, the brains of the two groups did not differ: they both showed a heightened level of beta activity, compared with their resting level. Both, in other words, were using inhibition to control and limit their thinking. But when Martindale looked at the results for the inspiration phase, he found that the groups were now quite distinct. The Uncreative group were still showing heightened beta activity. Their brains were, to put it crudely, trying to 'figure out' the story-line. The Creative group, however, showed a dramatic switch from beta to alpha. Their frontal lobes were exerting much less inhibitory control, so that the process of reverie could take its course, and come up with some novel connections. They weren't 'figuring', they were daydreaming. And they knew, intuitively, when to dream, and when to stop dreaming and shape up. Explaining the fact that novel ideas 'bubble up' into consciousness as insights or inklings, without any preceding rational train of thought, does not, after all, require the services of an external Muse, or even an inner daemon. It is what the brain does if you let it. Interestingly, it looked as if the Uncreative group were those who had simply forgotten how to make productive use of the full range of flexible modes that the brain has at its disposal. Happily, recent research by Paul Howard-Jones and myself at Bristol University seems to be suggesting that this form of rigidity is, for many people, quite easy to break.[38]

This view of the unconscious also makes sense of the 'shadow-lands' of intuition: those experiences that are somewhat conscious, but ill-formed, vague, allusive – and elusive. As we have seen, there is no problem, in principle, in seeing brain activity as resulting in conscious experiences of varying degrees of clarity. There is no sharp dividing line between conscious and unconscious. Some things – a pistol shot in a library, a sudden, blinding insight – stand out with stark clarity; others – a gnawing, unfocused anxiety, a sense of foreboding – do not. Sometimes there is no bright 'breaker' in the middle of consciousness, no white water at all, only a groundswell of unease or a gradually developing inkling or intimation of something that is not yet ready to reveal itself more explicitly. A baby that is not ready to be born nevertheless makes its presence felt by kicking in the womb; intuitions are the kickings of the unconscious brain.

And though hunches and 'feelings' are not necessarily 'right', neither are they entirely gratuitous. When people are asked to choose the heavier of two almost identical weights, they feel that they are guessing, yet their choices are much better than chance. The 'guess' has greater validity than they think.[39] Nobel science laureates overwhelmingly agree that taking their intuitions seriously has paid dividends. Michael Brown, laureate in medicine in 1985, spoke for many top scientists when he admitted that 'we felt at times that there was almost a hand guiding us . . . we would go from one step to the next, and somehow we would know the right way to go . . . and I really can't tell you how we knew that.'[40]

Neuroscientists have recently developed detailed models of how the brain could generate such intuitive signals, for example by computing the extent to which the activity in one part of its own networks, corresponding to the 'search space' for the solution to a problem, matches the pattern in another area, corresponding to the current problem-solving activity. Even though a clear solution has not yet been discovered, nevertheless the intuitive signal could reflect an overall measure of the extent of the mismatch. As progress is made, so the strength of signal increases to the point where it begins to flicker in the corner of consciousness, rather in the way that a 'You Have Mail' message flashes in the corner of your computer screen while you are working on something else.[41]

There is much more detail that one could add to the stories of how and why the brain makes emotions, intuitions and creative insights. My intention here has merely been to show that, on our current understanding of the brain, these experiences can be included within the range of what we can consider to be 'normal' and 'useful', and do not, in themselves, require any more exotic explanatory apparatus to account for them. I have also tried to show that the inhibitory mechanisms of the brain can confer on human beings much of their intelligence. Because of inhibition, we are able to manage the multiplicity of demands and opportunities that every moment brings. We can select and sequence our plans, and both maintain our concentration in the face of alternatives and distractions, and also remain open to the need, every so often, to reprioritise and change tack. And we can also decouple motivation from cognition, defer the moment of action, and thus explore implications and associations in ways that can be both analytical and logical, and synthetic and creative. All of this activity can be construed as essentially unconscious, with moments and passages of consciousness emerging as corollaries of brain states that have, for an instant, settled into stronger or more stable configurations.

All is not always so rosy, however. Just as physical strength is a boon that can be misused, so is cortical inhibition. And when it goes wrong, it can lead to some rather odd effects: some more of the human oddities that have traditionally been assigned to 'the unconscious'.

9

The Devil Incarnate: Madness and the Frontal Lobes

The mind plays tricks with her balance, like a juggling shopkeeper who slides his little finger slyly along one side of the beam, and by pressing upon it makes twelve ounces of plumbs draw up a pound of lead. It must be owned to our shame that we too frequently practise these scurvy tricks to cheat those who have dealings with us, and what is more fatal, to cheat ourselves into error and mischief . . . which we often get a habit of doing so covertly that we are not aware of the fraud ourselves.

– A. Tucker, 1768[1]

Like the brakes on a car, inhibition makes possible greater control – but only if it is used appropriately. When the car's brakes jam on, or the cable snaps, things go wrong, and so it is with the brain. Both over- and under-inhibition can cause trouble. As we saw in the last chapter, creativity depends on the brain's ability to modulate the strength and spread of its own inhibition. But some people cannot ease up on the inhibition pedal when it is smart to do so, and their creativity suffers as a result. Others, such as people who have frontal lobe damage, have lost or failed to develop the ability to make as much use of their inhibitions as they could, and they, on occasions, struggle in a different way. This chapter is about some of the varied ways in which inhibition goes wrong, and how, as a result, some of the more destructive oddities of human experience and behaviour which we have been trying to explain come about. By making use of what we now know about the brain (and especially the inhibitory powers of its frontal lobes), how much of what Freud called the 'psychopathology of everyday life' can we account for – without having to call upon spirits, super-egos and the like?

In the last chapter, I introduced the idea of inhibition in terms of the central workings of the brain. Inhibition strongly influences the direction in which patterns of neural activity travel across the neural landscape, how many of them can be active at any one time, and how tightly marshalled and corralled they are. We might call this the central or 'cognitive' aspect of inhibition. But inhibition also affects the more peripheral areas of the mind too: the 'back end', where plans are being turned into actions, and the 'front end', where the senses are making contact with the world and the body, and bringing in information about the external and internal states of play.

In evolutionary terms, inhibition may well have developed first at the back end of things, as a way of controlling overt behaviour. Group living depends on a degree of harmony, and this requires, some of the time, the ability to align your plans and intentions with other people. If you suddenly decide that you have had enough of the hot savannah and go off for a swim in the middle of the hunt, you are not likely to get your share of the subsequent feast. Cooperation depends on concentration, commitment and self-control, and all of these need the power to inhibit alternative courses of action, and their concomitant desires. Sexual and aggressive urges may have to be restrained in the interests of social order, and you may be risking your very life if you cannot keep your paws off the favourite consort of the alpha male. Meanwhile, it can be very useful to be able to inhibit impulses and expressions that might give your rivals vital information about what you are planning. It is a survival advantage to be able to keep a poker face, or to engage in diversionary tactics that throw competitors off the scent. Chimpanzees are accomplished body-language liars, and so, almost certainly, were our ancestors.[2] And it is also becoming clear that human beings, in particular, are born with the ability and the inclination to imitate those around them, and while this is a powerful source of learning, it is also another way of 'giving the game away' about your inner world of values and intentions, and therefore a good candidate for inhibition.[3]

Behavioural inhibition can go wrong when it is either over- or under-used. The disinhibition of imitation, for example, which can follow damage to certain areas of the brain's prefrontal cortex, leads people into compulsive aping of whatever is being said (called *echolalia*) or modelled (*echopraxia*) around them. They echo an interviewer's words, and may even get trapped in a repetitive groove, like a stuck record, of imitating themselves. In a simple test devised by the great Soviet neurologist A. R. Luria, such patients have the utmost difficulty in following an instruction like: 'When I tap the table once, I'd like you to tap once, but if I tap twice, I want you not to tap at all.' Children, incidentally, also have difficulty with such a task because the requisite inhibitory control has not yet matured in their brains. People who suffer from Tourette's Syndrome, in which they are unable to stop themselves blurting out all kinds of socially inappropriate thoughts and feelings, are also bedevilled by an inability to inhibit themselves. On the other hand, *over*-inhibition can be equally troublesome. Children who have not yet mastered the art of *selective* inhibition may overdo it, in the midst of a temper tantrum, and get locked into a kind of physical paralysis – what would be called catatonia, if they were adult schizophrenics – that can result in complete bodily rigidity, and perhaps the inability even to breathe (giving rise to what used to be called a 'blue fit').

At the input end, we have already encountered some of the ways in which neural inhibition can influence perception and attention. When inhibition is lax or unstable, it becomes impossible to maintain concentration, and perception becomes scattered and diffuse. When both attention and behaviour are uncontrollable, as occurs with some children, the resulting syndrome is commonly referred to as 'attention deficit and hyperactivity disorder', ADHD. It is important to remember, in this context, that what we are seeing may be a loss of flexibility of control, leading to inappropriate ways of attending, rather than a biochemically caused 'inability'. There are circumstances in which highly distractible attention is exactly what you need: for example in a situation that may be fraught with unpredictable and unknown dangers. To allow yourself to become engrossed in a good book, as night falls in an unfamiliar part of the jungle, is not so smart. Being 'jumpy' and 'on edge', in this situation, is appropriate and intelligent. Though the mechanism that underlies some children's scattiness involves a lack of neural inhibition, this does not mean that their brains need fixing with a sedative. Perhaps, for some of them, their experience has taught them that life is indeed a dangerous jungle, full of unexpected threats, and their jumpiness – rather like a rabbit out in the open and far from its burrow – is entirely justified. The fault lies in the learned triggering of disinhibition, rather than in the basic consistency of their brains' chemical soup.

Perceptual disinhibition may also account for some of the more unusual forms of human experience: hallucinations. We are, in the main, able to distinguish between what is a 'perception' and what is a 'hallucination', and this distinction is based on a number of considerations. We can predict what *follows* ('If I stand in front of an imaginary bus, it is not going to knock me down'), or find out whether *other people* are – more or less – seeing the same thing. And we also rely on the relative intensity or *richness* of the experience. When I am awake (we'll come back to dreams later) what counts as perception tends to be much more detailed than the contents of my fantasies or daydreams. And that is because, though many of the same circuits are active in the brain when I see and when I imagine, the *degree* of perceptual activation, during imagination, is attenuated. My imaginative brain produces a rather watered-down or bleached-out version of a scene. If this attenuating mechanism were to be switched off somehow, then the quality of my imaginings could begin to approach that of my perceivings much more closely – and I might then begin to confuse one with the other. And if conscious 'reality' is a video produced by the unconscious brain, just as much as my 'fantasy' is, then there is no problem in principle – no *philosophical* problem – about such errors of judgement. The only problems to be explained are *when* and *why* and *how*.

When am I likely to take my imaginings for my surroundings? There are a number of common 'predisposing factors' for such hallucinations. I am more likely to make such mistakes when I am ill, especially when I have a high fever; when my system is subject to high levels of stress; and when I am deprived of the normal diet of sensory and interpersonal input which enables me to keep my dominant perceptual model grounded in my interactions with the world, and in what other people are saying about it. In other words, I have trouble when my brain chemistry is disturbed, and when my normal touchstones and benchmarks for what to treat as 'real' are taken away from me. Many scientists have suggested that it is precisely this mixture of circumstances in which the mechanisms of inhibition are likely to malfunction.

Compelling auditory hallucinations, for example – imagining the voice of someone known or unknown, and then hearing your imagining as if it were 'real' – is much more likely to occur under conditions of stress, where the inhibitory resources of the brain may be stretched to the limit. When stressed, overt signs of panic may have to be controlled, and inner feelings of desperation or terror damped as well as possible, both consuming considerable amounts of the brain's inhibitory power. At the end of one's tether, there may simply be insufficient inhibition to go around, and some of the brain functions – such as imagination – that normally consume a portion of this resource may find themselves operating without the expected 'braking'. At the same time, there may also be a build-up in the circulating fluids of the body of breakdown products of adrenalin and other stress-released hormones. As these find their way to the frontal lobes, so some of the normal functions of the brain may be modulated or compromised: in particular, the flexible control of inhibition.

It might even be possible to pinpoint the location in the brain where a change like this is having its effect. Underlying the frontal lobes, and closely interconnected with them, is an area on each side of the brain called the anterior cingulate. A neuroimaging study carried out in 1998 found that the anterior cingulate in the right hemisphere became active when people *heard* a real sound, and when they were *hallucinating*, but not when they *imagined* the same sound. It looks as if, normally, this area would be inhibited when something was being imagined, but, perhaps as a result of stress, it can become disinhibited, and thus turn the experience of imagining into a full-blown hallucination.[4]

We need to weave into the story of inhibition at this point another of its influences on perception. We saw in chapter 7 that the apparent threshold between conscious and unconscious perception can vary. Some people are more sensitive to their borderline or subliminal stimulation than others, and for most of us this sensitivity is also dependent on how tense or relaxed we are. Under pressure, our sensitivity can go either up or down. When people are anxious, for example, some of them become hypersensitive to any information that bears, however remotely, on the possibility of threat, while others put up the conscious shutters and become – apparently – oblivious to anything upsetting that may be going on around them. In the phenomenon known as 'perceptual defence', for example, when they have to detect words flashed very briefly, many people require an exposure three times as long to 'see' a taboo word as they do to detect a neutral one. The idea of cortical inhibition shows us how this self-protective trick can be accomplished. The word is recognised unconsciously, as a result of which the brain instantly deploys a corollary pattern of inhibition that effectively raises the threshold for consciousness. It damps its own activity, and thus prevents certain experiences from rising above the horizon of the unconscious.[5]

Now, if we allow (as the evidence forces us to) the reality of subliminal perception, and combine it with the possibility, which we have just been discussing, of the disinhibition of imagination, we can make a stab at explaining how it is that hallucinated voices come to be associated with *prophecy*. The accurate, detailed, verifiable prophecy of events distant in space and time, of which we can be sure that the hallucinating person can have had no knowledge through normal channels, must remain a mystery (though these provisos exclude most if not all such claims).[6] However, Julian Jaynes gives a plausible example of how prophecy of a more mundane sort might be generated in the brain of someone, such as a schizophrenic, who is prone to such experiences. 'A janitor coming down a hall may make a slight noise of which the patient is not conscious. But the patient hears his hallucinated voice cry out: "Now someone is coming down the hall with a bucket of water." Then the door opens, and the prophecy is fulfilled.'[7] A few such experiences, and it is easy to see how the Voice may come to be credited with increasingly general, and increasingly impressive, supernatural powers.

The intensity of imaginings is also affected by cultural habits and beliefs. In Euro-American cultures, a fairly sharp distinction is drawn between Real and Imaginary, partly because seeing or hearing 'imaginary' things is so closely associated, in these societies, with madness. Surveys show that there are many people who do in fact experience such hallucinations (especially at times of stress), but they conceal them from others for fear of being thought insane (or, worse, from themselves, for fear of actually being so). In other cultures, the association between hallucination and insanity is not so strongly maintained. For them, the person who hears voices may be mad, but they may also be seen as experiencing an inconvenient but transitory period of possession, or they might even be channelling the wisdom of the ancestors or the gods. It depends.

When the need to make the Real/Imaginary distinction is not so hard and fast, it may also be that the knack of neural inhibition is not so fully developed, and so hallucinatory experiences are just more common and more visible in those societies – and therefore, via a kind of circular logic, less exceptionable and less in need of a pathologising kind of explanation. Whatever the combination of reasons, a survey carried out for the Society for Psychical Research in 1894 by Henry Sidgwick found that Russians reported twice as many hallucinations as did the British, and Brazilians experienced an even greater number, especially of auditory hallucinations.[8] (The behavioural side of inhibition also shows cultural variation. In some sub-cultures – such as those of the courtly intrigues of seventeenth-century France – dissembling is developed into a sophisticated art form, and a soft sigh may betoken near suicidal despair. In others, such as contemporary Italy maybe, the ability to prevent one's intentions from permeating one's body language seems hardly to have been mastered at all.)[9]

Jaynes speculates that either the cerebral machinery, or the learned knack (or both), of inhibition were significantly less developed in the days of the Homeric Greeks than they are today, and that the greater prevalence of uninhibited hallucinations – especially auditory ones – was readily interpreted as the 'voices of the gods'. In line with his argument that disinhibition is associated with stress, he notes, for example, that it is precisely in moments of intense stress – Achilles in battle, Medea faced with a monumental life-and-death decision – that the gods are most likely to intervene. And if, as he suggests, the hallucinated voice is actually an echo of a real-life figure of authority, then it carries with it – as it does for contemporary schizophrenic sufferers – an aura of power and the expectation of obedience.[10]

We cannot, of course, confirm that the Voice of Zeus was in fact

Achilles' own voice by holding a sensor to his neck to see if his throat was rumbling with the divine cadences. But you can do something similar with a living sufferer from schizophrenia, and if you do, you will find that such *sotto voce* activity does indeed accompany their hallucinations. The fact that the voice they hear is not usually their own voice, but that of a deceased relative, an ex-partner, or the Lord Jesus Christ, may simply reflect a combination of some mimicry in their sub-vocalisation, and a good deal of expectation-driven interpretation in their own hearing.[11]

In general, schizophrenia is often accompanied by an inability to control associations, so that the sufferer's mind is flooded with different possibilities for action and interpretation. The frontal lobes of the normal brain use their inhibition to keep track of context, so that those possibilities that are consistent with the current plan, or the currently unfolding scenario, get boosted, and those that are not get dampened. When you are fishing and someone says 'Let's go to the other bank', you do not stop to consider if she is talking about finding a cash dispenser. Your brain does not even find it necessary to remind you that the word 'bank' is ambiguous at all – though you know it perfectly well. But many schizophrenics continually have exactly this problem.

Gregory Bateson, a man who understood schizophrenia well enough to formulate the famous 'double bind' hypothesis, once described an incident in a hospital canteen involving a young male schizophrenic. As he reached the head of the queue for lunch, the woman serving smiled at him and said: 'And what can I do for you, my love?' Bateson watched as the young man froze for a moment, looked wildly around him, and then dropped his tray and blundered from the room. He was, argued Bateson, suddenly bewildered and terrified by the variety of sharp rocks that lay just below the calm surface of the assistant's apparently innocent remark. Was she offering sexual favours? Was she mocking him? Was she someone he knew intimately but failed to recognise? Or was she simply asking him what he wanted to eat? To respond on the basis of any one of these was to risk being shipwrecked by his own stupidity. Unable to chart a way through such dangerous interpersonal waters, he had no choice but to flee.

A perfectly normal situation has erroneously triggered a full-blown emergency, because his brain had stopped inhibiting improbable alternatives. As Bateson said, schizophrenics such as this young man are continually faced with the question: 'What on earth is going on?'[12] Many of the bizarre actions and interpretations of the insane can be seen not as the jerking of a puppet manipulated by an invisible but malicious puppeteer, nor as the inevitable outcome of an excess of black bile, but as desperate attempts to respond to a subjective world that refuses to settle down and make sense. And the latent ambiguity with which such people struggle is woven out of remote possibilities that the normal brain would have sensibly, preconsciously discarded. Cruelly, the kind of disinhibition that serves us well in the context of creativity – when the unlikely association is precisely what we need – runs riot in the mind of the schizophrenic, and cripples his or her life.

A simple experiment demonstrates this failure of inhibition dramatically. It is based on a game that psychologists call the Stroop Test, in which you are shown a series of words printed in different colours, and all you have to do is call out, as quickly as you can, the name of the colour. The trick is that some of the words are themselves colour names, and they may be printed in a different colour from the one they name, so your job is to call out 'Yellow' when you see the word 'Purple' printed in yellow, for example. Everyone is slower when they are confronted with such mismatches; we seem to be unable fully to inhibit the involuntary impulse to read the word, and thus we get confused about what to say because we have not one but two colour words activated in our minds at the same time. Sufferers from schizophrenia turn out to be much more 'thrown' by the Stroop Test than the population at large, showing that their powers of selective inhibition are even worse than ours.[13] They also show a greater than normal 'semantic priming effect'. A subliminal exposure of the word 'table' speeds the subsequent recognition of the consciously-presented word 'chair' even more than it does for the rest of us.[14]

However, schizophrenia is a complex disorder that seems to reflect a breakdown of the *control* of inhibition, rather than a simple dearth of it. From some points of view, schizophrenics look as if they suffer from too much inhibition rather than too little. The disinhibition of imaginative possibilities can be offset by a pathological increase in the inhibition of feeling and action. The mind runs wild while the body freezes up. As one schizophrenic famously said: 'It's not so much thinking out what to do, it's the doing of it that sticks me.'

Professor of Clinical Psychology Louis Sass says in *The Paradoxes of Delusion*: 'madness . . . is the end-point of the trajectory consciousness follows when it separates from the body and the passions, and from the social and practical world, and turns in upon itself.'[15] Schizophrenia is a condition in which consciousness becomes bizarre and fragmented, but also blocked and disembodied. The world looks unreal; other people appear like zombies; and the patient's own body becomes dead and remote. A schizophrenic girl complains that 'even the sea disappointed me a little by its artificiality.' Another woman speaks of her '*so-called* children' and 'a place *called* the laundry'.[16] Everything is distant and attenuated – except the swirling hyper-reality of self-consciousness. The inhibitory control that normally keeps the world and our thoughts tied reasonably closely together has slipped, like a worn clutch in a manual car, and the mental engine is racing wildly while the physical wheels slow to a halt. The frontal lobes are flailing about, both over- and under-inhibiting the rest of the brain, and leaving the person lost and without traction.

Can we be more precise about what has actually gone wrong in the schizophrenic brain, if not an infestation of demons or an eruption of libido? There are suggestions that the loss of control of inhibition may reflect an over- or under-production of dopamine. Dopamine is a neurotransmitter known to be involved in inhibition. In particular, it affects the breadth or focus of the dominant pattern of activation by suppressing its potential rivals. In other words, the dopamine system widens or narrows the 'beam' of attention, and the extent to which activity in one centre of the brain automatically spreads out to its neighbours. Corroboration of this idea comes from studies in which drugs that affect dopamine levels have been shown to 'normalise' the performance of schizophrenic patients in the Stroop and 'semantic priming' experiments described above.[17]

Challengingly, Sass argues that this modern twist on an ancient form of madness is the *reductio ad absurdum* of the dispassionate, postmodern, intellectualised way of being that the late twentieth century so admired. His book *The Paradoxes of Delusion* draws disconcerting parallels between the detailed recording by the nineteenth-century German judge Daniel Schreber of his own schizophrenia, and the philosophy of Ludwig Wittgenstein. Wittgenstein's primary concern was to free the analytical mind from a kind of frantic, ineffectual metaphysical buzzing, which he likened to that of a fly caught in a bottle. Both the philosopher and the schizophrenic may be paralysed by the compulsive exploration of disembodied possibility. Both have lost their 'common sense' – their ability to sense, in common with the world of matter and of other people. And the cure for both, Sass agrees with Wittgenstein, lies in the reuniting of consciousness with the bodily, social and physical roots from which it has become disconnected. It is not so much that demons in the unconscious are making trouble, as that the less conscious aspects of the person – intuition, feeling, embodiment – are being neglected in themselves. The problem is that a person's sense of identity has become obsessively tied to analytical self-consciousness, and the submerged bulk of their iceberg of humanity ignored and disowned.

Be that as it may, it is surely only a small step from these kinds of accounts of schizophrenia to a brain-based explanation for the experience of being possessed. In both, one hears a hallucinated voice as if emanated from a Real Other, rather than from one's own imagination. The key questions are where this Other is to be located, and how its pronouncements are received, both by the ones 'possessed', and by their community. If the source is placed outside – up in the sky, or in the mythical 'happy hunting ground' of the ancestors – all you have to attribute to yourself is the psychological satellite dish needed to pick up their signals. All you have to do is somehow tune your 'set' to the appropriate frequency and away you go. (Mediums, who claim to have superior control of the supernatural media, presumably have privileged access to certain esoteric pay-per-hear channels.)

If you place the alien source inside, however, then you have to imagine that some kind of invasive force or being has seized control of your own internal system, and is broadcasting its own propaganda through your speakers into your consciousness. Your own psychological apparatus has been commandeered by the possessor. And if you are more modern still in your interpretation, you can see the Source not as invasive but as insurgent – as a latent aspect of your own make-up that is yelling its own separatist claims through a stolen megaphone. Each of these stories can be seen as an acquired cultural overlay on the basic phenomenon of auditory hallucination. And each suggests a different kind of response. If the source is a god, he or she had better be appeased. If it is an invader, you might call for the exorcist. And if it is an internal rebellion, you mobilise the counter-insurgency forces of the super-ego to put down the uprising, or you send in the missionaries and mediators of the ego to see if you can effect a mass conversion and reconciliation.

Many of the oddities of human behaviour and experience involve shifts in a person's sense of self. Self-control, for example, has been subverted by an apparently alien force. I am not who I thought I was, and there is more – or less – to 'Me' than meets the

'I'. Can neuroscience account for such shifts of identity? To answer this, we have to revisit the question of why anything ever becomes conscious at all. What are the 'neural conditions of consciousness'? Several recent investigators have suggested that for an aspect of the active pattern of brainwaves to become conscious, it has to be linked in with a core pattern that is associated with the currently dominant sense of 'self'. One of the main characteristics of consciousness is, after all, that it strongly seems to be 'mine'. 'I' am the subject of my consciousness, and sometimes 'me' is an object of consciousness as well. I can be thinking about myself, or about the shopping, I can be aware of my feeling of irritation or of the car in front; but there is always that sense of 'I' to whom things are occurring. So it makes sense to assume that the brain imbues consciousness with a personal feeling.

What is this background sense of 'I'? Where does it come from? How is it represented in the brain? Perhaps the easiest way to see it is as a more or less coherent perspective on events: a point of view that can be characterised by a set of goals, fears and hopes that give rise to a backdrop of expectations and attitudes. When such a core set of priorities is active, some habits of responding, attending, thinking, imagining and remembering are primed, in line with the things that matter (from this point of view), and other habits are relatively inhibited. So – very crudely – suppose that my dominant identity revolves around wanting to be respectable, successful and in control, and being afraid of being rejected or looking weak or stupid. These priorities then skew my attention so that I am on the lookout for opportunities to impress, and for facial expressions that indicate disdain. They may prime certain ways of talking and standing, so that I look and sound 'cool'. They open up the sections of the brain's memory store that are compatible with this self-image, and, through collateral inhibition, shut off those that are most at odds with it. This active identity serves, if you will, to 'tilt' the whole functional surface of my brain so that I am ready to see, feel, notice and respond in certain ways, and to remember certain things; and, reciprocally, to suppress other habits and memories. 'I' is the overall sense of this dominant background 'point of view'.

For most of us, much of the time, this sense of identity is continuous – some of our hopes and fears glow more brightly from time to time, and then die down again, and the portfolio alters over time, but we are able to preserve the feeling of being, more or less, 'all of a piece'. But some people suffer experiences that are so totally incompatible with the 'deep structure' of this self-image that their brains have no option but to jump to a separate 'perspective', an alternative centre of identity, that affords a radically different viewpoint on the world. Prototypically, such triggering experiences may involve extreme or prolonged degradation and helplessness, accompanied by overwhelming feelings of terror, rage or disgust. Where the first 'self' was premised on at least a minimal amount of personal power, efficacy and respect, the second, built *in extremis*, is founded on worthlessness, hopelessness or unpredictability. If the first is somewhat domesticated, the second is profoundly feral. By setting up this alternative centre of identity, an abused person can say of their abuse, in effect: 'I know it is happening, but it is not happening to *me*': not to the 'normal', the 'essential me', at least.

Jamie, aged nine, has been repeatedly abused by his alcoholic father, witnessed savage beatings of his mother, and eventually watched his mother shoot his father dead. To start with, he tried to cope by inventing different planets in his head where he could go, 'but it's real now; it's no game any more'. On some of Jamie's planets, terrible things happened, but on his 'own' planet, he was safe, and he could become invisible. Now, Jamie can make himself invisible and come back to Earth and not be hurt. 'I know I can,' he said. 'You're just going to have to believe me. My friends believe it.'[18]

Such dissociations do not only arise from extreme conditions of abuse or trauma, however. Robert Louis Stevenson's well-researched case of Dr Jekyll and Mr Hyde, which we discussed in

Chapter 6, provides a fictionalised example. Jekyll, you remember, is very clear that his alter ego does not reflect an abusive childhood. It was simply, as he explains, that he 'found it hard to reconcile my imperious desire to . . . wear a more than commonly grave countenance before the public' with his 'concealed gaiety of disposition', and thus, even as a child, 'stood committed to a profound duplicity of life' accompanied by 'an almost morbid sense of shame'. As Jekyll says, 'it was thus rather the exacting nature of my aspirations than any particular degradation in my faults, that made me what I was, and, with even a deeper trench than in the majority of men, severed in me those provinces of good and ill . . .'[19]

Possession, too, may reflect a splitting of identity in the brain. There is nothing magical about the idea that a different constellation of perspectives and priorities can, for a while, take over the role that the normal 'I'-model plays of guiding what does and does not join the neural party underpinning consciousness. The vital questions are 'why' and 'how' and 'when' such a switch of drivers takes place, and one of the most common answers to 'when' is, as I have already pointed out, under stress, under the influence of certain disinhibiting drugs, and in states of trance that can be induced by the hypnotist's charm, or by taking part in ego-transcending rituals of prolonged dance or chanting. (In many cultures, trance reliably precedes the emergence of possession.)[20]

So, for a variety of reasons, it becomes possible for the brain to toggle between different perspectives, and as it does so, feelings and memories that would have been inhibited by one, and therefore disconnected from consciousness, become compatible with the other, and therefore accessible to consciousness. The brain is perfectly capable of resetting itself so that a whole new package of personal traits comes to the fore: speech cadences, physical prowess, compartments of memory, discomfiting insights into the private foibles of fellow villagers, unacceptable blasphemies and much more may be disinhibited. The brain cobbles together a collection of human characteristics that is so convincingly personlike that we cannot but imagine that a real other has taken over the controls. Many of the details of this approach to the oddities of experience remain to be worked out. But even this brief sketch indicates that brain-based explanations are perfectly possible, and offer an alternative to more nebulous kinds of unconscious sub-personalities such as the Freudian id, as well as to succubi and incubi.[21]

Actually, these shifts of perspective occur all the time, at a more mundane level, as changes in emotional mood. When we are suddenly angered, the world immediately looks different, our bodies feel different, we think, notice, remember and plan different things. When we are in love, the red haze is replaced with softer, rose-tinted spectacles, and we are infinitely ready to forgive and console. As the brain shifts between its built-in modes, so the emotional colour and the content of consciousness change concomitantly. Though normally such mood swings are not so intense, there are nevertheless times when we do indeed lose touch with our normal background identity, and feel 'beside ourselves' with rage, or 'transported' by the beloved. 'I don't know what came over me' is a vernacular recognition of the 'multiple personalities' that live within us all, and which, at root, are a vital part of our ability to ready ourselves for different kinds of fundamental emergency.[22]

As we saw earlier, emotions configure us in different ways, to meet certain challenges, and extreme 'flips' may even be built into the brain, as part of its survival equipment, to meet extreme challenges. We may even be designed to undergo these flips occasionally just for practice! Animals such as chimpanzees sometimes run amok for no apparent reason, and act, briefly, as if they are possessed, or having visions.[23] Maybe such bursts of 'madness' reflect the brain occasionally tripping itself into 'extreme survival' mode for the same reasons that organisations practise irregular fire drills, and national emergency services hold dress-rehearsals of major terrorist attacks.

There is another mechanism that seems to kick in *in extremis*, and this too can account for some unusual kinds of human experience. Both animals and humans seem to have a last-ditch brain state, beyond emotional and imaginative sub-personalities, that engages when all active attempts at coping or responding to events are (unconsciously) judged to be hopeless. In such a state, all motivational 'tilting' of the brain-scape stops, and a profound passivity settles on the animals or the person, so that they appear to lose the normal, engaged interest in what is going on around them, and even in their own survival. This state of 'shock' was described in 1857 by Scottish missionary David Livingstone (of 'Dr Livingstone I presume' fame) as a curious languor that overtook him while he was in the process of being mauled by a lion. While being violently shaken, like a mouse by a cat, Livingstone was overtaken by 'a sort of dreaminess in which there was no sense of pain nor feeling of terror', though he remained clearly and vividly conscious of what was going on. As we now know, a massive release of endorphins had dampened all feeling and motivation in the brain.[24]

When the brain is in neutral like this, people seem to lack a fundamental quality of personhood. They act like zombies: the 'living dead'. In cults like that of Haitian voodoo, a shared belief system may even be strong enough for such dramatic demotivation to be capable of being induced by a hypnotic curse. It is understandable that observers might wonder if a sufferer's personality has not been replaced, as in 'normal' possession, but simply stolen. In other cultures, such explanations will be all the more likely if there does not appear to be any obvious and adequate external cause. In war, we can label such uncanny disinterest 'shell-shock'. But where there are no shells, we call on the Devil to fill the explanatory gap.[25]

The brain builds not just one but a variety of models of the world, for different purposes. For example, the usually unconscious model of the world that directs the way we reach out to touch it is different from the usually conscious model of visual perception, which gives us an image of a three-dimensional space that is being 'observed' from a particular point of view – 'mine'. These two models do not 'represent' the world in the same way. If I unselfconsciously reach out to pick up the disks in the centres of the two displays, shown below, my fingers automatically position themselves in exactly the same way for both disks – despite the fact that my *conscious* impression is that the one on the left is bigger than the one on the right. The part of my brain that is manufacturing the visual world is fooled by the surrounding circles into adjusting the conscious impression. But the part of my brain that programmes my reaching and grasping is not fooled at all.[26]

Now, as I say, the conscious world that my brain normally serves up is one of a wide cone of 3D space, seen from a particular perspective: where I imagine my head to be. But I have much

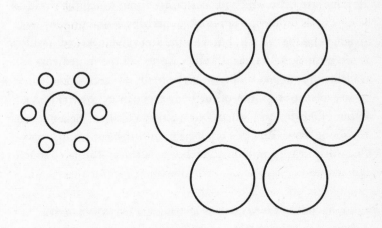

This illusion, attributed to English-born psychologist Edward Titchener, shows how the brain adjusts conscious perceptions to take account of context. The perceptual size of the central circle is expanded or shrunk depending on the size of its neighbours. The 'reaching and grasping' system doesn't bother with this integration: it just (in this example) wants to grab the middle coin. And so it is not fooled.

more information than that in my brain. As I sit here in my shed at the bottom of the garden, looking at a keyboard and a screen, I have a *latent* model that tells me what I *would* see if I were to look under the desk or turn round.[27] I know I have this model, because if I did look round and my house was gone, or it was on fire, I would immediately experience shock and panic. I also know that I could perfectly well imagine what I would currently look like to someone standing in the kitchen doorway, looking down the garden, through the shed window, at a small figure in a blue denim shirt scratching its head and puffing out its cheeks as its brain searches for the right sequence of words to complete this sentence. Put all this knowledge together, and I need not be too disconcerted by the idea that my brain might – again, perhaps in conditions of stress or disorientation – toggle into a state in which it serves up a version of the world in which the two disks *do* look the same size, or in which the perspective from which the world is being seen is different from normal, perhaps containing my own imagined body within it, but with the same vividness and 'reality' as the normal model has. In other words, all the ingredients are available, from what we know of the brain, to construct a brain-based explanation for out-of-the-body experiences. We still have to account for 'why' and 'when', but we have already made a start on explaining 'how'. And this is not even 'cutting-edge' neuroscience. Over forty years ago, Donald Hebb, prescient in this as so much else, wrote:

> It is not difficult at any time to imagine yourself as seen from some other point in space, nor difficult to imagine prehistoric monsters ploughing through a prehistoric forest. Normally in either case there are sensory cues from one's [actual] environment to inhibit the full development of the mental process concerned, so the scene remains 'imagination', [i.e.] has not the full characteristic of reality. But let the inhibition lose its effectiveness . . . and either of these constructs . . . may begin to

seem real. In the second case, the subject reports having a hallucination, but in the first he reports being somehow detached from his body, which is inherently a more disturbing event (in this culture) . . . Seeming to observe from one place, with his body in another . . . readily leads to the hypothesis that his mind is capable of wandering through space.[28]

The more florid kinds of oddity that we have been considering all involve a shift of perspective within the brain, whether that be physical, as in out-of-the body experiences, or psychological, as in cases of multiple personality and possession. The effect of the shift on consciousness is immediate and obvious. There are many oddities, however, that tend to leave the core sense of self in place, but affect the quality or reliability of experience in more indirect or partial ways. As with schizophrenia, problems may arise because either too much or too little control is being deployed by the frontal lobes. And the area of experience that is consequently over- or under-inhibited can be behaviour, feeling or perception, or a combination of these.[29]

The over-inhibition of the physical body, as we saw earlier, may lead to total bodily paralysis. It can also lead to psychosomatic problems associated with the attempt to suppress unwanted feelings by tensing muscle groups that would otherwise be elastic. Fear, for instance, is associated with facial trembling, and with a sinking feeling in the stomach, both of which can be attenuated by muscular means: stiffening the upper lip, as the traditional British soldier was taught to do as he marched into battle, and tensing of the abdomen. On the other hand, under-inhibition of behaviour can lead to a host of inappropriate and shameful displays of fear, anger, lust or disgust.

We have already mentioned some of the ways in which varying levels of inhibition affect the nature of perception. Too little inhibition, and concentration may be impossible to maintain, leading to scattered attention and broken trains of thought; too much, and the quality of perception itself can be severely degraded. We have seen how, in perceptual defence, the brain is able to maintain low recognition thresholds for threatening material, whilst immediately throwing up an inhibitory barrier that prevents anything upsetting from becoming a functional part of the core of neural circuitry that is subserving consciousness. We can retain our unconscious sensitivity to the world, and simultaneously create spots of (conscious) blindness. Some of these lacunae can be specific to 'rude words'. Others can blot out whole domains of feeling from consciousness, as is the case with people who manage to remain oblivious of their chronic anxiety, or their hair-trigger irascibility.

In more dramatic cases still, entire sensory channels can become disconnected from consciousness, as when people develop 'hysterical' blindness, deafness and so on. People suffering from hysterical blindness have nothing organically wrong with their visual system, yet in good faith they deny that they are having any conscious visual experience. That they are in fact unconsciously seeing is evident from the fact (which Pierre Janet noted in 1929) that they do not bump into furniture as they move around, nor walk in front of buses. It can also be inferred from the curious fact, established by Harold Sackeim and colleagues, that, when tested, some patients perform very significantly *below* chance level, while others – while they think they are guessing – actually score very highly. What seems to be happening is that, while both kinds of patient have genuinely managed to inhibit their own conscious visual experience, the former are adding a kind of additional insurance by reversing any impulses or vague intuitions which they may have. (As Sackeim puts it, 'in order to be so wrong, they must first be right'.) The latter group are not 'switching their responses' in this way, and are therefore astonished when they discover their level of accuracy. Interestingly, when the former group are informed of their give-away below-chance performance, they realise that they have overdone it, and their performance rapidly improves, so that it becomes closer to the genuinely random level! Neither group, however, as far as the experimenters could tell, seemed to comprise individuals who were consciously faking or malingering: all the manipulation of their experience seemed to be going on behind their own backs.[30]

While we can only guess why such dramatic self-protective manoeuvres might arise in the course of real life, the fact that the brain can indeed perform such feats is demonstrated through modern studies of hypnosis, in which parallel states of blindness, deafness and analgesia have been reliably produced. In a hyper-relaxed and trusting mood, a susceptible person is open to suggestions that can directly alter the pattern of selective inhibition that the frontal lobes are producing, thus dampening the conscious perception of vision, hearing and even pain.[31] As with the spontaneous hysterics, however, it seems clear that it is only consciousness that is being manipulated, and that unconscious perception continues undiminished.

In the 'hidden observer' effect, for instance, a person might be asked to keep one hand in a bucket of iced water for several minutes, a procedure that most people find rapidly to be quite uncomfortable. A successfully hypnotised person, however, will cheerfully leave her hand in the bucket as long as you like, and inform you – honestly, as far as you can tell – that she feels fine. However, if you probe her experience more indirectly you get a different story. Give the other hand a pen and a piece of paper, and simply ask the volunteer to write automatically without thinking, and the tell-tale hand will soon start inscribing things like 'Ouch! It hurts!' Psychological indicators such as skin conductivity also reveal heightened arousal, more commensurate with pain than with the professed relaxation.[32]

When consciousness is expurgated not so much of physical but of psychological or emotional pain, we talk of *repression*, and it should be obvious by now that finding a brain-based account of repression – and of the psychological trouble that repression can cause – is not, in principle, too difficult. The brain is full of back-projections, which allow downstream activity to influence the activity of its upstream neighbours (as well as *vice versa*). These connections enable the brain, in effect, to ' 'know' (not of course consciously) where activity in one cluster of neurons is likely to lead – and if the downstream destination is associated with the production of actions or experiences that, for one reason or another, are considered to be aversive, then inhibitory roadblocks can be set up which prevent the flow of activity from heading in that direction.[33]

The most effective inhibitory strategy simply switches the points, and diverts an unfolding train of thought onto a less threatening line, thereby replacing the dangerous possibility with an anodyne conscious substitute. Just as in perception the beam of conscious attention can be narrowed or swivelled away from unpleasant experiences, so similar manoeuvres can take place in the heart of the brain itself. One becomes self-distracting, and, by creating a diversion, the fact of repression is itself concealed. You avoid, and you avoid noticing *that* you have avoided. Thus, for example, people who are habitual (and therefore presumably expert) repressors are quicker to retrieve a happy memory after they have watched an upsetting film than people who have not practised switching the points so assiduously.[34]

Less successful are the inhibitory barriers that simply arrest the flow of neural activity, without opening up an alternative channel: less successful because in the ensuing moment when 'your mind goes blank', the blockage draws attention to itself – and therefore hints at the existence of the very danger from which you are trying to distract yourself.[35]

It is exactly these tell-tale hints that the psychoanalyst is trying to garner when she invites her patient to play 'free association', and 'say whatever comes into your head'. In the consulting room, the 'patient' (the medicalising, disempowering word that analysts still prefer for their clients) is deprived of the usual array of surrogate goals and interests with which he keeps himself busy, and therefore distracted – except, of course, the goal of 'understanding himself' and 'getting better' (which in itself may have been sufficient to keep him busily digging in the wrong place). But if he is willing to drop even this for a while, and play along with the therapist's suggestion, a very different network of desires and associations may become disinhibited – and set up currents that begin to draw the stream of consciousness towards the rocks. At some point, an inhibitory dam has hastily to be thrown up to check this dangerous drift – and the patient finds himself blocked. Ah ha, says the analyst, just as did Freud and Jung: what have we here? It is not so much the telling association, as the place where associating stops, that is of interest.[36]

The classical Freudian use of individual words, delivered apparently at random, as the triggers may, perhaps, heighten the need for such panicky measures, as there is no evolving context that the brain can use to predict what might be coming next. It can be caught napping, and more nakedly uninhibited. The chances are increased that either a forbidden association will be blurted out, or that the brain will deploy massive inhibition and freeze – in both cases, giving the game away, and pointing towards the unconscious seat of the problem.

If the patient's reflex resistance – i.e. his tendency to start throwing up ever more desperate prevarications and diversions – can be softened (and here the soothing presence, and even the hypnotic voice, of the analyst comes in handy), then the dammed ('damned'?) activity may build up, and begin to leak through. And if a functional, energetic connection can be made with whatever fearful, dissociated memory or desire has been hidden, it may finally be reunited with the core pattern underlying consciousness – and the buried 'memory', or the shameful desire, resurfaces. In this way, we can begin to give a brain-based account of the basic storyboard of classical psychoanalysis.

It is perfectly possible, as Pierre Janet argued, that the

disconnected centres of identity and activity in the brain can be outside consciousness, but still active. The fact that they are being prevented from linking arms with the throng of neurons that are underpinning current conscious experience does not stop them dancing in the darker corners of the brain. They are still capable of putting their motivational spin on the workings of the brain, and thus influencing the course of cortical events, even though they themselves are prevented from surfacing into consciousness. And thus they can have real impact on our involuntary actions, on the feeling states – the 'states of emergency' – to which we are prone, and on the trains of thought that rise unbidden into conscious awareness. Inhibition, in other words, is capable of editing and distorting how unconscious brain activity gives rise to consciousness, without necessarily dampening or damming the flow of activation in the brain itself. Excitation and inhibition do not just cancel each other out, like adding '+4' and '−4' and getting zero.[37]

To go back to my original analogy, they function like accelerator and brake in a car. Both can be 'full on' at the same time, and when they are, the resultant strain may risk shaking the vehicle to pieces. That, presumably, is why repression is not, after all, an entirely benign method of self-protection. Habitual repressors, people who exert high degrees of inhibitory control over their conscious experience, show exaggerated physical responses to alarming events, and are more likely to suffer from a variety of physical complaints, including hypertension and cancer. Having surveyed the literature for the prestigious *Psychological Bulletin*, Drew Westen concludes that 'inhibiting conscious access to one's emotions places the body, particularly the heart and the immune system, under considerable stress', and he notes, mordantly: 'Freud may be dead, but his theories are proving increasingly useful in predicting who will be joining him sooner rather than later.'[38] And there are social and behavioural costs of repression too. Because inhibition does not switch off the activation of troublesome areas of the brain, or the 'magnetic fields' of unconscious desire that keep drawing activation towards them, it sets up counter-fields, and thus creates complex cross-currents in the brain that may lead to unpredictable and unstable resolutions. When I am stressed, I am at my most dangerous, for one minute I am nice as pie, and the next a hurtful critic, and you may have no way of predicting when I am going to flip, and thus of protecting yourself from my waspishness.

It is worth noting that Freud himself, early in his career, devoted a good deal of energy to trying to work out a neurological underpinning for his developing approach to neurosis, and especially to repression. 'I am so deep in the "Psychology for Neurologists",' he wrote to his friend Wilhelm Fleiss on 27 April 1895, 'that it quite consumes me . . . Will anything come of it? I hope so, but the going is hard and slow.' Six months later, Fleiss received the first 100 handwritten pages of the manuscript that laid out what Freud's translator, James Strachey, would later call 'an extraordinarily ingenious working model of the mind as a piece of neurological machinery'. Freud himself was pretty pleased with it. A month before he sent his pages to Fleiss, he wrote: 'One strenuous night last week . . . everything fell into place, the cogs meshed, and the thing really seemed to be a machine which in a moment would run of itself . . . I don't know how to contain myself for pleasure.' Yet, only weeks after he had dispatched the manuscript, he wrote to Fleiss again, saying: 'I cannot conceive how I came to inflict it on you . . . it seems to me to have been a kind of aberration.' And indeed he rapidly lost heart and abandoned his 'Project'. He never reclaimed his notebooks from Fleiss; it was only after the latter's death in 1950 that they came to light.[39]

Freud was disappointed by the lack of enthusiasm that Fleiss and others showed for his neurological theorising, and he also found himself hamstrung both by the lack of physiological knowledge on which to draw, and also by some unrecognised misconceptions of his own. Most basic, perhaps, was his lifelong attachment to a misguided metaphor: he continually likened the mind to an optical instrument such as a compound microscope or a camera, with a series of dissociable components arranged in series. This led him to make a fundamental distinction between the 'perceptual system' at one end, the 'motor system' at the other, and the 'memory system' in between. So perception was the 'lens', for example, while memory was the photosensitive film or plate. Freud thought that they had to be kept separate like this.

We now know, however, as we saw in chapter 8, that the brain is not organised like that, and that perception, motivation, memory and action are tightly interwoven. Freud made a series of ingenious attempts to overcome the problems that were inherent in his own choice of metaphor, but eventually confessed himself stumped, and gave up. 'The mechanical explanation [for repression] is not coming off,' he wrote at the end of 1895, 'and I am inclined to listen to the still, small voice which tells me that my explanation will not do.' Thus, though Freud himself saw repression as the absolute cornerstone of psychoanalysis, he was unable to explain how it worked to his own satisfaction, and he constantly reverted, in his later writings, to the anthropomorphic metaphor of the 'censor' to 'explain' repression, which, of course, was no explanation at all.[40]

Yet in some ways, he was not so far off the mark. Freud was right in suggesting that the brain works as a network of neurons, joined by synaptic connections. He saw that each synapse had a certain threshold, below which incoming activation would not 'jump' the barrier to the next neuron, and he proposed, as many people do today, that activation would be distributed according to the resistance or 'weight' of the barrier. He suggested however that the resistance of a barrier could be raised or lowered ('primed' or 'inhibited') by another input, which he called a 'side-cathexis'. The 'ego', neurally represented, was just such a side-cathexis, capable of raising neuronal thresholds – and therefore preventing an impulse travelling in the direction of what he called 'unpleasure'.

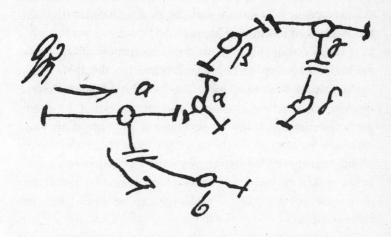

Freud's 1895 sketch of how the 'ego' could work in neural terms.

So, in Freud's sketch, you are invited to imagine that some activation arriving at *a* would, all other things being equal, travel across the easier junction towards *b*. However, *b* in this case represents an unpleasant memory, so the ego, represented by α, β, γ and δ, comes to the rescue by sending a wave of inhibition towards *a* which prevents it from discharging. Or, translated back into Freudian, 'It is easy to imagine how, with the help of a mechanism which draws the ego's attention to the imminent fresh cathexis of the hostile mnemic image [that's *b*], the ego can succeed in inhibiting . . . a release of unpleasure by a copious side-cathexis which can be strengthened according to need.' The major problem for Freud – the one on which the project foundered, was that, in 1895, he had no way of explaining how the ego's attention could be drawn to anything, without crediting the ego with quasi-human powers of perception. He did not know that a century later, the discovery of the vast amount of feedback, as well as feed-forward, in the nervous system, would give him the mechanism he needed. Because of this, a is able, quite mechanically, to anticipate that its outflow is likely to head towards b, and initiate the inhibition required to stop that happening.[41]

If Freud was unable to explain the mechanism of repression, neither could he explain how people learned to 'do' it. He had to assume that we are born with a rudimentary suite of defence mechanisms – a kind of innate 'primary repression' for example – presumably ready to be engaged as soon as they are necessary. Yet once we see that repression does not involve a complicated process of consigning memories and desires to a special prison within the mind, and hiring guards to make sure that they do not escape, the problem of how it can be learned becomes more tractable.

Repression reflects the deployment of inhibition within the circuitry of the brain, and we know that children are busy learning how to do that in a whole variety of ways, as they grow towards adolescence. 'Delayed gratification', for example, requires such inhibitory control, and four-year-old children have mastered it in different ways and to differing extents. In the famous 'marshmallow test', a child is left alone with a marshmallow on a plate, and is told that if the sweet is still there when the adult returns, she can have two – but if it has gone, that's it. Some four-year-olds clearly know 'how not to think about the sweet': they sing, turn their backs, converse with an imaginary friend, appoint a toy to 'guard' the marshmallow, and so on. Others have not yet developed these strategies of inattention, and they are much more at the mercy of their own impulses. As Richard Webster comments, we often underestimate the amount of effort that goes in to training children to develop skills of attending 'against the grain' of their own immediate impulses. 'It is only by learning to control a whole variety of interests, appetites, fantasies, desires, and temptations and to banish these temporarily from our awareness that it is possible to develop the intelligent, clear and rational frame of mind which is idealised within our culture.'[42]

From this point of view, childhood is, to a significant extent, an apprenticeship in learning what and how to notice, and what and how not to. Partly these habits are learned through the activities that children are given, and through the praise and encouragement that are meted out when they notice, or not, in approved ways. But they are also picked up through observing what the grown-ups do. Children are inveterate eavesdroppers and voyeurs, and they are built to imitate more successfully and more enthusiastically even than parrots or chimpanzees. Recent research has demonstrated (as if we needed to be told) the extent to which their brains are predisposed to copy what those around them are up to.[43]

And from infancy onward, one of the most important things that children are learning to imitate is what adults are attending to and talking about, and what they are not. Some noteworthy things are reliably commented upon: a ring at the door; a favourite TV programme, the preparation of food, bath-time rituals, and so on. But other things, that might have been the subject of conversation, slide by without being remarked upon, or are reliably associated with deliberate changing of the subject. If, by mistake, my parents found themselves watching a television programme of which they disapproved, the nature of their aversion, or the basis for it, was never discussed. All that happened was that one of them would 'casually' say to the other 'Is there anything else on?', or 'I think that can go off now, dear', perhaps followed by a suggestion that a cup of tea might be nice. Though in this case their discomfort with sex (for that's what it usually was, of course) did not rub off too badly on me, I am sure that I remain unaware of dozens of ways in which, for good or ill, their attentional habits have moulded my own.

With the aid of subliminal perception, and the brain's developing ability to anticipate its own states, I am now able to push things aside even before they have become conscious, so that I am unconscious of what it was that I have just avoided, and unconscious indeed that I have avoided anything. My world looks complete and seamless to me – I see no jagged edges where threatening paragraphs have been torn out. Just as an animal naturally senses what might be significant, and rejects the rest – my cat does not notice what is on the television unless it becomes too loud and disturbs his sleep – so children learn to carve a world of significance out of the infinite range of possibilities with which they are presented, and thus to create an anti-world of all the things that are to remain invisible. They are taught, in other words, what and how to repress. They learn the trick by watching their elders, just as they learn their accents and gestures.[44]

Early learning also helps to explain another concept that psychoanalysis tends to mystify: transference, the tendency for adults to look at people, especially the important people in their lives, through the lenses that were formed by their most significant childhood interactions. Susan Andersen and her colleagues at New York University have shown how children build up templates of their significant others in their brains, and then, if these are triggered, even subliminally, years later, will tend, as adults, to unconsciously apply the whole package to a new person.

For example, in one study, participants first generated a list of the most salient attributes of 'someone who has been very important to you for many years' – 'insightful', 'funny', 'self-critical', and so on. They then played a computer game against someone in another room who they had no contact with except through their electronic 'moves'. At the end, they were asked to give their impressions of their invisible adversary.

Immediately before the game some of the participants were given a subliminal flash of one of the key descriptors of their longtime 'significant other' – 'insightful', for instance. Sure enough, the results showed that those who had had the flash were likely not only to rate their playmate as more 'insightful', but as 'self-critical' and 'funny' as well. Andersen suggest that we have here another straightforward example of activation spreading between well-connected, very 'available' sub-networks within the brain. Once the important prototype is primed by the subliminal cue, the template as a whole becomes active, and collaterally suppresses other trait-descriptions that might be equally applicable.[45]

There is obviously a great deal more that needs to be explored about the relationship between human psychopathology and the brain. However, I think I have done enough in this chapter to show how far one can get with a relatively few, rather powerful, neurological concepts. In particular, the fact that the frontal lobes of the brain develop, across the childhood years, into sophisticated, selective, lightning-fast inhibitors of activity in other cortical areas – perceptual, emotional, motivational and behavioural – is well established. The inhibitory control of each of these areas of action and experience is capable of breaking down in a variety of ways, leading to a wide range of bizarre, upsetting and dysfunctional consequences, many of which have previously needed the invention of some mysterious mental place or interior agent to make sense of them. The emphasis in this chapter has deliberately been on the 'negative oddities': experiences that most people would rather be without. It is high time we turned to more positive matters.

10

The Sublime and the Subliminal

To those whose lives are devoted to getting into the unconscious mind, either to find out why they have problems or to find some transcendent truth, I say you will be looking for a long, long time. You might better spend your time reading a book on memory or neuroscience.

– *The Skeptic's Dictionary*[1]

The oddities of experience come in inspiring as well as distressing forms. Throughout history, people have been at least as interested in thinking about the wise, positive and productive mysteries of their experience, as the dark and perverse ones. Is it possible that they too can be seen as unusual products of the normal brain? Perhaps we can put the mad delusions of the schizophrenic down to a change in the neurochemical soup – but surely the visions of Hildegard of Bingen, or the felt profundity of archetypal dreams, require us to go beyond the machinations of the spongy meat between our ears? Well, let us see.

To begin with, we might ask how it is that the brain manages to be symbolic as well as literal. For many years, cognitive scientists – people who were used, in their professional lives, to stringing clear propositions together into logical arguments – assumed that that was how the brain worked too. The basic 'code' of the brain was like a language, and it 'thought' by linking clear statements together in logical ways. This view was largely inspired by the predominant but profoundly mistaken assumption that the mind (and therefore presumably the brain), was structured like a digital machine The brain was our on-board, 'neck-top' computer.

There were two problems with the computer metaphor, however. The first was that it was based on the Cartesian model of human reason, and therefore was very ill-equipped, right from the start, to offer any account of non-rational phenomena. So for a long time such experiences were just ignored. As the computer scientist (and one-time victim of the Unabomber) David Gelernter has said: 'The computer is the Procrustean bed of modern thought science. Aspects of human thought that don't fit are . . . lopped off. Thought science has been bent out of shape by the force field of computation . . . [But a] thought theory that never comes to grips with intuition, hallucination, spirituality or dreaming cannot possibly be a serious account of cognition.'[2]

And the second problem, put crudely, is that nobody ever found a syllogism in the temporal lobe, or a CPU in the prefrontal cortex. Even the parts of the brain that *are* specialised for language turn out to have been originally designed to control non-verbal forms of action and perception. A brain that is fundamentally designed to sense and act and survive can, given a bit of help, master the intricacies of human language and rational thought, but these are secondary, not primary.[3]

With its sophisticated powers of excitation and inhibition the brain can *emulate* a computer. It can do this in a number of ways:

- By restraining the on-line influence of its goals and concerns, the brain can think in a way that is more detached from immediate purposes.
- By restricting the lateral 'spread' of activation round a conceptual epicentre, I can operate on the basis of prototypes, and functionally discard all the variegated detail

that fleshes out the conceptual skeleton, and turns it back
into a real instance. I can spin arguments about 'the brain',
as I am doing now, without having to worry about the messy
reality.

- By activating my brain-model of 'you', and dampening my
own for a while, I can change the neural default settings of
perspectives and priorities, so that my trains of thought run
in different directions. I can 'put myself in your shoes', and
see different sides of the argument.

- And also by the judicious deployment of inhibition, I can
restrict the number of concepts and habit-tendencies that are
simultaneously active, and thus follow a more tightly
structured train of thought in a linear fashion.

It is, I suspect, largely education that cultivates these neural
knacks. Through a concerted and protracted programme of coaching, teaching and modelling, many youngsters' brains master the
trick of linear, focused reason.

But the fact that the educated brain can learn to set itself into
this useful mode does not mean that rational thought is its only, or
even its most important, modus operandi. As we saw in our brief
discussion of creativity, the ability to relax some of these neural
constraints – to *stop* doing the inhibitory trick – is essential if
fresh patterns, links and ideas are to be discovered. The mature
brain learns more by finding new connections between what it
already knows than by the earnest acquisition of new information,
and to do that, you need reverie just as much as you need reason.
If it is to be as smart as can be, the brain must remember how to
let itself paint with watercolours on wet paper, and let ideas bleed
into each other, as well as learn how to draw neat diagrams with a
sharp pen. On the old view, if the brain was fundamentally a
rational machine, it was hard to explain how and why it so often
seemed to operate in ways that were very different, and which the
rational view was forced to view as inferior: intuitive, poetic and

symbolic. But now we are freed of this restrictive intellectual perspective, and equipped with some general understanding of how very different the organic brain is from a silicon-based laptop. And we can think freshly about the nature and function of symbolism.

In chapter 7, I argued that the break between conscious and unconscious is not sharp. There may be a bright pinnacle to the mind's activity, but there is always a shading-off, around that peak, of activated assumptions, details and associations that comprise the margins, or the groundswell, of consciousness. And below that there is a wider set of connotations and concerns that are not conscious in themselves, but whose subliminal activity colours and nuances what and how we are seeing or thinking. The more I reduce the inhibitory ring that surrounds, corrals and defines the central core of conscious perception and thought, the wider and richer this half-seen penumbra can become. Instead of activation rushing down the inviting, narrow canyon of what seems logical or relevant, it can pool and spread, lighting up, even if only dimly, a background glow of memories, feelings and resonances.

That is what a symbol does. It is an idea or an image that begs to be experienced in terms of its associated tissue of partly personal and partly universal, partly semi- and partly sub-conscious, associations. It wants you to impregnate it with meaning, much of which is not going to surface itself into consciousness. It is the essence of a symbol, as of all art, that it can move you, and you can't say why. If you could, its numinous aura would disappear. As the cognitive scientist and expert on Jewish mysticism Brian Lancaster says, summarising the research, 'the picture of the mind which emerges . . . is of a preconscious realm characterised by multiplicity of meaning and intent, preceding the entry into consciousness of unitary concepts.'[4]

It is the essence of poetry that its juxtaposition of words simultaneously blocks a simple, literal reading, and invites their tacit ripples to interweave and interfere in interesting and affecting ways. As one poet to another, Adrian Mitchell wrote this little poem, 'Not Cricket', as an appreciation of the craft of Ted Hughes:

> Ted backsomersaulted to catch the meteorite lefthanded,
> Rubbed it thoughtfully on the green groin of his flannels
> And span it through the ribcage of the Reaper,
> Whose bails caught fire
> And jumped around the pitch like fire-crackers.
> Said the commentator:
> Yes Fred, it might have been a meteor –
> Could have been a metaphor.[5]

The cosy world of English cricket, the remote and massive power of the heavenly bodies, the unpredictable, disconcerting behaviour of fireworks, and the impressive, acrobatic skill of the poet, with a sideswipe at death and immortality: in the poet's hands, these incommensurable domains collide in a way that ordinary sense cannot possibly comprehend. Yet, if you are available, the multiple metaphorical pile-up captures your attention and slows you down, and then some unexpected moiré pattern, like spilled petrol on the road, composed of affection and respect, playfulness and insight, exuberance and death-defiance, begins to seep around the edges of your consciousness.

Interestingly, Hughes's own working method mimicked my metaphor for the working of the brain. He would place the germ of an idea for a poem in a circle in the centre of a blank page, and then scribble any other ideas or images that would surface in his own mind, like fish rising to take the bait, around it, sometimes allowing them to become the epicentres for their own activity, until he had fished his own mind to his satisfaction, and he had his raw material. In a talk on children's radio once, he said that we have to learn the subtle art of such mental fishing, or 'our minds lie in us like fish in the pond of a man who cannot fish'.[6] Later, when the celebrated theatre director Peter Brook, with whom Hughes was collaborating, asked him how he found his material, he replied: 'I listen to the patterns that arise in the deep level of the brain, when impulses become sounds and syllables – and before they shape themselves into recognisable words.'[7]

The mesh of associations that underpin a conscious symbol is deep as well as broad. In a good metaphor, two different domains of experience are juxtaposed in a way that further discloses the nature of one of them, or even both. Together they create a harmony that enriches the melody of each. But in art, when it moves as well as illuminates us, the symbolic tension created throbs with deeper notes as well. The archetypal bass-notes of the mind become part of the resonance. Can we locate these Romantic depths, too, in the brain?

A human being is a tangle of basic biological needs *and* acquired desires; of basic sensibilities *and* their parasitic skills of attention and perception; and of basic reflexes *and* their socialised development into complex portfolios of capability. What we become, as we grow up, is the inextricable resultant of what is carried in our genes, *and* what experience we have been exposed to. Just as any physical landscape reflects the gradual erosion of particular types of rock, that shear and crumble in particular ways, by particular types of geological and meteorological activity that exert different types of force, so the human mind is the resultant of genetics and experience. Human bodies are programmed to grow four limbs, not eight, and to develop muscles that can, with training, jump two metres into the air, but not, with any amount of training, ten. And so, we must suppose, the developing mind, too, reflects an evolutionary bedrock of 'survival themes', as well as the influence of the local cultural weather to which that bedrock has been subjected.

Evolution is a slow and invisible process, so firm decisions about what is inherent in the genetic substrate, and what comes with the weather, are hard to make, and always contested. There is wide agreement at last that trying to make firm distinctions between nature and nurture is a waste of time. However, it is not fanciful at all to suppose that the interaction of our genetic preconfiguring, and the ubiquitous experience-base of human babies, leaves us all with a largely universal set of fundamental survival 'issues' – on which the idiosyncrasies of particular cultures and families will be overlaid.[8]

Back in Chapter 8, we took a quick look at some of the basic emotional themes that constitute the genetic bedrock of the human psyche. Basic experiences of *hunger* and *thirst, cold* and *heat*, physical *confinement* and *hardship* signal survival threats, and trigger corresponding instincts and reactions. So do *pain, injury* and *illness*, leading to the licking of wounds and the vomiting up of toxins, accompanied by the rudiments of emotions such as '*sadness*' or '*disgust*'. Being threatened by an escapable enemy triggers '*flight* and *fear*', and by a beatable enemy '*attack* and *anger*'. And because *Homo sapiens* has, to a unique extent, bet its evolutionary life on the survival strategy of learning and knowing – since *ignorance* is dangerous and adaptation is smart – the presence of non-lethal strangeness triggers 'approach and investigate', with accompanying feelings of *interest, excitement* and *fascination*. When the brain cannot decide which one of these basic modes is appropriate, in the face of a threat that can't be immediately diagnosed and clearly categorised, we hover between approach and avoidance, close down all other systems, and attend very, very carefully. The emotional tone of this mode we might call '*anxiety*'.[9]

We also, way back in evolutionary history, decided to go with the survival strategy of sociability – not just the 'safety in numbers' approach of a herd of wildebeest, but the development of an expanding social network of reciprocal roles, relationships and responsibilities. Members of an ordered society enjoy the benefits of many survival buffers that the singleton – the 'lone ranger' – does not. But club membership comes at a price: the need to accept a place in the social structure (that may not be your ideal), and to be willing to carry out communal duties of foraging, defence and childcare, for example.

Private advantage is always at risk of clashing with these public duties, and the long-term benefits of membership may be swamped by the irresistible lure of short-term opportunities. In social living, the moment-to-moment motivational vector (under-lying the continual question 'What shall I do for the best?') becomes an order of magnitude harder for the brain to compute, and thus a host of new ways of 'getting it wrong' are born. There is always the risk

- that somebody's nurturing might give way to *indifference*;
- that care may be withdrawn and be replaced by *abandonment*;
- that social acceptance might be replaced by *rejection*;
- that trust (the vital glue of society) may crumble, leaving an atmosphere of *suspicion* or even *betrayal*;
- that status and respect might go, leaving public *shame* or *humiliation*;
- that support unreciprocated, or trust betrayed, might turn into *disdain* or *revenge*;
- that the withdrawal of protection might leave one *outlawed* and *exposed*, again, to the more primitive threats of *privation* or *predation* from which society has been protecting you.

All of these become lurking possibilities; part of the expanded repertoire of threats that is the price that must be paid for the advantages of social living. These misfortunes are entailed by civilisation. Being trodden on is the downside risk of being an ant; and being ashamed is the downside risk of being a human being.

Every dark threat brings with it a silver lining, of course. It comes bundled with an image of a person who protects, rescues or forgives you. There is

- the person who sees clearly the way to go when you are confused and anxious;
- the person whose greater strength or experience helps you beat off your enemies;
- the person who loves and accepts you when everyone else thinks you despicable;
- the person who takes you in and feeds and heals you;
- the person who believes you, and believes *in* you, when nobody else does.

And each new threat thus conjures into existence a new *positive feeling*, a new version of happiness, that corresponds to the relief of being rescued, protected or valued. The possibility of a host of rebound emotions opens up, of feeling safe, secure, satiated, comfortable, triumphant, powerful, knowledgeable, accepted, loved, proud or just simply well.

We can debate the details of this picture, but what I have presented, at high speed, is a sketch of an *archetypal world* that is built in to the basic architecture of the human brain. It is, as you will have anticipated, the world of myths, legends and fairy tales. It is the world of wicked witches and wise old wizards; of trolls and gremlins; or fairy godmothers and reckless princes; of highwaymen and heroes; of banishment, injustice and treason. These figures and their associated plots personify and dramatise the risks and dilemmas that every child is heir to, and which never quite go away. These themes can be overlaid, repressed or simply forgotten. We can fill our waking lives with dozens of surrogate projects that distract us from the primordial, ancestral dramas that are built into our brains, and into the ways they function. But they remain, deep swells and currents within the complex ocean of the brain's activity, always ready to nuance and inform what is going on on the surface.

This view of the archetypal world, with its dramatis personae, its symbols and its basic plot structure, is very close to the one that Carl Jung himself held, at least in the earlier part of his career. He insisted, for example, that the term 'archetype' was meant to denote 'an inherited mode of functioning, corresponding to the inborn way in which the chick emerges from the egg, the bird builds its nest, a certain kind of wasp stings the motor ganglion of the caterpillar, and eels find their way to the Bermudas. In other words, it is a pattern of behaviour.'[10]

Jung's view of the mind was much influenced by a dream he had in 1909, when he was sailing across the Atlantic, with Freud, on his first trip to America. The dream furnished him with an image, not of the ocean, but of a house with a series of ever-deeper cellars, in the lowest of which 'were scattered bones [including two human skulls] and broken pottery like the remains of a primitive culture'. While Freud tried to persuade his friend that the skulls symbolised an unconscious death wish against two of Jung's acquaintances, Jung held to a very different interpretation. The upper story symbolised consciousness, while

> The ground floor stood for the first level of the unconscious.
> The deeper I went, the more alien and the darker the scene
> became. In the cave, I discovered . . . the world of the primitive
> man within myself – a world which can scarcely be reached or
> illuminated by consciousness. The primitive psyche of man
> borders on the life of the animal soul, just as the caves of
> prehistoric times were usually inhabited by animals before men
> laid claim to them.[11]

It is noteworthy that Jung's evolutionary image of the 'collective unconscious' came to him in a dream, for it is in dreams themselves that these ancestral themes make themselves known most vividly to us. And we are beginning to get an idea of how and why the brain sleeps, and, some of the time, turns its sleeping activity into dreams.

There are umpteen theories of why we sleep, and a good deal of time has been wasted trying to decide which of them is 'right' (to the exclusion of the rest). The truth is, most of them have a degree of validity, and there is no reason why the sleeping brain should not serve a range of functions, just as the waking brain does. Sleep is clearly restorative, for example: reserves of hormones, such as the vital pituitary growth hormone, as well as cortisol and testosterone, get replenished during sleep. Skin repairs itself faster during sleep. Muscles are allowed to rest, waste products are discharged, energy is conserved, and sleeping animals, especially small and tasty ones, draw less attention to themselves in the dark, when they might otherwise be at risk.[12]

But the brain is also attending to its own organisation during sleep, especially during the phase known as 'rapid eye movement' or REM sleep, when the most interesting and well-developed dreams tend to occur.[13] Francis Crick amongst others has suggested that during REM sleep, the accumulated memory traces of the day are being sorted out, with some of them being erased and others reactivated, consolidated and integrated more coherently into the general-purpose memory store. The neurochemical balance of the brain changes, in REM sleep, in such a way that the aminergic systems, which are involved in acquiring information, are damped down, and cholinergic systems take over, working the temporary 'hot spots' of activity left over from the day into more long-lasting structural changes.

At the same time, a kind of neurochemical backwash weakens those residues of the day that turn out not to have any new information or functional significance. The philosopher Owen Flanagan suggests that the first, consolidation, process is like pressing Restore and Save on your computer, while the latter corresponds to Delete and Trash. Certainly, both these operations make sense, and there are plausible neural mechanisms that could underwrite them. The structure called the hippocampus, for example, is thought to be behind the Restore function, being able to reinstate the rather haphazard, hastily scribbled records of the day so that they can be sorted, edited and filed more permanently (like a diligent student copying up her lecture notes).[14]

REM sleep may also be involved in refining the power and precision of our perceptual systems. Babies have a much higher proportion of REM sleep than adults, and there is a great deal of activity going on, during REM sleep, in their visual cortex. It looks as if all this nightly activity is helping to fine-tune the wiring that underlies their sensory perception. In support of this is Geoffrey Hinton's surprising discovery that even artificial brains – computer simulations of neural networks – learn to recognise things faster and more accurately if they are allowed periods of 'dreaming' or 'fantasising' interspersed with their training. When they are 'awake', the sensory input to these networks is cumulatively altering the strengths with which the neurons are wired up, just as is happening in real brains. But when they are 'dreaming', they are, in effect, seeing how good they are at recreating what it was that they have previously been shown. How well does what they have *recorded* enable them to piece together the world as it was *experienced*? This practice at reinstating earlier perceptions allows the network to compare what it has learned with what it has been taught, and thus to correct its own performance, and this is obviously very helpful in developing its powers of discrimination.[15]

It may well be that these two functions of REM sleep, sharpening memory and perception, are both connected with the brain's underlying concern with its archetypal dangers and plots. To see how this might be so, we should note another couple of research findings about REM sleep and dreaming, First, the 'hot spot' records of the day that tend to get reactivated and consolidated at night are those which had some emotional significance or 'charge' attached to them – but where that significance was not acknowledged or explored at the time, so that, if you like, the charge was not *dis*-charged. Perhaps there was too much else going on, or perhaps the perception was quickly judged to be too threatening or difficult to attend to on the spot. Either way, the normal habits of waking attention could have produced an immediate wave of inhibition that stopped those circuits from resonating with others, and thus from gaining access to consciousness. Reactivating them 'off-line', later that night, when there is more time, less competition from competing priorities, and less inhibition generally in the brain, could enable activation to spread around them, and thus, in effect, to release what Freud would have called the temporarily 'cathected' activation that had got caught in the inhibitory ring, like fish in a net.

During sleep, although the brain remains very active, the frontal lobes are quieter than during waking, and thus all kinds of daily inhibitions are relaxed, and a greater variety of brain activities can emerge as candidates for entry into consciousness.[16] The externally driven model of the perceptual world is switched off, and can be replaced by fantasy. (We might note, at this point, that many of the recent 'insights' into sleep and dreaming, now cloaked in brain language, have been known for some time. To give just one example, the Persian sage Ibn Khaldûn wrote in *The Muqaddimah* in 1377: 'When the spirit withdraws from the external senses during sleep, it can activate forms of memory which can then become clothed by the imagination in the form of sensory images.'[17]

The daytime attenuation of fantasy, which differentiates it from 'real perception', is also removed, allowing fantasy to have the same degree of vividness and richness as perception – so dreams seem 'real'. The need to string moments of consciousness together in ways that preserve an overall sense of coherence, and of an unfolding narrative, is also somewhat reduced, allowing dreams to take their characteristic swerves and jumps. (Imagine a game of 'Consequences' in which a group of people are writing a story by the curious method of each person adding one word and then passing it on – but each contributor, as they select their word, can only see the immediately preceding four words. They could easily produce something, when it was finished, and the whole 'story' revealed, that looked rather like a dream.)[18]

The second research finding that we need to introduce at this point is the frequency with which dreams do in fact incorporate themes, and especially emotions, that are primordial or archetypal, in the biological sense.[19] In the most common dreams, people fall, are chased by wild animals, fail exams, appear naked in public, encounter loved ones who have passed away, and experience helplessness or failure as they battle against obscure forces to get to a meeting or catch a plane. These recurrent motifs involve the archetypal emotions – fear, shame, dependency and so on – that are often held in check during the day, for fear of genuine criticism. In dreams, however, there are no real others observing you, ready to judge or capitalise on your emotional reactions, so they can be disinhibited and 'felt' with an intensity that was earlier suppressed. Dreams touch all the archetypal emotional bases that I outlined above. The most prevalent emotion is anxiety, followed by anger, sadness, confusion and shame. Only 20 per cent of all dreams have a positive emotional tone.[20]

Dreams seem to pick up on, and rework, daily experiences that are both personal and emotionally charged. People tend not to dream about films they have just watched, however emotionally charged the action may have been. But neither do they dream about daily experiences that lack 'charge'. Many common daily activities, such as reading the paper or sending emails, rarely reappear as the raw material of dreams. So although fragmentary experiences of the previous day do undoubtedly resurface in dreams, they tend to be those details that could do with further emotional/motivational processing, as we saw above.

Another kind of disinhibition is also at work in dreams: the relaxation of the complex, corralling agenda of goals and purposes by which our days are structured, and which keeps our waking activity 'on track' and 'in the groove'. When this rigid neural

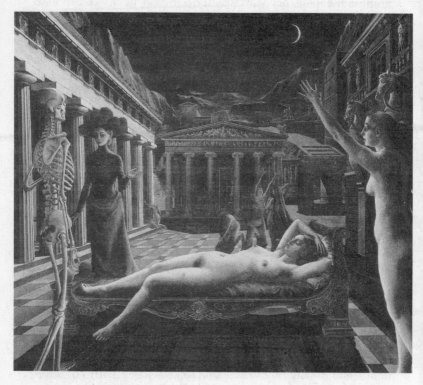

Sleeping Venus *by Paul Delvaux, 1944 (painted in Brussels during the Second World War). Delvaux shows how Venus, the beautiful, lovable, innocent girl, reworks the anguish of the daytime bombings into the night-time archetypes of her dreams.*

contouring is relaxed, not only do a greater, less tidy, range of ideas intermingle in the mind, but also they tend to get organised and 'lined up', not by the mundane cares of the day, but by the disinhibited magnetic fields of our deeper, archetypal desires and concerns. While the day has centred around the conscious desire for promotion, or the possibility of a sexual liaison, the dream may give vent to the fears of loneliness, guilt or betrayal that constitute the unacknowledged shadows of ambition or lust. Yet it does so indirectly, by adding symbolic emotional charge to objects, people or events that may lend themselves to it. Elements are co-opted into the dream that in some way can be given a supporting role in an archetypal drama. They reappear not as themselves, but as actors or ciphers that carry an unexpressed emotion, whether it be of unwarranted kindliness or of unfathomable menace. Thus the mechanism of disinhibition allows us to see how the unaided brain can throw up dreams that are 'wise', in that they remind us of the values and fears that sometimes get eclipsed by the brighter, more urgent lights of business and family life.

If we go back for a moment to Geoffrey Hinton's proposed function of 'dreaming', we can see how such dreams might have evolutionary value independently of any morning-after rumination or consulting-room interpretation. For Hinton, dreaming sharpens learning and perception, but it is the neural activity underlying the dream, and not the conscious experience of the dream itself, that does the functional work. Recall that Hinton's neural networks learn to recognise patterns that have been designated as 'significant' more readily if they are allowed to 'fantasise' them, and compare their fantasies with their perceptions. What could be more significant than patterns that act as signals or harbingers of our archetypal threats and resources? Perhaps what dreams are doing is using the residues of the day as a pretext to sharpen up their ability to recognise possible sources of threat or succour.

As the Finnish psychologist Antti Revonsuo, the originator of a similar approach to mine, sums it up: 'we dream about very severe and rather primitive threats ("ancient concerns") – they reflect the threat-simulation scripts embedded in the dream-production system as default settings, defining the types of threatening events that should be rehearsed most frequently.' And he adds: 'The dreaming brain is not adapted to solve problems such as finding a job, writing a thesis or preventing pollution. Such problems did not exist in the ancestral environment, so they are not the kinds of problems that the dream-production system would recognise, or know how to handle.'[21] Yet, as we know, such scenarios may very well be commandeered by our deeper hopes and fears as vehicles for their nocturnal expression and exploration.

The brain-based approach to dreams that I have outlined does not, of course, require that all dreams are significant. Some may indeed consist of disconnected bits of flotsam resurfacing from the day before. Nor does the idea that dreaming *is* the brain doing useful work prevent us from using the dream as a kind of Rorschach blot or Tarot reading the following morning, and exercising our imaginative and interpretive powers upon it. We may well be able to extract useful insights, in this way, from a dream that itself contains no coherent message or wisdom from the unconscious at all. And if we get stuck, we can even take it to a psychoanalyst, who is an expert at imputing obscure readings to meaningless patterns, and feel that her fee was money well spent.

However, my approach also allows that dreams may indeed be impregnated with reminders of neglected concerns that we would do well to hear and heed. Here, to conclude this discussion of dreams, is a prime example of the kind of dream I have been talk-ing about:

I'm on a car ferry travelling from Ireland to England. I am aware that I am a member of a group of undesirable aliens whom the secret service or army would like to arrest and persecute. I huddle into a position in a corner beside my sister. Suddenly, I notice two official-looking gentlemen, one in some sort of army uniform jumper, and the other in plain clothes, standing near us, although they don't appear to see us. I'm about to leave when a member of our lot signals to me to stay where I am. The signal however is ambiguous and I still move off. My sister stays behind as I head in the direction where some of our group are staying at the head of the boat. I am jumped on by the two officials . . . who grab me about the shoulders and say they have already arrested the people I was heading towards.[22]

The dreamer, Joseph Griffin, is in no doubt that this is an archetypal dream (in my sense), relating it to a visit the previous day by his wife and himself to a drive-through Safari Park. The slow-moving convoy of cars in the park clearly reminded him of recently boarding a car ferry for a trip to Ireland – the obvious basis of the dream analogy between the two events. Driving through the park, the car was surrounded by orang-utans who threatened to damage the car by climbing all over it. Griffin felt that he and his wife were intruders in the orang-utans' world – undesirable aliens, who might well be attacked for their temerity. The convoy stopped for some reason, and Griffin became seriously frightened that the nearest two apes were about to attack the car. He urged his wife (sister) to drive on, but it was unclear whether they should overtake the car in front. And so on. Griffin offers interpretations of several such dreams. But it is quite possible, on the present view, that his 'reading' of the dream is beside the point. The dream may have already done its work of focusing in on the archetypal feeling of being an 'alien', and of exploring the kinds of circumstances under which it might arise, and of the kinds of responses that might – or might not – be effective or appropriate. The analysis is superfluous, or at least supererogatory.

One of the remarkable things about dreams is the extent to which the normal sense of self remains. My feelings are more dramatic, perhaps, than I usually allow, but I am normally in my familiar body, looking at the world from a familiar perspective. I am present as the initiator of bold or bizarre actions; as the experiencer of the acute anxiety when I fail the test or my pants fall down. It is recognisably Me who resides at the centre of the dream world. Not so, however, in the kind of radical transformation of the quality of experiencing that is usually dubbed 'religious' or 'spiritual'. In such moments or periods of 'grace', something changes at the centre. The world looks different not because anything different is happening, but because I am looking at it with different eyes. Can the brain help us here, too, with these most profound of all oddities? While we don't yet have a satisfactory and comprehensive model, there are plenty of promising beginnings and plausible speculations.

I began, you recall, to define the 'self system' in the brain in terms of an acquired tangle of goals and values, and their reciprocal threats and fears. These mark a whole variety of possible events as desirable or even necessary, and a complementary set as undesirable or catastrophic. These goals 'work' by overlaying patterns of priming and inhibition on the 'brainscape' that effectively bend or tilt it so that activity tends to flow in certain directions and not others. Whenever these goals are 'switched on', like an electromagnet, the brain becomes furrowed, and whatever happens is likely to be captured, channelled and interpreted accordingly.

Experience and opportunity are seen in the light of these crisscross motivational forces – we tend to see what is relevant to our desires and fears, and to ignore the rest. Perception is simultaneously depleted, and skewed. Under the influence of our goals, the brain meets the world armed with a predetermined fistful of highlighters and erasers, and this superimposed selectivity affects what we are ready to see, and do, and feel. (As Hermann Hesse wrote in his diary in 1917, 'If I inspect a forest with the intention of buying it, renting it, cutting it down, going hunting in it, or mortgaging it, then I do not see the forest but only its relation to my desires, plans and concerns, to my purse . . . [Likewise] the man whom I look at with dread or hope, with greed, designs or demands, is not a man but a cloudy mirror of my own desire. Whether I am aware of it or not, I regard him in the light of questions that limit and falsify.')[23]

While our *archetypal* reactions are built in to the brain's modus operandi at a deep, structural level, the mass of *acquired* hopes and fears has to be represented in terms of these patterns of priming and inhibition – as do the defences, such as repression, which we looked at in the last chapter. It takes no energy to maintain a background fear of snakes, or disgust at the smell of putrefaction, but it does to maintain and service a fear of wearing the wrong trainers, or a revulsion at 'smut' on the TV.

These desires and aversions draw on the total pool of activation, both excitatory and inhibitory, that the brain has at its disposal at any instant – just as a burglar alarm draws on the total electrical power supply to your house. Now there is good reason, as we have seen, to suppose that the brain has to possess ways of limiting the size of this total pool of activation. After all, if it could increase indefinitely, you might end up with the entire brain switched on at once, and then it would be incapable of doing its job of prioritising and selecting, and would probably go into meltdown. (Some drug experiences can be rather like that.)

So there may well be a trade-off between the amount of activity that is locked up on 'sentry duty' in the brain, keeping watch for the appearance of threats and benefits, and being ready to capture or disarm them when they occur, and the amount that is left over to underwrite perception, action and cognition. The greater the state of emergency, the more able-bodied people have to be conscripted to the army, and the fewer are left to repair the streetlights or empty the garbage. It is a simple idea, but it might just account for why we cannot find the car keys, and become increasingly clumsy, the more stressed we are. There isn't enough activation to go round, amidst all the worrying (both conscious and, more importantly and extensively, unconscious).

A good many of these threat–need bundles are especially problematic because they are inherently contradictory or insatiable. As we noted before, I may simultaneously switch on the need to be liked, and the need for integrity. What am I to do, then, when my gang dares me to do something cruel? I may want both to be challenged and take risks, and to care about the world that I am leaving for my grandchildren. What, then, am I to do when I know that a really juicy business deal might well lead to a renewable energy patent being quietly bought up and mothballed? And what am I to do when an intrinsic aspect of my own functioning – sexual attraction, menstruation, tearfulness – is transmuted into a potential source of shame? Then I am kept busy fighting my right hand with my left.

And acquired desires – to be fashionable or knowledgeable, for example – if they become serious injunctions, also magic into existence shadowy threats of being found dowdy or ignorant that are everlasting and insatiable, precisely because they are relative, and constantly changing. (The exhausting, tail-chasing game of defining your personal worth in terms of an ever-shifting benchmark of 'relative abundance' and 'relative scarcity' was invented, according to the social historian Nicholas Xenos, in the fashionable salons of eighteenth-century Europe.)[24]

One of the ways to deal with these irreconcilable and insatiable clashes of value is to ignore one side of them. You can take something that you do value, and surround it with a ring of inhibition so that it does not reach consciousness. Every time it threatens to erupt, and therefore create more difficulty, complexity and irresolvable choices, you dive down a diversionary wormhole in the brain and busy yourself with something else. This does not deal with the clash, but it deals with the discomfort caused by your awareness of the clash. This kind of disconnection can cause trouble, though it may not, on the face of it, be as self-destructive as some of the more extreme forms of repression we looked at in the last chapter.

For example: one of the brain's problematic in-built priorities is (as I have just exemplified) *care*. Most of us are wired up to take care of our environment and our family and friends. It makes good evolutionary sense to take care of your 'living room', as we have seen, and there is evidence of unselfconscious altruism in many species and in young children. However, caring can be inconvenient, because it can conflict with a whole load of other, more self-centred, projects that you may be working on. The awareness of the conflict can be suppressed if the impulse to care is disowned and denied. However, this strategy will often generate the 'running cost' of a continual stream of small moments of guilt or regret – at people not helped, because it might have made you late for a meeting, or children's achievements given only perfunctory attention because you were too tired or preoccupied. Or a general denial of care may erupt as an absurd, sentimental affection for a pet or a vegetable patch.

The self system boosts the apparent importance of these acquired drives through a manoeuvre that we might call 'identification'. Identification transmutes 'wants' into 'needs' and disappointments into mortal threats. And it does so by expanding the idea of 'identity' – my self, Me – to include them. Whatever I make integral to my identity becomes potentially as important (when that connection is 'switched on') as a bereavement or an encounter with an armed robber. Identified with my knowledgeableness, ignorance cannot simply be shrugged off. I am *obliged* to spend time accumulating information, to compete fiercely with TV quiz-show contestants, and to avoid situations where I might be exposed. Identified with my youthfulness, an incipient wrinkle becomes as threatening as a brown bear in the bathroom. Identification upgrades disappointments to disasters and preferences to necessities.

Languages help immeasurably in this process of need-escalation, especially when they contain equivalents of 'I' and 'am'. To say 'I am clever' (and to have the certificate of your Oxford 'First' lovingly framed on the study wall to prove it) is to propose an incontrovertible and persistent fact, parallel to saying 'I am flesh and blood', or 'I am a man'. If *I* truly *am* clever, then to be stupid is to not be me – to be negated, to die a little. The avoidance of that *petite mort* therefore becomes a survival imperative. And there must also be some internal entity – our old friend the 'soul', perhaps – that corresponds to this 'I', and which 'has' attributes, such as being alive and being smart. We learn to say 'I see', and thus to create an invisible experiencer who is 'doing' the seeing, and receiving its fruits: film producer and audience rolled into one. 'I can' and 'I do' attribute efficacy to this inner agent, while 'I tried' reinforces the feeling of internal agency by allowing that, sometimes, it doesn't work. 'I have' extends the dominion of identity outside the skin, so that damage to a car, or the theft of a manuscript, can also be hooked up to the archetypal power of the emotions, and I experience these events as dire violations of my very self.

Everybody's history writes for them a different specification of their mandatory or ideal self. Everybody varies in the composition and strength of their portfolio of attachments. Someone, sometime, could be so identified with his soft furnishings that a splash of red wine on a new carpet elicits virtually the same kind and strength of reaction that might more appropriately attach to the news that his teenage daughter is missing. Someone else, identified with their verbal fluency, might never dare to give a speech without a written script in their back pocket. (The French singer Françoise Hardy, in her twenties, once dried on stage, and still, in her sixties, refers to it in interviews, and has not given a live concert since, though she still records.)

But the pattern of priming which our brains deploy, and which determines what we shall value and what we shall fear, also varies, depending on our mood, on how secure we feel, and how old we are. At some moments our brains may be functionally carved by our desires into tightly packed peaks and canyons that force their activity into predetermined channels. At others – when we feel calm and loved, perhaps – the inhibition relaxes, and our attention can meander through much softer terrain. We might imagine a continuum of brain function running from 'full of conditioned hopes, fears, standards and rules with which we are strongly identified' to 'empty of the above'. And we could suppose that most of us live, most of the time, at some variable mid-region on this continuum, with a pretty full agenda of psychological as well as practical and interpersonal projects, some 'hot spots' in our psyches that we would rather not touch, but still some time and space to smell the coffee and have a laugh.

Now imagine what might happen, in the internal economy of such a brain, if its convoluted and chronically active self system could be switched off – decathected, to use the Freudian term. Suddenly the anxious preoccupation with a whole raft of self-centred threats and needs would disappear. Self-consciousness – looking at oneself critically through the assumed-to-be-judging eyes of other people – would die away. Perhaps even the habitual, linguistically derived sense of the inner experiencer and instigator might go, leaving only a feeling of wonder at the fact that your experience and action continue to unfold as it were by magic, without your 'self' being at the controls.

As the babble of conflicting goals quietens down, so 'what to do for the best' might appear less problematic. If care is indeed one of our natural, residual concerns, then that, disinhibited, might immediately come to the fore. We might be startled to find that we feel affectionate, loving even, towards a café full of strangers. And, as pockets of locked-up inhibition are released in the brain – like those sentries being stood down – we might find that the suddenly available surfeit of activation rushing into our sensory systems feels rather like a blaze of fire in the body, or a suffusing of perception with brightness and detail.

We might, in other words, find ourselves in the middle of a full-blown spiritual experience, such as those described by the mystics – Eckhart, Boehme – we quoted in chapter 5. There, I just gave a flavour of how these writers were obliged to reach for some notion of the unconscious to account, however inadequately, for the powerful strangeness of their experiences. Here, in order to see how far the brain can take us, I need to distil out, a little more clearly, what some of the key features of such experiences seem to be. Across the world and its history, despite differences of culture and language, some core consensus can be discerned.

The first is an unusually strong sense of *aliveness*. Such experiences are very frequently characterised by a heightened sense of energy and vitality. It is, people say, as if an habitual, hardly noticed sense of being dampened is dispelled, and the body and the senses flood with life. The spiritual and Romantic literature continually reminds us that the origin of the word 'spirit' is closer to that of a high-spirited child, or a spirited horse, than it is to any kind of anaemic piety.

The second quality could be called an affinity with *mystery*. It involves a curious, almost paradoxical sense that all is well with the world, despite not knowing how things are going to turn out. People feel more able to meet whatever comes, and experience a lessening of the anxious need to predict and control. The need to find security in opinions and beliefs is substituted by an interest in depth and truth – wherever they may lead. Open-mindedness and inquisitiveness replace fundamentalism and dogmatism. The unknown, and thus the unconscious, become less alien and therefore less frightening.

The third quality I shall call *belonging*: a sense of being at home, at ease in the world, that seems to be independent of actual places and situations. This felt sense of 'belonging' replaces a nagging background sense of *longing* – as David Steindl-Rast puts it, a feeling of being somehow orphaned or displaced in the world – with a stronger sense of security. Wherever I am feels like 'my place'; whoever I am with are 'my people'. When this is the case, attitudes of suspicion or competition are replaced with what

This detail of an illuminated manuscript from the early thirteenth century shows the famous mystic Hildegard of Bingen in a state of spiritual rapture.

appears to be an unforced inclination towards kindliness and care. Compassion, love even, do not have to be 'worked on'; they emerge as entirely natural corollaries of belonging. Here is a chunk that I excised from the earlier quotation from Herman Hesse's essay 'Concerning the soul', about the eye of desire dirtying and distorting. (I've tinkered with it to get rid of the gendered language in the original.)

> At the moment when desire ceases and contemplation, pure seeing, and self-surrender, begin, everything changes. People cease to be useful or dangerous, interesting or boring, genial or rude, strong or weak. They become nature, they become beautiful and remarkable, as does everything that is an object of clear contemplation. For indeed, contemplation is not scrutiny or criticism, it is nothing but love. It is the highest and most desirable state of our souls: undemanding love.'

Fourth, there is a sense of enhanced *peace of mind*. If I may allow myself one anecdote: I remember sitting in a meditation hall in North London waiting reverently with forty or so others for the appearance of an illustrious Japanese Zen teacher called Maezumi Roshi. Eventually he arrived and processed slowly to the front, where he took a long time to settle himself just so on his podium. Satisfied at last, he raised his eyes to us and said: 'So, what you all doing here, huh?' We laughed nervously, and after another pause, he said: 'You here because your mind not at ease.' And we all nodded enthusiastically. It was true. Spirituality, in this view, holds out the promise that it is possible, though a mixture of grace, insight and effort, to shed some of the mundane anxiety and confusion that Buddhists call *dhukkha*, and to find oneself more often in a state of inner harmony and clarity, and less often conflicted and self-conscious.

And finally, underlying all these four shifts in the quality of experience seems to be an expansion in the sense of identity, so that instead of feeling like an anxious bubble, in constant danger of being jostled or pricked, people claim to feel more union or wholeness, both within and without, and this brings with it more kinship and more trust. It is no coincidence that the many documented descriptions of spiritual experience are couched in such glowing language, for those who report them overwhelmingly appraise them as positive and valuable. While from the outside it is possible – as Freud and others have done – to interpret accounts of the Common Experience sceptically or pathologically, from the inside there is little doubt that something precious, even momentous, has occurred.

So could it be that the long tradition of such spiritual experiences reflects not a revelation of God, but a happy accident in the frontal lobes of the brain? Or rather, could it be that these are just different languages for describing one and the same experience? There are certainly those who think so, and who have claimed to be able to correlate aspects of spiritual experience with underlying changes in the activity of the brain. The American investigators Eugene d'Aquili and Andrew Newberg have shown that alterations in the experience of the boundaries of the 'self' are paralleled by a drop in activity in the superior parietal region of the cerebral neocortex. Two Russian scientists have shown that a state of relaxed, defocused happiness – the release from anxious self-concern – is reflected in an increased harmony of cortical activity. Studies of 'transcendental meditation' have shown a similar increase in the coherence of the EEG. Feelings of bliss are accompanied by a greater 'joined-up-ness' of the brain's activity. And the Canadian neuroscientist Michael Persinger has claimed that he can induce certain aspects of spiritual experience by artificially influencing the electromagnetic fields in the brain, especially by altering the balance of activity between the two hemispheres.[25]

As Persinger himself is the first to point out, none of these correlations proves that God is *not* out there. Any such results could perfectly well reflect the activity of the brain as a *receiving* system, rather than as a *generating* system. But as these results accumulate, and we begin to understand more about how such experiences can at least be represented in the brain, it does put God further and further on the back foot. His adherents have to work that bit harder to explain why it is Him, rather than some as yet to be explained biochemical change, that initiates the brain events that then show up as spiritual experience.

The question remains: are these exotic experiences just occasional aberrations and happy accidents, or do they tell us anything deeper about the way we are built? Certainly those who have had them tend to agree that they are experiencing in a way that is more, not less, 'in touch with reality', but that sense could perfectly well be part of a recurrent delusion. However there are indications, again from current cognitive science, that they may, at least to a degree, be right.

Central to spiritual experience, it appears, is a feeling of being much more 'ecological' than you had thought. Instead of being a disembodied pinprick of conscious intelligence, trapped in a corrupt body and alone in the world, people feel as if their identity has expanded to include both the body and the external world. The Cartesian dualism breaks down, and the sense of self spreads out – in two senses. First, there is the explosion of care and belonging: 'These are my people; this is my place.' And second, there is a concomitant shift in how one perceives the source and nature of one's intelligence. Mind expands to include mystery; it contains its unknown regions as well as its consciousness. The unconscious is embraced, welcomed and 'owned'. And intelligence stops being associated exclusively with reason, and is felt to extend down into the body and out into the world. I am smart, to the extent that I am, because – I now realise – I am a component, an integral part, of a smart system that includes body and world.

The intelligence of the body is abundantly clear. We have already explored how the physical feelings of emotion, far from being subversive, are part of our evolutionary intelligence. We may sometimes read situations wrongly, and feel feelings that are unjustified or inappropriate, but the inability to feel pain or fear or love makes one socially and biologically stupid. Damasio's research has shown just how vital our physical feelings and intuitions are.[26]

A clear example is provided by the therapeutic procedure known as 'focusing', developed by American psychotherapist Eugene Gendlin. Back in the 1970s, Gendlin discovered three important facts about therapy. The first was that people who were benefiting from their therapy – regardless of what 'school' their therapist belonged to – were those who were able spontaneously to slip into a kind of quiet, reflective conversation with themselves. They did not trot out a pat story, but took their time to explore meanings and search for a fresh way of putting things. Secondly, this conversation involved listening to the subtle promptings and feelings that were manifesting in their own bodies. They noticed slight changes in the quality of feeling in their abdomen or throat, say. And thirdly, Gendlin discovered that this receptive internal dialogue could be taught. People could learn to attend to this physical shadowland, the glimmerings of meaning that were not yet well-formed enough to make a conscious story, but which could be nurtured along.[27] One is reminded of A. E. Housman's response to a request from an American student to 'define poetry'. He replied: 'I could no more define poetry than a terrier could define a rat, but that I thought we both recognise the object by the [physical] symptoms which it provokes in us.'[28] The body has to be included within the organ of intelligence.

And so does the external world itself. As they say these days, intelligence is *distributed*.[29] We are all smart, in large measure, because we have access to a whole variety of tools and resources, and know how to use them. Snooker cues, biros, personal organisers, filing cabinets, tape measures, vegetable peelers, scalpels, bulldozers, buoyancy jackets, telephones, microscopes, cyclotrons, the internet, maps, cellos, psychedelic drugs, cement, dictionaries . . . our accomplishments, great and small, depend on a continual process of interaction with the outside world. We are smart because we know how to make smart use of stuff, and where to get it. The stuff around determines the kind of smart that we are. And as we learn to make smart use of stuff, so our minds are shaped by the tools we find ourselves using. We develop the mentality of a cellist or a surgeon, varieties of what the French call the *déformation professionnelle*. So it would be stupid to take away a techie's computer, or a Nobel laureate's laboratory, or David Beckham's boots, come to that, and then say: '*Now* show me how clever you are'! René Descartes notwithstanding, the idea that intelligence is all in the isolated brain bears no more scrutiny than the idea that it is all in the conscious mind.[30]

The idea that the mind flows out beyond the confines of the skin is not by any means new. The invention of written text, back before the story of the unconscious even began, has profoundly altered the way we think. Being able to freeze a thought on paper, a wax tablet or a screen allows the development of both solitary and collective rumination. I can show you my draft, and your reactions will enable me to think what I could not have done without the mediating tool of text. An artist makes models and sketches, and in doing do, amplifies the power of her own imagination. She can see more possibilities, more layers of meaning, as she plays with her sketch, and any account of her creative process must include her cycling between her drawing and her imagination. As the blind person's cane (or the gamer's console) becomes, to all intents and purposes, an extension of their body, so does the artist's pencil and her pad.

Recent technological advances serve only to dramatise this exploded view of the human being. A cochlear implant can not only correct a hearing loss; it can enable me to hear sounds that the rest of you cannot. New aircraft flight-decks can tie the pilot so tightly to the technology that merely glancing at a dial can cause a bit of software to check and adjust the reading. It will soon be possible to buy clever spectacles, connected by wireless technology to a computer database that, for example, will recognise the face in front of you, and project the person's name and their most salient characteristics, across the top of your visual field. So where does the 'mind' stop? Not only are its operations essentially unconscious, but they cannot even be corralled within the biological envelope of the brain and skin.[31]

More than anything else, intelligence is *socially* distributed. If I need my reference books, how much more do I need my colleagues, my sounding boards, my sparring partners, my role models? In a creative discussion, mind becomes communal. No one has all the information and no one is in control, but by listening, contributing and thinking aloud, we can go places where none of us could have gone alone. We kick ideas around, build on each other's flights of fancy, veer off at tangents and feed back in our experience sometimes slowly and delicately, and sometimes so fast that we have that vertiginous feeling of being way out beyond the safety net, keeping each other airborne like a virtuoso troupe of acrobats. Our minds are so intricately woven together that it may even take a while for each of us to 'find ourselves' again when the creative caper stops. In creativity we fuse, just as we do in love. And it is both thrilling and disconcerting.[32]

So we do not know our own minds; and we do not (always) own them either. They are as much unconscious as conscious; as much physical as mental; as much communal as individual. We seem to have come a long way from the arch-rationalism of the Enlightenment. As the philosopher Andy Clark says,

> we must begin to face up to some rather puzzling (dare I say metaphysical?) questions. For starters, the nature and bounds of the intelligent agent look increasingly fuzzy. Gone is the central executive in the brain – the real boss who organises and integrates the activities of multiple special-purpose subsystems. And gone is the neat boundary between the thinker (the bodiless intellectual engine) and the thinker's world. In place of this

comforting image . . . it may for some purposes be wise to
consider the intelligent system as a spatio-temporally extended
process not limited to the tenuous envelope of skin and skull . . .
The flow of reasons and thoughts, and the temporal evolution of
ideas and attitudes, are determined and explained by the
intimate, complex, continued interplay of brain, body and
world.[33]

And we have come a long way, too, from the disembodied soul:
the immaculate fleck of divinity that is in us but not of this world.
Instead of having recourse to a transcendental realm, a parallel universe in which everything is True and Good, we seem to be able to
relocate spirituality, not just in the brain, but in the recovery of an
intimate, ecological, empathic relationship with *this* world of
wood and gristle and fellow-feeling.

11

Turning the Mind on Its Head

No activity of mind is ever conscious.
– Karl Lashley

Jane Andrews, a former servant of the Duchess of York, killed her boyfriend by hitting him with a cricket bat, and then plunging an eight-inch kitchen knife into his heart. At her trial she pleaded 'diminished responsibility' on the grounds that buried memories of years of sexual abuse by her brother were bubbling up in her mind, stirred perhaps by some visits to a Chelsea psychotherapist. These visits, sadly, she claimed, had ended too soon, leaving 'the secret locked away' in her unconscious until after the killing. Yet it was the seething of these unconscious memories which stimulated the rage that impelled her deadly outburst. She explained that the childhood experiences were 'unravelling', and 'affecting her mental state', though she did not yet have conscious access to their content. It was only 'heavy sessions', after she had been jailed for life, that 'unlocked the full facts of [the] sexual abuse, and the impact it had on her', said her lawyer, launching the appeal against her conviction. The argument was only permissible because the law had come to recognise the unconscious. Forty-eight years earlier, Ruth Ellis, also on trial for murdering her lover, was not able to plead 'diminished responsibility' and she became the last woman in the UK to suffer capital punishment.

Parliament introduced the defence two years after she was hanged.[1]

Human beings remain a mystery. That is not going to change. They lash out. They remember vivid details of their childhoods in therapy or under hypnosis. They hear voices. They forget names they know perfectly well. They see visions. They are moved to tears by sunsets. They have weird dreams. They fear harmless things. They have premonitions. Bizarre and profound ideas burst into their heads. They can't get tunes out of their minds. They respond to instructions while under general anaesthetic. They love the strangest people, and they hurt the ones they love. They create the most astonishingly beautiful things. They rape their neighbours. In spite of our science and our rationality, irrationality abounds.

Or perhaps not 'in spite of', but 'because of'. The more prescriptive the cultural model of the 'normal' mind – the more clear-cut the boundary that is drawn between the unexceptionable and the odd – the more odd the odd becomes, and the more it cries out for explanation. We still live in such prescriptive times. Our default model of the mind still puts reason at the centre. Systematic thinking and clear articulation dominate our most respected cultural institutions and professions: government, medicine, education, the law. 'Premeditation' makes an offence worse. If the police had found recent receipts for a hunting knife, and for duct tape with which the victim's hands had been bound, Jane Andrews's appeal would have been dead in the water. Planning is prima facie evidence of sanity, of intention, of *mens rea*, the guilty mind.

The attempt to maintain the fiction of intention generates a range of difficulties. Is the tobacco industry any more or less culpable because its senior managers take great care *not* to draw consciously the conclusions that seem obvious to more disinterested parties? When the negligence behind the rail crash, the chemical explosion or the *Challenger* disaster arises from wishful thinking or commercial pressures, rather than from deliberate 'evil', should that make a difference? Should a drink-driver be guilty of manslaughter rather than murder because, though he 'chose' to drink, he did not 'intend' to run down those children? Should people whose minds are sophisticated enough to be able to prevent their left hand knowing what their right hand is doing be treated more leniently by the law than those who have not learned to manipulate their own consciousness in this way? If the law gives minds the incentive to turn a blind eye to their own activities, why not jump at the chance?

While this dubious understanding of our own psychology holds sway, it is not surprising that a Heath Robinson collection of ancillary explanations for the oddities piles up. The gods, or God, continue to intervene. Magic remedies such as homeopathy continue to do a brisk trade. Witches are not so much in evidence, but feng shui and aromatherapy are doing well. New mysterious agents continue to be invented, though we might now call them 'viruses' and 'chemicals'. (Following media reports of a possible toxin in Coca-Cola, many children across the UK experienced symptoms of poisoning, though the original reports were soon shown to be untrue.)[2]

And various versions of the unconscious, construed as the dissociated rumpus room or the locked ward of the mind, live happily on in our language. We have a super-ego to explain our guilt; an id to cause our neuroses and 'repressed traumatic memories' to account for our bad behaviour; a collective unconscious to generate the symbolism of myths and dreams. And now we have brain states as well, to help us out when we are puzzled by ourselves: serotonin imbalances, frontal lobe dysfunctions and (my favourite) 'minimal brain damage' – so slight you cannot see it, but definitely there, or those kids would not be so unruly (sorry, 'hyperactive').

The unconscious remains sandwiched somewhat uneasily between the spirits and the brain, reflecting the fact that, though we now think we have probably got one, we are still not sure if we like it. Faced with the possibility that we might actually have one of these mental cesspits, and carry it around with us wherever we go, the other two kinds of explanation seem rather more attractive. If I have been possessed by a passing spirit, I can always try to argue that it was just bad luck that it picked me. And the same with physical disease: I need not feel ashamed of getting measles (though syphilis is a different matter), nor need I if I am diagnosed as '*suffering from* Attention Deficit Hyperactivity Disorder', or even schizophrenia. It may be tough, but it ain't my fault. Bad luck that it was the brain that caught it, this time round, and not the liver. It is because the unconscious is only wheeled out to account for the wacky stuff that it stays alien. It can do the necessary explanatory job, but it still isn't really 'me'. That is the point of it.

Yet the evidence and ideas I have reviewed in the last few chapters suggest that the unknown substrate of what makes me tick is very much broader than this Freudian mixture of sporadic nuisance and convenient excuse. The problem is much worse than we thought, because it begins to look as if the unconscious brain–body – context system ('brain' for short) is in charge not just sometimes but all the time. When all the oddities are mounted up, and we take them seriously, we come up with an image of our own minds that places unconscious intelligence at the very centre, rather than on the margins. The oddities are not just a jumble of curiosities; they point to fundamental misconceptions in the Cartesian folk psychology of 'normal' human nature. The idea of the calm, well-lit Executive Office of rational consciousness as the mind's centre of operations, occasionally interrupted by the id or inspired by the muse, is a misleading image. The brains behind the operation turns out to be the brain itself – augmented by its blistering array of social and technological 'mindware upgrades'.

When we try to look downwards into the 'darkling pool' of our own minds, we see only metaphors reflected in the surface. So we need the best, the most accurate, the most helpful images we can find. New images of the relationship between consciousness and the unconscious are needed. The idea that they are two equivalent – but warring – realms in the mind, one light and the other dark, won't do. Depicting 'the unconscious' as a place – the 'depository' of memories, searched by the conscious librarian; the 'locked ward' of waywardness guarded by a nervous attendant – does not do justice to its intrinsic dynamism and intelligence. There is no evidence that we have anything like an invisible person inside us – no librarian, no lunatic, no censor, no CEO – separate from the brain. These are outdated metaphors, like 'élan vital', the Tooth Fairy and Mount Olympus. It no longer works to see the atom as a currant bun, nor heat as a subtle substance that flows from hot to cold bodies. And it no longer works to explain the oddities of human experience in terms of an 'upstairs, downstairs' architecture, or a supernatural soap opera, or a demonic sub-personality at odds with the conscious Me.

Fresh images are beginning to emerge. Cognitive scientists now liken consciousness to the dashboard of a car, the cockpit displays of an aircraft, or simply the screen of a computer. Conscious perceptions are not video images from the 'security cameras' of the senses; conscious thoughts are not the musings of the CEO. They are readings that summarise the state of some of the unconscious processes that are going on 'under the bonnet'. As I look around, what I 'see', consciously, is not 'what's there'; it is a representation of what the brain is currently treating as novel, or useful, or important. As I 'think', the strings of words that seem to slide across my consciousness, like subtitles on the screen, are likewise read-outs from decision-making processes that are, in themselves, always and ever beyond my ken.

'No activity of mind is ever conscious', said the great American psychologist Karl Lashley, though of course many of these activities *generate* consciousness. No intention is ever hatched in consciousness; no plan ever laid there. Intentions are premonitions; icons that flash in the corner of consciousness to indicate what may be about to occur. As that wise sceptic Ambrose Bierce said in his *Devil's Dictionary*, an intention is 'the mind's sense of the prevalence of one set of influences over another set; an effect whose cause is the imminence, immediate or remote, of the performance of the act intended by the person incurring the intention'. (Bierce comments on his own definition, 'when figured out and accurately apprehended, this will be found one of the most penetrating and far-reaching definitions in the whole dictionary'. And it is beginning to look as if he may well be right.)[3]

The brain actually produces two kinds of thing: physical effects and mental experiences. Its patterns of activation spin around, and then they cause changes in the body – muscle contraction, hormone release, enzyme activation – and in consciousness – emotions, perceptions, thoughts, images and so on. Sometimes it produces actions without accompanying conscious experience; sometimes consciousness without any corollary action; and sometimes both. And when it produces both, sometimes they seem to be coordinated, and sometimes not. In fact there is often some degree of mismatch, simply because the kinds of brain activity that eventuate in 'thoughts' are not the same kinds of activity that result in 'actions'. For example, you recall the experiment on reaching for the disks in the middle of the Titchener circles, where the grasp of the hand unconsciously adjusts to the actual size of the disks, while the conscious perception is distorted by the contrast between the central circle and the size of the circles surrounding it. Or: when young men's pulse rates have been raised by walking across a rather scary rope bridge, they tend to fancy the first young woman that they then meet! They mistakenly attribute their own physiological arousal to sexual attraction – a more consciously acceptable motive than fear. They do not *think* it or *surmise* it: they actually *experience* their anxiety as attraction.[4]

Unconscious forces are everywhere, determining social patterns as much as individual ones. For example, people tend to like things that are familiar – but only if they are not aware that it is mere familiarity that is at work. That's one reason why swings in fashion are so powerful and so ephemeral. A clothing style catches on when people are beginning to pick up on an emerging trend – but before everyone is wearing it, and they become conscious that it *is* a trend. By the time it has achieved visible popularity, the *fashionistas* would not be seen dead in it. The same applies to choosing baby names. How come, in 2002, that thousands of people in the UK independently decided that Bethany and Amelia were attractive and original girls' names, and Cameron and Bradley were pretty cool for boys? Probably because there is a positive feedback loop happening. As a name begins to become popular, it is more likely to come to mind. But if you realise that it comes to mind because lots of other people are choosing it, you are likely to discard it. ('Oh not Jessica, sweetheart – every second baby is called Jessica these days!") Or if a famous person becomes too famous, their name stops being attractive. (In the US, the number of Hillarys peaked in 1992, and plummeted as soon as the Clintons moved into the White House.)[5] One part of the unconscious is informing the choice in a way that would not happen if the part that is informing consciousness 'knew about it'.

There is a good deal of evidence that the part of the unconscious brain that concocts *explanations* for why we did something – what neuroscientist Michael Gazzaniga calls the 'interpreter' – is not the same part of the brain that decided to do it. The former part does not have direct access to the workings of the latter. All the interpreter can do is notice what you actually did, or felt, and then construct a plausible story about How Come. Gazzaniga suggests that for most of us the interpreter is located in the left hemisphere of the brain, and he has been able to show it at work in so-called 'split brain' patients, those who have had the two sides of the brain disconnected. If you flash the word 'Laugh!' to one of these patients in such a way that it only goes into the right hemisphere, they laugh, but the left hemisphere does not know why, because it did not see the word. If you ask the patent why they laughed, the interpreter, quick as a flash, makes something up. The patient says: 'You guys come up and test us every month. What a way to make a living!' And, like the young men on the bridge, they do not know that this is a confabulation – they genuinely believe that they are reporting the actual cause of their laughter.[6]

So consciousness may be the dashboard of the mind – that is, of the unconscious biotechnological system – but far from being infallible and transparent, it turns out, some of the time at least, to be inaccurate and untrustworthy. It reflects something of what is going on down there, but it does so 'through a glass darkly'. And one of the main reasons why its reports are partial and skewed is that, through consciousness, we are seeing the mind at its most inhibited. We see what has been preselected by the backroom boys as being of potential danger, delight, or at least relevance to current goals – and thus what we experience is essentially reflected in Hesse's 'cloudy mirror' of our own hopes, fears and expectations, both those that have been hard-wired by evolution, and those we have absorbed from our own culture.

The evidence suggests that the brain manufactures the sharpest consciousness

- when it is being selective;
- when it is busy sequencing and prioritising;
- when we are at our most circumspect;
- when we are startled and alarmed;
- when the smooth flow of activation from sensation to reaction is blocked, and we have to pause and reconsider;
- when what we are about to do matters terribly, and we have to be sure to get it right;
- when the unexpected happens (the stairs creak at 3 am), or the expected does not (the clock stops ticking);
- when our self-respect is dented, and we feel, acutely, pangs of guilt or remorse;

- when we are made *self*-conscious and suddenly awkward by a chance remark;
- when we are getting our story straight, rescuing our self and presenting it in a favourable light.

Conversely when the brain relaxes, when the frontal lobes quieten and allow patterns of activation to diffuse and flow more freely, awareness diffuses too, and we drift into the foggy borderlands of reverie, and on into the recurrent loss of consciousness we refer to as sleep. And then, in dreams, as we have seen, the brain chews over the day, seeking out significance, and thus becomes more emotional, more selective and more value-laden again. The metaphorical surface of the brain puckers up, becomes more rutted, setting up more clearly etched channels for its activity to run along: in dreams we see the brain back at its grooviest.

But for whose benefit are these conscious indicators generated? Surely they must be for 'me', to make use of or take into account. Otherwise what is the point? Evolution could surely not have designed something as ingenious as this intricate display system if there was not going to be anybody sitting in the pilot's seat to 'read' them. So do we need the ghost in the machine after all? Does the soul have to be sneaked back in? Or can we dare to suggest that consciousness is merely a *concomitant* of certain important kinds of activity in the brain; an evolutionary miracle, a happy accident that had and has no design? Sure, the kinds of reverberation that *underlie* consciousness are of obvious and extreme utility. It is only our ability to inhibit ourselves – to pause, prioritise, consider options – that enables us to juggle our plethora of goals with more or less success. But is it 'me' doing that, or is it my brain? Does the brain just serve up spread-sheets and sketches for the Cartesian ghost in the machine to deliberate upon? Or is the experience of deliberating simply what passes across the screen, while the microchip is busy performing computations that are infinitely more speedy and more subtle?

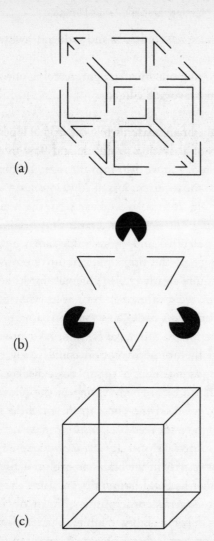

Three reminders that the brain serves up conscious experiences that may not be 'true', and over which the conscious 'me' has no control. (a) reproduces the cube from page 207 in which the brain falsifies the evidence in order to corroborate its 'decision' that what you are looking at is a cube obscured by diagonal bars. (b) shows a similar figure, the Kanizsa triangle. Try as you might, armed with as much physical information as you can get, you cannot make the illusory edges and contrasts go away. (c) is the familiar Necker cube, about which the brain has trouble making up its mind. Stare at it, and it flips backwards and forwards, now one face is the front, now another.

Actually, there is no way of deciding the issue. It certainly seems as if 'I' am busy, somewhere inside here, weighing up factors, making decisions, and presumably issuing orders to my larynx and my spleen to make their contribution to my cunning plan. But there is a lot that 'seems' that isn't so. It seems as if the sun goes round the Earth. It seems as if there are bright bars obscuring the cube. And it seems as if I am in control. But here is philosopher Daniel Dennett musing on the phenomenology of decision-making: noting what actually occurs in consciousness, if we watch carefully:

Are decisions voluntary? Or are they things that happen to us? From some fleeting vantage points they seem to be the pre-eminently voluntary moves in our lives, the instants at which we exercise our agency to the fullest. But those same decisions can also be seen to be strangely out of our control. We have to wait to see how we are going to decide something, and when we do decide, our decision bubbles up to consciousness from we know not where. We do not witness it being *made*; we witness its *arrival*. This can lead to the strange idea that Central Headquarters is not where we, as conscious introspectors, are; it is somewhere deeper within us, and inaccessible to us. E. M. Forster famously asked 'How can I tell what I think until I see what I say?' – the words of an outsider, it seems, waiting for a bulletin from the interior . . . [And] once we recognise that our conscious access to our own decisions is problematic, we may go on to note how many of the important turning points in our lives were unaccompanied . . . by *conscious* decisions. 'I have decided to take the job,' one says. And very clearly one takes oneself to be reporting on something one has done recently, but reminiscence shows only that yesterday one was undecided, and today one is no longer undecided; at some moment in the interval the decision *must have happened*, without fanfare. Where did it happen? At Central Headquarters, of course.[7]

What we observe, if we look closely, is a process that can flip backwards and forwards like a Necker cube: we see ourselves making decisions, and then we see decisions – images, thoughts, regrets, fantasies – welling up into consciousness by themselves. We see a mystery. And perhaps because we are inveterate story-tellers, we are dissatisfied with the latter perspective, the one of astonished receptivity, rather than busy authorship, so we invent a Doer behind the Deed. Dennett again:

> Faced with the inability to 'see' (by 'introspection') where the centre or source of our free actions is, and loath to abandon our conviction that we really do things (for which we are responsible), we exploit the cognitive vacuum, the gaps in our self-knowledge, by filling it with a rather magical and mysterious entity, the unmoved mover, the active self.[8]

What we call our 'self' is an agglomeration of both conscious and unconscious ingredients. We have Needs: basic requirements and basic threats to attend to, like finding shelter and avoiding predators. We have Senses: our range of species-specific sensitivities that rapidly gets customised into our 'point of view'. We have a repertoire of Cans: zones of control, where there is a tight correlation between what the brain tells the body to do, what the muscles actually do, what proprioceptive information results, and what changes in the world are reported back by the senses. We have a personal portfolio of Haves, of possessions: objects, places, even animals and other people, in which we feel we have some special investment, and over which we feel we can exercise some kind of remote control. We have our unique profile of Dos: our signature repertoire of habits, traits and preferences. We may not think much about our Needs, Senses, Cans, Haves and Dos – we may not have them very well formulated, so they can function as objects of conscious scrutiny – but they nevertheless combine to define who we are.

And then there are ingredients that are more commonly conscious. There are my Wants: the collection of projects, goals and interests that organise my choices and my time. There are my Oughts: the duties, commitments and obligations that tell me who I am supposed to be, whether I want to be or not. There are my Coulds: the range of possible selves and possible futures that I can conceive of; the life courses that seem available and appropriate (to a working-class boy; to a retired accountant . . .). There is my special trail of Was-es: the autobiographical thread of memories and memorabilia that seem to secure my continuity; to reassure me that there is an important sense, despite the shrinking hair and expanding waist, that I am the same person as the seven-year-old boy in the holiday snap, playing cricket on the beach. And finally there is my ongoing ticker-tape of Thinks: the conscious commentary that accompanies my actions, and which seems – though Dennett tells me otherwise – to select and influence the way they go.

None of these is in dispute. Of course who I am is woven out of all these threads. The only question is how I put them together. What do I make of them? The conventional response is to tidy them all up by inventing a tiny word with the grand title of The First Person Singular Pronoun – 'I', to you and me – and to turn all the various ingredients of the self into Auxiliary Verbs. So the English-speaking child has to learn how to talk about herself as the Subject of all these different kinds of Predicates. I do not just 'have' or 'experience' needs: I Need (a drink, a pee). I Sense (hunger, roast chicken). I Can (tie my shoelaces, count to ten). I Have (a hamster called Polly, new trousers). I Do (like my room tidy, have Shreddies for breakfast). I Want (to be friends with Anna, to get into the team). I Ought (to write to Granny, to do my piano practice). I Could (aim to be a nurse, but not a civil engineer or a hot-air balloonist). I Was (a terror when I was two, in hospital with asthma when I was six). I Think (I'll go downstairs, that Sophie was really mean).

Used over and over again, these constructions hold out an over-whelming temptation: to assume that the 'I' is the same in all of them. So instead of having an intricate web of things that make me Me, I have to create a single imaginary hub around which they all revolve, and to which they all refer. When I think about a cake, I do not make the mistake of assuming that there is something called 'the cake' which is separate from all the ingredients (bound together in interesting ways). But when I think about my Self, 'I', on the conventional view, I do. The assembled oddities of human nature point to the fact that it is not just the mind that bursts out of the Cartesian straitjacket into which it has been forced; it is the very core of self, of human identity, that threatens to escape. I am darker, and more dispersed, and more various, and more change-able, than I am supposed to be – than I would *have* to be, if the Great I Am were as real and coherent as the theory says.

The attempt to keep this fiction going, to 'hold it together', can become quite tiring and bothersome. If I AM essentially reason-able, then wild dreams and mystical experiences become a problem. If I imagine that my zones of control – over my own feel-ings, for example – are wider and more robust than they are, then I am going to get in a tangle trying to 'control myself'. If I once decided that Who I Am is Clever, then my increasingly familiar Senior Moments aren't funny. If I AM determined to be Pretty, then ageing becomes my enemy in a different way. If I was brought up to be the innocent ray of sunshine in a moody family – to think of myself as the one who brings happiness and makes things light – then my moments of surliness or selfishness are not just unfortunate, they put me at odds with myself. By playing Jekyll too hard, I make myself Hyde. Creating the hub of 'I' locks everything together, and prevents it moving. It stops Me expand-ing to include the unconscious, or graciously shrinking to accommodate old age. I can't enjoy my waywardness, nor see it as an intrinsic part of Me (a valid and valuable form of psychological weather; the heat haze and the thunder of the mind).

Try this. It is an experiment invented by V. S. Ramachandran, director of the Center for Brain and Cognition at the University of California, San Diego, and author of *Phantoms in the Brain*. It will give you a two-foot nose. You will need two friends (call them Anne and Bill) and two chairs, placed one behind the other. Bill sits in front, you behind with your eyes closed. Anne takes your right hand and uses your right index finger to make a pattern of taps and strokes on Bill's nose. At the same time, she uses her left hand to stroke and tap your nose in exactly the same rhythm. After about a minute of this, if you are susceptible, you will feel the stimulation at the tip of your own nose – which is now where Bill's nose is! Your brain has matched the fact that your right index finger is tapping two feet away, with the experience that is coming in from Anne's taps on your nose, and put them together in the only way it can: by giving you a Pinocchio-like proboscis. Just as the brain is happy to invent occluding bars in front of a cube, so it is willing to monkey around with your body sense, if the evidence seems to warrant it. The question is: do you experience this as funny or unnerving, or perhaps a bit of both?[9]

The orthodox sense of self is thrown by such experiences, and tends to suffer a sense-of-humour failure. It sees all waywardness as an affront, and tends to become earnest or myopic in response. In a nutshell: it is bad enough to have a nightmare, without your rattled sense of self telling you that you are going mad. Weird experience can never be just funny (as the Pinocchio effect can be), or matter-of-fact (as possession is in Bali), or transiently inconvenient (as a bad dream is), or wonderful (as a mystical experience can be), or just mysterious (as a premonition might be). For the locked-up self they have to be denied, explained or dealt with. All the evidence is that a more relaxed attitude towards the bounds of self makes for a richer, easier and more creative life. Perhaps, after all, waywardness in all its forms is in need not so much of explanation, but of a mystified but friendly welcome. We can explain it if we wish, and the brain is beginning to do a reasonable job. But the *need* to explain, when not motivated by the dispassionate curiosity of the scientist, is surely a sign of anxiety: of the desire to tame with words that which is experienced as unsettling.

I said earlier that we need the most accurate and the most useful models of the mind, through which to see ourselves. It is true, but there is an issue here that I glossed over before. The most accurate and the most useful are not the same thing. The Underground map of London is highly inaccurate, wrong in almost every respect; yet it is an extremely useful map precisely because it is so crude and stylised. And so, having driven the model of the mind as far as we can currently go in the direction of accuracy – of scientifically validated detail – we might close by drawing back and asking if this image, for all its sophistication, is the best, or the only, one we need. There are dozens of maps of London, all good for different purposes. The traveller has no problem switching between the Tube Map and the '*A to Z Street Map*'; she experiences no epistemological crisis as she does so. Why should we restrict ourselves to just one map of the mind? Should we not, after all, allow ourselves a set of complementary perspectives as we try to make sense of our personal and social waywardness?

Remember that the Balinese today happily switch between Western and indigenous approaches to various forms of trance, possession and what we would think of as physical and mental illness. Like many people who find themselves camped at the crossroads of cultures, they solve the problem of deciding which way to go, which account of waywardness to subscribe to, by refusing to choose. A headache can be treated with an aspirin. But a persistent headache, accompanied by melancholia or withdrawal, may well signal the disapproval of the ancestor spirits, and the need for a ritual of repentance or atonement. Is there a sense in which we too would be better off if we were to let go our exclusive commitment to the scientific perspective, and allow ourselves the same fluidity? Might there, after all, be some method in the messy mixture of models of the unconscious which our society is heir to?

Here's a suggestion. The scientifically founded view of the individual mind as intrinsically more mysterious, more embodied and more variable than the Cartesian bubble of rationality, is an improvement when it comes to thinking about our own experience. It allows us to be more relaxed about our own wayward tendencies, and more interested in them. We can expand our identities to embrace the mystery, rather than being rattled by it. The stories we create, whether of ids or frontal lobes, Freudian repression or neural inhibition, can be constructed more leisurely and held more lightly. They can encourage genial acceptance of our vagaries, rather than anxious efforts to control the uncontrollable. (Just as the phrase 'a senior moment' helps to take the embarrassing sting out of the momentary loss of a familiar name, so a more widespread vernacular appreciation of the broader, deeper view of mind could encourage a greater equanimity in the face of all kinds of waywardness. Not that serious dysfunction is not hard to deal with; but that the *additional* distress generated by the fact that it does not fit the normative 'official doctrine' only makes matters worse.)

When all is said and done, explanations based on scientific models of brain and mind are predominantly individual. The mechanisms, and to a large extent the causes, of waywardness are placed inside us. And the language of the modern brain–mind does not offer much in the way of a public language which we can collectively sign up to. The language of science deliberately has no symbolism, no resonance. Though it continually fails, its aim is to be literal and transparent. It offers no way to make cultural, as opposed to scientific, sense out of madness, creativity or spiritual experience. And that may be a loss. Though the public exorcisms of the seventeenth century were subject to all kinds of manipulations, by both priests and victims, nevertheless the whole mythology of devils and demons had its positive side too. Possession could be seen to have a sociological, as well as a psychological, dimension.

Though it is hard to see the witch-hunts of Salem, now, as anything other than pernicious, the language in which they were couched did allow a collective discourse, as well as an individual interpretation. When Freud took possession and turned it into neurosis, the private perspective was developed, but at the expense of the public one. The phenomenon was pathologised and dragged out of sight. Where exorcism offered a chance for a whole community to think about its values, procedures and its health, therapy becomes private and invisible, and runs the risk of loading all the responsibility for waywardness inside the 'victim', and concealing its social or cultural dimensions. For a teenage girl to 'become possessed' could be seen as a stigma. But it could also provide a framework within which she could 'behave badly' (in the face, perhaps, of sexual repression and confusion) and let off steam. The framework could – and sometimes did – allow her society to cut her a bit of slack. It is not clear that getting drunk and vomiting in a city centre on a Saturday night is a vast improvement. There are costs to the public framework of devils and possession, but there are benefits as well. Without it, there is less containment. Things do not make so much sense. One feels more alone with one's waywardness.

The arena where this tension between cultural utility and scientific accuracy is at its strongest today is that of the law. From the scientific point of view, the attempt to maintain a strong line between behaviour that is deliberate or intended, and for which one can be held responsible, and behaviour which is in some sense involuntary, and for which one can be excused, looks increasingly doomed. Was Jane Andrews in the grip of uncontrollable forces – eruptions of passion caused by childhood events for which she could not be held accountable – or was she 'in her right mind', as she clubbed her lover to the ground? The only intelligent answer is: we don't know. If even the simplest decision to move a finger up or down is initiated by the brain before the conscious mind is privy to the 'intention', how can we possibly maintain the fiction that Thought is *ever* the instigator of Action?

Yet if we allow that Thought and Action both bubble out of a darker place to which we have – can have in principle – no conscious access, how on earth can anyone ever be held to account? No doubt Hitler and Saddam had 'bad' childhoods, just as Fred and Rosemary West, and Jane Andrews, did. But does that mean that societies have no right, no mandate to regulate themselves? That it is inhumane to punish the drunk driver, unintentional killer of two small children, who had just been chucked by her boyfriend? If she was not 'in her right mind' when she ordered the third double vodka, nothing that ensued could have been her 'fault'. The science of the unconscious leaves us in a terrible social mess, if it is taken to undermine the crucial notions of 'responsibility' and 'intent' on which many judicial systems are founded.

Perhaps here we need the complementarity: the unapologetic right to treat people *as if they were responsible*, for the greater good. Though single thoughts never lead to distinct actions – that cause-and-effect model of the mind is orders of magnitude too simple – nevertheless the brain is forever calculating the odds. It reads newspapers, it watches the news, it knows about punishment and prison. And it computes contingencies and likelihoods that can weight in the intricate, intuitive, unconscious balance that underlies our every twitch. So it is perfectly acceptable for a society to do whatever it can, in defence of its values, to try to maximise the weight of such considerations – knowing that, in the heat of some future moment, their weight may well not be enough to tip the scales and prevent a crime. We *act as if* responsibility could be assigned because the fiction enables us to punish certain kinds of acts, and, most importantly, to broadcast and dramatise the humiliation and privation of the punished, *pour encourager les autres*. In regulating and maintaining the social order, the 'truth' about human nature is what works. And such a strategy is both highly dangerous, allowing all kinds of oppression and legalised skulduggery, and partially effective.

There might even be a place for the gods and the ancestor spirits, to help to reinforce cultural agreement about what is Right and Wrong. The scientific unconscious, the biotechnological mindware that runs the show, is amoral. There is nothing in the neuro-cognitive story that tells us what to do or how to behave. Moment to moment, the brain adds up a bewildering array of influences and expectations, and computes a best-guess course of action. And sometimes it blows a conscious bubble that seems to justify that course. But there is nothing intrinsic to this image of the mind that makes it overwhelmingly want to behave 'well', in social terms – unless we can embed in the brain–mind a moral narrative, an image of a moral world, that can interrupt the smooth computations of the brain and give it, literally, 'pause for thought'. As you rush to action, the learned story may trip you up, and as you gather yourself to carry on, so the higher ideals that are embedded in the narrative (in the conduct of the heroes, and the hideous fate that befalls the villains and the unwary) come to mind, and serve to adjust the weights on the unconscious balance in favour of The Good.

So 'Olympus Inc' and the Ancestral Spirits are devices that encourage the preservation of a particular social order, for good or ill, by biasing the brain's internal calculations. In a benign society, the stories work in and on the brain to temper flaring passions and selfish impulses, for the general good. In a corrupt regime, the myths serve only to further the interests of the temporarily lucky few. Most societies are a messy mixture of the two. The scientific view of the unconscious leaves you up this complicated creek without a compass or a paddle. The supernatural views can open you to oppression and exploitation. Maybe we do need both, to mitigate the excesses of the other.

But maybe also the tangle of views we have inherited about the wayward mind does not give us the best possible balance. My argument does not quite legitimise the messy status quo. We do not want to eliminate our cultural stories – our gods and devils, our angels and ancestors – entirely. Their magic is valuable and enriching of cultural life, even though their potential for abuse is not. I want the poetry of the mind, as well as the science, and those who think that the latter will overwhelm the former, and the sooner the better, do not understand that cultures need to regulate and enrich themselves, just as much as nerve cells do.

But the Enlightenment view of the mind is in urgent need of moderation. Its lopsided adherence to explicit, deliberate, conscious reason as the acme of intelligence is flawed. It leads to a contempt for symbols – for language that resonates in the intricate depth of the brain – and an overestimation of dull, literal prose. It leads to students being taught to pull poetry and dreams apart; to plunder them impatiently for their 'meaning', and to a neglect of Keats's art of 'negative capability' – the ability to dwell in 'uncertainties, Mysteries, doubts, without any irritable reaching after fact and reason'.

It leads to schools and universities losing sight of wisdom in their pursuit of mere cleverness, or, worse, mere knowledgeability.

It leads to art becoming didactic, rather than layered and allusive.

It leads, in business, to an inability to wait and ponder, and to an epidemic of 'premature articulation'.

It leads to transient, fruitful states of confusion, in which the brain is slowly crystallising complexity into comprehension, being woefully misinterpreted as stupidity or indecision. In other words, it leads to minds that have no time for perplexity, and thus shoot their own creativity in the foot.

It leads to doctors and midwives being taught to distrust their intuition, because the official doctrine cannot understand intuition as anything other than sloppy and second-class thinking.

It leads, in the law courts, to the dangerous assumption that the truth will reliably emerge from two teams of clever people trying, with a host of unacknowledged wiles, to win an argument.

It leads to the sonorous symbolic prose of the Bible being superseded by something thin and pale that can be merely understood, and to a profound mistrust by religion of the mysterious and the mystical.

And it leads to a kind of flimsy political culture in which no one ever has the time or the inclination not to know, and so buying and selling jumped-to conclusions becomes a substitute for thinking. No wonder so many people disengage from a discourse that has such a transparent lack of depth.

All these and many other social ills stem from a cultural view of the mind that is not at ease with its own unconscious depth: with its own inherent waywardness. It is time for a little rebalancing. It is not that we need to allow our minds to be more wayward. It is simply that we need to realise that we were never as much in control as we thought. And that that is perfectly fine.

Notes

Chapter 1

1 Lancelot Law Whyte, *The Unconscious Before Freud*, Julian Friedmann: London, 1979.

2 Daniel Dennett, *Consciousness Explained*, Little, Brown: Boston, 1991.

3 This distinction between 'common sense' and (explicit) 'theories' is commonly used in anthropology. See, for example, Robin Horton, *Patterns of Thought in Africa and the West*, Cambridge University Press: Cambridge, 1993; Paul Hellas and Andrew Lock (eds.), *Indigenous Psychologies*, Academic Press: London, 1981.

4 In Dorothy Holland and Naomi Quinn (eds.), *Cultural Models in Language and Thought*, Cambridge University Press: Cambridge, 1987.

5 Roy D'Andrade, *The Development of Cognitive Anthropology*, Cambridge University Press: Cambridge, 1995. See also a classic article by Clifford Geertz, 'On the nature of anthropological understanding', *American Scientist*, 1975, vol. 63, pp. 47–53.

6 Angeline Lillard, 'Ethnopsychologies: cultural variations in theories of mind', *Psychological Bulletin*, 1998, vol. 123, pp. 3–32.

7 J. Deardoff, 'Mom wins asylum for son with autism', *Chicago Tribune*, 21 February 2001.

8 W. I. Johnson, 'Work together, eat together: conflict and conflict management in a Portuguese fishing village', in R. Andersen (ed.), *North Atlantic Maritime Cultures*, Mouton: The Hague, 1979.

9 Yvonne Cook interviewing Lance Hayward, *The Independent*, 1 April 1999.

10 Michael Bywater, 'Genocidal? Must be bad potty training', *The Observer*, 28 March 1999.

11 William James, *Principles of Psychology*, Dover Press: New York, 1984.

12   Quoted in D. B. Klein, *A History of Scientific Psychology*, Routledge
     and Kegan Paul: London, 1970.
13   E. R. Dodds, *The Greeks and the Irrational*, University of California
     Press: Berkeley, 1951.
14   Even professional anthropologists fall into these traps. The American
     anthropology professor Pascal Boyer accuses Angeline Lillard, from
     whom I quoted earlier, of 'taking explicit cultural models as descrip-
     tions of how minds actually work in different cultures, which of course
     they are not' (personal communication).

Chapter 2

1   Erik Hornung, 'The discovery of the unconscious in ancient Egypt',
    Spring: An Annual of Archetypal Psychology and Jungian Thought, Spring
    Publications: Dallas, Texas, 1986.
2   Peter Kingsley, *Ancient Philosophy, Mystery and Magic*, Clarendon Press:
    Oxford, 1995.
3   Steven Mithen, *The Prehistory of the Mind*, Thames and Hudson:
    London, 1996.
4   Bruno Bettelheim, *The Uses of Enchantment*, Thames and Hudson:
    London, 1976.
5   Margaret Stutley, *Shamanism: An Introduction*, Routledge: London,
    2003.
6   Quoted in Diane Purkiss, *Troublesome Things: A History of Fairies and
    Fairy Stories*, Allen Lane, The Penguin Press: London, 2000.
7   Walter de la Mare, *Behold, This Dreamer!*, Faber and Faber: London,
    1939.
8   Peter Wason and Philip Johnson-Laird, *Psychology of Reasoning: Structure
    and Content*, Harvard University Press: Cambridge, MA, 1972.
9   See, for example, Richard Nisbett and Lee Ross, *Human Inference:
    Strategies and Shortcomings of Social Judgement*, Prentice-Hall:
    Englewood Cliffs, NJ, 1980; Thomas Gilovitch, *How We Know What
    Isn't So*, The Free Press: New York, 1991. The fact that we are so unde-
    niably adept at seeing what we believe does not, of course, mean that
    what we believe is always a fiction. We believe in dozens of real things
    as well as dozens of imaginary ones. Just because you're paranoid, it
    doesn't mean they're not out to get you.
10 Nicholas Humphrey, *A History of the Mind*, Vintage: London, 1992.
11 Richard Byrne and Andrew Whiten (eds.), *Machiavellian Intelligence:
    Social Expertise and the Evolution of Intellect in Monkeys, Apes and
    Humans*, Clarendon Press: Oxford, 1988; Simon Baron-Cohen, *Mind-
    blindness*, MIT Press: Cambridge, MA, 1995.

12 Scott Atran, 'The neuropsychology of religion', in Rhawn Joseph (ed.), *Neurotheology: Brain, Science, Spirituality, Religious Experience*, University Press California: San José, CA, 2002.

13 See Julian Jaynes, *The Origin of Consciousness in the Breakdown of the Bicameral Mind*, Houghton Mifflin: Boston, 1976.

14 This 'Just So Story' of the 'bicameral mind' parallels that of Jaynes, op. cit.

15 This bit of the story, crudely put, follows Atran, op. cit. Though I have presented it, for entertainment's sake, in rather two-dimensional 'conspiracy' language, there is no implication that this is how the supernatural world actually evolved. But its effects, in supporting existing leaders, and opening up enticing possibilities for the priesthood profession, could well have been just as described.

16 Quoted in Alain Schnapp, 'Are images animated: the psychology of statues in ancient Greece', in Colin Renfrew and Ezra Zubrow (eds.), *The Ancient Mind: Elements of Cognitive Archaeology*, Cambridge University Press: Cambridge, 1994.

17 Ivan Leudar and Philip Thomas, *Voices of Reason, Voices of Insanity*, Routledge: London, 2000.

18 For the importance of narratives in human psychology, see Jerome Bruner, *Acts of Meaning*, Harvard University Press: Cambridge, MA, 1990.

19 This translation of Homer is provided by Kathleen Wilkes, *Real People*, Clarendon Press: Oxford, 1988, p. 206.

20 Many of these derivations are drawn from Owen Barfield, *History in English Words*, Faber and Faber: London, 1953.

21 For aspects of such a history, see, for example, Nicholas Humphrey, *Soul Searching: Human Nature and Supernatural Belief*, Chatto and Windus: London, 1995; Diana Purkiss, *Troublesome Things: A History of Fairies and Fairy Stories*, Penguin: London, 2000. For the anthropological perspective, see R. Murray Thomas, *Folk Psychologies Across Cultures*, Sage: London, 2001.

22 Jonathan Andrews and Andrew Scull, *Customers and Patrons of the Mad-Trade: The Management of Lunacy in Eighteenth-Century London*, University of California Press: Berkeley, CA, 2003.

23 Michael Lambek, *Human Spirits: A Cultural Account of Trance in Mayotte*, Cambridge University Press: Cambridge, 1981.

24 D. P. Walker, *Unclean Spirits: Possession and Exorcism in France and England in the Late 16th and Early 17th Centuries*, Scolar Press: London, 1981.

25 See Mark Altschule (ed.), *The Development of Traditional Psychopathology*, Wiley: New York, 1976, p. 202.

26 Victor Turner, quoted in Bennett Simon, *Mind and Madness in Ancient Greece*, Cornell University Press: Ithaca, NY, 1978, pp. 281–2.

27 Luh Ketut Suryani and Gordon D. Jensen, *Trance and Possession in Bali: A Window on Western Multiple Personality Disorder and Suicide*, Oxford University Press: Kuala Lumpur, 1995.

Chapter 3

1 From a conversation between Goethe and Riemer, quoted in Bruno Snell, *The Discovery of the Mind*, Dover: New York, 1953, p. 31.

2 Otto Rank, *The Double*, University of North Carolina Press: Chapel Hill, NC, 1971, p. 84.

3 Erik Hornung, 'The discovery of the unconscious in ancient Egypt', *Spring: An Annual of Archetypal Psychology and Jungian Thought*, Spring Publications: Dallas, TX, 1986.

4 Robin Horton, 'Destiny and the unconscious in West Africa', *Africa*, 1961, vol. 31, pp. 110–16.

5 The usages of these proto-psychological terms are complex and disputed. For more detailed expositions, see Kathleen Wilkes, *Real People*, Clarendon Press: Oxford, 1988; E. R. Dodds, *The Greeks and the Irrational*, University of California Press: Berkeley, 1951; R. B. Onians, *The Origins of European Thought*, Cambridge University Press: Cambridge, 1951; Snell, op. cit.

6 Julian Jaynes, *The Origin of Consciousness in the Breakdown of the Bicameral Mind*, Houghton Mifflin: Boston, 1976.

7 Jaynes, ibid., p. 93, suggests that there are good physiological reasons why conditions of stress are precisely those under which people are most likely to experience auditory hallucinations – and therefore to believe that their unusual actions, *in extremis*, are being directed through the voices and vibes of the gods.

8 Jaynes, ibid., p. 275.

9 R. B. Onions, *The Origins of European Thought*, Cambridge University Press: Cambridge, 1951, note 3, p. 103.

10 Jean Smith, 'Self and experience in Maori culture', in Paul Heelas and Andrew Lock (eds.), *Indigenous Psychologies*, Academic Press: London, 1981. See also Elsdon Best, *Spiritual and Mental Concepts of the Maori*, Ward: Wellington, New Zealand, 1922.

11 Jaynes, op. cit., p. 283.

12 This point was first made, very likely, in 1851 by the renowned cultural historian Edward Tylor (see Nicholas Humphrey, *Soul Searching*, Chatto and Windus: London, 1995, p. 190). Humphrey also quotes Leonard Zusne: 'Once the premise of immortality, immateriality and

transcendence is granted, every magic act on the part of the transcending self becomes possible: after all, it belongs to a different world, one that is not bound by the limitations of gravity, density, and time and space in general.'

13 Part of this story of the soul parallels that provided by Michael Daniels, 'The transpersonal self: a psychohistory and phenomenology of the soul', *Transpersonal Review*, 2002, vol. 3, pp. 17–28.

14 Dodds, op. cit.

15 Quoted in Snell, op. cit., p. 59.

16 The information on Medea is drawn from Snell, op. cit., and from Euripides, *Alcestis and Other Plays*, translated by John Davie, introduction by Richard Rutherford, Penguin: London, 1996. The interpretations are my own.

17 Gordon Burns, *Happy Like Murderers*, Faber and Faber: London, 1998.

18 Snell, op. cit., p. 47.

19 Snell, op. cit., p. 52.

20 Snell, op. cit., p. 53.

21 Jaynes, op. cit., p. 287.

22 J. Barnes, *Early Greek Philosophy*, Penguin: Harmondsworth, 1987, p. 86.

23 Brian Morris, *Anthropology of the Self: The Individual in Cultural Perspective*, Pluto Press: London, 1994.

24 Quoted in Snell, op. cit., p. 101.

25 Quoted in Frederick B. Artz, *The Mind of the Middle Ages*, Alfred A. Knopf: New York, 1965, p. 10.

26 Ibid., p. 9.

27 Bertrand Russell, *History of Western Philosophy*, Allen and Unwin: London, 1946, p. 56.

28 Plato, *Phaedrus and Letters VII and VIII*, translated and introduced by Walter Hamilton, Penguin: London, 1973, p. 52.

29 Plato, ibid., pp. 50–1, 61–2.

30 Plato, *The Republic IX*, translated by Robin Waterfield, Oxford University Press: Oxford, 1994, and Edward L. Margetts, 'The concept of the unconscious in the history of medical psychology', *Psychiatric Quarterly*, 1953, vol. 27, pp. 115–38. My translation combines elements in both these sources.

31 Plato, *Timaeus*, quoted in Bennett Simon, *Mind and Madness in Ancient Greece*, Cornell University Press: Ithaca, NY, 1978, p. 171.

32 Dodds, op. cit., p. 239.

33 Gilbert Murray, *Five Stages of Greek Religion*, Clarendon Press: Oxford, 1925, ch. iv. Quoted in Dodds, op. cit., p. 245.

34 Dodds, op. cit., p. 253.

35   Donna Tartt, *The Secret History*, Penguin: London, 1993, p. 44.
36   Margetts, op. cit., pp. 118–19.

Chapter 4

1   G. C. Lichtenberg, *Deutsche National Literatur*, 1778, vol. 141, p. 47, quoted in Lancelot Law Whyte, *The Unconscious before Freud*, Julian Friedmann: London, 1079, p. 114. Whyte, ibid., p. 114.
2   Patinus, *The Enneads*, quoted in Whyte, op. cit., p. 79.
3   St Augustine, *Confessions*, translated by R. S. Pine-Coffin, Penguin: London, 1961, pp. 214–18.
4   St Ambrose, *Epistolae*, quoted in Eric Jager, *The Book of the Heart*, University of Chicago Press: Chicago, 2000, p. 25.
5   Origen, *Commentarii*, quoted in Jager, op. cit., p. 21.
6   Quoted in David Jeffrey, *By Things Seen: Reference and Recognition in Medieval Thought*, University of Ottawa Press: Ottawa, 1979, p. 16.
7   Jager, op. cit., p. 63.
8   Owen Barfield, *History in English Words*, Faber and Faber: London, 1962, p. 127–8.
9   Ian Watt, *The Rise of the Novel*, Penguin: Harmondsworth, UK, 1972, p. 231.
10 Perez Zagorin, *Ways of Lying: Dissimulation, Persecution and Conformity in Early Modern Europe*, Harvard University Press: Cambridge, MA, 1990, p. 295.
11 Andrew Whiten and Richard W. Byrne (eds.), *Machiavellian Intelligence*, Cambridge University Press: Cambridge, 1997.
12 Machiavelli, *The Prince*, Cambridge University Press: Cambridge, 1988, pp. 59, 62.
13 Both these quotations come from Zagorin, op. cit.
14 John Vyvyan, *The Shakespearean Ethic*, Chatto and Windus: London, 1968, p. 128.
15 ibid., p. 132.
16 Many of these quotations were collected by Whyte, op. cit., pp. 84–6.
17 This is quoted in Richard Webster, *Why Freud Was Wrong*, HarperCollins: London, 1995, p. xiii.
18 Vyvyan, op. cit., p. 156.
19 Vyvyan, op. cit., p. 162.
20 Barfield, op. cit., p. 138.
21 My account of Descartes draws on René Descartes, *Discourse on Method and The Meditations*, translated and introduced by F. E. Sutcliffe, Penguin: London, 1968; Patricia Smith Churchland, *Brain-Wise*, MIT Press: Cambridge, MA, 2002; Kathleen Wilkes, *Real*

People: Personal Identity Without Thought Experiments, Clarendon Press: Oxford, 1988.

22 Amelie Rorty, *Essays on Descartes' Meditations*, University of California Press: Berkeley, CA, 1986; Churchland, op. cit., p. 10

23 Descartes, op. cit., p. 159. How mind and body communicate was the bugbear of dualism right from the start. Princess Elizabeth of Holland wrote to Descartes in 1643: 'it would be easier for me to admit matter and extension to the soul than to concede the capacity to move a body and be moved by it to an immaterial thing.' Leibniz confessed that he 'could not find any way of explaining how the body makes anything happen in the soul, or vice versa', and reckoned that 'Descartes had given up the game at this point.' Both quotes in Churchland, op. cit., p. 8.

24 Quotations from Descartes, op. cit., pp. 103–5, 112, 132, 153–6.

25 Janet Malcolm, *Psychoanalysis: The Impossible Profession*, Knopf: New York, 1981, p. 6.

26 C. Adam and G. Milhaud (eds.), *Correspondance de Descartes*, vol. VII, Presse Universitaires de France: Paris, 1936, pp. 349–50; quoted in Solomon Diamond (ed.), *The Roots of Psychology*, Basic Books: New York, 1974, p. 278. These codicils to Descartes remind me of the surprise with which students always greet the news that B. F. Skinner wrote a wonderful paper on the central role of intuition in the creative process called 'On "Having" A Poem'. It is salutary to remember that the figures who we now popularly demonise were at least as complex and clever as we are.

27 Whyte, op. cit., pp. 88–90. The quotation about Olympus is Whyte's own comment.

28 John Locke, *Essay Concerning Human Understanding*, 1690, quoted in D. B. Klein, *A History of Scientific Psychology*, Routledge and Kegan Paul: London, 1970, pp. 394–5.

29 Wilkes, op. cit., p. 216.

30 Wilkes, ibid., p. 219.

31 David Hume, *A Treatise of Human Nature*, quoted in Diamond (ed.), op. cit., p. 61.

32 Whyte, op. cit., p. 97.

33 Baruch Spinoza, *A Political Treatise* (1678), in R. M. H. Elwes, *The Chief Works of Benedict de Spinoza*, G. Bell and Sons: London, 1883, vol. 1, pp. 279–80.

34 Thomas Hobbes, *The Questions Concerning Liberty, Necessity and Chance*, 1656, quoted in Daniel Dennett, *Elbow Room: The Varieties of Free Will Worth Wanting*, Clarendon Press: Oxford, 1984, p. 15.

35 Hume, quoted in Klein, op. cit., p. 598.

36   Sir Kenelm Digby, *Two Treatises, In The One Of Which, the Nature of Bodies; In The Other, The Nature of Man's Soule, Is Looked Into*, quoted in Diamond, op. cit., p. 555.

Chapter 5

1   J. P. F. Richter (Jean Paul), 1804, *Sämtl*, quoted in Lancelot Law Whyte, *The Unconscious before Freud*, Julian Friedmann: London, 1979, p. 33.

2   Gregory of Nyssa, *On The Making of Man*, in H. A. Wilson (ed.), *A Select Library of Nicene and Post-Nicene Fathers of the Christian Church*, London, 1893; quoted in Solomon Diamond, *The Roots of Psychology*, Basic Books: New York, 1974, p. 502.

3   See Erich Fromm, *The Forgotten Language*, Gollancz: London, 1952, p. 105–7.

4   Aristotle, *De Anima*, quoted in Fromm, op. cit., pp. 109–10.

5   Cicero, *On Divination*, quoted in Fromm, op. cit., p. 113.

6   Lucretius, *De rerum natura*, quoted in Diamond (ed.), op. cit., pp. 499–500.

7   Artemidorus, quoted in Fromm, op. cit., pp. 111–12.

8   Antony Easthope, *The Unconscious*, Routledge: London, 1999, p. 12. The quotation about landscapes is from Sigmund Freud, *The Pelican Freud Library*, vol. IV, Penguin: Harmondsworth, p. 524.

9   Easthope, op. cit., pp. 10–12.

10 Ken Wilber, Jack Engler and Daniel Brown, *Transformations of Consciousness*, Shambhala: Boston, 1986, pp. 178–83. The effect of one-pointed meditation, and perhaps of mindfulness too, is reminiscent of this 'spiritual poem' of Epictetus:

> So-and-so's son is dead.
> What happened?
> His son is dead.
> Nothing else?
> Not a thing.
>
> So-and-so's ship sank.
> What happened?
> His ship sank.
>
> So-and-so was carted off to prison.
> What happened?
> He was carted off to prison.

But if we now add to this:
'He has had bad luck,'
Then each of us is adding to this observation
On his own account.

(Quoted in Pierre Hadot, *Philosophy as a Way of Life*, Blackwell: Oxford, 1995, p. 188.)

11 Ralph Waldo Emerson, *Essays*, 1844, quoted in Edward Reed, *From Soul to Mind: The Emergence of Psychology from Erasmus Darwin to William James*, Yale University Press: New Haven, CT, 1997, p. 259.

12 See Owen Flanagan, *Dreaming Souls: Sleep, Dreams, and the Evolution of the Conscious Mind*, Oxford University Press: Oxford, 2000.

13 Marin Cureau de la Chambre, *Les Charactères des Passions*, Paris, 1645, quoted in Diamond, op. cit., pp. 505–6.

14 William Smellie, *The Philosophy of Natural History*, Edinburgh, 1799, quoted in Diamond, op. cit., pp. 508–10.

15 This quotation comes from an article by Alfred Adler, quoted in D. B. Klein, *A History of Scientific Psychology*, Routledge and Kegan Paul: London, 1970, p. 67.

16 E. B. Bynum, *The African Unconscious: Roots of Ancient Mysticism and Modern Psychology*, Teachers' College Press: New York, 1999, pp. 81–2.

17 This discussion of Parmenides and the techniques of incubation is based on Peter Kingsley, in *The Dark Places of Wisdom*, Element: Shaftesbury, UK, 1999. Parmenides' poem is quoted on pp. 60–1. Kingsley also argues that the better-known 'Parmenides' of Plato's dialogue is a gross misrepresentation, created (knowingly or unknowingly) through Plato's desire to be seen as Parmenides' heir.

18 See Peter Abbs, *The Educational Imperative: A Defence of Socratic and Aesthetic Learning*, Falmer: London, 1994.

19 Hadot, op. cit., p. 19. Hadot notes that even to try to make a coherent philosophical system out of Aristotle is to make the mistake of assuming that his writing originally had the same status and intent as a published, peer-refereed piece of philosophical work today. 'Aristotle's writings are indeed neither more nor less than lecture-notes; and the error of many Aristotelian scholars has been to . . . imagine instead that they were . . . intended to propose a complete exposition of a systematic doctrine' (p. 195).

20 Ludwig Wittgenstein, *Philosophical Investigations*, Oxford University Press: Oxford, 1953.

21 Carl Jung, quoted in Robert I. Watson, *Basic Writings in the History of Psychology*, Oxford University Press: Oxford, 1979, p. 352.

22 Hugh Blair, *Lectures*, 1783, quoted in *Turner at Tate Britain*, Tate Publications: London, 2002.

23 Edmund Burke, *Philosophical Enquiry into the Origin of Our Ideas of the Sublime and the Beautiful*, 1757, quoted in *Turner at Tate Britain*, op. cit., p. 8.

24 Quoted in Whyte, op. cit., pp. 125–6.

25 This line of thought is developed much more fully by Reed, op. cit.

26 See James Hillman's introduction to Carl Gustav Carus, *Psyche: On the Development of the Soul*, originally published 1846, republished Spring Publications: Dallas, TX, 1970, p. xiii.

27 ibid.

28 Jung, quoted in Watson, op. cit., p. 354.

29 ibid., p. 355.

30 Quoted in Ian Watt, *The Rise of the Novel*, Penguin: Harmondsworth, UK, 1972, p. 198. It is symptomatic of the current fascination with consciousness, and the continuing neglect of its unconscious foundation, that Watt's analysis of Richardson's *Clarissa* is discussed by contemporary English literary critic David Lodge, in his *Consciousness and the Novel* (Secker and Warburg: London, 2002), without any reference to the unconscious.

31 Watt, op. cit., p. 261.

32 ibid., p. 265.

33 ibid., p. 269.

34 ibid., p. 267; Diderot translation by G. C.

35 Otto Rank, *The Double*, University of North Carolina Press: Chapel Hill, NC, 1971, p. 53.

36 N. Lukianowicz, 'Visual thinking and similar phenomena', *Journal of Mental Science*, 1960, vol. 108, pp. 979–1001.

37 Graham Reed, *The Psychology of Anomalous Experience*, Hutchinson: London, 1972, p. 54.

38 Versions of the double are still alive and well. Stanislaw Lem plays with the device in his 1992 novel *The Investigation*, in which the hero Gregory is walking along a deserted arcade when he notices coming towards him

> a tall lean man whose head was nodding as if he were talking to himself. Gregory was too busy with his own thoughts to pay much attention to him, but he kept him in sight out of the corner of his eye . . . Gregory looked up. The man's pace slowed but he kept coming, albeit hesitantly. Suddenly they stood facing each other no more than a few paces apart . . . He moved as if to walk past the stranger but found his path blocked. 'Hey,' Gregory

began angrily, 'what the . . .' his words faltered into silence. The
stranger was . . . himself. He was standing in front of a huge
mirrored wall marking the end of the arcade . . . Gregory stared
at his own reflection for a moment . . . 'Had a good look?' he
muttered to himself, then turned on his heel in embarrassment
and headed in the direction he had come from. Halfway up the
arcade, Gregory couldn't resist an irrational impulse to turn and
look back. The 'stranger' stopped also. He was far away now
among some brightly lit, empty shops, heading down the arcade,
busy with his own affairs in the mirror world . . .'

(Stanislaw Lem, *The Investigation*, André Deutsch: London, 1992.)

39 Dostoevsky, quoted in John Cohen, *The Lineaments of Mind*, W. H.
    Freeman: Oxford, 1980, p. 110.
40 See Andrew Motion, *Keats*, Faber and Faber: London, 1997, pp. 165,
    232. I am grateful to Stephen Batchelor for drawing these quotations
    to my attention.
41 Carl Jung, 'Civilisation in Transition', *Collected Works*, vol. xix,
    Routledge and Kegan Paul: London, 1964, para. 565.
42 Quotations from the apophatic mystics are from Anne Bancroft, *The
    Luminous Vision*, Unwin Hyman: London, 1989; and J. Ferguson,
    An Encyclopedia of Mysticism, Thames and Hudson: London, 1976.
43 Stephen Batchelor, *The Awakening of the West: The Encounter of
    Buddhism and Western Culture*, HarperCollins: London, 1994, p. 256.
44 D. T. Suzuki, *The Zen Doctrine of No Mind*, Rider: London, 1969,
    p. 56. See also Philip Yampolsky, *The Platform Sutra of the Sixth
    Patriarch*, Columbia University Press: New York, 1967.
45 Suzuki, op. cit., pp. 133, 143.
46 Harold Monro, 'The Silent Pool', from Walter de la Mare, *Behold, This
    Dreamer!*, Faber and Faber: London, 1939.

Chapter 6

1 Sigmund Freud, *The Interpretation of Dreams*, 1900, in J. Strachery
   (ed.), *The Standard Edition of the Complete Psychological Works of
   Sigmund Freud*, vol. 4, Hogarth Press: London, 1963.
2 Charlotte Brontë, *Jane Eyre*, Wordsworth Editions: Hertfordshire,
   1992, pp. 258–9.
3 Roy Porter, *Madness: A Brief History*, Oxford University Press: Oxford,
   2002, p. 10.
4 Bennett Simon, *Mind and Madness in Ancient Greece*, Cornell
   University Press: Ithaca, NY, 1978, p. 66.

5 Porter, op. cit., p. 50.

6 Simon, op. cit., p. 105.

7 Aulus Cornelius Celsus, *De medicina*, translated by W. G. Spencer, Harvard University Press: Cambridge, MA, 1935, pp. 289–91.

8 Simon, op. cit., p. 169.

9 Pico della Mirandola, *On the Dignity of Man*, translated by Charles Wallis, Bobbs-Merrill: Indianapolis, 1937.

10 Luis Vives, *De anima et vita*, Brussels, 1538, quoted in Solomon Diamond (ed.), *The Roots of Psychology*, Basic Books: New York, 1974, pp. 521–3.

11 Porter, op. cit., p. 106.

12 ibid, p. 72.

13 Dante, *Purgatorio*, translated by W. W. Vernon, quoted in L. L. Whyte, *The Unconscious before Freud*, Julian Friedmann: London, 1979, p. 81.

14 Robert Burton, *The Anatomy of Melancholy*, quoted in Mark Altschule (ed.), *The Development of Traditional Psychopathology*, Wiley: New York, 1976, p. 28.

15 Arthur Schopenhauer, *The World as Will and Idea*, translated by R. B. Haldane and J. Kemp, Trubner: London, 1883, vol. I, quoted in Edward L. Margetts, 'The concept of the unconscious in the history of medical psychology', *Psychiatric Quarterly*, 1953, pp. 125–7.

16 Schopenhauer, op. cit., vol. III, pp. 168–9.

17 M. Ryan, *Lectures on Population, Marriage and Divorce as Questions of State Medicine*, Renshaw and Rush: London, 1831, p. 48.

18 *The Goncourt Journals, 1851–1871*, translated by Robert Baldick, Doubleday: London, 1953, p. 193.

19 Charles W. Paige, 'The adverse consequences of repression', quoted in H. A. Bunker, '"Repression" in pre-Freudian American psychiatry', *Psychoanalytical Quarterly*, 1945, vol. 14, p. 473.

20 See Donald Mackinnon and William Dukes, 'Repression', in Leo Postman (ed.), *Psychology in the Making*, Knopf: New York, 1964.

21 Edward Reed, *From Soul to Mind: The Emergence of Psychology from Erasmus Darwin to William James*, Yale University Press: New Haven, CT, 1997, p. 163.

22 Henri Ellenberger, *The Discovery of the Unconscious*, Basic Books: New York, 1970.

23 Jonathan Miller, 'Going unconscious', in Robert Silvers (ed.), *Hidden Histories of Science*, Granta Books: London, 1997, p. 5.

24 Quoted in Theodore Sarbin, 'Attempts to understand hypnotic phenomena', in Leo Postman (ed.), *Psychology in the Making*, Knopf: New York, 1964. Sarbin's article formed the basis of Jonathan Miller's more popular exposition.

25 James Braid, *Neurhypnology, Or the Rationale of Nervous Sleep Considered in Relation with Animal Magnetism*, J. Churchill: London, 1843, p. 47.

26 Hamilton and Huxley quotes from Miller, op. cit., pp. 19, 25.

27 Ellenberger, op. cit.

28 During Freud's internship at the Salpêtrière, Charcot whispered to him on one occasion, apropos the cause of mental illness: 'C'est toujours la chose génitale.' He appeared to take the great man at his literal word. See Porter, op. cit., p. 189.

29 Ellenberger, op. cit., p. 315–17.

30 Henry Maudsley, *The Physiology and Pathology of the Mind*, Appleton and Co: New York, 1867, p. 124.

31 ibid., p. 161.

32 ibid., pp. 284–5.

33 ibid., pp. 9–11.

34 Actually we should not blame Freud for the 'scientisation' of the psyche. It was his American translators who took Freud's straightforward, almost homely, labels, and turned them into something technical and arcane. Freud's 'ego' was originally just *das Ich* – the 'I'. The 'id' – a word he pinched from Nietzsche – was simply the 'it': the part of me that is 'not me'. And the 'super-ego' was *das Über-Ich* – the 'above' or 'higher' part of me that represented my aspirations and injunctions. We might also note that Freud generally spoke of the psyche as *das Seele*, the soul, which was again systematically secularised, in translation, as the 'mind'. See Bruno Bettelheim, *Freud and Man's Soul*, Chatto & Windus: London, 1983.

35 This vivid, and not entirely unfair, image is due to the British psychologist Don Bannister. See Don Bannister and Fay Fransella, *Inquiring Man*, 3rd edition, Routledge: London, 1986.

36 Barrington Gates, 'Abnormal psychology', in Walter de la Mare, *Behold, This Dreamer!*, Faber and Faber: London, 1939, p. 551.

37 See, for example, Richard Webster: '[Freud] continued to regard . . . sexual and sadistic impulses not as an intrinsic part of the "conscious soul" but as a residue of man's animal past which had now been relegated to the "Unconscious". In this way Freud preserved the moral dualism of the Judeo-Christian tradition, but now located that dualism within the mind itself.' Webster, *Why Freud Was Wrong*, Harper Collins: London, 1995, p. 465. To maintain this split, Freud was obliged to focus exclusively on the perverted or pathological aspects of sexuality. For example, by describing young children's undeniable pleasure in sensuality as 'sexuality', he was able to make this healthy aspect of their early experience sound exotic, dangerous and problem-

atic, and was thus able to keep it out of the 'ego-soul'. One is reminded of Quintilian's maxim 'scientia facit difficultatem': 'it's the theory itself that creates the difficulties'. Jung's treatment of sexuality was much less convoluted.

38　Frank Tallis, *Hidden Minds*, Profile: London, 2002, p. 63.

39　Perhaps we could quote Shakespeare back at Freud, and say: 'Thy wish was father, Sigmund, to those thoughts.'

40　Webster, op. cit., p. 261.

41　Sigmund Freud, 'A seventeenth century demonological neurosis', *The Penguin Freud Library*, vol. 14, *Art and Literature*, 1923/1985, Penguin: London.

42　Ibid.

43　Freud, *The Interpretation of Dreams*, in Strachey op. cit., p. 510.

44　These two ways of carving the mind cut across each other in ways that were never really spelled out: both the ego and the super-ego could be conscious, preconscious or subconscious, it appeared, while the id seemed only to be subconscious. For present purposes, we do not need to clear this up, thankfully.

45　Freud, *The Interpretation of Dreams*, in Strachey op. cit, pp. 77, 611.

46　Freud, *New Introductory Lectures on Psycho-analysis*, in Strachey op. cit., vol. 22, pp. 174–6.

47　For detailed deconstructions of some of Freud's projections – as in his 'interpretations' of slips of the tongue – see Sebastiano Timpranaro, *The Freudian Slip: Psychoanalysis and Textual Criticism*, NLB: New York, 1976.

48　Wilhelm Fleiss, quoted in Paul Hellas and Andrew Lock (eds.), *Indigenous Psychologies*, Academic Press: London, 1981, p. 229.

49　Quoted in Ernest Jones, 'The psychopathology of everyday life', *American Journal of Psychology*, 1911, vol. 22, pp. 479–80.

50　Nancy Procter-Gregg, 'Schopenhauer and Freud', *Psychoanalytical Quarterly*, 1956, vol. 25, p. 197. Quoted in Leo Postman (ed.), *Psychology in the Making*, Alfred Knopf: New York, 1964, p. 665.

51　D. B. Klein, *A History of Scientific Psychology*, Routledge and Kegan Paul: London, 1970, p. 769.

52　Tallis, op. cit., p. 47. Freud wrote to Marie Bonaparte, of Janet's request: 'No, I will not see him. I thought at first of sparing him the impoliteness by the excuse that I am not well . . . But I have decided against that . . . Honesty the only possible thing; rudeness quite in order.' (Quoted in Kenneth Bowers and Donald Meichenbaum, *The Unconscious Reconsidered*, Wiley: New York, 1984, p. 11.)

53　Whyte, op. cit., pp. 169–70.

54　Quoted ibid., p. 169.

55 Freud, in Strachey op. cit., vol. 26, 1964, p. 193; quoted in Webster, op. cit., p. xii.

56 Adam Phillips, *The Observer*, 17 September, 1995, quoted in Webster, ibid., R. S. Woodworth, *Dynamic Psychology*, Columbia University Press: New York, quoted in Klein, op. cit., p. 774.

57 Webster, op. cit., p. xiii.

Chapter 7

1 Sir William Hamilton, *Lectures on Metaphysics*, vol. I, quoted in L. L. Whyte, *The Unconscious before Freud*, Julian Friedmann: London, 1979, p. 147. Sigmund Freud, *The Interpretation of Dreams*, vol. 4, Penguin Freud Library, Penguin: Harmondsworth, 1900/1991, p. 11.

2 H. F. Carlill, *The Theatetus and Philebus of Plato*, Swan Sonnenschein: London, 1906, p. 76–8.

3 Mary Carruthers, *The Book of Memory*, Cambridge University Press: Cambridge, 1990, p. 247.

4 ibid., pp. 44–5.

5 Immanuel Kant, *Anthropology*, 1798, section 5, quoted by E. L. Margetts, 'The concept of the unconscious in the history of medical psychology', *Psychiatric Quarterly*, 1953, vol. 27, p. 124.

6 Samuel Butler, *Unconscious Memory*, 1880; 3rd edition Fifield: London, 1920.

7 Nora Chadwick, *The Celts*, Penguin: Harmondsworth, 1970, pp. 260–1.

8 Quoted in John Cohen, *The Lineaments of Mind*, W. H. Freeman: Oxford, 1980, p. 101.

9 Edouard Claparède, 'Recognition and "me-ness"', 1911; reprinted in D. Rapoport (ed.), *Organisation and Pathology of Thought*, Columbia University Press: New York, 1951, pp. 58–75.

10 Antonio Damasio, *The Feeling of What Happens*, William Heinemann: London, 2000.

11 Elizabeth Warrington and Lawrence Weiskrantz, 'New method of testing long-term retention with special reference to amnesic patients', *Nature*, 1968, vol. 217, pp. 972–4. For an overview, see Daniel Schacter, 'Implicit memory: history and current status', *Journal of Experimental Psychology: Learning, Memory and Cognition*, 1987, vol. 13, pp. 501–18.

12 Ignace Gaston Pardies, *Concerning the Knowledge of Beasts*, 1672, Paris; quoted in Solomon Diamond, *The Roots of Psychology*, Basic Books: New York, 1974, pp. 405–6.

13 Gottfried Leibniz, *New Essays Concerning Human Understanding*, 1704, quoted in Diamond, op. cit., p. 415.

14 Nicolas Malebranche, *De la recherche de la vérité*, Paris, 1675; Ralph
    Cudworth, *The Intellectual System of the Universe*, 1678; John Norris,
    Practical Discourses (Cursory Reflections), all quoted in L. L. Whyte, op.
    cit., pp. 95–7.

15 See Raymond Fancher, *Pioneers in Psychology*, Norton: New York,
    1979, p. 67. One of the most prominent heiresses of this enlightened
    view is Annette Karmiloff-Smith: see her *Beyond Modularity: A
    Developmental Perspective on Cognitive Science*, MIT Press: Cambridge,
    MA, 1992.

16 Quoted in Whyte, op. cit., p. 99.

17 Duns Scotus, *On the First Principle*, quoted in *Brett's History of
    Psychology*, MIT Press: Cambridge, MA, 1912.

18 Anthony Marcel, 'Slippage in the unity of consciousness', in CIBA
    Symposium 174, *Experimental and Theoretical Studies of Consciousness*,
    Wiley: Chichester, 1993.

19 Gottfried Leibniz, *New Essays Concerning Human Understanding*,
    Cambridge University Press: Cambridge, 1982, p. 166.

20 Ambrose Bierce, *The Devil's Dictionary*, Bloomsbury: London, 2003;
    Daniel Wegner, *The Illusion of Conscious Will*, MIT Press: Cambridge,
    MA, 2002.

21 Hermann von Helmholtz, *A Treatise on Physiological Optics*, 1867;
    edited by J. P. C. Southall, Dover: New York, 1925, vol. III, pp. 2–5.

22 For an overview of blindsight studies, see Lawrence Weiskrantz,
    Blindsight: A Case Study and Implications, Clarendon Press: Oxford, 1986.

23 I am relying here on the discussion in Frank Tallis's *Hidden Minds*,
    Profile: London, 2002, pp. 150–2. The idea that subliminal messages
    probably prime existing tendencies, and obviate more conscious con-
    trols, now widely accepted, is due originally to John Kihlstrom, 'The
    cognitive unconscious', *Science*, 1987, vol. 237, pp. 1445–52.

24 Richard Hardaway has concluded, in a major review article published
    in 1990, that the evidence of a 'slight but consistent effect' in such
    studies is overwhelming. 'Future research designed to replicate basic
    experimental effects is deemed superfluous', he says. See Richard
    Hardaway, 'Subliminally activated symbiotic fantasies: facts and arti-
    facts', *Psychological Bulletin*, 1990, vol. 107, pp. 177–95. Quoted in
    Tallis, op. cit., p. 159.

25 C. J. Patton, 'Fear of abandonment and binge eating: a subliminal
    psychodynamic activation investigation', *Journal of Nervous and
    Mental Disorders*, 1992, vol. 180, pp. 484–90. It is interesting that,
    when these kinds of results were first submitted to professional jour-
    nals in America in the 1960s and 70s, the papers were rejected as
    being 'simply unbelievable'. Lloyd Silverman, the originator of the

'Mummy' studies, demanded, and eventually got, an independent investigation, which concluded that his studies were 'of an extremely high standard and obviously fit for publication'. (Quotes from Tallis, op. cit., p. 160.)

26   J. F. Dovidio, K. Kawakami, C. Johnson, B. Johnson and A. Howard, 'On the nature of prejudice: automatic and controlled processes', *Journal of Experimental and Social Psychology*, 1997, vol. 33, pp. 510–40.

27   Timothy D. Wilson, *Strangers to Ourselves: Discovering the Adaptive Unconscious*, Belknap Press: Cambridge, MA, 2002.

28   J. R. Lackner and M. Garrett, 'Resolving ambiguity: effects of biasing context in the unattended ear', *Cognition*, 1973, vol. 1, pp. 359–72.

29   R. S. Corteen and B. Wood, 'Autonomic responses to shock associated words', *Journal of Experimental Psychology*, 1972, vol. 94, pp. 308–13.

30   Anthony Marcel, 'Slippage in the unity of consciousness' in CIBA Symposium 174, *Experimental and Theoretical Studies of Consciousness*, Wiley: Chichester, 1993.

31   For a review of this research, see Dixon, *Preconscious Processing*, Wiley: Chichester, 1981; Robert Bornstein and Thane Pittman (eds.), *Perception Without Awareness*, Guilford Press: New York, 1992. For a rebuttal of subliminal perception, see Daniel Holender, 'Semantic activation without conscious identification in dichotic listening, parafoveal vision, and visual masking: a survey and appraisal', *Behavioral and Brain Sciences*, 1986, vol. 9, pp. 1–66.

32   Wilhelm Wundt, *On the Methods of Psychology*, 1862, in T. Shipley (ed.), *Classics in Psychology*, Philosophical Library: New York, 1961, p. 57.

33   Claude Perrault, *Du Bruit*, 1680, quoted in Diamond, op. cit., p. 179–81.

34   Butler, op. cit., pp. 87–91.

35   Oliver Wendell Holmes, 'Mechanism in thought and morals', published 1877, quoted in Whyte, op. cit., pp. 171–2.

36   E. R. Dodds, *The Greeks and the Irrational*, University of California Press: Berkeley, 1951, p. 81.

37   Bruno Snell, *The Discovery of the Mind*, Dover: New York, 1953, ch. 13.

38   Carruthers, op. cit., p. 166.

39   ibid., p. 50.

40   Whyte, op. cit., pp. 93–4.

41   A. E. Housman, 'The name and nature of poetry', quoted in Brewster Ghiselin (ed.), *The Creative Process*, University of California Press: Berkeley, CA, 1952.

42   J. W. von Goethe, *Letters*, quoted in Whyte, op. cit., p. 128.

43 Brian Eno, *A Year with Swollen Appendices: The Diary of Brian Eno*, Faber & Faber: London, 1996.

44 See Steven Smith and Steven Blankenship, 'Incubation and the persistence of fixation in problem solving', *American Journal of Psychology*, 1991, vol. 104, pp. 61–87.

45 John Livingston Lowe, quoted in Ghiselin (ed.), op. cit., p. 228.

46 Max Ernst, quoted in William MacKay, *Envisioning Art: A Collection of Quotations by Artists*, Barnes & Noble: New York, 2003.

47 See Jonathan Schooler and Joseph Melcher, 'The ineffability of insight', in S. M. Smith, T. B. Ward and R. A. Finke (eds.), *The Creative Cognition Approach*, MIT Press: Cambridge, MA, 1995. Henry Moore, 'Notes on sculpture', quoted in Ghiselin, op. cit., p. 73. See also Arthur Koestler, *The Act of Creation*, Macmillan: New York, 1964.

48 Julian Jaynes, *The Origins of Consciousness in the Breakdown of the Bicameral Mind*, Houghton Mifflin: Boston, 1976, p. 47.

49 Kihlstrom, op. cit, pp. 1450.

50 All quotes in this paragraph are taken from 'The id comes to Bloomsbury', by Daniel Pick, *The Guardian Review*, 16 August 2003, pp. 26–7.

51 Stephen Sondheim and James Lapine, *Into the Woods*, Theatre Communications Group: New York, 1989.

52 Jennifer Mundy (ed.), *Surrealism: Desire Unbound*, Tate Publishing: London, 2001.

53 *Weekend Herald*, New Zealand, 9–10 November 2002.

54 Andrew Powell, 'Soul consciousness and human suffering', *Journal of Alternative and Complementary Medicine*, 1998, vol. 4, pp. 101–8.

55 See Patricia Churchland, *Brain-Wise: Studies in Neurophilosophy*, MIT Press: Cambridge, MA, 2002, pp. 171–2.

Chapter 8

1 Harold Monro, *Collected Poems*, Duckworth: London, 1933.

2 Genesis, 6,5.

3 This quotation, and much of this brief history, is based on the selection of sources cited in Solomon Diamond (ed.), *The Roots of Psychology*, Basic Books: New York, 1974.

4 William Shakespeare, *Love's Labour's Lost*, IV.2.

5 See John Cohen, *The Lineaments of Mind*, W. H. Freeman: Oxford, 1980, pp. 75–6.

6 When I was a boy, my practical joke kit contained a device composed of a small rubber cushion and a rubber bulb connected by a fine tube.

You placed the cushion under someone's dinner plate, and at an opportune moment, squeezed the bulb, causing the plate to rise up and jiggle about. I did not know at the time that this was a prototype of the nervous system with which the majority of my forebears would have been familiar.

7   René Descartes, quoted in Cohen, op. cit., p. 83.

8   René Descartes, *The Passions of the Soul*, 1650, quoted in Diamond, op. cit., p. 528.

9   David Hartley, *Observations on Man*, 1748, quoted in L. L. Whyte, *The Unconscious before Freud*, Julian Friedmann: London, 1979, p. 111.

10 See Edward Reed, *From Soul to Mind*, Yale University Press: New Haven, CT, 1997.

11 John Bovee Dods, quoted in Reed, op. cit., p. 2.

12 E. T. A. Hoffmann, *Master Flea*, quoted in Reed, op. cit., pp. 49–50.

13 Robert Baldick, *Pages from the Goncourt Journal*, Oxford University Press: Oxford, 1988, p. 27.

14 William B. Carpenter, *Principles of Mental Physiology*, 1874, quoted in Whyte, op. cit., p. 155.

15 Francis Crick, *The Astonishing Hypothesis: The Scientific Search for the Soul*, Simon and Schuster: London, 1995, p. 3.

16 For more detail on action systems, see John McCrone, *Going Inside*, Fromm International: New York, 2001. In general, much in this section concurs with McCrone, and with the recent work of Paul and Patricia Churchland: see Paul Churchland, *The Engine of Reason, The Seat of the Soul*, MIT Press: Cambridge, MA, 1996; Patricia Churchland, *Brain-Wise: Studies in Neurophilosophy*, MIT Press: Cambridge, MA, 2002.

17 This functional view of emotion builds on the work of such researchers as Antonio Damasio, *Descartes' Error: Emotion, Reason and the Human Brain*, Putnam: New York, 1994, and *The Feeling of What Happens: Body, Emotion and the Making of Consciousness*, William Heinemann: London, 2000; George Lakoff and Mark Johnson, *Philosophy in the Flesh: The Embodied Mind and Its Challenge to Western Thought*, Basic Books: New York, 1999; Joseph LeDoux, *The Emotional Brain*, Weidenfeld and Nicholson: London, 1998; Keith Oatley, *Best Laid Schemes: Toward a Psychology of Emotion*, Cambridge University Press: Cambridge, 1992; and John Lambie and Anthony Marcel, 'Consciousness and the varieties of emotional experience: a theoretical framework', *Psychological Review*, 2002, vol. 109, pp. 219–59.

18 See Patricia Churchland, op. cit., p. 258.

19 M. F. Zigmond, F. E. Bloom, S. C. Landis, J. L. Roberts and L. R. Squire, *Fundamental Neuroscience*, Academic Press: San Diego, 1999.

20 William James, *The Principles of Psychology,* vol. I, Henry Holt: New York, 1890, reprinted Dover: New York, 1950, p. 246.

21 The 'ocean' metaphor improves upon the kaleidoscope metaphor in allowing for this shifting, dynamic undertow to consciousness. What we are aware of, in any moment, are the 'breakers' of our brain activity, behind each of which lies a partly or completely invisible groundswell of less strongly activated memories and predictions.

22 Jonathan Schooler and Tonya Engstler-Schooler, 'Verbal overshadowing of visual memories: some things are better left unsaid', *Cognitive Psychology,* 1990, vol. 22, pp. 36–71.

23 Pawel Lewicki, Maria Czyzewska and Thomas Hill, 'Nonconscious information processing and personality', in Dianne Berry (ed.), *How Implicit Is Implicit Learning?,* Oxford University Press: Oxford, 1997, p. 57.

24 For a review of such achievements, and how they are developed, see Paul Churchland, op. cit.; Peter McLeod, Kim Plunkett and Edmund Rolls, *Introduction to Connectionist Modelling of Cognitive Processes,* Oxford University Press: Oxford, 1998.

25 This study was reported to a meeting of Oxford University's Ostler Society in 1963, attended by one of Gilbert Ryle's young American graduate students by the name of Daniel Dennett. Dennett describes the study in his book *Consciousness Explained,* Little, Brown: Boston, 1991, p. 167.

26 D. K. Meno, A. M. Owen, E. J. Williams, P. S. Minhas, C. M. Allen, S. J. Boniface, J. D. Pickard, I. V. Kendall, S. P. Downer, J. C. Clark, T. A. Carpenter and N. Antoun, 'Cortical processing in persistent vegetative state', *The Lancet,* 1998, vol. 352, p. 800.

27 See P. J. Whalen, S. L. Rauch, N. L. Etcoff, S. C. McInerey, M. B. Lee and M. A. Jenike, 'Masked presentations of emotional facial expressions modulate amygdala activity without explicit knowledge', *Journal of Neuroscience,* 1998, vol. 18, pp. 411–18.

28 D. A. Leopold and N. K. Logothetis, 'Activity changes in early visual cortex reflect monkey's percepts during binocular rivalry', *Nature,* 1996, vol. 379, pp. 549–53; and Norman Dixon, *Preconscious Processing,* Wiley: Chichester, 1981, p. 12.

29 S. Murphy and R. Zajonc, 'Affect, cognition and awareness: affective priming with suboptimal and optimal stimuli', *Journal of Personality and Social Psychology,* 1993, vol. 64, pp. 723–39.

30 See, for example, M. I. Posner and C. R. Snyder, 'Facilitation and inhibition in the processing of signals', in P. M. A. Rabbitt and S. Dornick (eds.), *Attention and Performance V,* Academic Press: London, 1975; J. H. Neely, 'Semantic priming and retrieval from lexical

memory: roles of inhibitionless spreading activation and limited capacity attention', *Journal of Experimental Psychology: General*, 1977, vol. 106, pp. 226–254. Much of this research is summarised in Max Velmans, 'Is human information processing conscious?', *Behavioral and Brain Sciences*, 1991, vol. 14, pp. 651–725.

31 This summary is based on McCrone, op. cit., p. 267.

32 David Ferrier, *The Functions of the Brain*, 1876, London, quoted in Diamond, op. cit., pp. 423–4.

33 Bruce Cuthbert, Scott Vrana and Margaret Bradley, 'Imagery: function and physiology', *Advances in Psychophysiology*, 1991, vol. 4, pp. 1–42.

34 Jack Nicklaus, *Play Better Golf*, King Features: New York, 1976.

35 David Westley, 'When and why the penny drops: activation and inhibition in sudden insight', paper delivered to the British Psychological Society Consciousness and Experiential Psychology Section Conference, London, September 1998.

36 About a third of a second after the onset of a visual stimulus, electrodes on the scalp can detect this general wave of inhibition sweeping across the brain – what John McCrone calls 'the sound of the whole brain hushing'. See McCrone, op. cit., p. 183.

37 Geoff Cumming, 'Visual perception and metacontrast at rapid input rates', D.Phil. thesis, University of Oxford, 1971; Daniel Robinson, 'Psychobiology and the unconscious', in Kenneth Bowers and David Meichenbaum (eds.), *The Unconscious Reconsidered*, Wiley: London, 1984.

38 Colin Martindale, 'Creativity and connectionism', in S. H. Smith, T. B. Ward and R. A. Finke (eds.), *The Creative Cognition Approach*, MIT Press: Cambridge, MA; Paul Howard-Jones and S. Murray, 'Ideational productivity, focus of attention and context', *Creativity Research Journal*, 2003, vol. 15, pp. 153–66. Howard-Jones and I are currently replicating Martindale's study using functional magnetic resonance imaging technology.

39 C. S. Pierce and J. Jastrow, 'On small differences in sensation', *Memoirs of the National Academy of Science*, 1884, vol. 3, pp. 75–83.

40 Quoted in Peter Fensham and Ference Marton, 'What has happened to intuition in science education?', *Research in Science Education*, 1992, vol. 22, pp. 114–22.

41 Bruce Mangan, 'Taking phenomenology seriously: the "fringe" and its implications for cognitive research', *Consciousness and Cognition*, 1993, vol. 2, pp. 89–108; and 'What feeling is the "feeling of knowing"?', *Consciousness and Cognition*, 2000, vol. 9, pp. 538–44; Russell Epstein, 'The neural-cognitive basis of the Jamesian stream of thought', *Consciousness and Cognition*, 2000, vol. 9, pp. 550–75.

Chapter 9

1 A. Tucker, *Light of Nature Pursued*, 1768, quoted in L. L. Whyte, *The Unconscious before Freud*, Julian Friedmann: London, 1979, p. 113.

2 David Bjorklund and Katherine Harnishfeger, 'The evolution of inhibitory mechanisms and their role in human cognition and behaviour', in Frank Dempster and Charles Brainerd (eds.), *Interference and Inhibition in Cognition*, Academic Press: San Diego, 1995. For work on lying chimps, see Richard Byrne and Andrew Whiten (eds.), *Machiavellian Intelligence: Social Expertise and the Evolution of Intellect in Monkeys, Apes and Humans*, Clarendon Press: Oxford, 1988.

3 For a review of this research, see Susan Hurley and Nick Chater (eds.), *Imitation*, MIT Press: Cambridge, MA, 2004; Michael Tomasello, *The Cultural Origins of Human Cognition*, Harvard University Press: Cambridge, MA, 1999.

4 Richard Bentall, quoted in Sharon Begley, 'Religion and the brain', *Newsweek*, 7 May 2001, pp. 52–7.

5 For the effects of tension/relaxation on sensitivity to faint stimuli, see Michael Snodgrass, Howard Shevrin and Michael Kopka, 'The mediation of intentional judgments by unconscious perceptions: the influences of task strategy, task preference, word meaning and motivation', *Consciousness and Cognition*, 1993, vol. 2, pp. 169–93; Mark Price, 'Now you see it, now you don't: preventing consciousness with visual masking', in P. G. Grossenbacher (ed.), *Finding Consciousness in the Brain: A Neurocognitive Approach*, Wiley: Chichester, 2001; Norman Dixon, *Preconscious Processing*, Wiley: Chichester, 1981, pp. 197–99.

6 See Nicholas Humphrey, *Soul Searching: Human Nature and Supernatural Belief*, Chatto and Windus: London, 1995.

7 Julian Jaynes, *The Origin of Consciousness in the Breakdown of the Bicameral Mind*, Houghton Mifflin: Boston, 1976, p. 90.

8 Henry Sidgwick, 'Report on the census of hallucinations', *Proceedings of the Society for Psychical Research*, 1894, vol. 34, pp. 25–394. Quoted in Jaynes, op. cit., p. 87.

9 I have borrowed this 'joke' from Marcel Kinsbourne, 'Imitation: from enactive encoding to social influence', in Hurley and Chater (eds.), op. cit.

10 Jaynes (op. cit., p. 105) tries to localise the 'speaking centre' in the right cerebral hemisphere, and the 'hearing centre' in the left, so that hallucinations are actually one side of the brain talking to the other. But there is really no need for this.

11 See Kinsbourne, op. cit.; and Marcel Kinsbourne, 'Voiced images,

imagined voices', *Biological Psychiatry*, 1990, vol. 27, pp. 811–12.

12 Gregory Bateson, *Steps to an Ecology of Mind*, Ballantine: New York, 1972. See also Chris Frith, 'Consciousness, information processing and schizophrenia', *British Journal of Psychiatry*, 1979, vol. 134, pp. 225–35. Jeffrey Gray, 'Schizophrenia and scientific theory', in *Experimental and Theoretical Studies of Consciousness*, CIBA Symposium 174, Wiley: Chichester, 1993.

13 Stephan Lewandowsky and Shu-Chen Li, 'Catastrophic interference in neural networks: causes, solutions and data', in Dempster and Brainerd, op. cit., p. 331.

14 M. Spitzer, I. Weisker, S. Maier, L. Hermle and B. Maher, 'Semantic and phonological priming in schizophrenia', *Journal of Abnormal Psychology*, 1994, vol. 103, pp. 485–94. Manfred Spitzer elaborated a view of schizophrenia similar to mine in chapter 11 of his *The Mind Within The Net: Models of Learning, Thinking and Acting*, MIT Press: Cambridge, MA, 1999.

15 Louis Sass, *The Paradoxes of Delusion: Wittgenstein, Schreber and the Schizophrenic Mind*, Cornell University Press: Ithaca, NY, 1994, p. 12. See also Sass's *Madness and Modernism: Insanity in the Light of Modern Art, Literature and Thought*, Basic Books: New York, 1993; and the review of these books in *The London Review of Books*, 2 November 1995, by Iain McGilchrist.

16 Sass, *Paradoxes* op. cit., pp. 23–4.

17 R. J. Dolan, P. Fletcher, C. Frith, K. Friston, R. Frackowiak and P. Grasby, 'Dopaminergic modulation of impaired cognitive activation in the anterior cingulate cortex in schizophrenia', *Nature*, 1995, vol. 378, pp. 180–2; Jonathan Cohen and David Servan-Schreiber, 'A theory of dopamine function and its role in the cognitive deficits in schizophrenia', *Schizophrenia Bulletin*, 1993, vol. 19, pp. 85–104.

18 Quoted in Luh Ketut Suryani and Gordon Jensen, *Trance and Possession in Bali: A Window on Western Multiple Personality, Possession Disorder, and Suicide*, Oxford University Press: Oxford, 1995, p. 204–5.

19 Robert Louis Stevenson, *The Strange Case of Dr Jekyll and Mr Hyde*, quoted in ibid., p. 199. It is worth noting that Stevenson may himself have experienced such dissociations. He certainly thought of his own mind in terms of unconscious sub-personalities. He attributed his own creativity to a helpful band of 'brownies' or 'little people' 'who do one-half my work for me while I am fast-asleep, and in all human likelihood do the rest for me as well, when I am wide-awake and fondly suppose I do it for myself.' He called them 'unseen collaborators whom I keep locked in a back garret, while I get all the praise, and they but

a share of the pudding' (ibid., p. 200).

20   See for example Suryani and Jensen, op. cit.

21   This sketchy account is based largely on David Spiegel and David Li, 'Dissociated cognition and disintegrated experience', in Dan Stein (ed.), *Cognitive Science and the Unconscious*, American Psychiatric Press: Washington, DC, 1997.

22   See the earlier discussion on the functions of emotions. Also Jaak Panskepp, *Affective Neuroscience: The Foundations of Human and Animal Emotions*, Oxford University Press: New York, 1997; Douglas Watt, 'Emotion and consciousness: implications of affective neuroscience for extended reticular thalamic activating theories of consciousness', http://server.philvt.edu/assc/watt/default.htm

23   Jane van Lawick-Goodall, *My Friends, The Wild Chimpanzees*, 1967 (quoted in Suryani and Jensen, [op. cit.,] p. 32). My cat, like many domestic moggies, also has such brief bursts of madness.

24   The quotation from David Livingstone's *Missionary Travels* of 1857 is used by Daniel Goleman to introduce a discussion of endorphins in his book *Vital Lies, Simple Truths: The Psychology of Self-Deception*, Simon and Schuster: New York, 1985.

25   For a recent study of zombies, see Marina Warner, *Fantastic Metamorphoses, Other Worlds*, Oxford University Press: Oxford, 2002.

26   David Milner and Melvyn Goodale, *The Visual Brain in Action*, Oxford University Press: Oxford, 1995, pp. 167–70.

27   In fact, much fascinating recent research shows that even the conscious model in the wide cone is largely composed of this latent information, rather than the rich tapestry of detail which I *think* is there. Studies of 'inattentional blindness' and 'change blindness' show that I am actually aware only of what I am momentarily focusing on, and all the rest is composed of promissory notes and instructions about how to reinstate the detail if I want to. See Kevin O'Regan and Alva Noë, 'A sensorimotor account of vision and visual consciousness', *Behavioral and Brain Sciences*, 2001, vol. 24, pp. 883–917.

28   Donald Hebb, 'The American revolution', *American Psychologist*, 1960, vol. 15, pp. 735–45. More recently Susan Blackmore has developed the theory that 'out-of-the-body experiences' (OBEs; like 'near-death-experiences', NDEs) are 'constructions of the living – or dying – brain'. See her *Dying to Live: Science and the Near-Death Experience*, Grafton Books: London, 1993, chapter 8. The crucial test of any brain-based theory of OBEs is whether you can see anything from your new perspective that you could not possibly have known, guessed or plausibly imagined to be there. Supernaturalists believe there is evidence you can. Brain theorists don't think there is, as yet, any good evidence.

29 Mardi Horowitz has recently suggested that, while some people may get stuck in an over- or under-inhibited mode, other neurotic conditions reflect an inability to maintain appropriate focus, so that sufferers may swing between the two poles in ways that do not reflect the needs of the situation. See M. Horowitz, C. Milbrath and M. Ewart, 'Cyclical patterns of states of mind in psychotherapy', *American Journal of Psychiatry*, 1994, vol. 151, pp. 1767–70.

30 Harold Sackeim, Johanna Nordlie and Ruben Gur, 'A model of hysterical and hypnotic blindness: cognition, motivation and awareness', *Journal of Abnormal Psychology*, 1979, vol. 88, pp. 474–89. An engaging fictionalised discussion of hysterical blindness is provided by William Wharton in his *Last Lovers*, Farrar Straus Giroux: New York, 1991.

31 Alternatively, sensory experiences can be created or enhanced under hypnosis, and the genuineness of the experience is paralleled by observable changes in the brain. When hypnotised people are asked to visualise a particular colour, for example, PET scans show increased blood flow in exactly those areas of the visual cortex that respond to actual perception of the same colour. The research was reported by David Spiegel to the American Association for the Advancement of Science, February 2002 (*The Guardian*, 18 February 2002).

32 Ernest Hilgard, 'A neodissociation interpretation of pain reduction in hypnosis', *Psychological Review*, 1973, vol. 80, pp. 396–411.

33 Evidence that the brain does in fact make use of anticipatory signals to regulate its own activity has been provided by Philip Wong and Howard Shevrin, see June 1999 *Journal of the American Psychoanalytic Association*.

34 J. M. Boden and R. M. Baumeister, 'Repressive coping: distraction using pleasant thoughts and memories', *Journal of Personality and Social Psychology*, 1997, vol. 73, pp. 45–62.

35 Similar arguments have been developed by Marylene Cloitre, 'Conscious and unconscious memory: a model of functional amnesia', in Dan Klein (ed.), *Cognitive Science and the Unconscious*, American Psychiatric Press: Washington, DC, 1997; Marcel Kinsbourne, 'Integrated cortical field model of consciousness', in *Experimental and Theoretical Studies of Consciousness*, CIBA Symposium 174, Wiley: Chichester, 1993; Mick Power and Chris Brewin, 'From Freud to cognitive science: a contemporary account of the unconscious', *British Journal of Clinical Psychology*, 1991, vol. 30, pp. 289–310; and Goleman, op. cit.

36 Jung, for example, carried out extensive studies of the lengths of time it took people to respond to the stimulus word, in a free association

task, and claimed that a dramatically lengthened response time was indicative of having run up against a repressed set of ideas that he called a 'complex'. These moments of blockage were also associated with changes in physiological indicators, such as skin conductivity, of which the patient himself was unaware. See Carl Jung, 'The association method', in C. E. Long (ed.), *Collected Papers on Analytical Psychology, 2nd edition*, Routledge and Kegan Paul: London, 1917. These studies are summarised in Donald Mackinnon and William Dukes, 'Repression', in Leo Postman (ed.), *Psychology in the Making*, Knopf: New York, 1964, chapter 11. Freud was completely unimpressed by any such laboratory studies. When Saul Rosenzweig sent him some positive results in 1934, Freud churlishly replied: 'I cannot put much value on these confirmations because the wealth of reliable observations on which [my] assertions [about repression] rest make them independent of experimental verification. Still, it can do no harm.' (See Mackinnon and Dukes, op. cit., p. 703.)

37 This has been demonstrated even in standard laboratory tasks. People are unable to recall words from a list that you have asked them to 'forget', showing that they have been successfully inhibited from reappearing in consciousness. However, other tests of memory reveal that they retain their activation and are perfectly well remembered. See E. Bjork, R. Bjork and M. C. Anderson, 'Varieties of goal-directed forgetting', in J. M. Golding and C. M. MacLeod (eds.), *Intentional Forgetting: Interdisciplinary Approaches*, Erlbaum: Mahwah, NJ, 1998; Daniel Wegner, 'You can't always think what you want: problems in the suppression of unwanted thoughts', *Advances in Experimental Social Psychology*, 1992, vol. 25, pp. 193–225; Drew Westen, 'The scientific legacy of Sigmund Freud: toward a psychodynamically informed psychological science', *Psychological Bulletin*, 1998, vol. 124, pp. 333–71.

38 Westen, op. cit., p. 342. For a review of the health risks of being a 'repressor', see Lynn Myers, 'Identifying repressors: a methodological issue for health psychology', cited in Lynn Myers, 'Deceiving others or deceiving themselves?', *The Psychologist*, 2000, vol. 13, pp. 400–403.

39 All the quotations concerning the Project are taken from Frank Sulloway, *Freud, Biologist of the Mind*, Burnett Books: London, 1979, pp. 113–25.

40 For a more detailed discussion of this problem, and Freud's struggles to overcome it, see Matthew Erdelyi, *Psychoanalysis: Freud's Cognitive Psychology*, Freeman: New York, 1985.

41 The 'Project for a scientific psychology' has been discussed in the light

of contemporary neuroscience by Karl Pribram and Merton Gill, *Freud's Project Reassessed*, Hutchinson: London, 1976; and Patricia Herzog, *Conscious and Unconscious: Freud's Dynamic Distinction Reconsidered*, International Universities Press: Madison, CT, 1991.

42 Richard Webster, *Why Freud Was Wrong*, HarperCollins: London, 1995, p. 246.

43 See Susan Hurley and Nick Chater (eds.), *Imitation*, MIT Press: Cambridge, MA, 2004; Michael Tomasello, *The Cultural Origins of Human Cognition*, Harvard University Press: Cambridge, MA, 1999.

44 A detailed discussion of how adults coach children in the art of repression, effectively reinterpreting some of Freud's own case material, is provided by Michael Billig, *Freudian Repression: Conversation Creating the Unconscious*, Cambridge University Press: Cambridge, 1999.

45 Noah Glassman and Susan Andersen, 'Activating transference without consciousness: using significant-other representations to go beyond what is subliminally given', *Journal of Personality and Social Psychology*, 1999, vol. 77, pp. 1146–62.

Chapter 10

1 Robert T. Carroll, *The Skeptic's Dictionary*, Wiley: New Jersey, 2003.

2 David Gelernter, *The Muse in the Machine*, Fourth Estate: London, 1994, pp. 15, 42.

3 This paragraph summarises a long and hard-fought change in the basic assumptions about the nature of mind, and its relation to the brain. But it is clear now that the rationalists, like Jerry Fodor and Noam Chomsky, have lost, and the brain has replaced the computer as the core metaphorical embodiment of mind. For reviews of the shift, see Francisco Varela, Evan Thompson and Eleanor Rosch, *The Embodied Mind*, MIT Press: Cambridge, MA, 1992; George Lakoff and Mark Johnson, *Philosophy in the Flesh*, Basic Books: New York, 1999; Patricia Churchland, *Brain-Wise: Studies in Neurophilosophy*, MIT Press: Cambridge, MA, 2002.

4 Brian Lancaster, 'New lamps for old: psychology and the 13th century flowering of mysticism', *Transpersonal Psychology Review*, 2001, vol. 5, pp. 3–14.

5 From *The Epic Poise*, edited by Nick Gammage, Faber and Faber: London, 1999, pp. 192–3.

6 Ted Hughes, *Poetry in the Making*, Faber: London, 1967.

7 Peter Brook, in Gammage (ed.), op. cit., p. 154.

8 For a clear statement of this 'deep interactionist' position, see Annette Karmiloff-Smith, *Beyond Modularity: A Developmental Perspective on*

Cognitive Science, MIT Press: Cambridge, MA, 1992. Karmiloff-Smith argues convincingly against naïve nativist claims, such as those of Steven Pinker, that we can identify 'the gene for altruism' or 'the gene for aggression'. For a well worked out case study of the genetic disorder Williams syndrome, see Annette Karmiloff-Smith, 'Elementary my dear Watson, the clue is in the genes . . . Or is it?', *The Psychologist*, 2002, vol. 15, pp. 608–11. For Pinker's claims, see for example Steven Pinker, *How the Mind Works*, W. W. Norton: New York, 1997.

9   This is about as far as the current state of knowledge in neuroscience can follow. For a summary of the basic emotion systems, and how they might be underpinned by the brain, see Jaak Panksepp, *Affective Neuroscience: The Foundations of Human and Animal Emotions*, Oxford University Press: New York, 1997. Jeffrey Gray suggests that disgust relies on an area of the brain known as the insula; fear resides in the amygdala and the hypothalamus; anger makes use of the 'periaqueductal grey'; and anxiety relies on the hippocampus. As I have said before, my general argument here does not depend on the assignment of functions to specific brain locations. See Jeffrey Gray, *Consciousness: Creeping Up on the Hard Problem*, Oxford University Press: Oxford, 2004.

10   Carl Jung, *Collected Works*, vol. 18, para 1228; quoted by Anthony Stevens, *Archetypes Revisited*, Brunner-Routledge: London, 2002, p. 18. Stevens's view is compatible with the present one, though he does not emphasise the evolutionary functions of emotion in the way that I have.

11   Carl Jung, *Memories, Dreams, Reflections*, Routledge and Kegan Paul: London, 1963, p. 156.

12   See Owen Flanagan, *Dreaming Souls: Sleep, Dreams and the Evolution of the Conscious Mind*, Oxford University Press: Oxford, 2000.

13   It is now known that dreamlike experiences occur throughout the night, but those outside the REM periods tend to be more fragmentary, lacking the characteristic narrative form of full-blown dreams.

14   Francis Crick and Graeme Michison, 'REM sleep and neural nets', *Behavioral Brain Research*, 1995, vol. 69, pp. 145–55. For the role of the hippocampus in memory consolidation, see John McCrone, *Going Inside*, Fromm International: New York, 2001.

15   Geoffrey Hinton, Peter Dayan, Brendan Frey and Radford Neal, 'The "wake-sleep" algorithm for unsupervised neural networks', *Science*, 1995, vol. 268, pp. 1158–61.

16   Pierre Maquet, Jean-Marie Péters, Joël Aerts, Guy Dolfiore, Christian Degueldre, André Luxen and Georges Franck, 'Functional neuroanatomy of human rapid-eye-movement sleep and dreaming', *Nature*, 1996, vol. 379, pp. 163–6.

17 Ibn Khaldûn, *The Muqaddimah: An Introduction to History*, translated by Franz Rosenthal, Routledge and Kegan Paul: London, 1958.

18 It may be that REM sleep retains a degree of inhibitory constraint that gives some dreams, at least, a kind of narrative structure; and that this is what distinguishes REM from non-REM sleep, where dream contents are much more fragmentary. See Allan Hobson, Edward Pace-Schott and Robert Stickgold, 'Dreaming and the brain: Toward a cognitive neuroscience of conscious states', *Behavioral and Brain Sciences*, 2000, vol. 23, pp. 793–842.

19 In a rather sophisticated theory, David Kahn and colleagues venture that: 'even subtler influences might be operative in the dreaming brain. These could include, for example, narratives and symbols laid down . . . early in the development of the brain, perhaps through personal experience or even by genetic patterning.' David Kahn, Stanley Krippner and Allan Combs, 'Dreaming and the self-organizing brain', *Journal of Consciousness Studies*, 2000, vol. 7, pp. 4–11.

20 Most of the details in this and the following paragraph are from Antti Revonsuo, 'The reinterpretation of dreams: an evolutionary hypothesis of the function of dreaming', *Behavioral and Brain Sciences*, 2000, vol. 23, pp. 877–901. Neuroimaging studies in both animals and human beings have even begun to correlate specific forms of brain activity with the conscious content of dreams. Rats trained to run a maze in a particular way show the reappearance of the selfsame pattern during that night's REM sleep. Said Matthew Wilson from MIT: 'The correlation is so close the researchers found that as the animal dreamt, they could reconstruct where it would be in the maze if it were awake, and whether the animal was dreaming of running or standing still' (*The Independent*, 20 February 2002). Equivalent results in people are discussed by Sophie Schwartz and Pierre Maquet, 'Sleep imaging and the neuro-psychological assessment of dreams', *Trends in Cognitive Sciences*, 2002, vol. 6. pp. 23–30.

21 Revonsuo, op. cit., pp. 895, 898.

22 Joseph Griffin, *The Origin of Dreams*, The Therapist Ltd: Worthing, West Sussex, 1997, pp. 74–5. Griffin offers a similar brain-based account of dreaming to the present one.

23 Hermann Hesse, *My Belief*, Jonathan Cape: London, 1976, p. 37.

24 Nicholas Xenos, *Scarcity and Modernity*, Routledge: London, 1989.

25 Andrew Newberg, Abass Alavi, Michael Baime, Michael Pourdehnad, Jill Santanna and Eugene d'Aquili, 'The measure of regional cerebral blood flow during the complex cognitive task of meditation: a preliminary SPECT study', *Psychiatry Research: Neuroimaging Section*, 2001, vol. 106, pp. 113–22; see also Eugene d'Aquili and Andrew

Newberg, *The Mystical Mind: Probing the Biology of Religious Experience*, Fortress Press: Minneapolis, 1999; L. I. Aftanas and S. A. Golocheikine, 'Human anterior and frontal midline theta and lower alpha reflect emotionally positive state and internalised attention: high-resolution EEG investigation of meditation', *Neuroscience Letters*, 2001, vol. 310, pp. 57–60; Frederick Travis and Keith Wallace, 'Autonomic and EEG patterns during eyes-closed rest and transcendental meditation practice: the basis for a neural model of TM practice', *Consciousness and Cognition*, 1999, vol. 8, pp. 302–18; Michael Persinger and K. Makarec, 'The feeling of a presence and verbal meaningfulness in context of temporal lobe function: factor analytic verification of the Muses?', *Brain and Cognition*, 1992, vol. 20, pp. 217–26. For a rather variable collection of articles, see Rhawn Joseph (ed.), *Neurotheology: Brain, Science, Spirituality, Religious Experience*, University Press: California, 2002.

26   Antonio Damasio, *The Feeling of What Happens: Body, Emotion and the Making of Consciousness*, William Heinemann: London, 2000.

27   Eugene Gendlin, *Focusing-Oriented Psychotherapy: A Manual of the Experiential Method*, Guildford Press: New York, 1996.

28   Quoted in Brewster Ghiselin (ed.), *The Creative Process*, University of California Press: Berkeley, CA, 1952, p. 56.

29   See e.g. Gavriel Salomon (ed.), *Distributed Cognitions*, Cambridge University Press: Cambridge, 1993.

30   These arguments are developed by, for example James Wertsch, *Voices of the Mind: A Sociocultural Approach to Mediated Action*, Harvard University Press: Cambridge, MA, 1991.

31   These examples are culled from Andy Clarke's excellent book *Natural-Born Cyborgs: Minds, Technologies, and the Future of Human Intelligence*, Oxford University Press: Oxford, 2003.

32   For the essentially social nature of intelligence, see Edwin Hutchins, *Cognition in the Wild*, Bradford: Cambridge, MA, 1996. For collective creativity, see Vera John-Steiner, *Creative Collaboration*, Oxford University Press: New York, 2000.

33   Andy Clark, *Being There: Putting Brain, Body and World Together Again*, Bradford/MIT Press: Cambridge, MA, 1997, pp. 217–221.

Chapter 11

1   'Abuse in childhood made Duchess's aide kill her lover', *The Independent*, 24 September 2003. In fact, Jane Andrews lost her appeal, and remained in prison, not because the psychological defence was ruled invalid – on the contrary – but because the appeal court said

that it should have been made *more* of at her original trial. For a further discussion see the 'Justice for women' website at www.jfw.org.uk.

2   'Watch out: hysteria about', *The Independent*, 8 July 1999. Quoted in Peter Spencer, 'Of witch crazes and health scares', *The Psychologist*, 2003, vol. 16, pp. 596–7.

3   Cognitive scientists who have recently written in this vein are Russell Epstein, 'The neural-cognitive basis of the Jamesian stream of thought', *Consciousness and Cognition*, 2000, vol. 9, pp. 550–75; Bruce Mangan, 'What feeling is the "feeling of knowing"?', *Consciousness and Cognition*, 2000, vol. 9, pp. 538–44; Daniel Wegner, *The Illusion of Conscious Will*, MIT Press: Cambridge, MA, 2002.

4   D. G. Dutton and A. P. Aron, 'Some evidence for heightened sexual attraction under conditions of high anxiety', *Journal of Personality and Social Psychology*, 1974, vol. 30, pp. 510–17.

5   This analysis is based on Timothy Wilson's, in *Strangers to Ourselves: Discovering the Adaptive Unconscious*, Belknap Press: Cambridge, MA, 2002.

6   Michael Gazzaniga, *Mind Matters: How Mind and Brain Interact to Create Our Conscious Lives*, Houghton Mifflin: Boston, 1988.

7   Daniel Dennett, *Elbow Room: The Varieties of Free Will Worth Wanting*, Clarendon Press: Oxford, 1984, pp. 78, 80.

8   ibid, p. 79.

9   See V. S. Ramachandran and S. Blakeslee, *Phantoms in the Brain: Human Nature and the Architecture of the Mind*, Fourth Estate: London, 1999.

Index

References to 'I' have been indexed under self. For metaphors of individual subjects, see under the general heading 'metaphors'.

Credits

p. 13 *Punch*; p. 29 Bridgeman Art Library; p. 36 Mary Evans Picture Library; p. 51 Alinari; p. 63 The Art Archive, p. 71 Sotheby's Picture Library; p. 94 National Gallery; p. 103 AKG; p. 128 Bridgeman Art Library; p. 134 The Art Archive; p. 146 Mary Evans Picture Library; p. 157 Bridgeman Art Library; p. 173 Wellcome Trust; p. 174 Wellcome Trust; p. 225 Science and Society Picture Library; p. 237 AKG; 243 Science and Society Picture Library; p. 244 Science Photo Library; p. 318 Tate/Foundation P. Delvaux – St Idesbald, Belgium/DACS, London; p. 329 AKG.

You can now order superb titles directly from Abacus: